I0812284

Architecture of Nature
Nature of Architecture

Diana Agrest

Published by Applied Research and Design Publishing.
An Imprint of ORO Editions.
Publisher: Gordon Goff

www.appliedresearchanddesign.com
info@appliedresearchanddesign.com

Copyright © 2021 Irwin S. Chanin School of Architecture of The Cooper Union, and Diana Agrest held jointly with Applied Research and Design Publishing.

All rights reserved. No part of this book may be reproduced, stored in a retrieval system, or transmitted in any form or by any means, including electronic, mechanical, photocopying of microfilming, recording, or otherwise (except that copying permitted by Sections 107 and 108 of the U.S. Copyright Law and except by reviewers for the public press) without written permission from the publisher.

You must not circulate this book in any other binding or cover and you must impose this same condition on any acquirer.

Book Author: Diana Agrest

Excerpt from *Book 1: Basin and Range* from *Annals of the Former World* by John McPhee. Copyright © 1998 by John McPhee. Reprinted by permission of Farrar, Straus and Giroux.

Excerpt from *The Return of the Repressed* by Diana Agrest from *The Sex of Architecture*, edited by Diana Agrest, Patricia Conway and Leslie Kanes Weisman. Copyright © 1996 Harry N. Abrams, Inc. Used by permission of Harry N. Abrams, Inc., New York. All rights reserved.

Book Design: Studio Lin, NYC
Project Manager: Jake Anderson

10 9 8 7 6 5 4 3 2 First Edition
ISBN: 978-1-939621-94-8

Color Separations and Printing: ORO Group Ltd.
Printed in China.

AR+D Publishing makes a continuous effort to minimize the overall carbon footprint of its publications. As part of this goal, AR+D, in association with Global ReLeaf, arranges to plant trees to replace those used in the manufacturing of the paper produced for its books. Global ReLeaf is an international campaign run by American Forests, one of the world's oldest nonprofit conservation organizations. Global ReLeaf is American Forests' education and action program that helps individuals, organizations, agencies, and corporations improve the local and global environment by planting and caring for trees.

Architecture of Nature
Nature of Architecture

Diana Agrest

With Yael Agmon

With contributions by D. Graham Burnett, Peter Louis Galison, Caroline A. Jones and John McPhee

The Irwin S. Chanin School of Architecture
The Cooper Union for the Advancement of Science and Art

Expanding Boundaries: Architecture, Nature, Science, Representation

Diana Agrest

New Horizons

The journey that is this book, exploring the complex questions around the subject of nature, can be traced back to two encounters with vast and almost geologically opposite landscapes. It begins from a love of the big horizons of the Pampa and the silent sections of the ravine in the Quebrada de Humahuaca bordering the Andean Plateau three thousand meters above sea level, from seemingly infinite views of the horizon on the low plains and an elevated plateau whose stratigraphic section traces Earth's history.

View of the Serranías de Hornocal in the Quebrada de Humahuaca, a narrow ravine located in the northwest of Argentina in the province of Jujuy, showing its stratigraphic record dating back to the Cambrian and Pre-Cambrian periods and its unique geomorphological characteristics. Photo: INAG.

While still a young student I undertook a thousand-mile road trip from Buenos Aires all the way to the northwest of Argentina, traversing extraordinary landscapes ranging from the bucolic plains and long horizons of the Pampas, a vast flat plain of 300,000 square miles, to the dramatic steep climbs along narrow mountain roads all the way to the Altiplano, the Andean Plateau, in the province of Jujuy. I remember crossing brooks, riding through the water current and rough terrain in a beat-up old station wagon, and suddenly being in front of the most extraordinary colors I had ever seen: the stratigraphic register of the Andean mountains appeared as layers of color accumulated over long geological time. It was pure section. When I turned the car motor off there was absolute silence, a sense of suspension in time.

The Pampas is all plan and endless horizon, marked occasionally by tall grasses or the famous Ombu tree, where the eye can extend in any direction without boundary. Seeing it recalled a previous experience, travelling as a child by train for two days through the dry desert region of Patagonia, when the stillness of the flat landscape with its uninterrupted horizon imposed itself over the movement of the train as it framed the landscape in time. This horizon now appears to me as the reified history of architectural representation, a horizontal plane and the line of a horizon which define each other according to the position of the viewer. The line, the line of vision, the lines of construction, the horizontal and vertical planes: plan and section.

View of the horizon from the road in La Pampa, Argentina with typical tall grasses. Photo: Diana Agrest.

This book is about the Earth striated by lines of all kinds in sectionals, accumulations of so many now invisible plans. As a young architect I left New York on a trip to Tunisia, traveling by car all the way from the city of Tunis to the south, reaching the Berber village of Matmata on the edge of the Sahara by a road that probably had not been used since the French Foreign Legion was there, a road dry with deep cracks and so much dust that one had to put wet towels on the car windows. After hours of travel on an already dark road, no village to be seen, a small light became noticeable in the distance. When I reached it, there was only the mouth of a cavernous, narrow space, leading to an open courtyard. Nothing had prepared me for what I saw next as I looked up: the dense starry sky of the Sahara framed by the circular walls of the courtyard; the celestial dome.

View of the Patagonian desert in the province of Neuquen, Argentina, as seen from the train. Photo: Diana Agrest.

These were the dwellings of the Berber people, carved into the desert ground, that in the bright white light of the morning resembled the undulating terrain of a cratered lunar landscape. There was no distinction between architecture and nature. The Quebrada and Matmata were two very different experiences. While one was of an extraordinary dimension and a pure record of Earth's history, the other was of a symbiosis between the vastness of desert and sky and a human intervention into the natural conditions of the place: the sun, the compacted sand, the dry air. Both were about section, a section cutting from the Earth framing a space that extended to the cosmos. These experiences were atmospheric in a double sense of the word: in the actual physical atmosphere, the dryness, the burning sun, the extreme temperature changes from daytime to nighttime, the light, sharp or dazzling as it was refracted by stars in the dry nights or through dust in the dry day; but also in the atmospheres created by both these conditions as such and as marked and reframed by human habitation. Matmata's impact on me was compounded, collapsing in a way the Pampas and the Quebrada.

General view of Matmata, in the Sahara Desert in the South of Tunisia, with Berber dwellings. Ca. 1972. Photo: Diana Agrest.

From the City to Nature

For most of my life in architecture I have focused on the city and urban discourse in its many dimensions, and it is in fact through the city that I "discovered" nature. This discovery took form in 1989, many years after I saw Matmata, in a project for Visionary San Francisco in which the most important "visionary" move was to eliminate buildings, and to do so at a time when a bunch of buildings was the prevailing surrogate for a city. As if by legerdemain, "nature" reappeared after having been absent from urban discourse for fifty years. A kind of folding together or sectional rewriting of my three early experiences, this project led me to investigate the question of nature from historical, philosophical, scientific, and gender perspectives. I called this project, for San Francisco's China Basin area, "The Return of the Repressed: Nature."[1] It was the realization of the essential place of nature in American culture and history, from the philosophical underpinnings of the country's founding texts to nature's manifestation in the colossal magnitude of the American landscape, from the country's natural richness and beauty, to the religious beliefs articulated through the esthetic philosophy of the sublime and reified in painting, that led me to pursue this exploration. From the relationship between nature/culture to that between nature/architecture, as well as from the nature/culture continuum to the nature/urban continuum, nature is freed from the binary sets of oppositions within which it has been defined, becoming itself the object of study.

Berber cave dwelling carved in the ground, Matmata, Tunisia, 1972. Photo: Diana Agrest.

Nature and Architecture

There has always been an active relationship between nature and architecture, but this interaction takes a prominent position at the present moment of climate change and environmental crisis. Nature, as an object of study in its many complex modes of interaction with architecture—scientific, philosophic, economic, political, ideological—is directly, implicitly, and critically reexamined in this book

Nature has played a key role in the history and theory of Western architecture, appearing as a constant motif in architectural texts from its very beginnings in Vitruvius. In Alberti's foundational 15th-century text, *The Ten Books of Architecture*, nature is seen as a basic element in the development of architectural theory and principles. Alberti imbues architecture with divine attributes through a set of complex representational operations where nature is the shifter between god and architecture, where proportion is the shifter between nature and man, and finally where man's body is the shifter that articulates nature and architecture.[2] In the 17th century, with Newton, Leibniz and the concept of infinitesimal calculus, science as a discipline explains nature in terms that are reified in architectural discourse, through new concepts such as infinite and continuous space and the erosion of physical boundaries as well as the baroque period's expansion of perspectival views and thus the horizon itself.[3]

In the modernist architecture theories of the early 20th century, such as Le Corbusier's Radiant City of 1929, urbanism acquires a new prominence, and nature comes to occupy an important and complex position as both a concrete pragmatic consideration and a metonymic construct—"architecturalized," flattened in space and synchronic in time. Nature is taken over and repressed, tamed, by urban discourse's ideology and represented by a controlled geometric "neutral plane," a "neutral green," not only in Radiant City but also in many post-WWII and subsequent urban developments for most of the 20th century. Just as urbanism became planning, nature in the 1960s became the "environment" via systems theory. The environment did not just include natural conditions and resources, but social and anthropological dimensions as integral parts of the urban realm. These approaches were not about architecture being in consonance with the natural environment air, light, sun, health, as in Radiant City, but about that environment itself conceived as a system and organized as a discourse by regional planning (a discourse that was, and still is, the intermediary between the political and the physical world—a political instrument of control). Systems theory pervaded every discipline, including the sciences.[4]

Diana Agrest, "The Return of the Repressed," General Plan. China Basin, San Francisco. 1989, Proposal - General Plan.

Representation, Nature, Science, and Architecture

Can the visual function there too as a form of research, not just popularization or illustration? Can there be a different kind of knowledge, an epistemological contribution...that supplements and enriches our understanding of science-in-practice?—Peter Galison

Rethinking the question of nature here is a matter of finding the right questions rather than looking for immediate answers. It is about thinking and rethinking inherited ideologies and assumed truths through the creative use of representation as a tool for thought in the production of architectural knowledge.

Nature has always been incorporated and embedded "within" architectural discourse in different forms. In this work, nature disengages itself as a free radical from the ideological constraints of architecture to become itself the object of study via one common mechanism, essential to the production of knowledge in both science and architecture, representation. In taking nature as an object of study, this exploration pursues a transdiscursive approach. Intersections through different discourses, be they scientific, philosophical, or historical, are intrinsic to the investigation of the concepts that bear upon our own understanding of nature. In so doing, we are expanding the very discourse of architecture itself. These discursive intersections, resulting from our readings of nature, manifest and sometimes reveal the entanglements in natural phenomena as their materiality, forces, and modes of generation overlap and affect each other.

A common ground between architecture and science in the understanding of nature is the central role of representation as a tentacular domain of knowledge.[5] The question of how representations of nature act as tools in scientific discoveries—and regarding the ensuing opposition between art and science, modes of seeing and objectivity—have until now been the subject of debates by historians of science, philosophers, and art historians. The relationship between art and science has influenced the development of scientific knowledge as it relates to the study of natural phenomena, opening the question of the role of representation in taking nature as an object of study in the field of architecture.

From the beginning representation has been intrinsic to architecture. Knowledge can be produced by "seeing" with different eyes, not just by talking or writing, not by photographing disaster, not by enacting what amount to temporary "solutions" to counteract our own destructive impulse, but rather by discovering the always mutating conditions of natural systems themselves that transcend the boundaries of our own discipline. In doing so, out of necessity and desire, we intersect with other discourses whose object of study is nature itself. Historically defined by dialectically bridging the opposition between art and science, stabilizing the oscillating relationship between those terms in the scientific representation of nature, architecture is both, and as such, it is in a privileged position to undertake this reading of nature with the means of production and representation of the architect.

It is oscillating on this line of the horizon that representation, science, and architecture come together. The horizon, so vividly present in the Pampas, is the element, the concept, that connects nature, the boundary between Earth and the atmosphere, and the human visual apparatus. It permits the recording of the perception of space in the perspectival construction and delimitation of space, and the recording of movement and time as marked by the Earth's limit, its outer boundary perceived as a continuous line. A line that, being made of points, is at the heart of the concept of the infinitesimal and the quest for an understanding of nature through mathematics, logic, philosophy, and religion. A line recording the motion and location in our constant planetary orbiting, and in so doing, generating the quest for an understanding of time—at least until Einstein's construction of the modern concept of time.[6] The horizon is framed in one case by our visual apparatus and in the other by the conceptual one of mathematics and logic.

Frederick Edwin Church, "The Andes of Ecuador," 1855. Reynolds House Museum of American Art, Winston-Salem, NC.

From early drawing based on direct observation of nature, to specialized drawing, to mechanical tools such as photography, to current sophisticated techniques and methods of observation and recording, diverse techniques manifest the constant presence and importance of visual representation in the evolution of science. In our work as architects, the world opened by the computer, a further extension of our eyes and hands, brings with it the question of coding and decoding; and that decoding entails the transposition of representations from one notational system to another. No longer is Galileo drawing the craters of the moon as he observed them through the telescope as chiaroscuro in 1609, as indexical as he could afford in the transition from the visual to the manual.[7] There are many more degrees of separation now. The eye itself does not see, and the direct synaptic connections between eye and hand are not activated. Different modes and systems in layers of coding and decoding occupy the space and function formerly held by the eye, transforming the very concept of representation. In this codification process the digital and the analog image alternate in a constantly mutating process. Our eyes and tools can interpret data of any kind, from charts and numbers to banal computer renditions of complex phenomena. "We" do the translation using a complex notational system, that of architecture, which is neither pictorial, nor "representational" in the strict sense of reproducing what is there, but is presentation, production, a different way of revealing what is codified in other data systems that are not visual.

Constructions of Nature

One of the prevailing questions of the recent past is the relationship between the Earth and humans. How many ways are there to elaborate and understand the complexity of that relationship? What is the place of humans on Earth in relation to all other living organisms—and how does this relationship change in Earth's timescale relative to human time? Many positions and approaches to these questions have been developed in different fields of knowledge and artistic production. Herein lie great differences, from philosophical elaborations, fatalistic, realistic, or relativistic in relation to Earth, to different approaches in the environmental sciences, to activist environmentalism with preventive and protectionist aims. Is this a concern for our planet or for us humans (at least some of us)?

Earth has changed and transformed drastically over its 4.5 billion years, and life on Earth has existed and evolved for almost as long. The forces of nature have extraordinary power, and the constant transformation of natural materials and formations continues and is of a degree that we cannot always control or fully predict, despite all our scientific and technological advances. In the geological time of the Earth, oceans have appeared and transformed, mountains have risen as oceans and rivers have disappeared, great plains have been eroded, continents have moved and keep on moving in the continuous dynamics of Earth's plates. But if we link geological time to historical time, we can't fail to notice that the catastrophic transformations through constant, ruthless exploitation have been taking place for millennia in the process of our expansion, reproduction, and survival, and it has continued, amplified, and accelerated until the present, manifested in the destruction of the natural environment that takes place every second.

Although it has a very old scientific and philosophical lineage, ecology was one of the first fields to understand nature as a system, studying the relationships, interactions, and processes of regulation between both living and nonliving organisms. While ecology is not synonymous with environment, its broader application, in consonance with systems theory, gave rise to the modern concept of environment and environmental approaches in various domains, including planning and urban ecology. Thus the term "environment" in consonance with systems theory filtered into our own discipline and came to replace "nature" in the scene of architecture. As Leo Marx writes, "In 1970, with the first Earth Day, ... the threat to the human habitat that had started after the destruction in Hiroshima and the nuclear arms race, attracted nationwide attention and an environmental movement emerged."[8]

The Gaia Hypothesis appeared as one of the most significant recent ecological constructions of nature, not only in itself but also in its vast influence. Gaia was first presented by John Lovelock in 1965 as the concept he called the Earth feedback hypothesis, which considered Earth as a self-regulating organism and as a system of living organisms and coincided with NASA's first images of the planet from space. In 1974 John Lovelock and Lynne Margulis joined their approaches as Margulis introduced biological concepts such as the effect of microbial life on the atmosphere, defining Gaia as "the series of interacting ecosystems that compose a single huge ecosystem at the Earth's surface...best regarded as alive." Her definition presupposes "a self-regulating, autopoietic, system," though Donna Haraway would later state that "Gaia is a system that is sympoietic mistaken for autopoietic." Gaia thus opens to a new understanding of the processes that are affected by human intervention.[9]

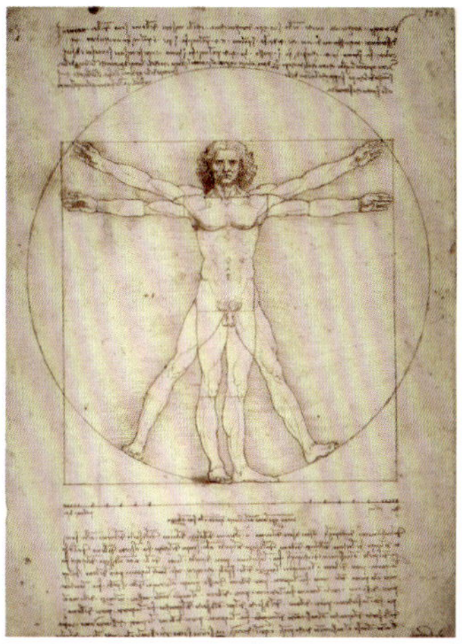

Leonardo da Vinci, "The Vitruvian Man," ca. 1487. Gallerie dell' Accademia, Venice, Italy, pen and ink on paper, 14 by 10 in.

One of the most recent constructions of nature proposes the notion of the Anthropocene, in which the effect of anthropogenic activity on Earth is of such magnitude that it merits being considered as a new geological epoch succeeding the Holocene, the epoch in which we were supposedly and stratigraphically still living. The Anthropocene has been an important call for attention, expanding rapidly since its original usage as a term in the 1980s by the biologist Eugene F. Stoermer to its formalization by atmospheric biologist Paul J. Creutzen in the year 2000. But there have also been numerous critical rebuttals, from earth scientists who stipulate that it has not yet been proven stratigraphically to a view shared by many in the social sciences and humanities that it is being coopted by the forces of capitalism and its industrial, financial, and military powers. In response, alternative notions such as the Capitalocene have been proposed.[10] The destruction of the natural environment takes place every second and has been taking place for millennia in the process of reproduction, settlement, and survival—the role of human intervention in dramatic environmental change is undeniable. While the Anthropocene as a position has directed attention to critical environmental issues, as a construction of nature it also carries an ideology of problem-solving and object-making that serves the powers that be.

As seen from the perspective of architecture, the idea of the Anthropocene (as a way to designate this not yet clearly defined period) is problematic, as it places Anthropos, man, at the center again. Even if Anthropos translates as 'human,' historically it has been used to characterize a male-dominated Western culture and society. Both feminist and non-feminist scientists, scholars, and artists have taken issue with this approach based on scientific, historical, political, and cultural perspectives. In the field of architecture there is certainly a loaded background in the way nature has been integral to the construction of Western architectural theory through man and man's body. In this historical context, nature has been constructed as female, where the body of woman, as an embodiment of nature, was metaphorically and literally subjected to abuse, taming, burning, etc.[11] Naming this period "Anthropocene" in one move replaces woman as embodying nature and places man at the center of the latest construction of nature (even as a guilty party) and an entirely new geological epoch.

Can we ever escape being thus framed? Maybe by accepting, in the spirit of a revised Gaia of complex, constantly transforming, and entangled systems, that we humans are but one species of living organisms but not necessarily the central one. The accelerating scale of human intervention is now unprecedented, but it is not just about us. The Earth does not particularly care about us and will go on with or without us, as scientist and scholars such as Donna Haraway, Lynn Margulis, and Dorion Sagan have vividly expressed in relation to Gaia, or as William Cronon has in writing about the imagined purity of the wilderness that preceded human intervention.[12]

The Work

Rather than looking for immediate answers, *Architecture of Nature/Nature of Architecture* is an attempt to search for and ask what the right questions are. In that spirit we make a parenthesis, stepping aside for a moment to take inventory and expand our knowledge and disciplinary boundaries, understanding the Earth as a living organism in its forces and complex material interactions, before and after human intervention, a perspective that is not about the taming of nature but about getting to know its untamable dimensions.

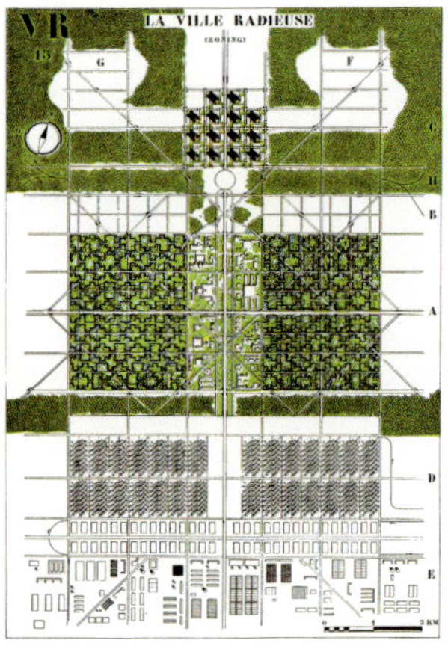

Le Corbusier, The Radiant City, 1929–30. General Plan, La Ville Radieuse, Editions L'Architecture d'Aujourd'hui, Boulogne, 1933, © FLC-ADAGP.

From the vantage point of architecture, two questions pertinent to the subject of nature must be addressed simultaneously. The first is the question of nature itself as it appears in the exploration of extreme natural phenomena. The second has to do with the means of representation by which this exploration is achieved. The work of discovery starts with observation of extreme natural phenomena. Drawing and modeling have been used as (specific) tools that, informed by the eye of the architect, reveal a different reality. These and other tools of representation have always been and still are essential to architecture; they are tools for thought. Through them the work re-thinks the transformative power of nature in relation to the limits of our field. Here they are the tools for reading and re-writing. This process of exploration and discovery starts with observation of the different modes by which natural phenomena have been registered and represented, from indexical recordings to codified data, taking these observations as raw material and recording what we read in them to be elaborated with our tools. In this double operation, recording becomes productive re-writing through representation.

In their research, 18th- and 19th-century scientists would go into the field, drawing what they saw and producing documents such as scientific atlases.[13] We as architects don't start from direct observation in the field. We work with existing data, selected from the various fields of science where natural phenomena are explored, and re-theorize them within our own discourse. That data, ranging from textual to numeric or graphic information, is the raw material on which we effect a transformation through our tools of representation, reading through many different intersecting parameters and narratives; it is representation as production, not as "re-presentation" of an objective "out there." Representation as production, as a creative exploration, mirrors the kind of simulation performed by actual models, which are not faithful representations but loci for the exploration and expansion of possibilities. They have the capability to be sensed, as Galison and Jones would say, in a haptic way that connects us to the larger scale of electromagnetic fields in which we are embedded and where life occurs. Drawing is of the essence, as it brings out questions of modes of seeing, instrumentality, observation, objectivity, and historical concepts of nature itself and its meaning in relation to the larger context of a period.

The term nature is used in this book's approach as an equivalent to Earth, confronting the materiality of nature and the forces at work in it and examining conditions that existed in periods dating back millions or billions of years. This colossal and mysterious background inevitably evokes feelings better described by the sublime, the horror and fear as we confront this background and the current environmental catastrophes. Focusing on the question of nature from the philosophical and scientific discourses that have explained, throughout history, the transformations that have led to the present conditions of the natural world as they affect our modes of habitation, the work explores a dimension of space, time, and scale, issues that take a preeminent position in the selection of natural phenomena. From this perspective nature presents a completely different concept of time, from universal and cosmic time to Earth's geologic time (the history of the Earth itself and the origin of life in it) to the construction of the concept of time in Einstein's general theory of relativity. Looking at a dimension of time where changes are measured in millions and hundreds of millions of years, and in which 10,000 years is just a recent occurrence, helps put in perspective the work we do and the ideas that support it in a time when actions are judged by the speed with which a result is obtained. Space is usually vast in the context of places that took billions or millions of years to develop and thousands for transformations to even be perceptible (until the most recent history where processes of transformation have accelerated). Time, as inseparable from space-time, is of a cosmic dimension that relates to the universe, taking architectural discourse by implication to a scale that transcends the disciplinary boundaries of architecture, planning, or landscape. Phenomena such as volcanoes, deserts, canyons, rivers, glaciers, fault lines, salt lakes, caves, oceans, sequoias, radioactive winds, mangroves, algae, and coral reefs are the locus of this exploration. Nature is itself the object of study.

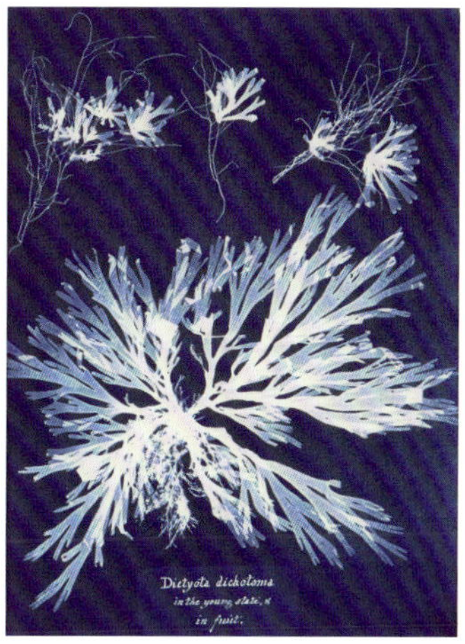

Anna Atkins, "Dictyota dichotoma, in the young state; and in fruit," from *Photographs of British Algae: Cyanotype Impressions*, part XI, ca. 1849. Spencer Collection, The New York Public Library. New York Public Library Digital Collections.

The study of this type and scale of phenomena has been undertaken by environmental scientists, including geologists, oceanographers, geographers, biologist, and ecologists. In placing work from architecture within a transdiscursive field, there is an opportunity to contribute to this exploration with a fresh view. At the core of this work is the question of representation, based on scientific studies in various domains from the environmental sciences to the history of science and philosophy. Architectural drawings and models in particular sections have been used as (specific) tools that, informed by the eye of the architect, reveals a reality different from those of the specialized fields. In each case, specific modes of representation are developed and used in a manner that arises out of the conditions presented by the phenomena themselves, ranging from handmade sketches to measurable geometric configurations and topological renditions. In a process of reading and re-writing, it is with facts and data that the work is produced. Architectural modes of seeing reveal nature's (Earth's) sectional organization and articulate its diverse systems and transformative processes. Horizontal and vertical sections as well as three-dimensional drawings expose the forms in which gasses are locked into and heat our atmosphere, as in the study of permafrost, the formation, advance, and retreat of glaciers, the formation of volcanoes in the Aleutian arctic, or salt domes that form over the course of two hundred million years. These drawings are sometimes measurable in time and sometimes reveal conditions better described topologically. Processes of transformation, chains of events, and possible effects are part of this exploration, but it does not necessarily bear an obvious relation to other fields that deal with environmental forces.

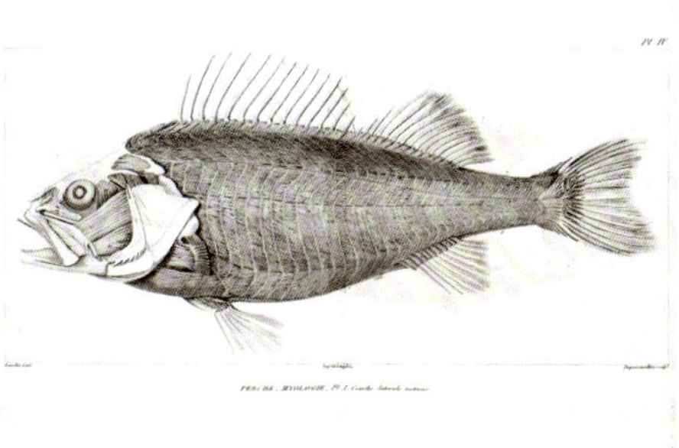

M Valenciennes and Georges Cuvier, Baron, "Perch: Myology, external lateral layer," in *Histoire Naturelle des Poissons*, 1828. F. G. Levrautt, Paris. General Research Division, The New York Public Library. New York Public Library Digital Collections.

How do we read time with our tools as it manifests itself on so many different scales, from eons to epochs, in periods or years, daily, hourly, or in a matter of seconds, but transformative time spans regardless? So many scales and levels of time determined by so many parameters in compartmentalized boundaries (biomes): time for butterflies or for bees, or of digestion for a boa constrictor, or for the formation of a tornado, or for geysers to erupt; the speed and duration of currents and tides; the time for clouds to form; the lifetime of a sequoia and the period of its daily cycle of nutrition, interconnected in myriads of unseen and even unpredictable entanglements; the time for a tsunami to unfold from a glacier to the ocean, or the time for a lake to dry and generate dunes, or the time for those dunes to move one hundred feet in massive formations, or the time for algae to reproduce and grow and the span of the sea life that lives on it, or for coral to form reefs and atolls—and all of this in the constant turning and swinging of and within the field of electromagnetic push and pull.

We can see the unfolding of some of these issues in time and in section when an instantaneous change in materiality brings together the scales of the atom and that of the whole Earth in a single instant, such as the most dramatic case of nuclear testing, seen underwater or from above, in the Bikini Atoll and the radioactive winds that engulfed and circulated around the globe, or the long-lasting effects of radioactivity in the life of the Marshall Islands. We can see the large scale and very slow process of millions of years and three different epochs in which the Lechuguillas cave formed, in a process beginning from fractures during the leaking of hydrogen sulfide through the Earth's crust and continuing through chemical and microbial processes to create an extraordinary cave system. Measurable in time and space, these sections register processes of transformation.

If the human figure (but not living organisms) is absent in these drawings, the reason might be found in the example of a volcano, which in section goes to the magma chambers several miles below the surface of the Earth. Next to a structure like this one, the human figure becomes a nonentity. Such natural phenomena and inanimate formations have taken billions of years to develop, well before genus Homo. While we are not looking as scientists, our work does focus on living organisms as an essential part of the Earth, in ways that present very different types of "entanglements" or complex ecological systems. This is true in the case of mangroves growing in anoxic conditions, where an ecological process, in which they become one with the land in its struggle against erosion, is carefully considered sectionally at scales from their microscopic entanglements to their larger territorial growth and impact. Drawings also reveal the extraordinary physical structure of the sequoia which depends for its existence and reproduction on a delicate balance between atmospheric conditions, water, and land, in a complex ecology operating across different scales and elements, from air and fog to the nutrition mechanism in its needles and trunk, to its decomposition once fallen, which creates the conditions for its reproduction. Projects such as the Coral or Clouds projects or the SF scenario of an artificially provoked mega-volcanic explosion in Mount St. Helens are in the tradition of the visionary potential of architecture and its advancement through visionary ideas.

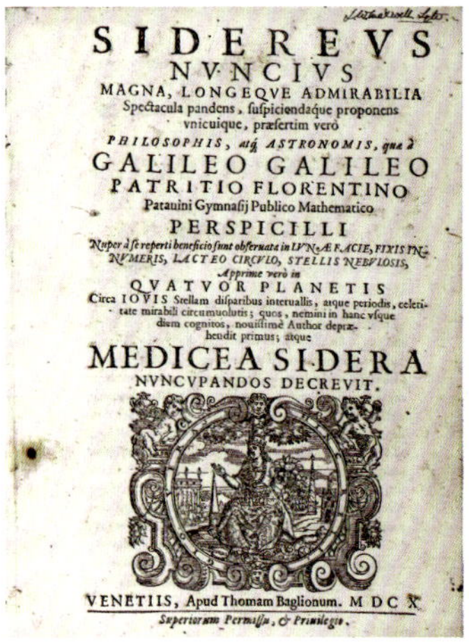
SIDEREVS NVNCIVS
MAGNA, LONGEQVE ADMIRABILIA Spectacula pandens, suspiciendaque proponens vnicuique, præsertim verò
PHILOSOPHIS, atq; ASTRONOMIS, quæ à
GALILEO GALILEO
PATRITIO FLORENTINO
Patauini Gymnasij Publico Mathematico
PERSPICILLI
Nuper à se reperti beneficio sunt obseruata in LVNÆ FACIE, FIXIS INNVMERIS, LACTEO CIRCVLO, STELLIS NEBVLOSIS,
Apprime verò in
QVATVOR PLANETIS
Circa IOVIS Stellam disparibus interuallis, atque periodis, celeritate mirabili circumuolutis; quos, nemini in hanc vsque diem cognitos, nouissimè Author depræhendit primus; atque
MEDICEA SIDERA
NVNCVPANDOS DECREVIT.
VENETIIS, Apud Thomam Baglionum. M DC X.
Superiorum Permissu, & Priuilegio.

Galileo Galilei, cover of *Sidereus Nuncius*, Apud Thomam Baglionum, 1610. Smithsonian Libraries. First printed account of Galileo's discoveries through the telescope.

In organizing the book without chapters, sliding from specific phenomena and processes in some relative order, the intention is to emphasize the relativity of boundaries as well as the sense of complex relationships and effects between different and apparently very diverse phenomena—from ocean currents to coral reefs to algae and sequoia, and from fog to clouds, and from nuclear explosions or fire to ice, and from undersea ice to the complex material and thermal changes of state as well as the movement, earthquakes, and landslides that it takes for salt domes to be formed. One could even, at the scale of these massive phenomena, follow the traces of everything at work with everything else in the constant change and transformations of the Earth.

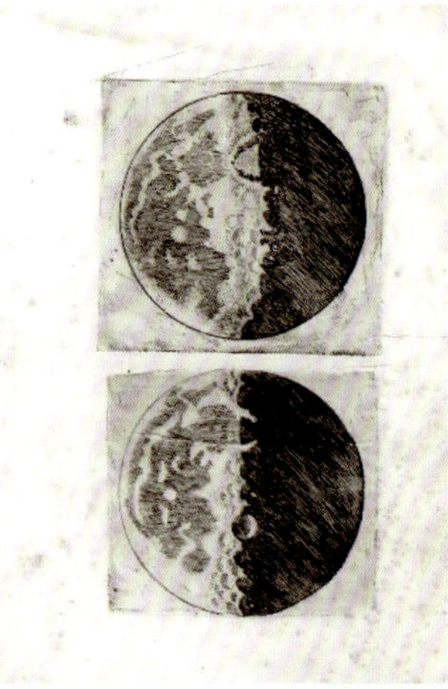

Galileo Galilei, copper engravings showing the uneven lunar surface and earthshine from the *Sidereus Nuncius*, Apud Thomam Baglionum, 1610. Smithsonian Libraries.

At the core of this reading of nature is the complex weaving of so many timeframes and scales. Everything is moving all the time. The line is never still. An endless choreography of bodies in space-time, a multidimensional opera in a total theater where the stage moves and changes as the drama unfolds, through events that articulate different rhythms, times, and tempos while defining spaces as the traces that overlap and intersect, these presentations of nature are revealed by our expanded perspective. And then, as a corollary to this work, there is our human time, our mini-choreographies of reproduction and survival over a narrative of "run for your life." We are trying here to establish a bridge between those two worlds.

Intersections

Intersecting fields open our views and foster a transdiscursive approach that expands the boundaries, possible ways of looking at, new understandings of, and developments of what we do. "Nature, Science and Architecture: From Representation to Presentation," was developed in the form of an interview/conversation that took place after both Peter Galison and Caroline A. Jones looked at the studio work that is the subject of this book. I asked both of them to contribute, as their joint work as well as their individual work deals with questions of representation, science, and art, subjects at the core of this book. This interview/conversation covers a range of different subjects around those issues, including Peter Galison's delineation of the question of objectivity and exploration of the relationship between art and science in scientific representation, ranging from the role of representation and its epistemic value in the development of science, to the three phases of truth, to nature, mechanical objectivity and trained judgment, and the concomitant correlated issues of objectivity vs. subjectivity and the self. An important question of a different kind is raised by Caroline Jones concerning issues of the role and place of humans in our entanglements with the dynamic forces of the Earth and the anthropogenic effects on it, the sublime in the representation of catastrophic disasters, and the value of analogy in the relationship between art and science. Of great interest is Galison's description of his most recent interest, the new natures emerging in what he calls the sacrificial sites of nuclear disasters, from Chernobyl to Fukushima. All of this opens onto the political implications of the subject of nature, which are at the heart of the undertaking of this book albeit in a less explicit way.

In “Sea Walls,” a conversation with Diana Agrest, Graham Burnett relates this work to Humboldt’s explorations in the 19th century and thinks of it as a kind of Humboldtian work for the 21st century, where representation is at the center of the endeavor. He brings up and draws from personal experience to pursue the questions of scale and the sublime that in a way articulate the deep psychological experience of fear, relating his young daughter’s experience confronting the promontories of Capri as seen from the water to the deep philosophical questions that it evokes in relation to nature—and to architecture, in the beautiful example of the temple of Serapis at Pozzuoli.

John McPhee’s set-piece on time is from the "Basin and Range" section of his book, in which he writes about the experience of traversing the land with archeologists. McPhee’s prose transmits the sense of seeing through layers of Earth’s history back into the same terrain in other epochs, as though with X-ray vision. His work resonates with the work of exploration we have been developing in our research, as drawings unfold these hidden layers of Earth’s history in its many geophysical states and configurations, a work in which time in its myriad manifestations occupies a central role.

My own text, “The Return of the Repressed: Nature,” written in 1991 and published in 1996,[14] but as relevant to my understanding of critical issues in our discipline now as it was then, stands here as a kind of autobiographical piece that led to a new phase in my work, from a focus on the urban to nature in relation to urban discourse, and expounded in yet another iteration on the question of gender in relation to the concept of nature, in this case in terms of the historically situated representations and conceptions of nature as female as well as issues of gender and science. As it concerns nature, science, representation, and architecture it points to the development of the subject of nature as an object of study in itself for the discipline of architecture.

Endnotes

1. Diana Agrest, "The Return of the Repressed: Nature," in *The Sex of Architecture*, Diana Agrest, Patricia Conway and Leslie Kanes Weisman, eds. (New York: Abrams, 1996), 49-68.
2. The concept of "shifter" in terms of the articulation of codes is developed in Diana Agrest, "Design versus Non-Design," in *Oppositions* 6(1976).
3. Gilles Deleuze, *The Fold: Leibniz and the Baroque* (Minneapolis: University of Minnesota Press, 1992); Gilles Deleuze, *Le pli: Leibniz et le Baroque* (Paris: Editions de Minuit, 1988).
4. Norbert Wiener, *Cybernetics or Control and Communication in the Animal and the Machine* (Cambridge, MA: MIT Press, 1948); Ludwig von Bertalanffy, Anatol Rapoport, Ralph W. Gerard, Kenneth Boulding, *Founding of Society for the Advancement of General Systems Theory* (California: American Association for the Advancement of Science, 1954); W. Ross Ashby, *Introduction to Cybernetics* (London: Chapman and Hall, 1955); Ludwig von Bertalanffy, *General System Theory: Foundations, Development, Applications* (New York: George Braziller Inc., 1968).
5. The use of this term is inspired by Donna Haraway, "Tentacular Thinking: Anthropocene, Capitalocene, Chthulucene," in *Staying with the Trouble* (Durham and London: Duke University Press, 2016), 30-57.
6. Peter Galison and Caroline S. Jones, eds., *Picturing Science, Producing Art* (Abingdon, UK: Routledge, 1998), 1-22. In the introduction to the book, the editors touch upon a subject that, although from a different perspective, is in a way at the core of the work in the "Architecture of Nature/Nature of Architecture" Advanced Design Research Studio that I created and led at Irwin S. Chanin School of Archtecture, The Cooper Union for the Advancement of Science and Art.
7. Erwin Panofsky. "Galileo as Critic of the Arts: Aesthetic Attitude and Scientific Thought," in *Isis* 47, no. 1 (Mar. 1956): 3-15; Paolo Molaro, "On the Earthshine Depicted in Galileo's Watercolors of the Moon," in *Galilæana* X (2013): 73-84.
8. Leo Marx, "The Idea of Nature in America," in *Daedalus, Journal of the American Academy of Arts and Sciences* 137, no. 2 (Spring 2008): 8-23, 16A.
9. James E. Lovelock "Gaia as Seen from the Atmosphere," in *Atmospheric Environment* 6 (1972): 579-80; James E. Lovelock, *Gaia: A New Look at Life on Earth* (Oxford: Oxford University Press, 1979); James E. Lovelock and Lynn Margulis, "Atmospheric Homeostasis by and for the Biosphere: The Gaia Hypothesis," in *Tellus, Series A* 26 (February 1974): 2-10.
10. Paul Crutzen and Eugene Stoermer, "The 'Anthropocene,'" in *Global Change Newsletter, International Geosphere-Biosphere Programme Newsletter* 41 (May 2000); Donna Haraway, "Anthropocene, Capitalocene, Plantationocene, Chthulucene: Making Kin," in *Environmental Humanities* 6 (2015): 159-165; Jason Moore, "Anthropocene, Capitalocene, and the Myth of Industrialization," *jasonwmoore.wordpress.com*. https://jasonwmoore.wordpress.com/2013/06/16/anthropocene-capitalocene-the-myth-of-industrialization/ (accessed Jun. 6, 2018).
11. Evelyn Fox Keller, *Reflections on Gender and Science* (New Haven, CT: Yale University Press, 1985); Carolyn Merchant, *The Death of Nature: Women, Ecology and the Scientific Revolution* (New York: Harper & Row, 1980); Isabelle Stenger, *Catastrophic Times: Resisting the Coming Barbarism* (London: Open Humanities Press and Meson Press, 2015); Donna Haraway, "Anthropocene, Capitalocene, Chthulucene: Staying with the Trouble." Lecture, Anthropocene: Arts of Living on a Damaged Planet from UC Santa Cruz, Santa Cruz, May 9, 2014.
12. William Cronon, "The Trouble with Wilderness; or, Getting Back to the Wrong Nature," in William Cronon, ed., *Uncommon Ground: Rethinking the Human Place in Nature* (New York: W. W. Norton & Co., 1995), 69-90. As Lynne Margulies and Dorion Sagan write, "Gaia is not the nurturing mother or fertility doll of the human race. Rather, human beings, in spite of our raging anthropocentrism, are relegated to a tiny and unessential part of the Gaian system. People, like brontosauruses and grassland, are merely one of the many weedy components of an enormous living system dominated by microbes." Lynn Margulis and Dorion Sagan, *Dazzle Gradually: Reflections on the Nature of Nature* (Hartford, VT: Chelsea Green Publishing, 2007), 183.
13. Lorraine Daston and Elizabeth Lunbeck, *Histories of Scientific Observation* (Chicago: University of Chicago Press, 2011); Lorraine Daston and Peter Galison, *Objectivity* (New York: Zone Books, 2010).
14. Diana Agrest, "The Return of the Repressed: Nature," in *The Sex of Architecture*, ed. Diana Agrest, Patricia Conway and Leslie Kanes Weisman (New York: Harry N. Abrams, Inc., 1996), 49-68.

Liquid Tectonics

Yellowstone Caldera, Wyoming
Chung-Wei Lee

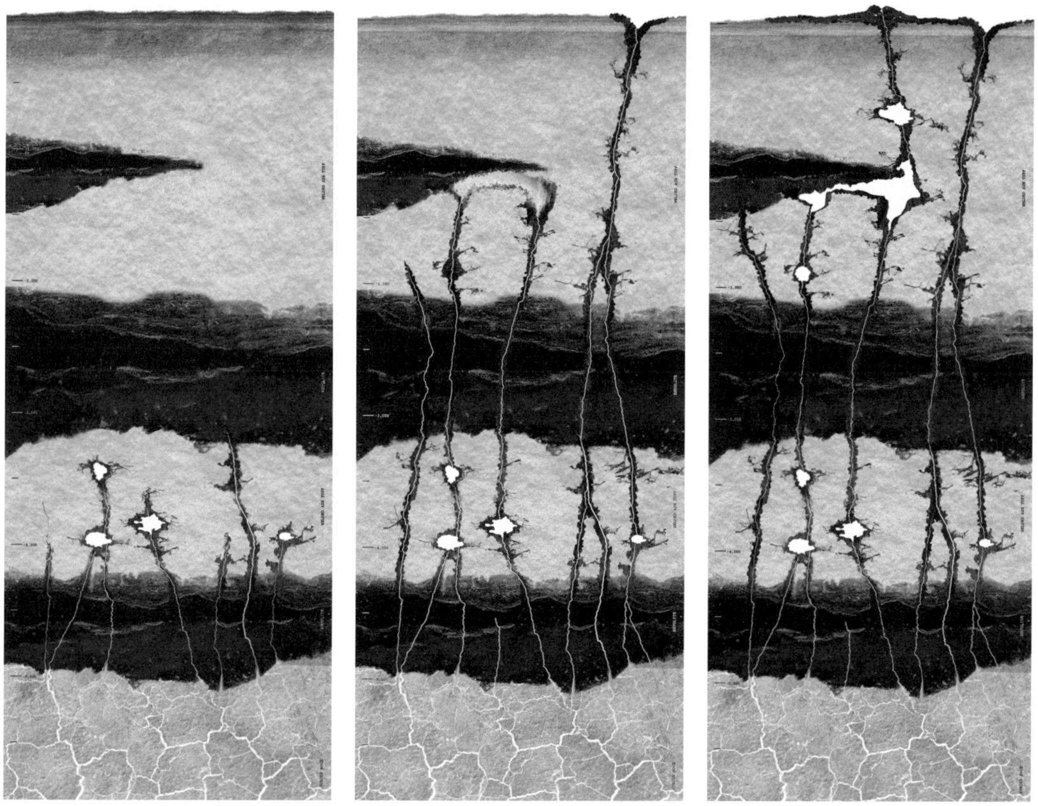

This project seeks to reveal modes in which heat triggers geological change. Rocks, often perceived as solid and static, can be melted and transformed by heated groundwater, which, when under pressure, can be aggressive and dynamic.

The Yellowstone caldera, about 40 miles in diameter, was formed over the past two million years as a result of three major super eruptions. It is considered one of the most geologically active places on Earth, as it sits above the Yellowstone hotspot in the Earth's mantle. Yellowstone's famous geysers and hot springs are just a few examples of the geothermal activity and geological transformations underway in the area. Here, water and rocks are altered by heat, which causes state changes and morphological transformations. As the Earth's mantle transfers heat to the surface, it creates layers of rhyolite lava, which contain an abundance of silica and are therefore rigid and impermeable.

The interaction of rocks, heat, and water produces an intricate system of water circulation, which drives geological change and also sustains ecosystems and local ecologies. This inquiry explores how the interaction between thermal conditions and geology might create new scenarios, relationships, materials, and transformations.

Top: Sections of the formation of a geyser showing the penetrations of superheated water through the layers of rhyolite. This transports silica upwards and creates the piping structures formed by the silica precipitations that will eventually channel the hot ground water to the Earth's surface.

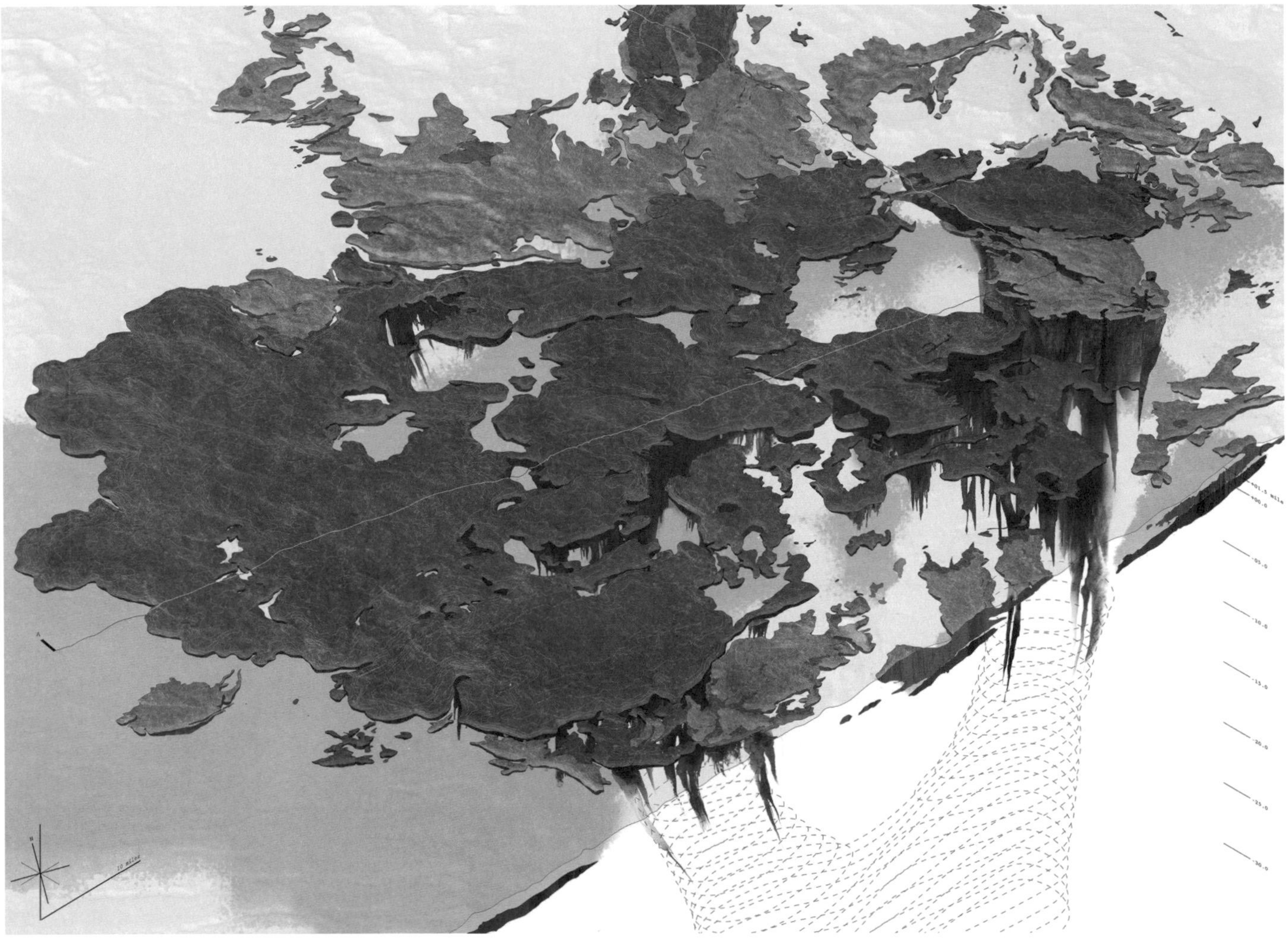

+01.5 mile
+00.0
-05.0
-10.0
-15.0
-20.0
-25.0
-30.0

Yellowstone
Caldera
2.0 Ma
PLAN OF GROUNDWATER AT -1,000ft
10 MILES

Opposite top: Isometric drawing of the water circulation system triggered by the heat of magma. The flow of water is determined by the rhyolite rock structure.

Opposite bottom: Plan of ground water at -1,000 feet. Areas in blue and white represent the permeation of water and dry areas of rhyolite rocks, respectively.

Above: Axonometric drawing showing rhyolite lava eruptions. The Lava Creek erupted around 640,000 years ago as the uppermost part of the magma chamber. Rhyolite lava erupted through the fractures that covered the caldera creating several layers of usually rigid and impermeable rhyolite.

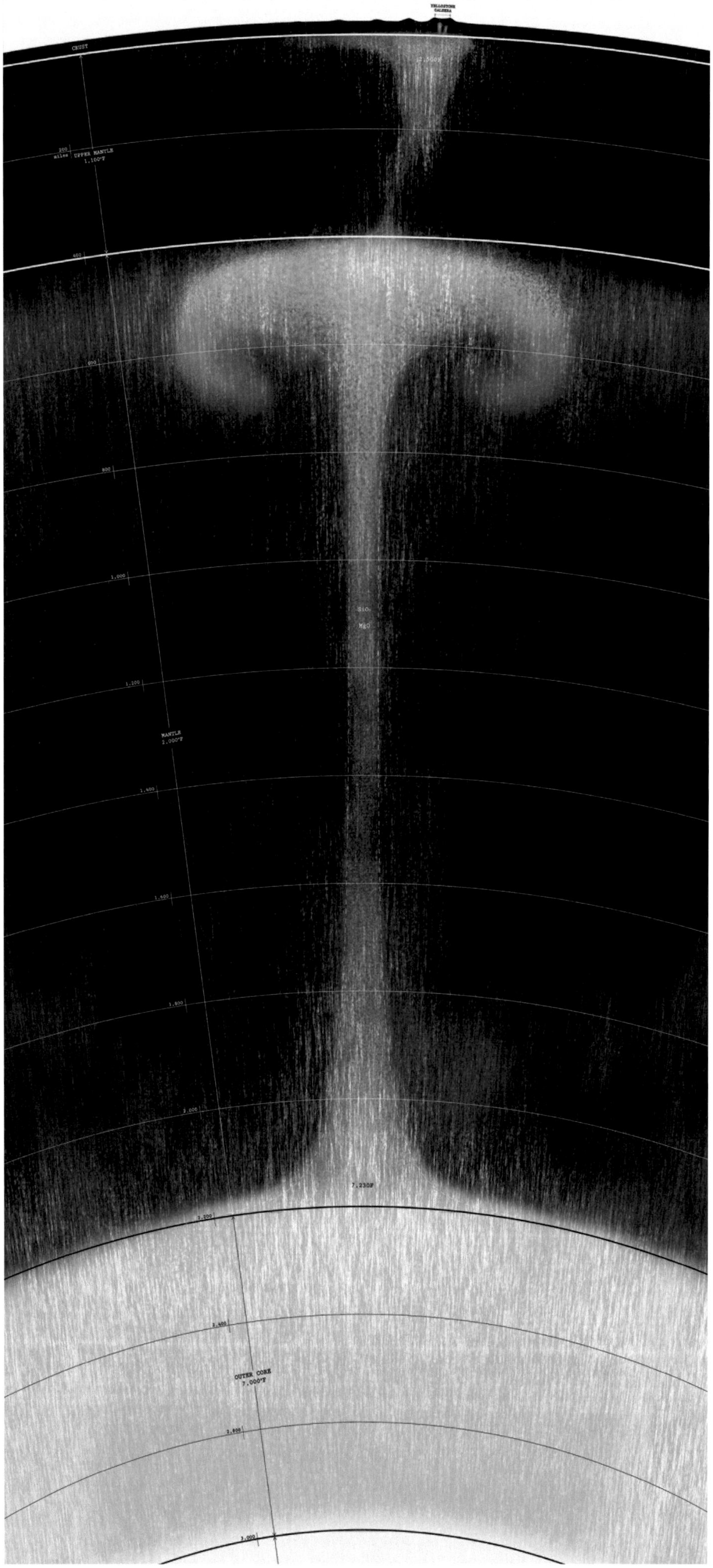
YELLOWSTONE
CALDERA
CRUST
200
miles
UPPER MANTLE
1,100°F
400
600
800
1,000
1,200
MANTLE
2,000°F
1,400
1,600
1,800
2,000
7,230F
2,200
OUTER CORE
7,000°F

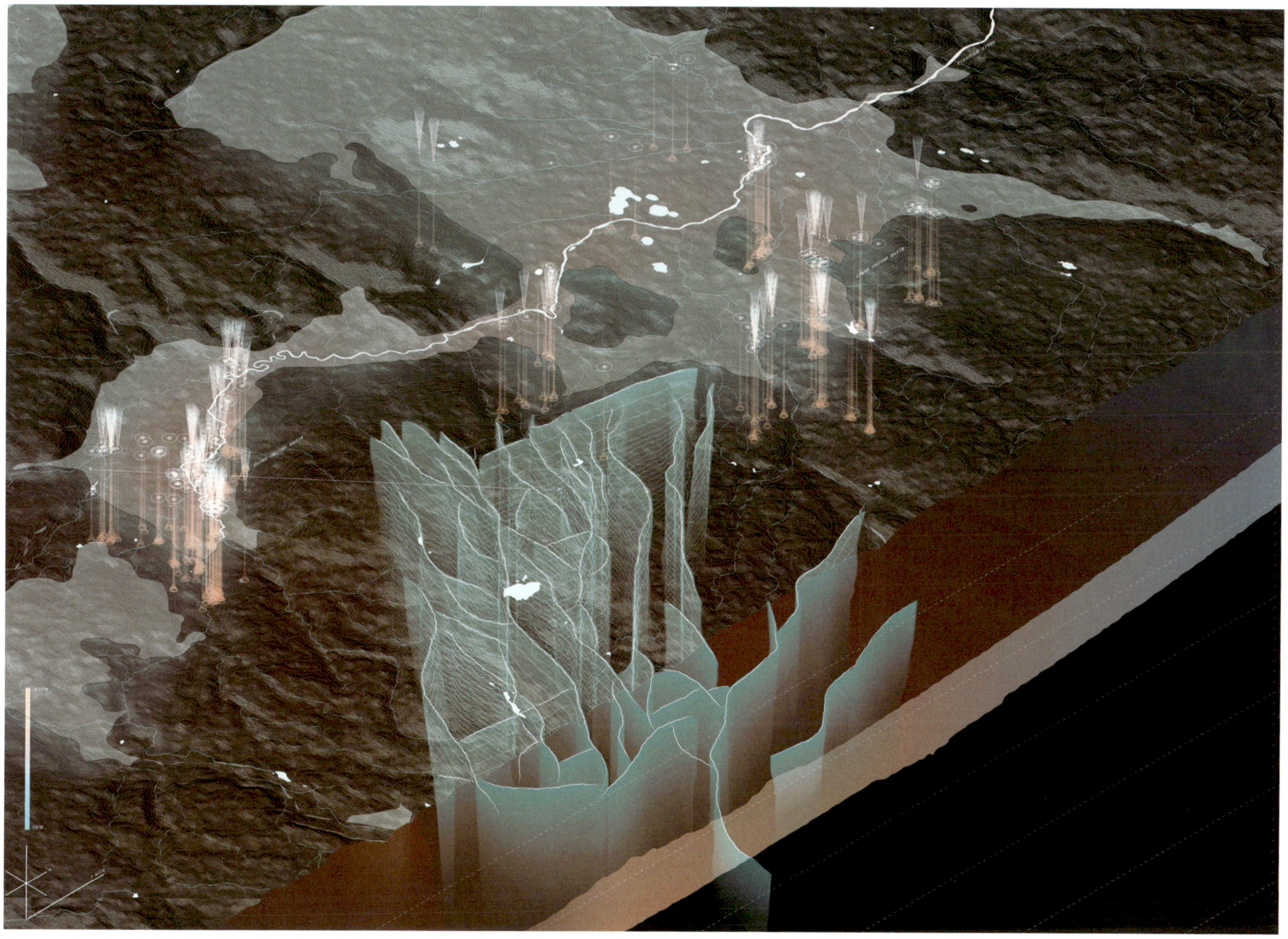

Opposite: Section through the Yellowstone hotspot system from the Earth's core to the surface. Convection brings abundant silica up to the surface in the form of rhyolite lava.

Above: Isometric drawing showing water circulation from the surface to 10,000 feet below the ground in the Upper and Lower Geyser Basin and depicting the surface water recharge of the aquifer through fault lines, while geysers and hot springs discharge the superheated water in order to release pressure.

Above: Section showing water circulation upwards, following the rhyolite rock structure with permeable and non-permeable rock.

Above and Left: Model depicting a morphed structure made with plaster, ice, and aluminum wire. A block of ice with drilled cores was inserted into a bucket of boiling plaster. The plaster was subsequently squeezed out, penetrating the ice through the drilled cores and forming a rigid structure. The interaction of a frozen material and a boiling one produced two reactions—melting and solidification—and ultimately shaped a new structure.

Phantom Surge

Seguam Island, Aleutian Arc, Alaska
Stefan van Biljon

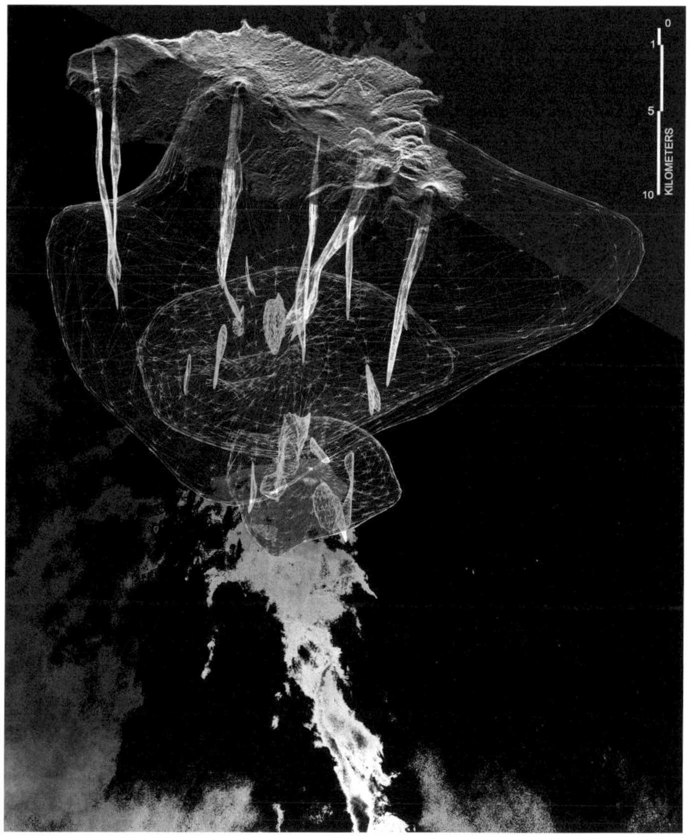

This exploration is concerned with the disjunction between Seguam Island's diminutive surface scale and the titanic geological engines that shape it. Though dramatic at a human scale, Seguam's topography is but a ripple in geological scale, produced by a titanic metabolism of time, pressure, and heat beneath the Earth's surface.

The Aleutian Arc is a 3,000-kilometer stretch of volcanic islands in Alaska, stretching southwest of Anchorage between the Bering Sea and the north Pacific Ocean. Located in the middle of this long archipelago, Seguam is a small volcanic complex (≈200 km^2) that became subaerial 318,000 years ago. 170 kilometers south of Seguam, the Pacific Ocean tectonic plate is subducting beneath the North American plate at the ≈7-km-deep Aleutian trench. As the oceanic plate is forced into the depths of the Earth's convecting mantle, a volatile mixture of sea water, pressure, and incredible heat delaminates the plate along its oblique descent. Magma percolates upward to form immense subterranean lakes of molten rock and gas. Such lakes, or magma lenses, form along lines separating rock density. Lenses are connected vertically by magma columns, and upon surface eruption, form volcanic islands like Seguam.

Through this reading, Seguam Island reveals younger volcanic vents born from the remains of previous incarnations. After a cataclysmic collapse 9,000 years ago, Seguam's surface was levelled and reconfigured beyond recognition. Slowly (≈6.8 cm/year), the magmatic conveyor belt morphing Seguam is working in darkness to produce a new continent.

Top: Isometric view of Seguam Island's subaerial volcanoes being fed with magma via conduits extending from a long-lived basaltic magma lens located ≈12 km below sea level.

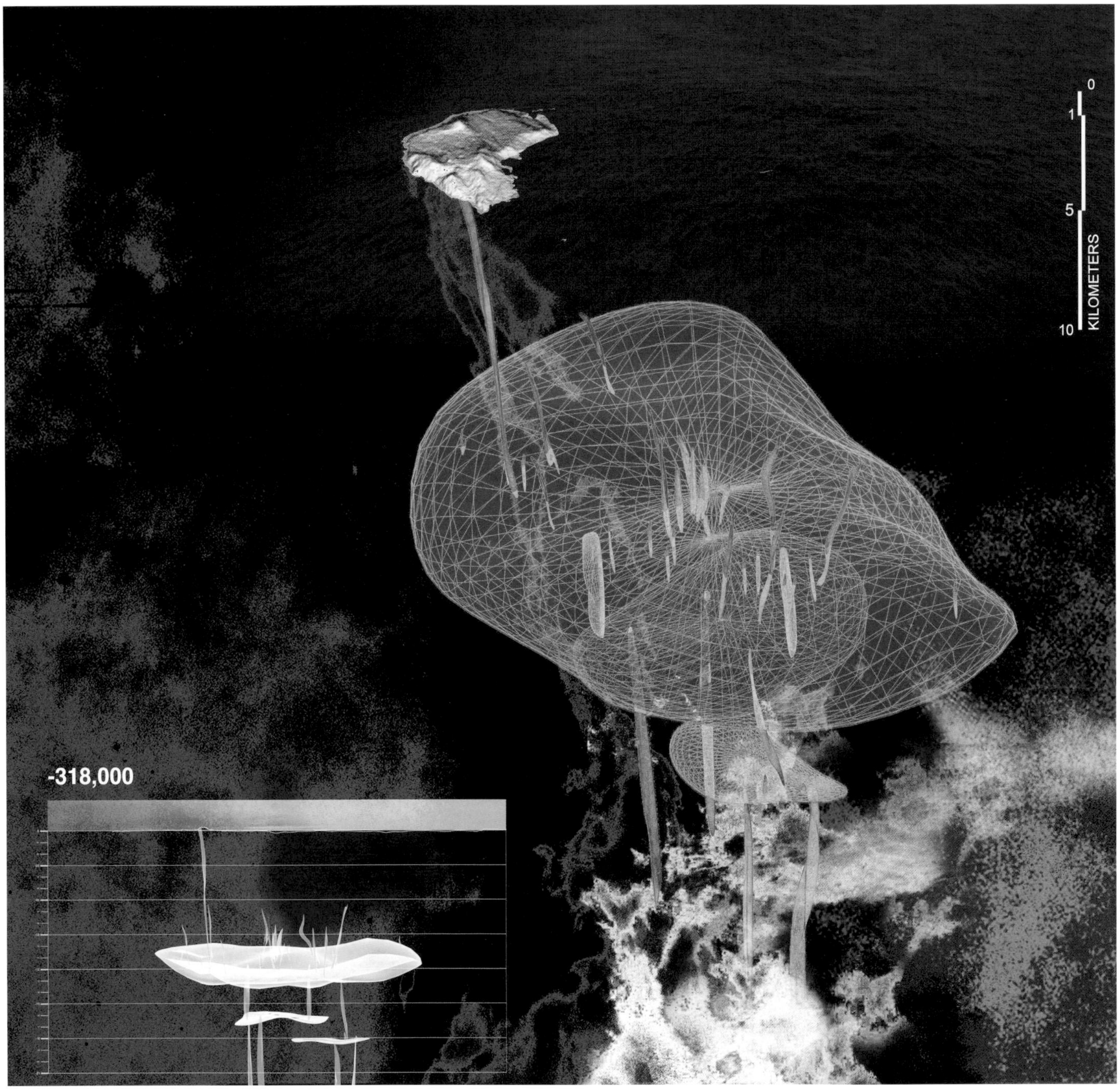

Above: Isometric view of Seguam Island's geological morphology approximately 318,000 years ago. A single magma conduit extends from the long-lived basaltic melt lens (≈12 km below sea level) to form Seguam's first subaerial landmass.

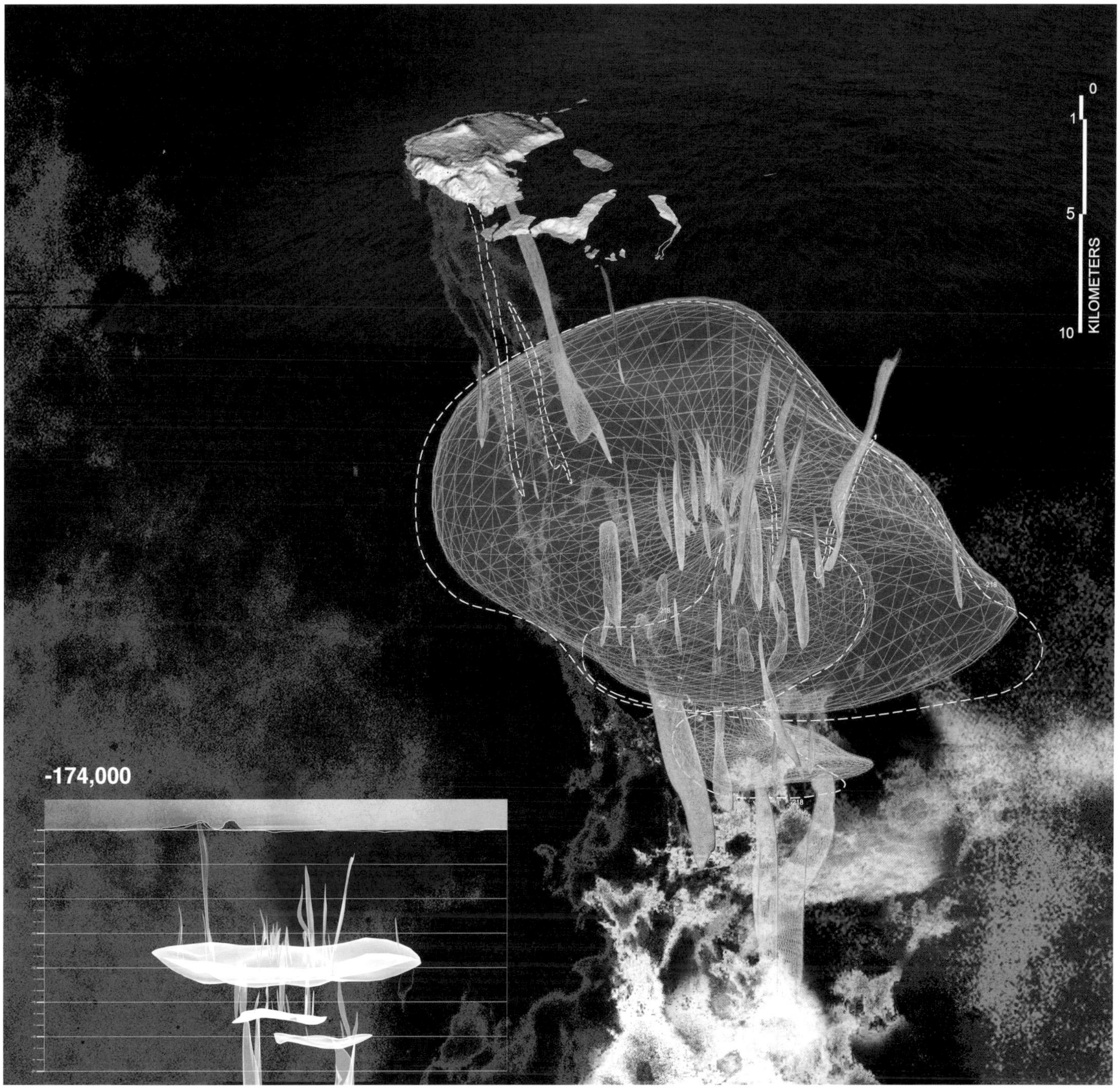

Above: Isometric view of Seguam Island's geological morphology ≈174,000 years ago. Several younger magma conduits sprout from the long-lived basaltic melt lines.

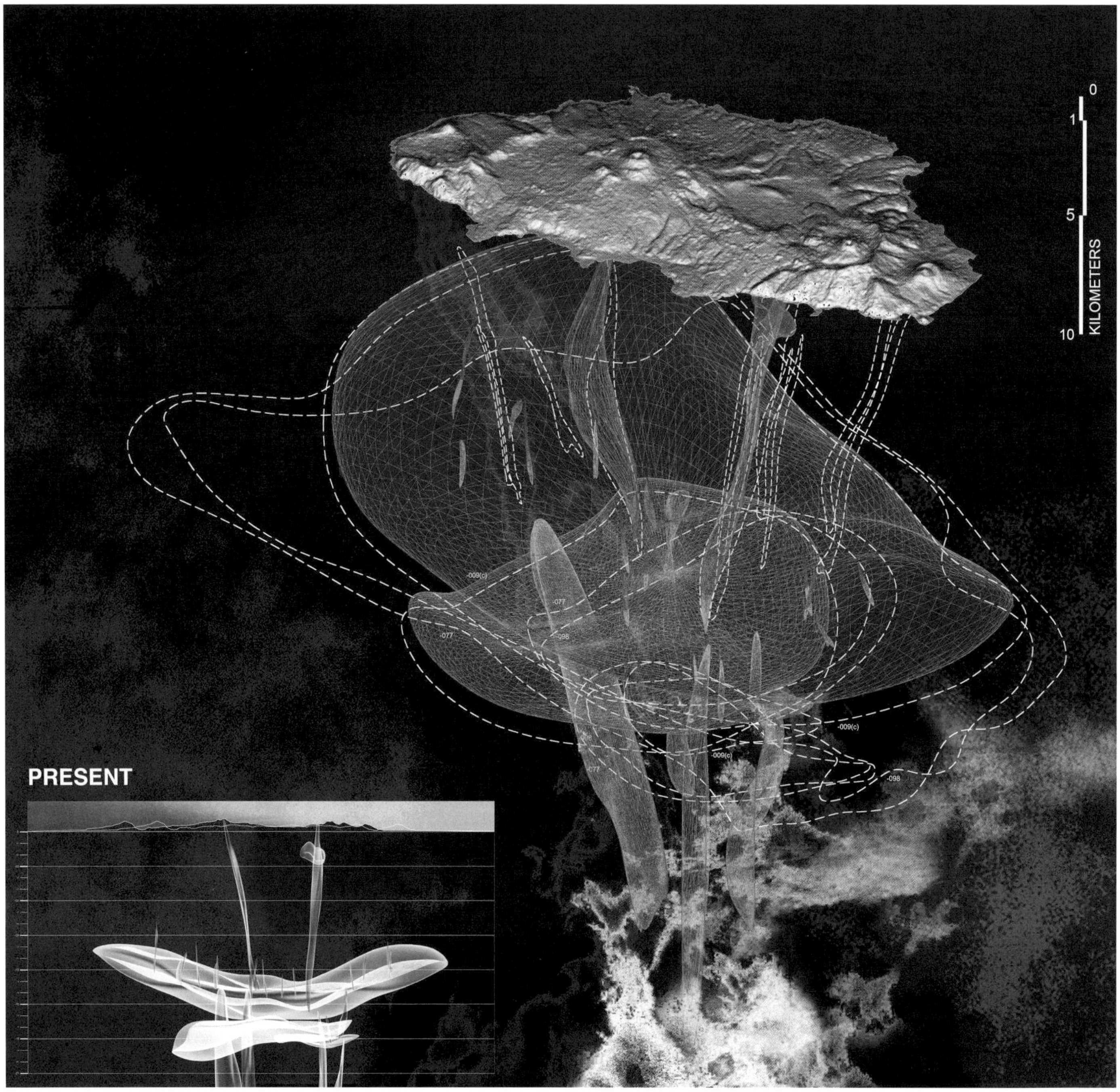

Above: Isometric view of Seguam Island's geological morphology in the present day. Broken lines trace the phantoms of Seguam's past forms.

Subduction and Transformations of the Mantle Rock

Mt. St. Helens, Washington
Hsing-O Chiang

This project explores the effects as water penetrates the rift between colliding tectonic plates and spills into the deep mantle. This process is the result of the physical and chemical interactions involved in subduction as the oceanic lithosphere converges with the Earth's lithosphere, sliding into the mantle due to gravity and temperature differential. Subduction, which generates a chain reaction that results in volcanic eruptions, has been occurring in this region for 200 million years. Powerful forces, resulting from the collision of the oceanic Juan de Fuca and the continental North American plates, cause massive rock formations to crumble. Ocean water then penetrates this geological rift. When water reaches a depth that allows its temperature to rise to 1400°C, a chemical reaction causes the rock to liquefy and form vast quantities of magma. High-pressure buildup pushes the magma upwards until it reaches the surface of the Earth's crust, giving birth to the mountainous volcanic landscape of the Arc.

Mount St. Helens, part of the Cascade Volcanic Arc that stretches from southwestern British Columbia to northern California, presents an ideal opportunity for these explorations. With a geological substratum 210,000 feet below sea level, and a height of 8,366 feet above sea level, the mountain covers 90 square kilometers and is comprised of rock over 40,000 years old. The volcano's most recent eruption was on May 18, 1980.

Top: Section of the Cascadia Subduction Zone, an active subduction zone extending northward along the Pacific Coast from northern California to British Columbia, showing the movement of the Juan de Fuca plate under the continental (North American) plate. The oceanic crust of the Pacific Ocean has been sinking beneath the continent for about 200 million years, and currently does so at a rate of approximately 40 mm/yr.

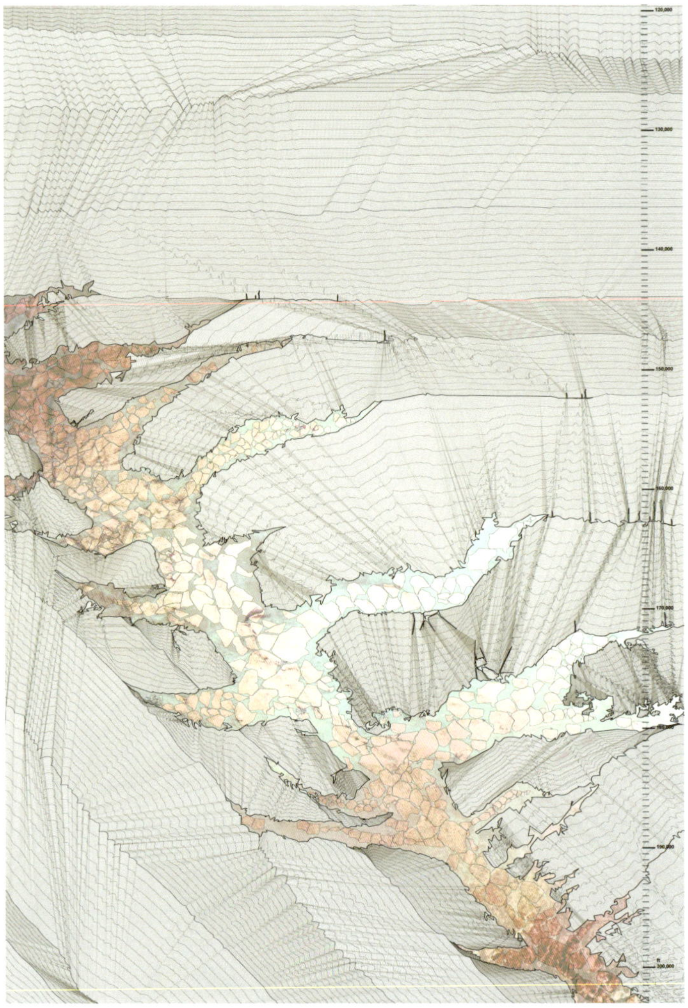

Above left: Detail section of the Juan de Fuca oceanic plate at a depth of 120,000 to 210,000 feet, as it subducts beneath the westward-moving North American continental plate.

Above right: Detail section of the Juan de Fuca oceanic plate at a depth of 120,000 to 210,000 feet. At about 180,000 feet deep, materials in the subducting plate begin to reach their melting temperatures and a process of partial melting begins. This partial melting produces magma chambers above the subducting oceanic plate. These buoyant magma chambers are less dense than the surrounding mantle.

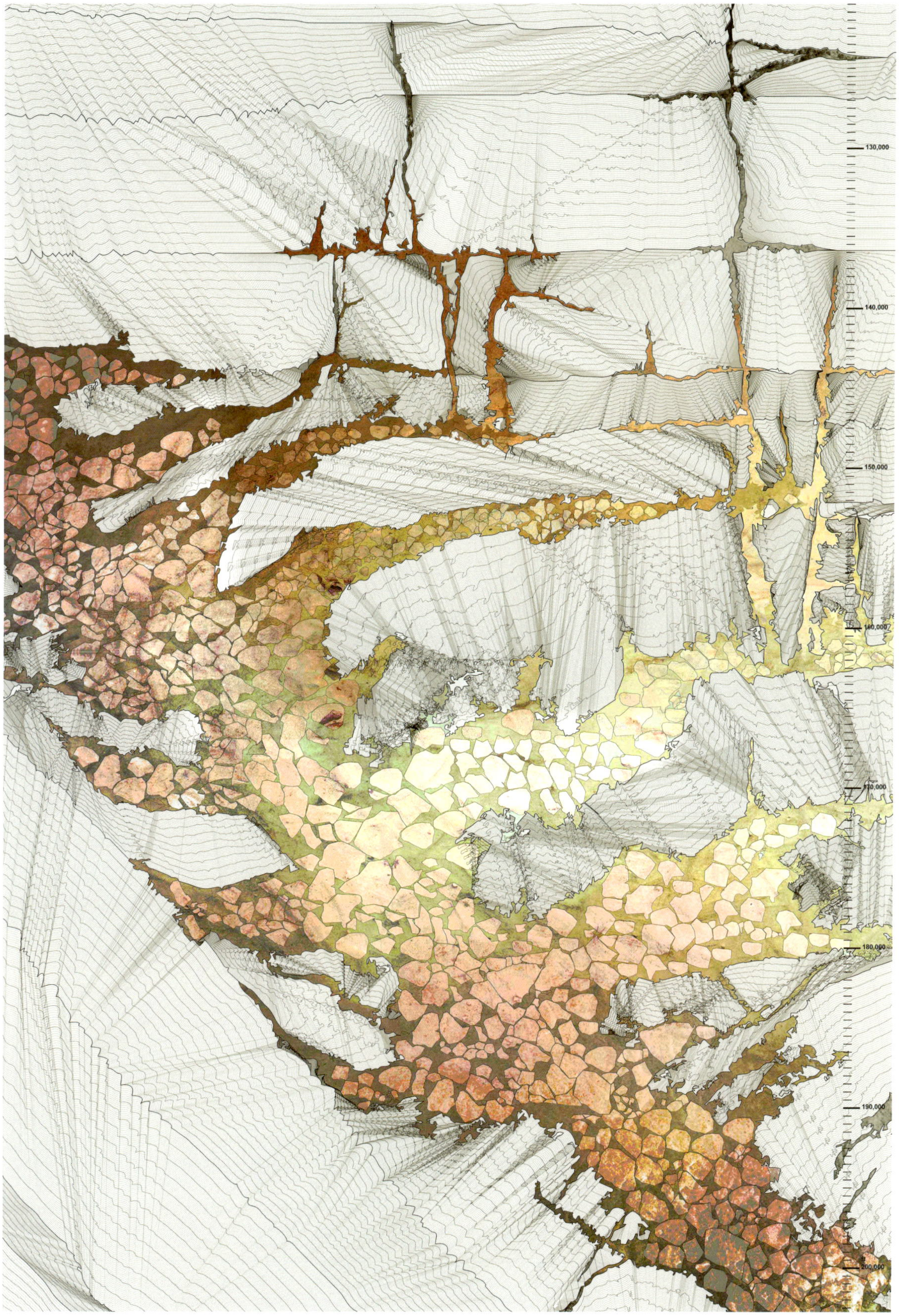

Above: Detail section of the Juan de Fuca oceanic plate at a depth of 120,000 to 210,000 feet, showing how magma chambers are produced by the melting process above the subducting oceanic plate.

Above left and right: Model showing solid rock in the mantle in three dimensions. Under the pressure of the continent, mantle rock seeks cracks to reach the surface.

Above: Detail section of the Juan de Fuca oceanic plate at a depth of 120,000 to 210,000 feet, showing the buoyant magma chambers. These chambers are less dense than the surrounding mantle materials in the asthenosphere, 200 kilometers below the Earth's surface. The buildup of pressure pushes them upwards.

Fire and Ice

Mount St. Helens, Washington
Minibum Koo

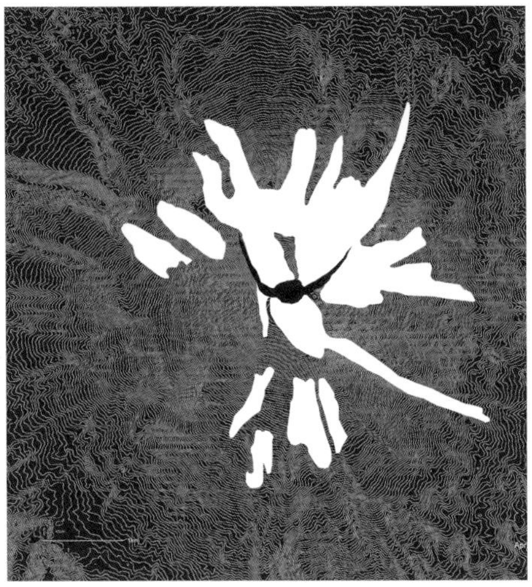

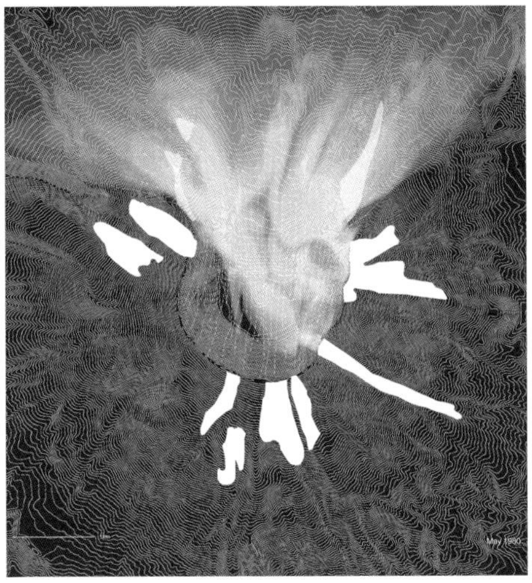

The Mount St. Helen volcano is characterized by the continuous interaction between extreme elements—hot magma and cold ice. This project explores thermal transformation in the layers of the Earth in Mount St. Helens at the moment of eruption when these thermal layers were punctuated and melted and then returned to a stable state. Mount St. Helens is a strato-volcano rising 8,366 feet above sea level, where it is covered with glaciers causing an extraordinary explosion in a volcanic eruption when liquid magma meets the solid ice of the glacier. This process has a profound and diverse impact on the Earth, affecting the ground, oceans, and the atmosphere.

Mount St. Helens's eruption in the spring of 1980 happened in two stages, with a first explosion followed by a second one about seven weeks later when the magma reached the bottom of the glacier and blew up one third of the mountain. Since 1980, lava from ongoing eruptions has added over 200 million cubic yards of material to the crater floor, and the crater glacier has also grown with snowfall and avalanches. New volcanic activity began in 2004. Based on this, a provocative scenario is proposed on a possible future interaction at Mount St. Helens as a bigger explosion triggered by an acupunctural approach of inserting the glacier into the magma body. A great eruption would then burn up all the magma in the northwest area of the volcano, eliminating the risk of another explosion. As an epilogue, a caldera would form on the top, with the width of 9.21 kilometers, four times larger than the current crater.

Top left and right: Sequential plans showing the interactions of the glacier and the magma at Mount St. Helens from 1979 to 2004.

Opposite right: Section of the melting glacier to a depth of 900 meters, where it came in contact with the magma on May 18, 1980.

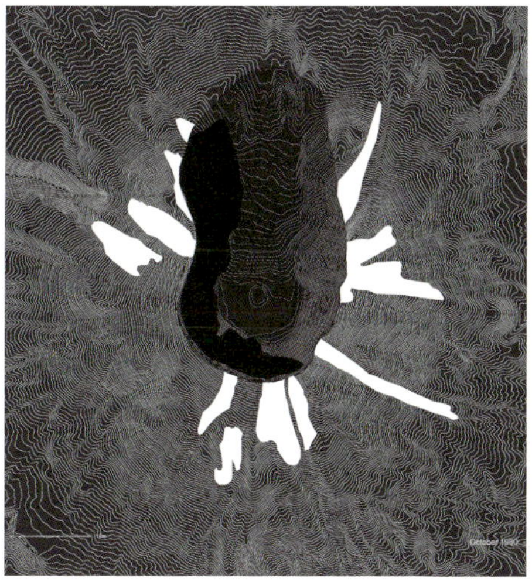
October 1980

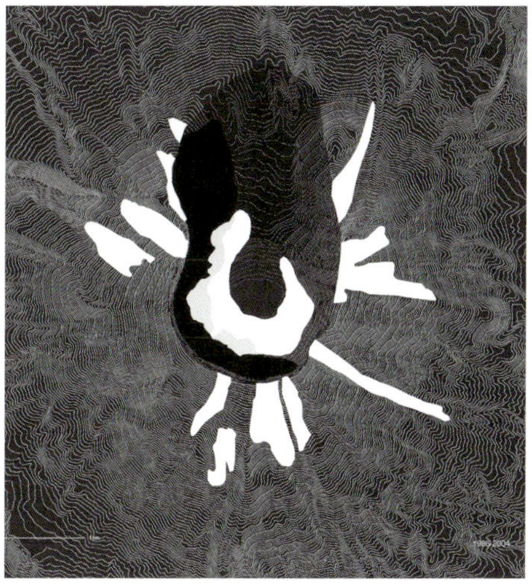
1980-2004

OCTOBER 2004

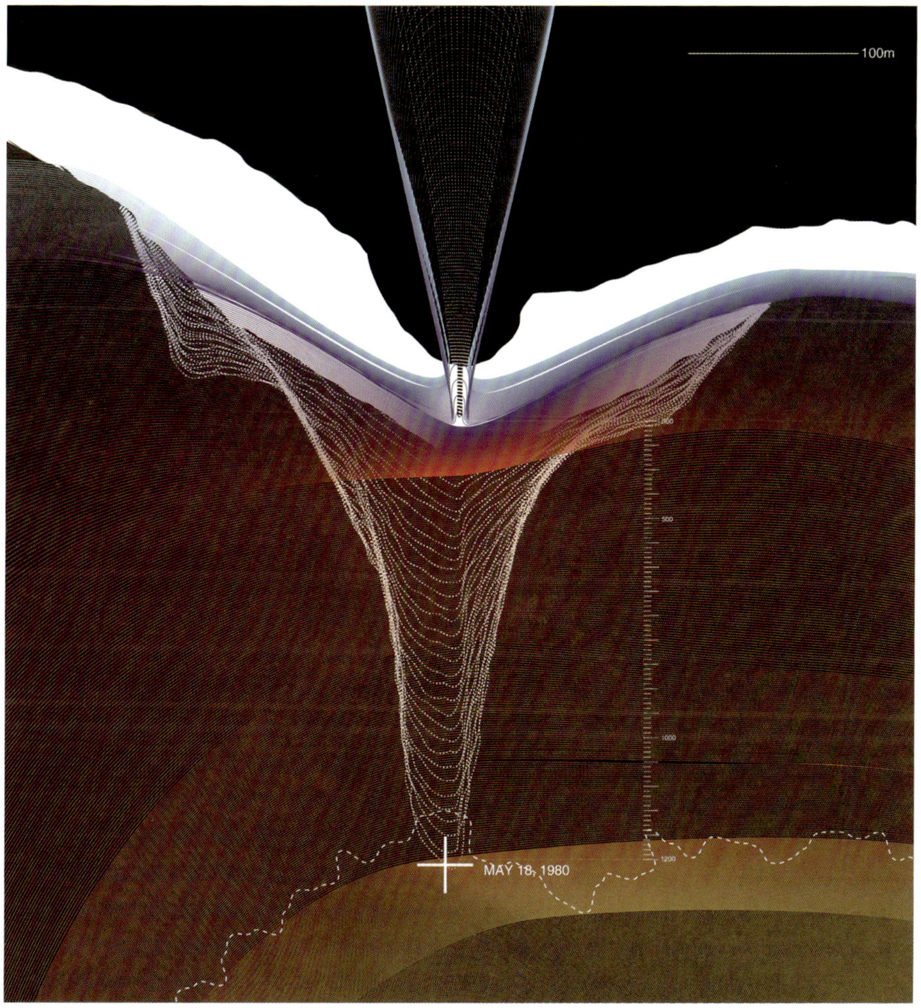
100m
500
1000
1200
MAY 18, 1980

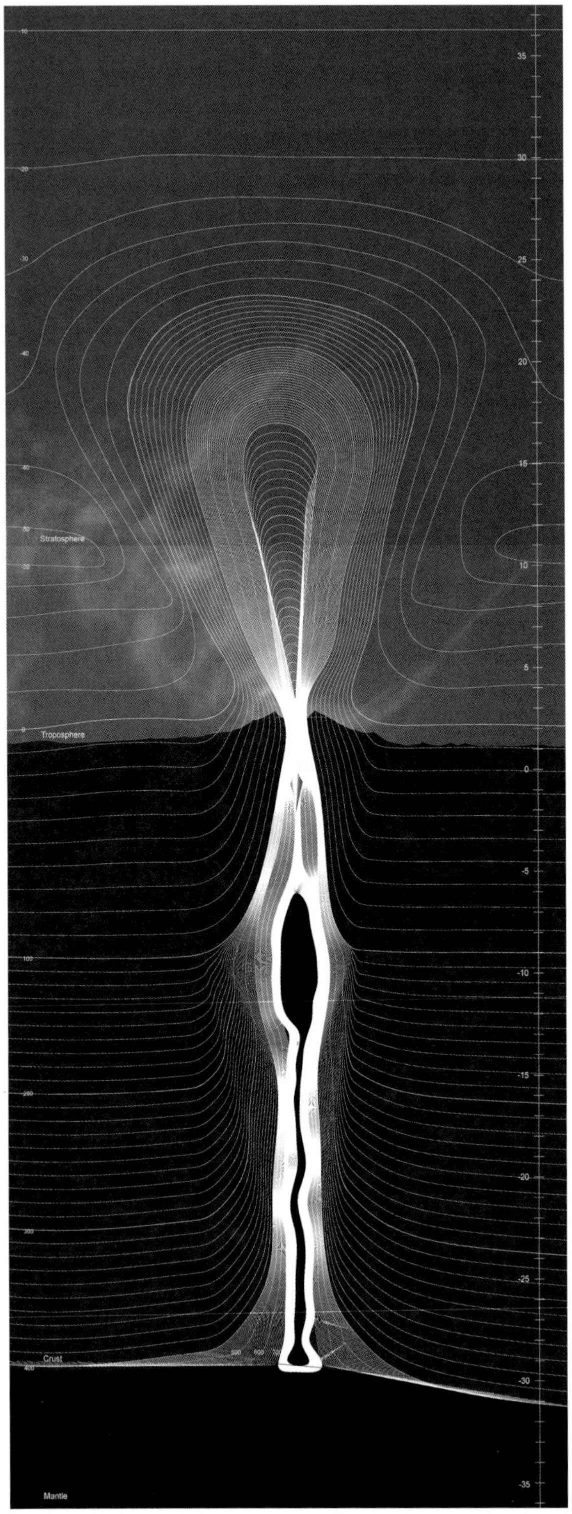

Above: Volcano section showing the penetration of the magma upwards through layers of the Earth and thermal contour lines.

Above: Three-dimensional rendition of the sound impact as it bounced between the atmosphere and the ground, alternating in rings of loud and silent zones.

Above: Plan of artificially triggered blast showing the effect of the pyroclastic density current from the explosion. At temperatures ranging between 100°C to 850°C, magma descended twelve miles in one minute, stripping the mountain of trees and soil.

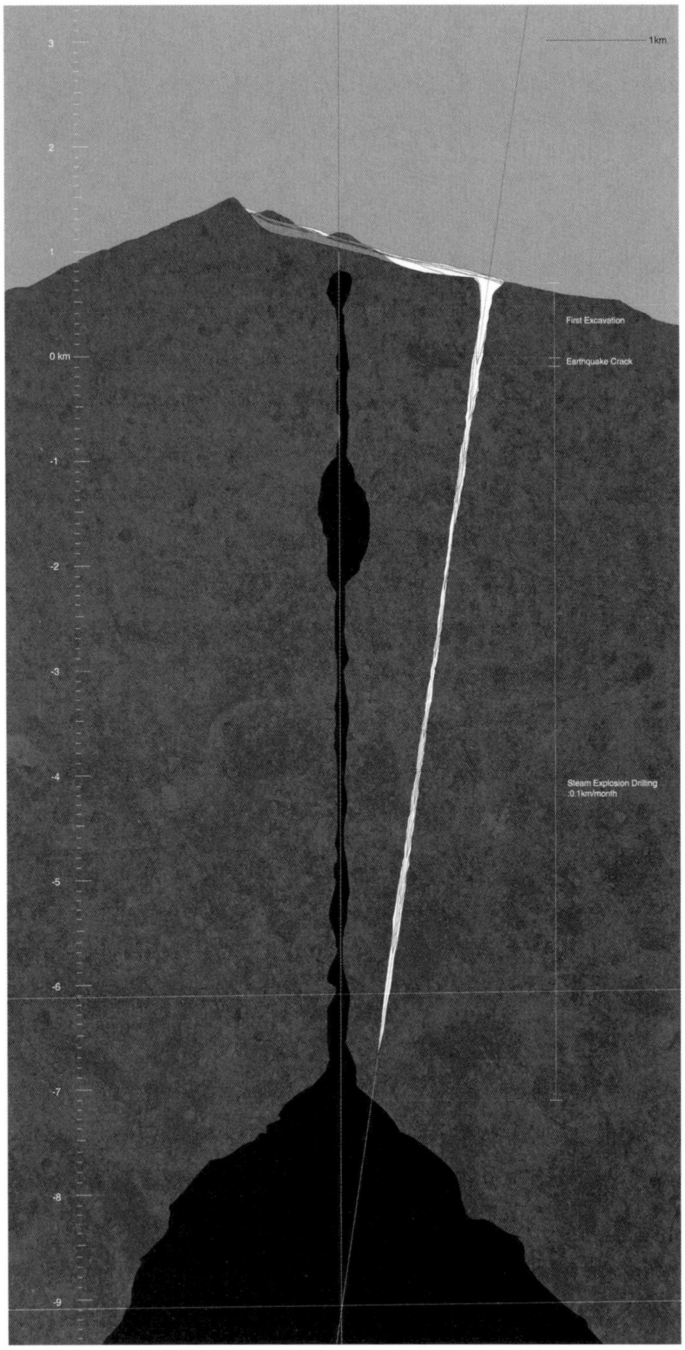

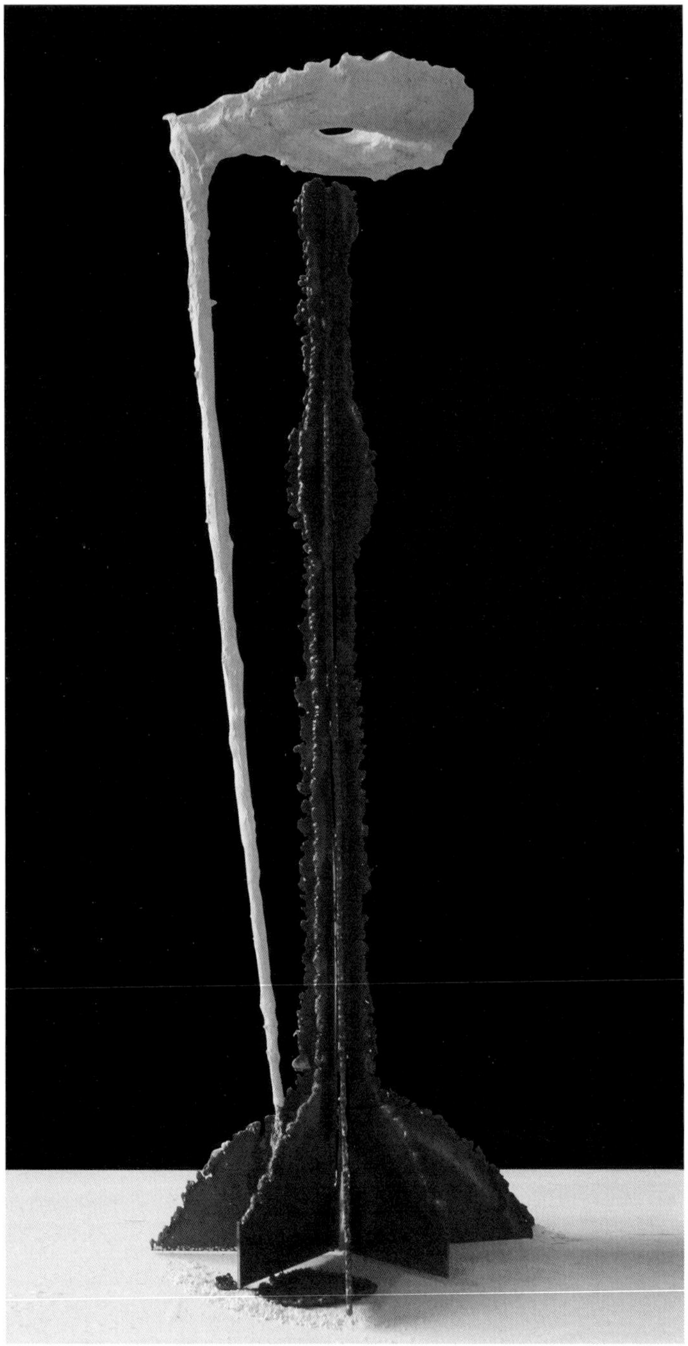

Above: Section through the puncture. The glacier will descend about 0.1 km/month until it meets the body of the magma and generates an explosion.

Above: Model of a hypothetical puncture at the core of the mountain, showing the penetration of the glacier into the magma chamber.

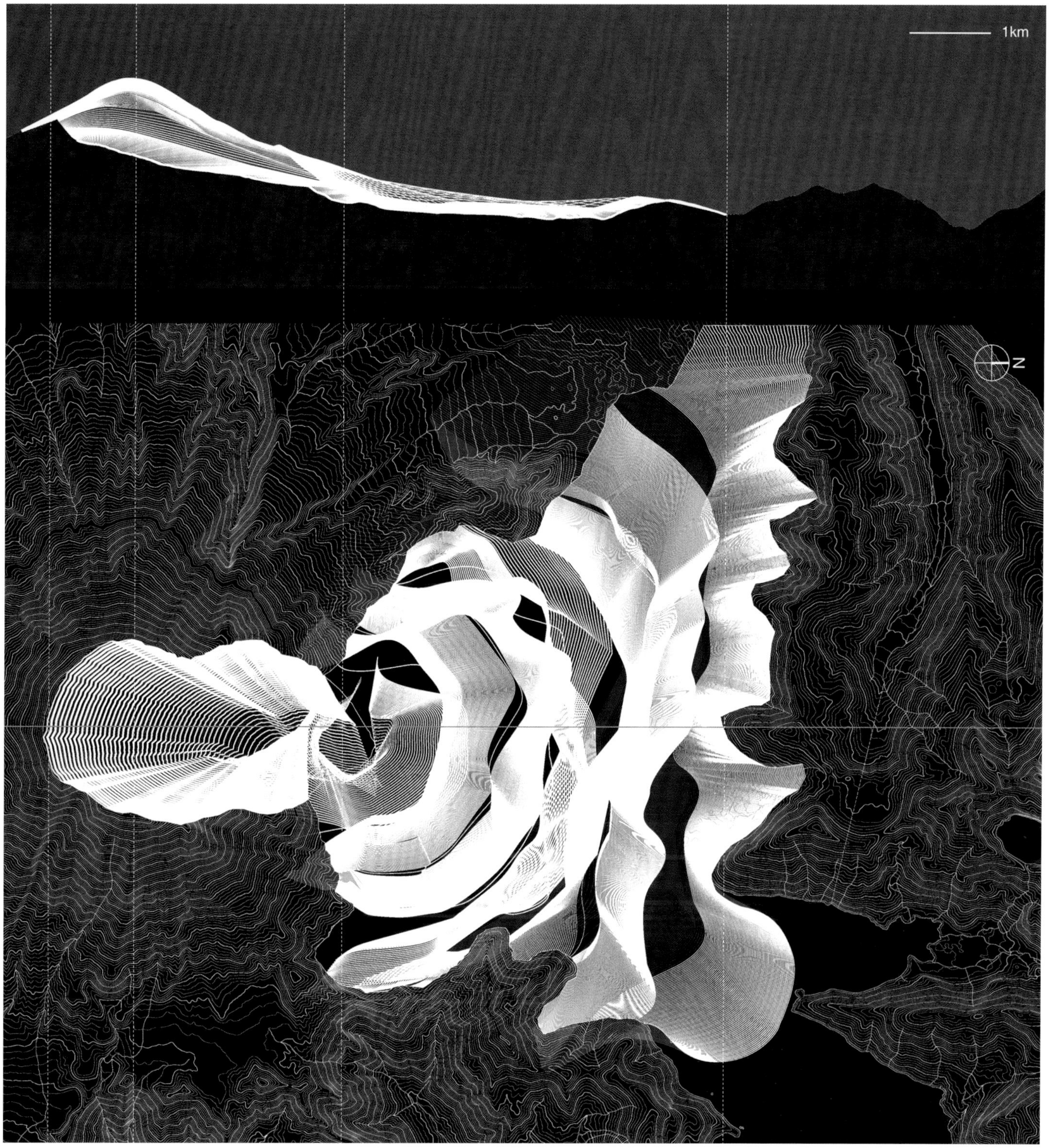

Above: Plan of the landslide after the explosion. Mudflow, a mixture of rocks lubricated with glacier, fell at a rate of 60 miles per hour.

Fire and Water

Crater Lake, Mount Mazama, Oregon
Aikaterini Olga Kefalogianni

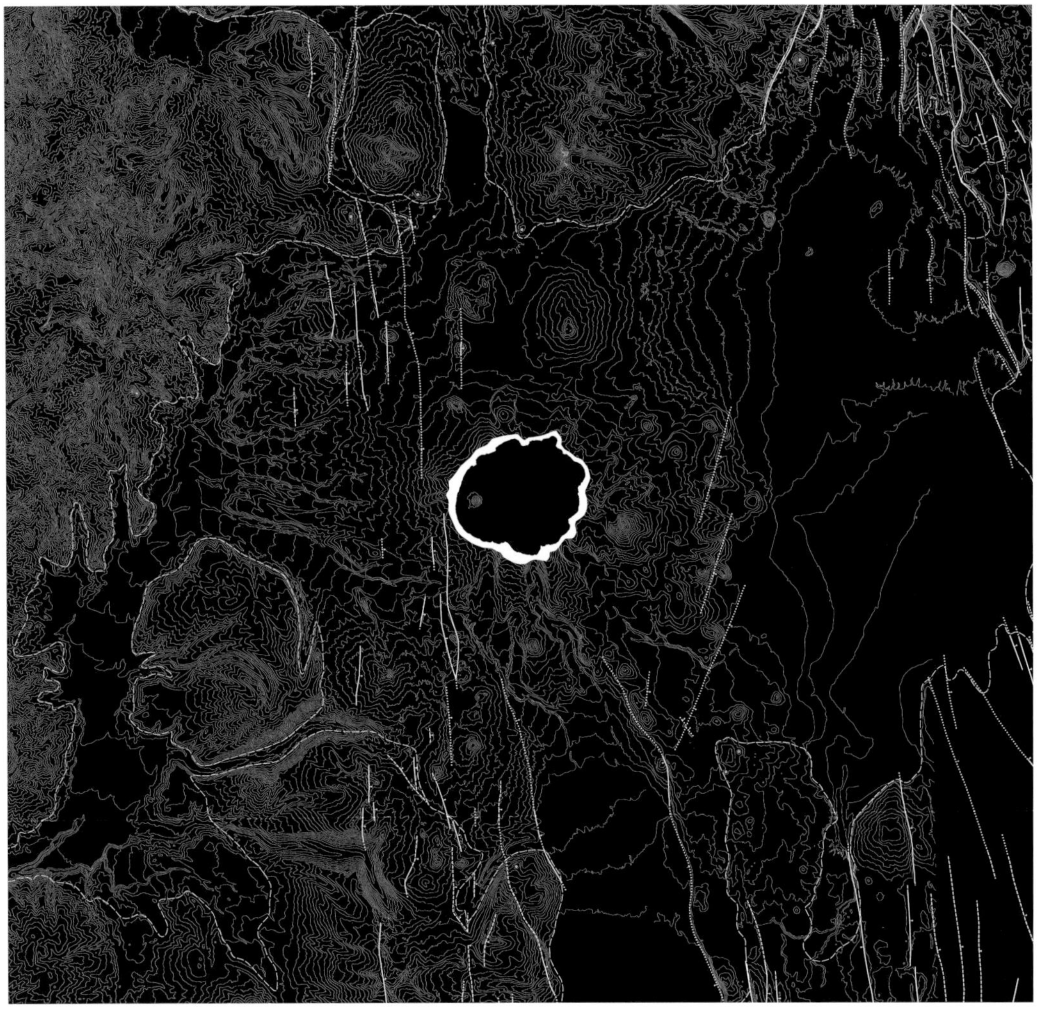

Crater Lake rests in the remnants of a collapsed volcano, Mount Mazama, in the Cascade mountain range in Oregon. One of Earth's clearest and deepest lakes, Crater Lake was formed by the opposing forces of fire and ice, catastrophe and regeneration, stability and transformation, collection and distribution, discontinuity and fluidity.

About half a million years ago in the Pleistocene Epoch, Mount Mazama formed as magma rose from below the Earth's surface. The volcano developed gradually as an irregular cluster of overlapping volcanoes that reached a height of 12,000 feet above sea level. But after an explosive eruption 7,700 years ago, Mount Mazama was radically transformed. As volcanic material was ejected from the magma chamber, the summit collapsed inward, forming a caldera six miles across and four thousand feet deep. In total, ten to thirteen cubic miles of the mountaintop disappeared. Over the next 250 years, snow, rain, and groundwater filled the volcano's caldera to create Crater Lake. Without any inlets or tributaries, the water enclosed in the volcano is totally clear, allowing sunlight to penetrate deep down. A fine balance between precipitation, evaporation, and underground seepage maintains a stable water level.

The basin of Crater Lake remains an active volcanic terrain. Future changes may come, but their nature and extent is unknown. This project attempts to decode the synergies involved in the creation of this present volcanic landform and explore its potential future through drawings and models that "re-write" the remarkable story of the Crater Lake's formation.

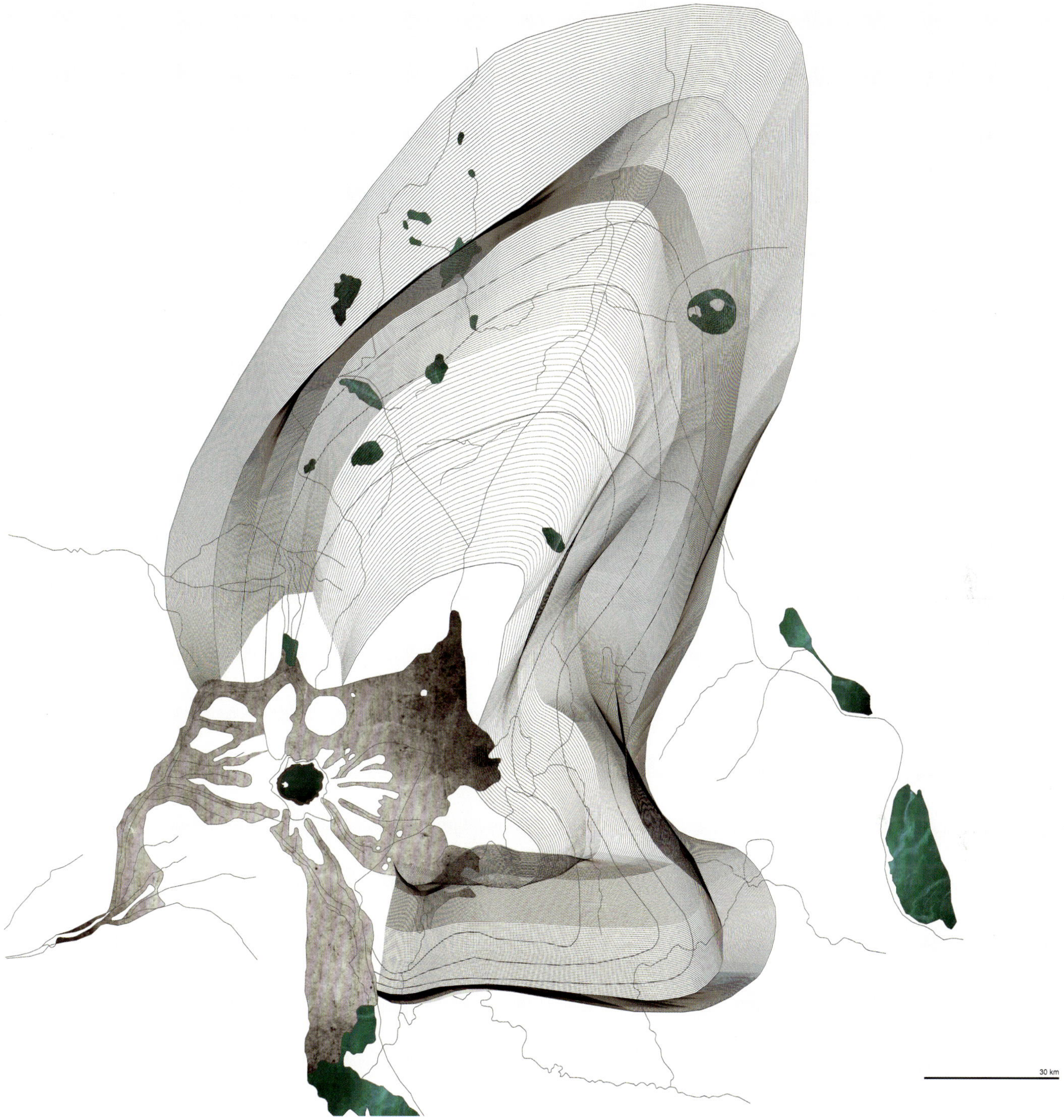

Opposite top: Plan of Mount Mazama's cone exposure in cross section after the volcano's explosion.

In the eruption, Pyroclastic flows of pumice and ash devastated the surrounding area, including all of the river valleys that drained to Mount Mazama from as far as 40 miles away. A blanket of pumice and ash fell to the northeast of the volcano at least as far as central Canada.

Above: Plan—Distribution of volcanic material and network of surrounding water bodies.

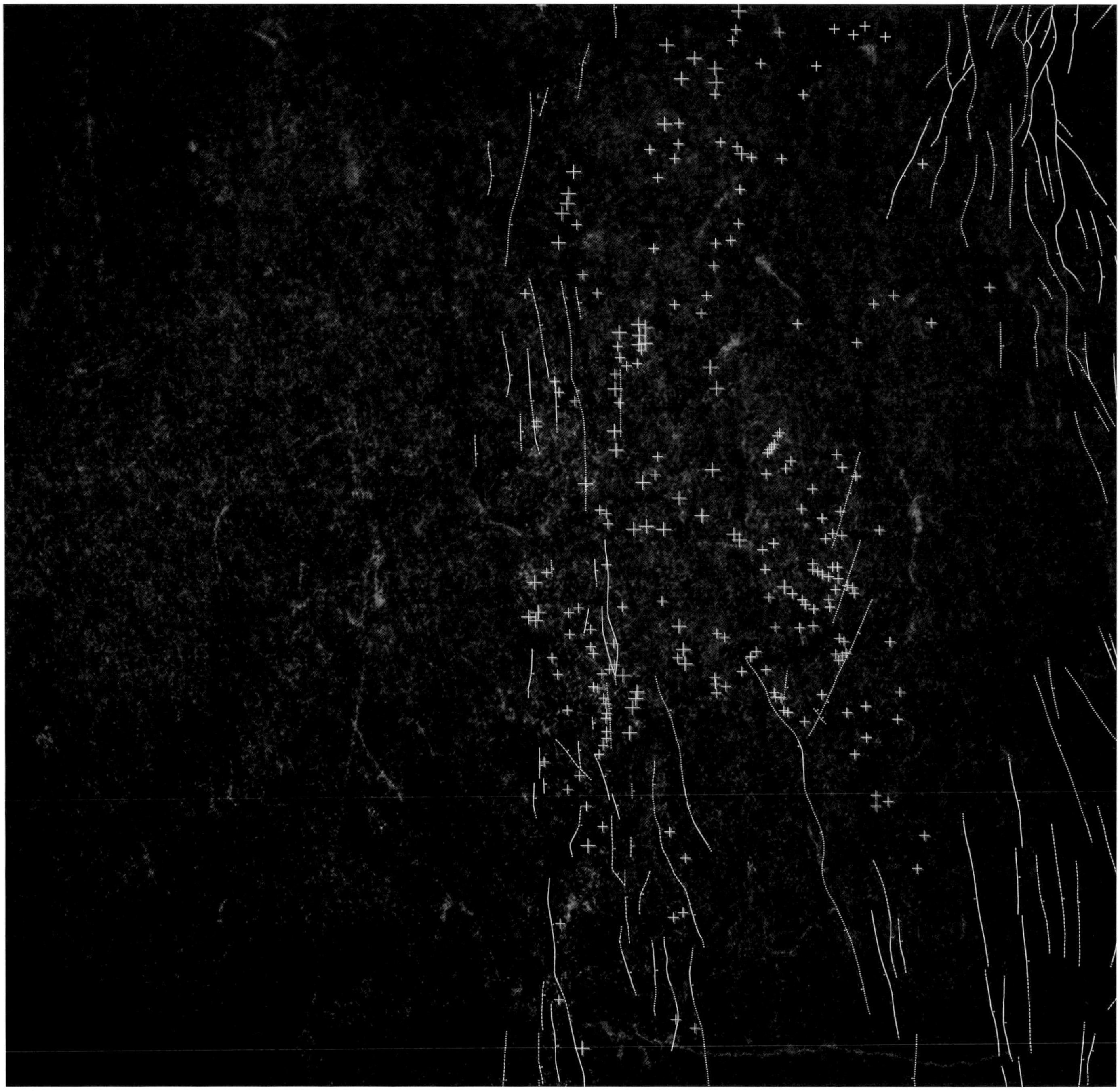

Above: Plan—Fissure vents and fault lines, comparing vertical fluidity and horizontal discontinuity.

Opposite top and bottom: Model of the generation of volcanic landforms. Vents and magma chambers are transporters and underground reservoirs, respectively, of the material that generates and continuously transforms volcanic landforms.

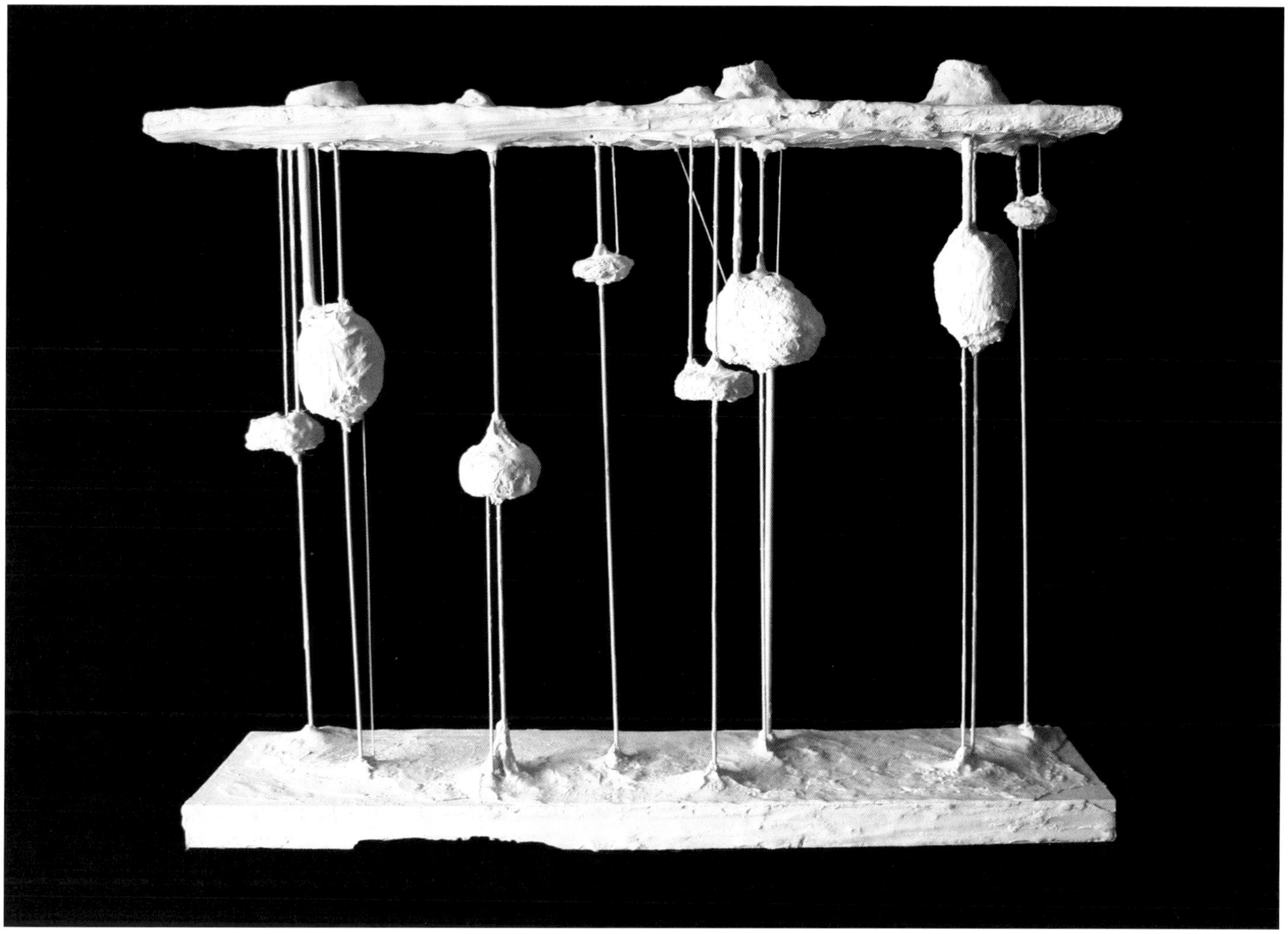

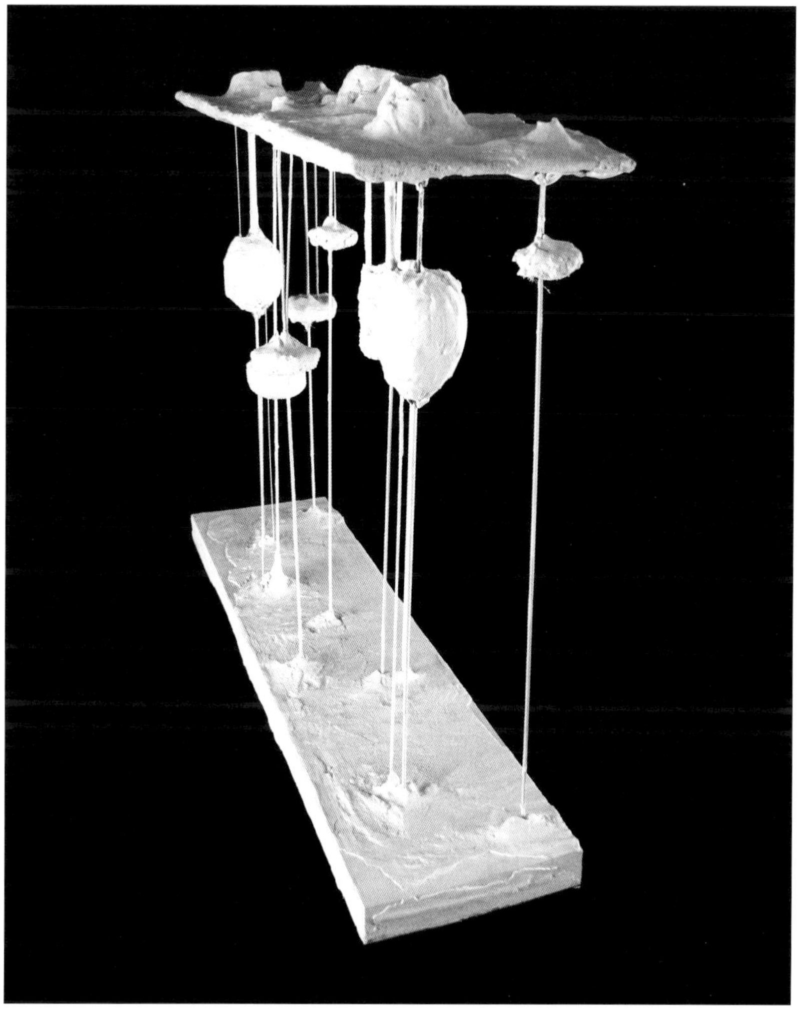

Oblique Tectonics

Kilauea Volcano, Hawaii
Lawrence Lek

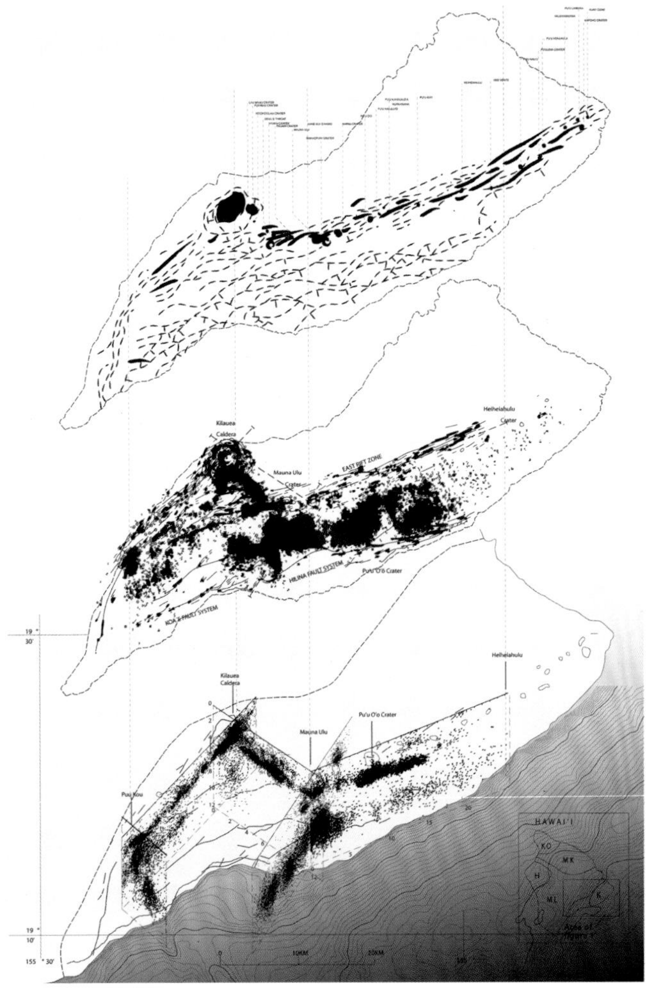

Oblique Tectonics traces the unseen structures and patterns that lie beneath the surface of Kilauea, the youngest and most active volcano of the "Big Island" of Hawaii. The project visualizes the internal architecture of the volcano by interpolating seismological data from the US Geological Survey, revealing a sedimentary process built up over millions of years of activity. Drawings, models, and diagrams reveal a three-dimensional palimpsest of magmatic geometry: the intertwined relationship between ancestral lava and the hidden tectonics of the Earth. It is an inherently unstable system: architecture characterized by regular eruptions and landslides.

The Hawaii island chain is the visible outcrop of a much larger geological formation. This ridge is built entirely from volcanic magma, with each eruption caused by pressure building within the Earth. The magma then solidifies into solid rock as it cools underwater. Many of these magma intrusions remain invisible, never breaking out on the surface; instead, they swarm together, compressed into knife-like granite extrusions known as dikes that cut into previous layers. The buildup of pressure from these intrusions creates cracks on the surface rock, through which subsequent eruptive lava flows. Over thousands of years, the accumulation of pressure can lead to catastrophic landslides in which entire flanks of the island collapse into the sea, causing tsunamis that could devastate the Californian and Japanese coastlines. By reconfiguring the tectonics of the subterranean landscape, a "negative architecture" of subterranean fissures could prevent catastrophic earthquake-driven landslides from occurring, and divert lava flows to form a new archipelago of islands at the boundary of Kilauea.

Opposite top: Superimposed plans showing subterranean tectonic activity that affects surface lava flow. From below: seismic movements over one month; seismic movements over one year; surface fissures and faults; topography; surface flows.

Above: Oblique tectonics: Kilauea volcano with three generations of superimposed subterranean lava flows. Each rising magma plume gets channeled into vertical fissures until it meets a resistant layer of rock, and then it spreads horizontally.

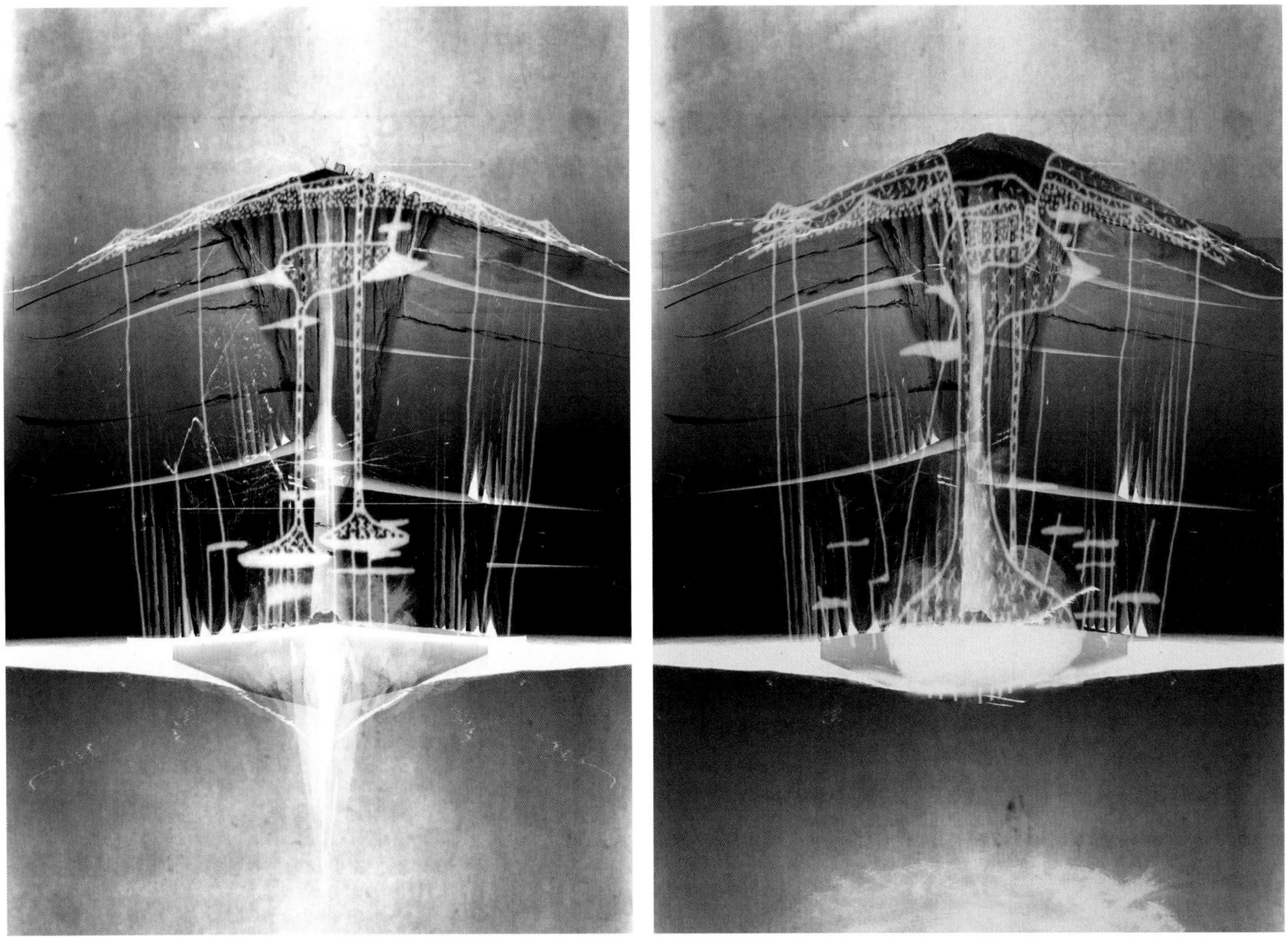

Above and opposite: Visible volcanic activity is the net result of invisible forces culminating over thousands of years. This drawing sequence shows a rising magma plume being channeled into an existing network of ridges and dikes created from earlier eruptions. The net effect pushes the entire structure upwards and outwards.

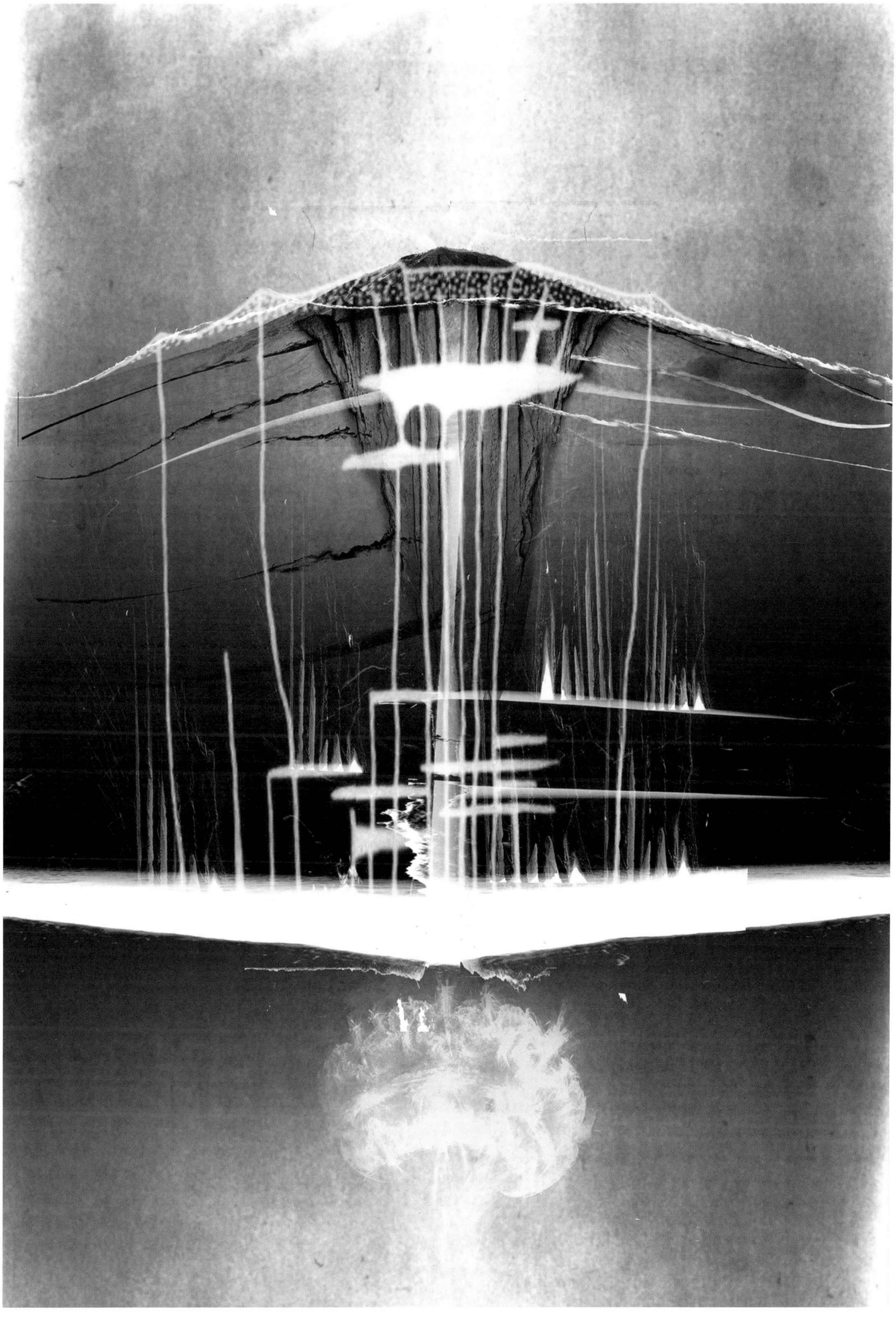

Moving Plates and Stationary Hotspots

Hawaiian Islands Archipelago
Wei Che Yu

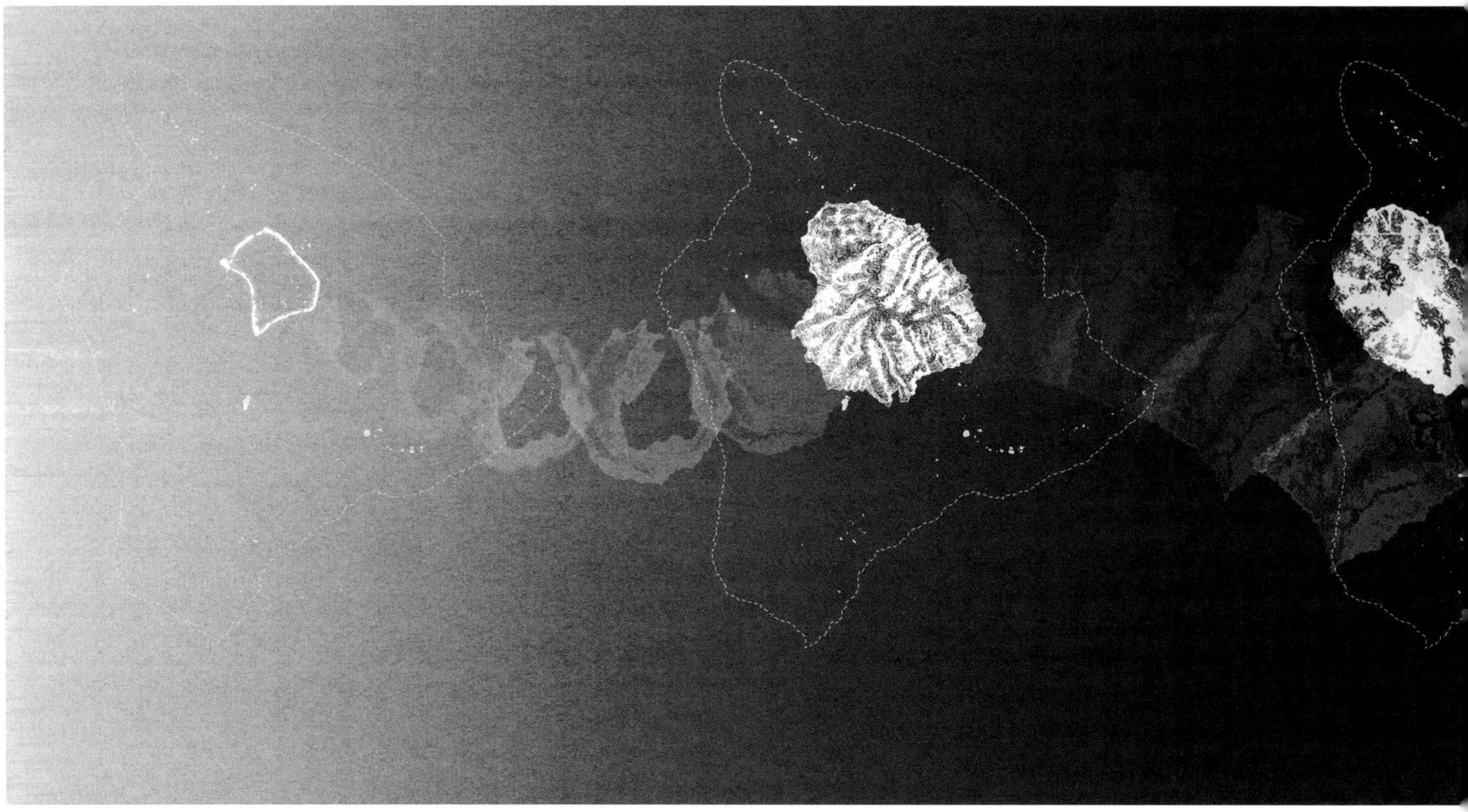

The Hawaiian Islands, a volcanic archipelago in the Pacific Ocean, have grown continuously over the past thirty million years. Located on a seventy million year old geologic "hotspot" 1,200 miles deep in the middle of the Pacific tectonic plate, the islands are formed as the plate moves while the hotspot remains stationary. The interaction between the moving plate and stationary hotspot generates volcanic activity, and ultimately a long trail of volcanoes stretching over 3,600 miles. Volcanic activity has also shaped these islands as layers of lava from successive eruptions have given them their specific morphological characteristics.

This exploration focuses on a specific aspect resulting from such volcanic activity, the generation of lava tubes. Lava caves or tubes are tunnels that form within the lava when the outer surface of a lava flow cools and hardens while the molten lava within continues to flow and eventually drains out through the newly formed tube. This process in the Hawaiian Islands reveals as well the possibilities that may result from the physical and chemical interactions between hot volcanic material, rainwater and the ocean water. In addition to exploring the geological processes at work on this archipelago, this project proposes a scenario whereby the interacting forces between hot lava and cold water may be harnessed for the production of energy.

Above: Plan of the transformation of the Big Island of Hawaii from its inception to its decline as it follows a dynamic path across the Pacific Ocean. The Big Island has grown continuously at the rate of one kilometer every three and a half years.

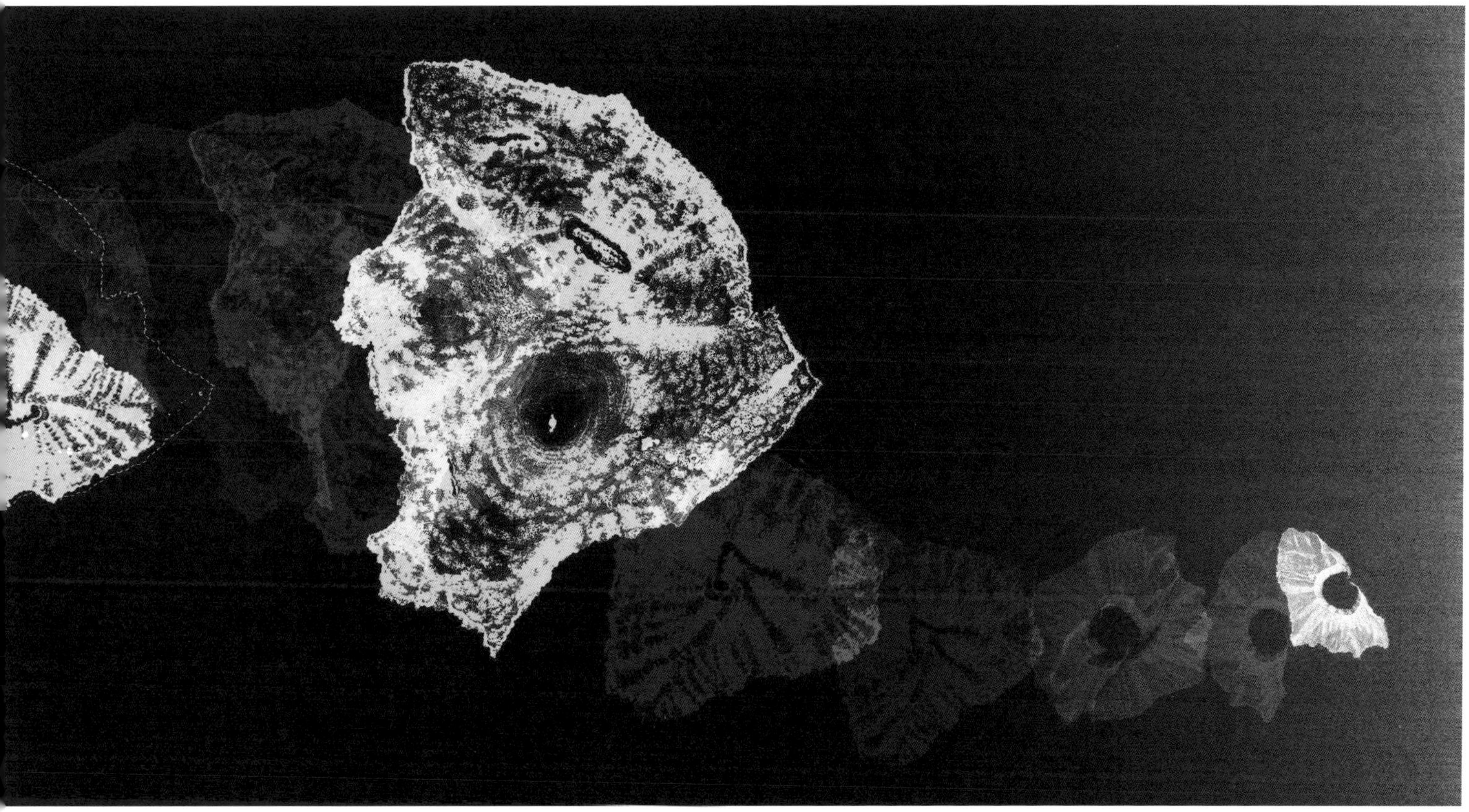

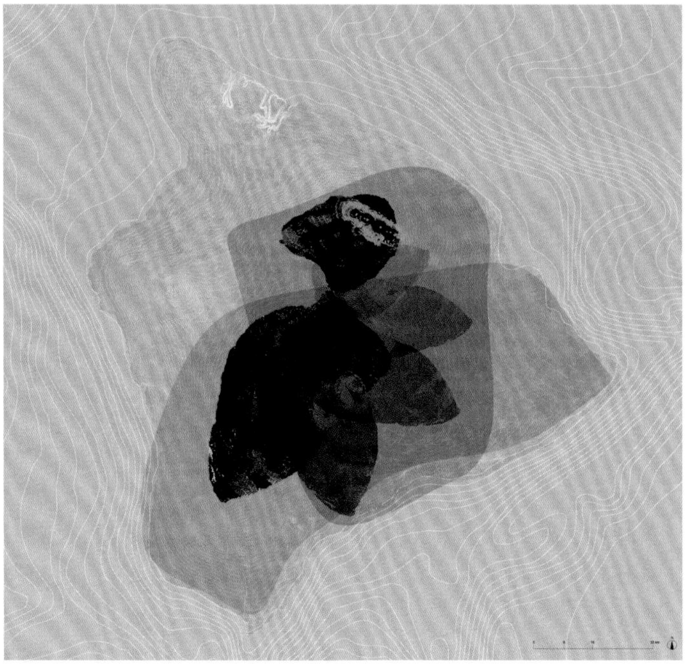

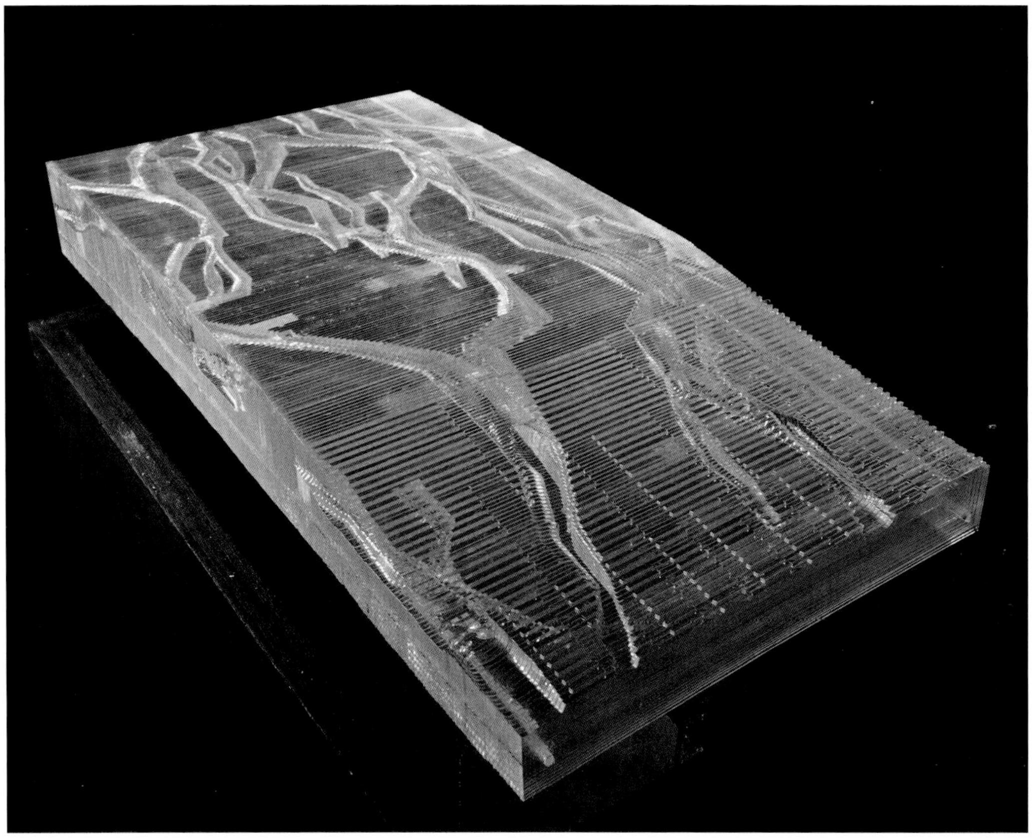

Top: Plans of the Big Island of Hawaii over the past 50,000 years showing how the island has transformed as the Pacific tectonic plate has moved in two directions.

Bottom: Model; lava tubes, plexiglass.

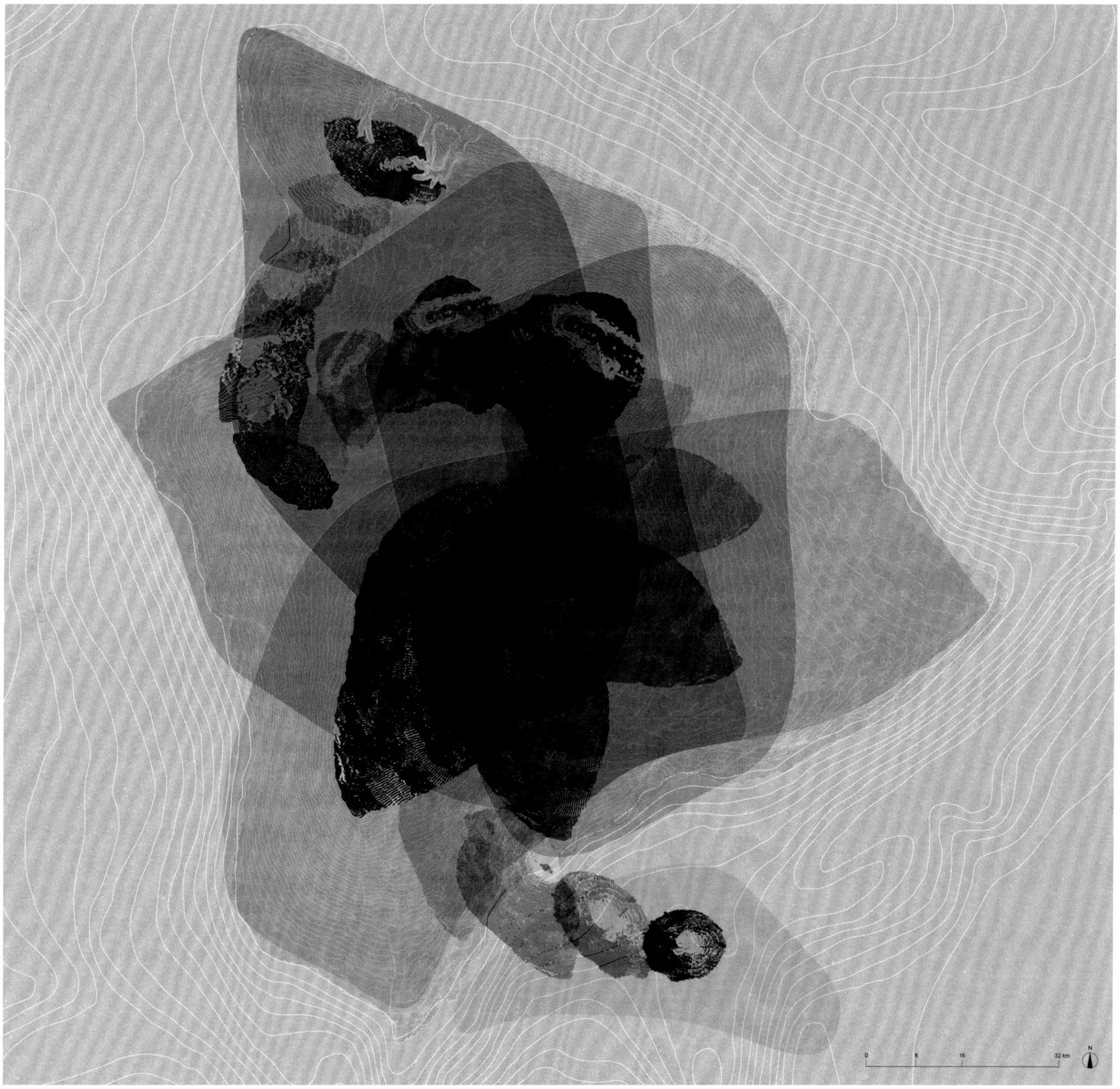

Above: Section showing the movement of the Hawaiian archipelago. Over the past seventy million years the combined processes of magma formation, volcano eruption and growth, and continuous movement of the Pacific Plate over the stationary Hawaiian "hot-spot" at its center have left a long trail of volcanoes across the floor of the Pacific Ocean.

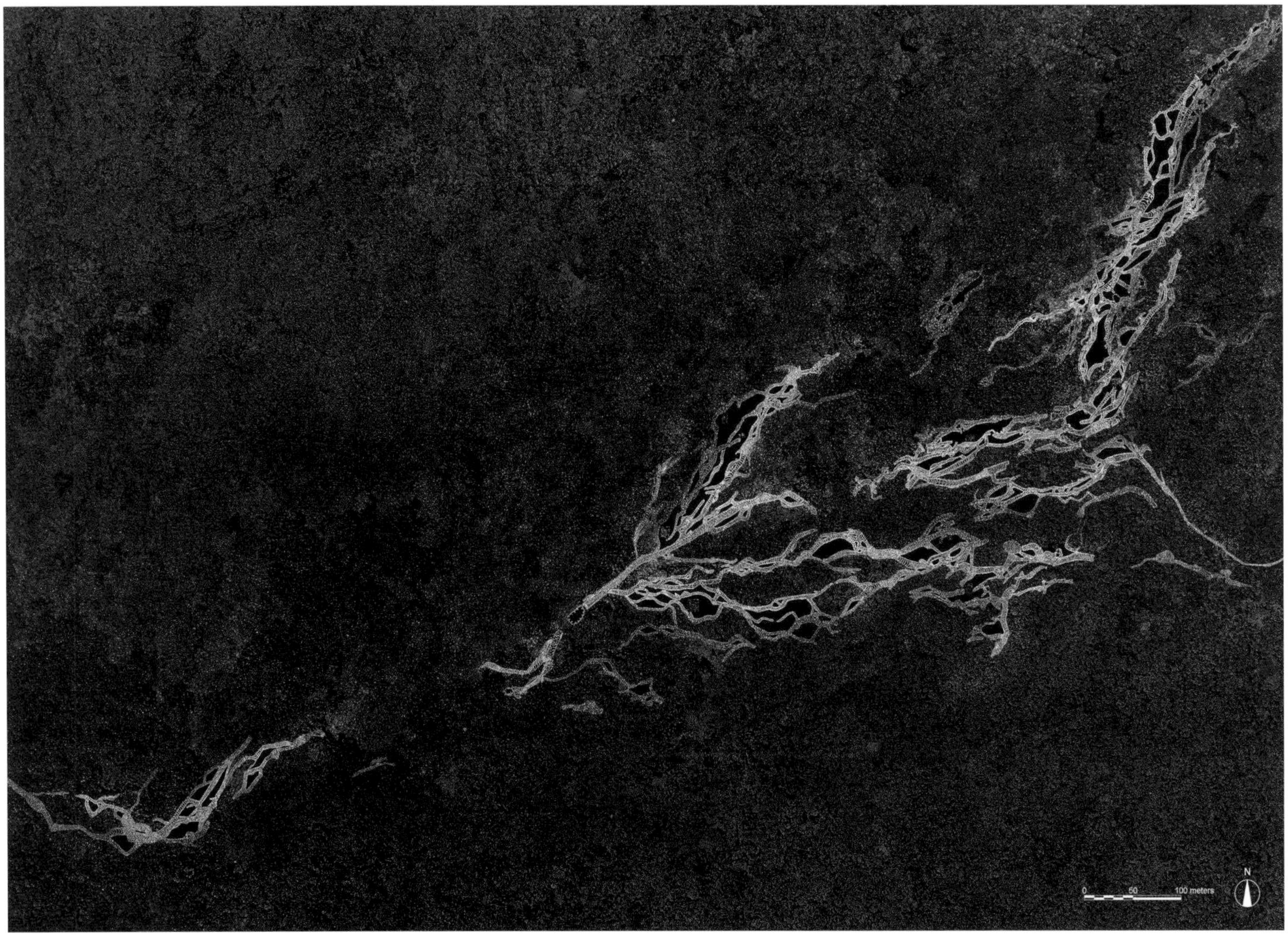

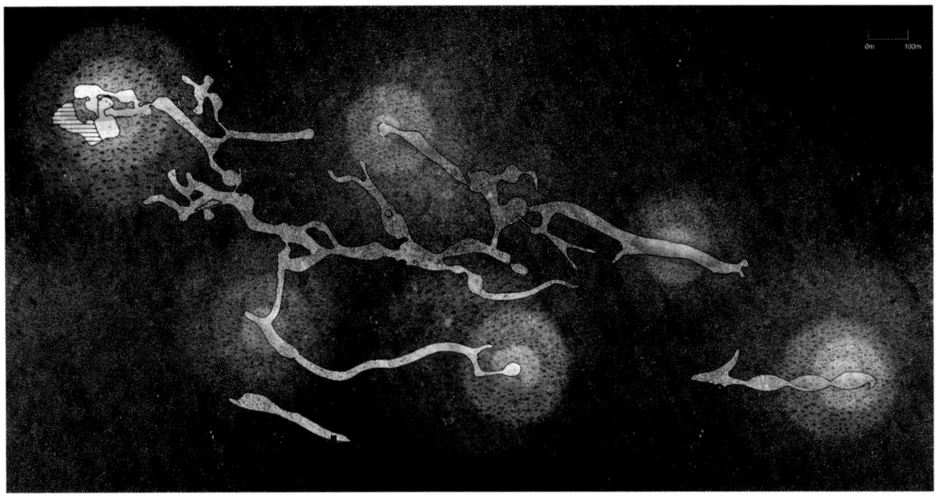

Top: Ground-level plan of lava tubes, mapping the underground path of lava tubes in relation to the above ground island topography.

Bottom: Plan of the interaction between rain water and lava, which could provide a potential energy source.

Opposite: Section of water in the lava tubes as it transforms into steam as the water is heated through its contact with lava.

Life, Death, and Regeneration of Coral Reefs

Hawaii and the Marshall Islands, Pacific Ocean
Hancheng Chen

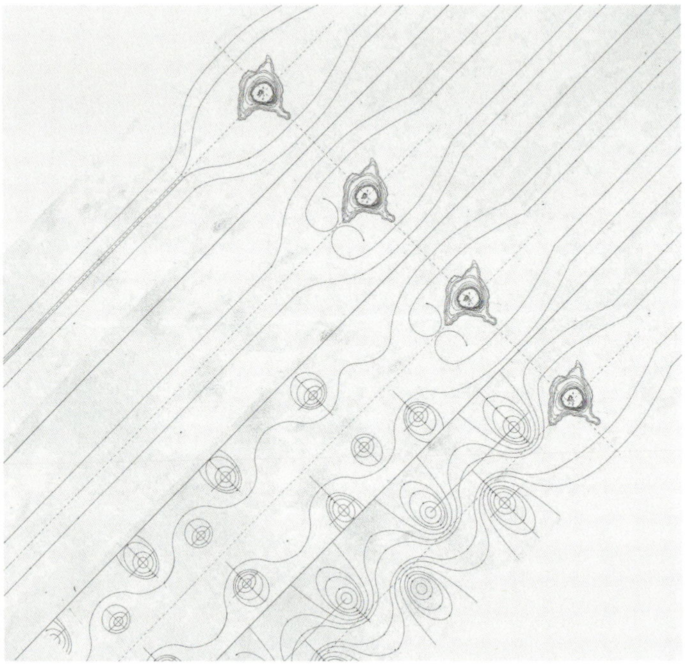

Coral reefs cover less than one percent of the ocean floor; nevertheless, more than one million species of plants and marine animals are associated with coral reef ecosystems. The Hawaiian Islands and the Marshall Islands are the locus for research and for speculation on possible new manners of coral growing. This project explores the reef environment through data analysis and computational fluid dynamics simulations of the particular current pattern by examining data such as water temperature, current direction, and coral polyp accumulation within the coral topography in both locations. This topography emerged from the movement of the tectonic plates, volcanic activity, and the accumulation of coral polyps formed forty million years ago.

The Marshall Islands, a chain of 1,156 volcanic islands covering an area of 750,000 km^2 in the Pacific, is the locus for an experimental proposal on a new manner of coral growing. A catalytic system is proposed based on the potential of ocean currents to generate low voltage electricity, which conducted through a steel wire initiates an electrolytic reaction causing mineral crystals naturally found in seawater to grow on the wire structure, creating propitious conditions for coral to attach and grow. This will generate, in turn, an environment that will foster a wide range and diversity of marine life. In an ongoing process, this scenario foresees the regeneration and expansion of coral reefs.

Top left: Map of the present water pattern in the northwestern Hawaiian Islands. The narrow straits between islands create so-called Von Kármán Vortex streets—a repeating pattern of swirling vortices caused by the unsteady separation of the flow of a fluid around blunt bodies. This traps more organic matter and food resources for coral reefs. In addition, these vortices provide potential energy for generating electric power. Reference data from NOAA's coral reef ecosystem division.

Top right: The water pattern is affected by the Reynolds number, the mathematical result of multiple factors including water speed, density, viscosity, and island scale. Reference data from NOAA's coral reef ecosystem division.

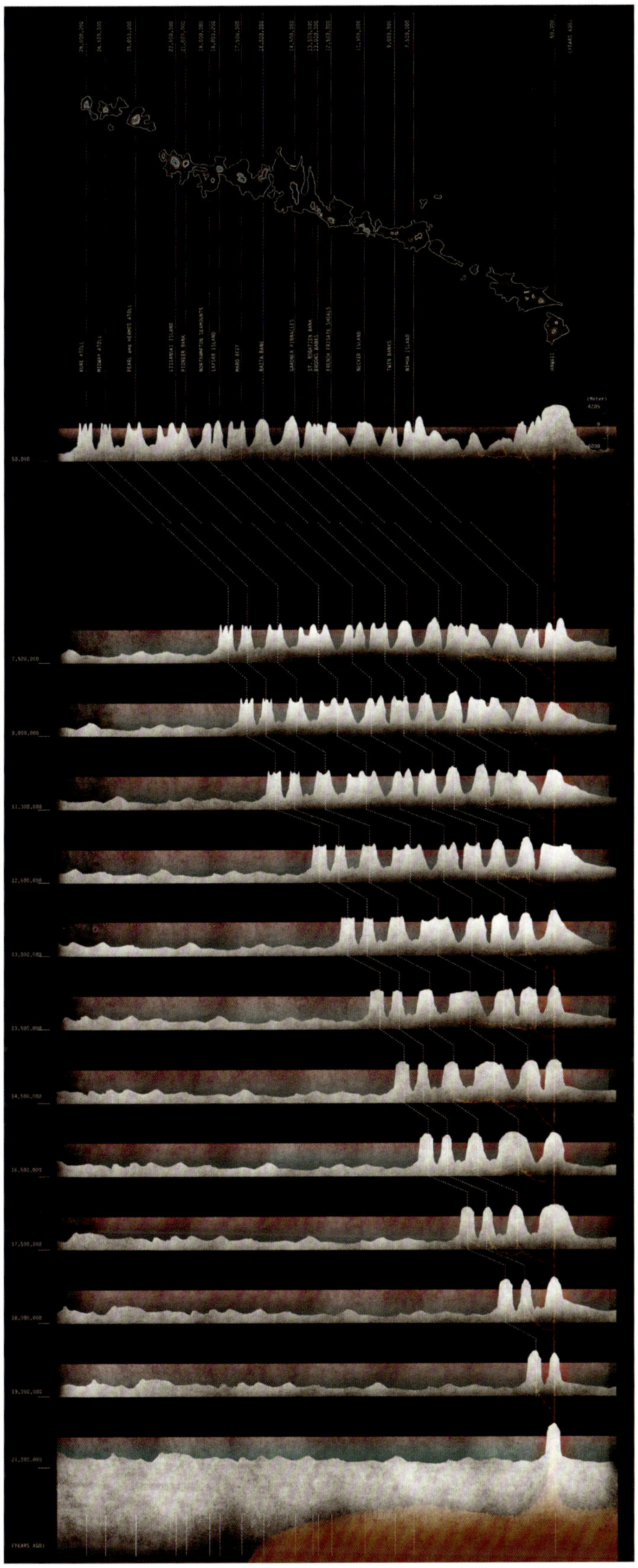

Above: Section of the formation of the northwestern Hawaiian Islands from forty million years ago. The red area at the bottom indicates the hot spot, which remains stationary while the tectonic plate above continues moving. The eruptions of the hot spot create volcanic islands at different periods of time, which will become extinct as they move away from the hot spot.

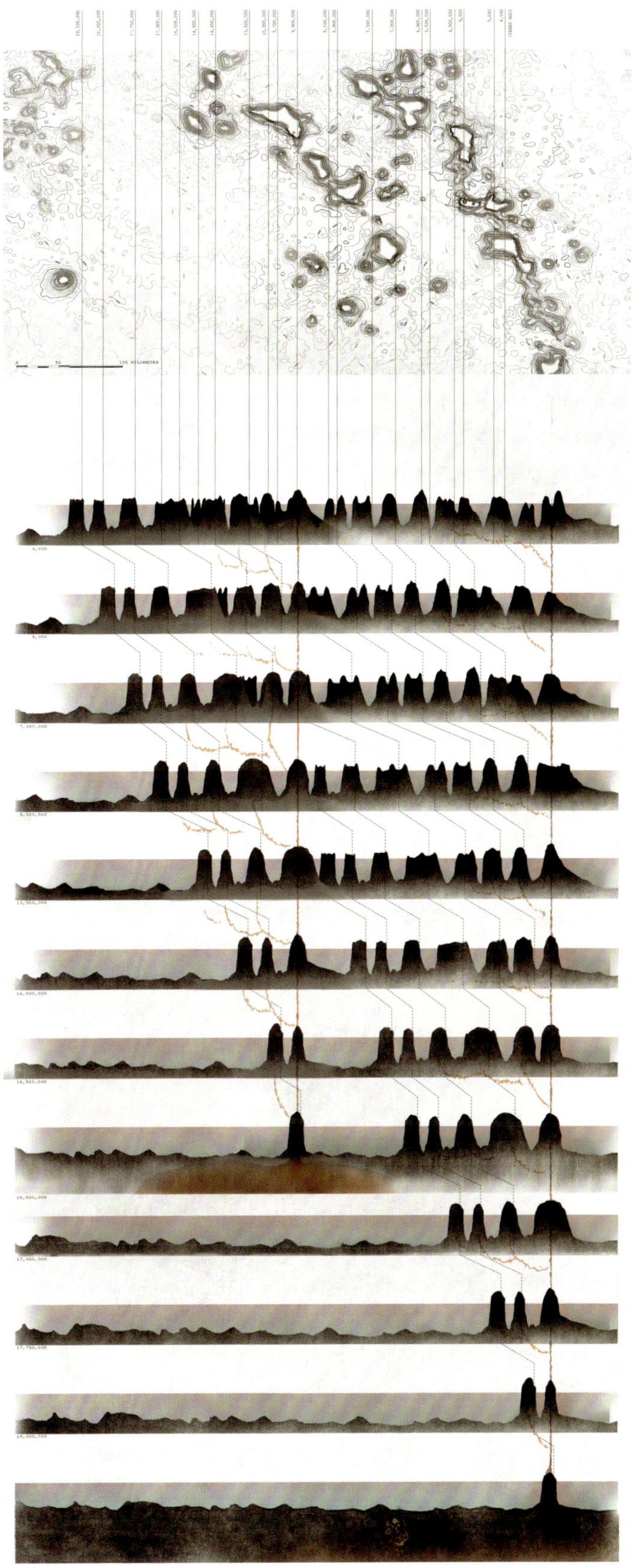

Above: Section of the formation of the Marshall Islands from forty million years ago. Two stationary hot spots erupted intermittently around forty and twenty-two million years ago, creating two rows of islands from southeast to northwest, following the direction of tectonic plate movement. Nuclear weapon testing in the twentieth century left minor craters, which can barely be seen at this scale.

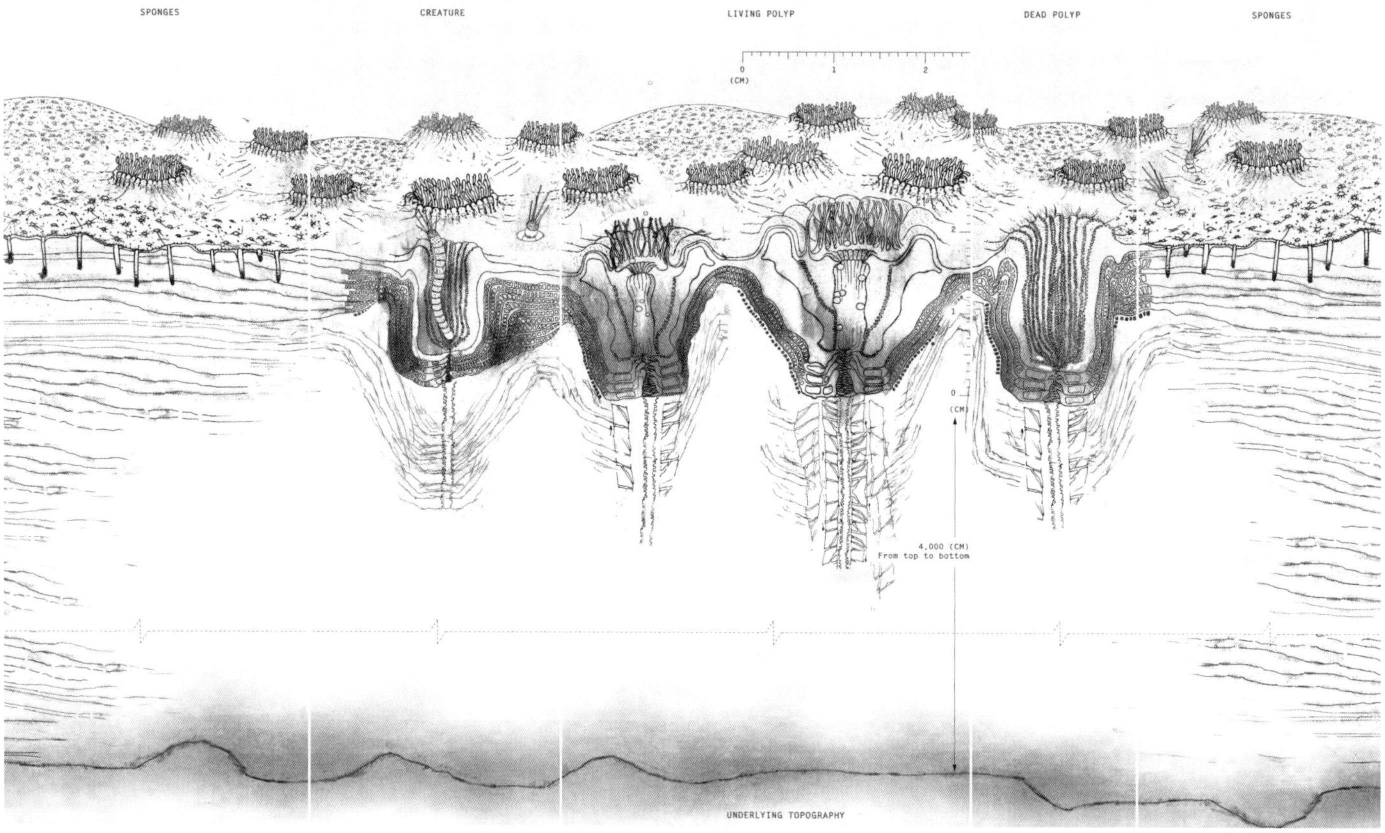

Top: Corals are formed by a colony of genetically identical polyps. They are small and soft-bodied organisms in the class Anthozoa of phylum Cnidaria, yet they form the biggest single organic structure on Earth. This structure, composed of calcium carbonate secreted by polyps, is even stronger than concrete. Most corals are colonial. The initial polyp attaches itself to a hard surface medium such as stone or artificial structure and the new polyps bud off from the initial polyp. They also reproduce by fragmentation. Hand drawing of reef structure study (4:1 scale).

Bottom: Model study showing the structure of a coral reef—front view (4:1 scale).

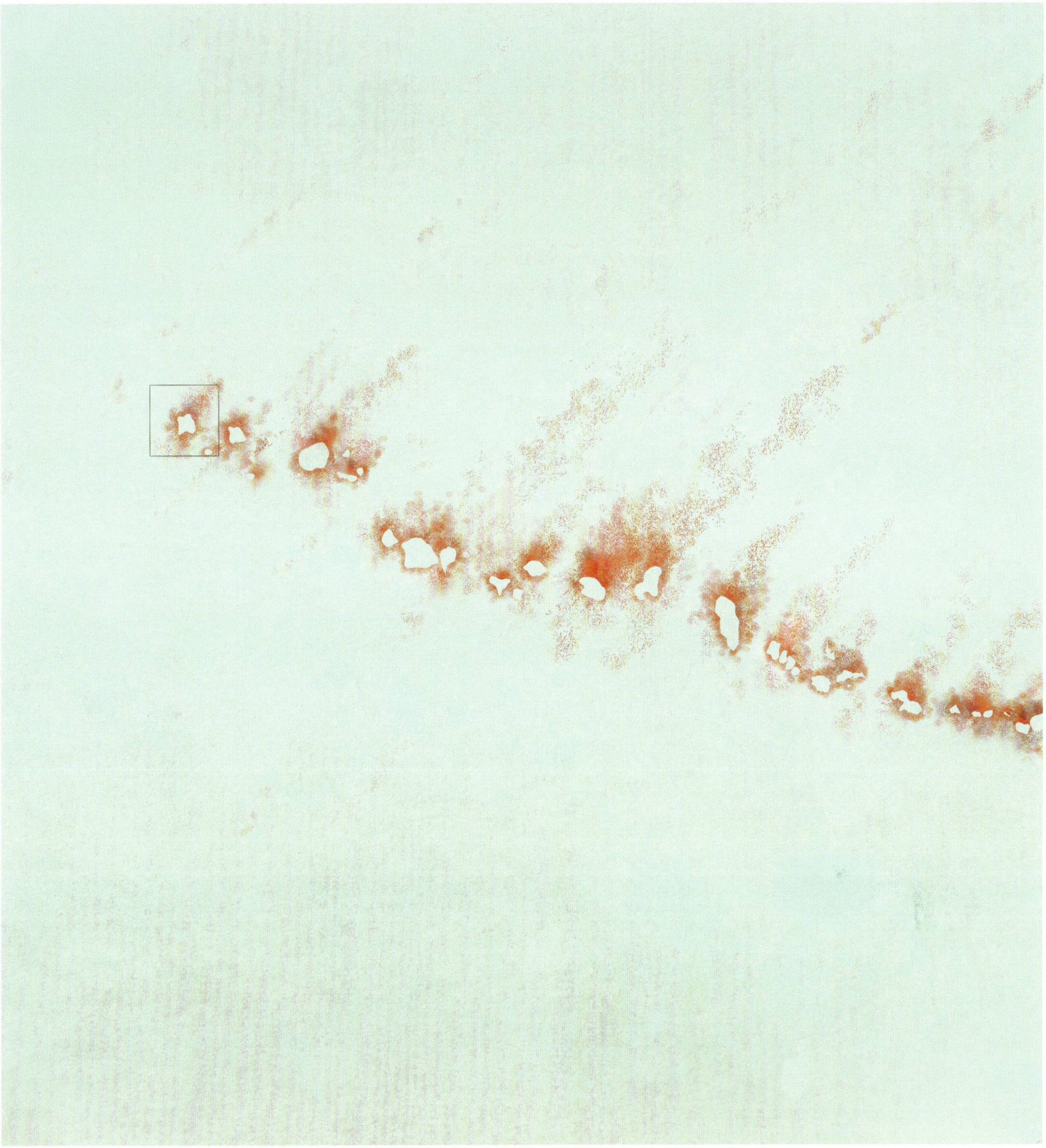

Above: Map of the present accumulation of coral polyps in the northwestern Hawaiian Islands' coral reef ecosystem division. The islands create optimal conditions for the growth of coral polyps. The windward side has warmer water temperatures and abundant food resources, encouraging the coral polyps to stay and reproduce. Reference data from NOAA's coral reef ecosystem division.

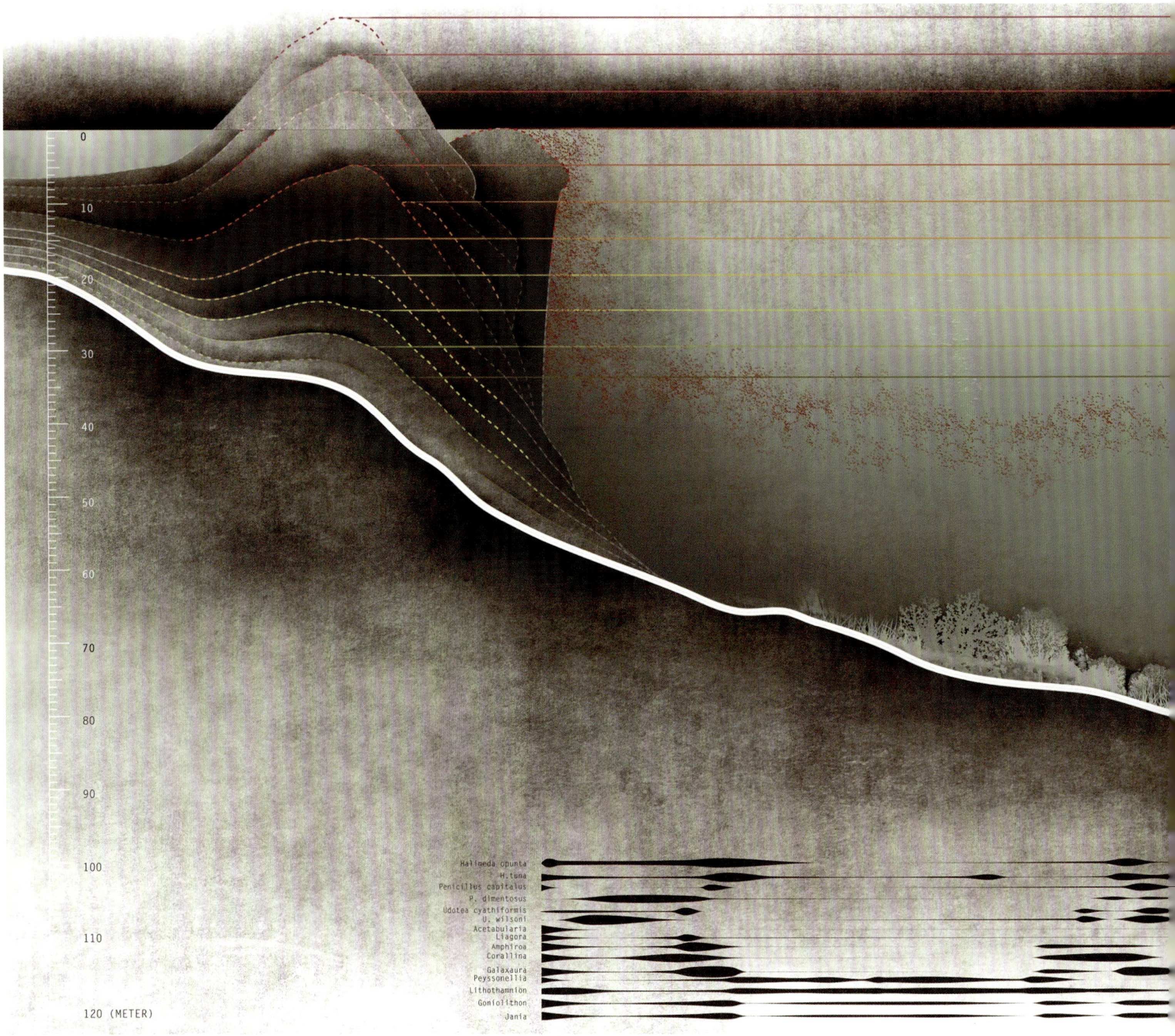

Above: Section of Kure Island and the relationship between coral polyps and sea level change due to climate change over the past thirty million years. The line chart in white indicates the change of sea level. It is intersected with the horizontal, colored lines indicating temperature. The lines extended to the island's section indicate the optimal areas for coral growing. As the temperature becomes warmer, around 84° Fahrenheit, the sea level rises, and coral polyps climb higher as well.

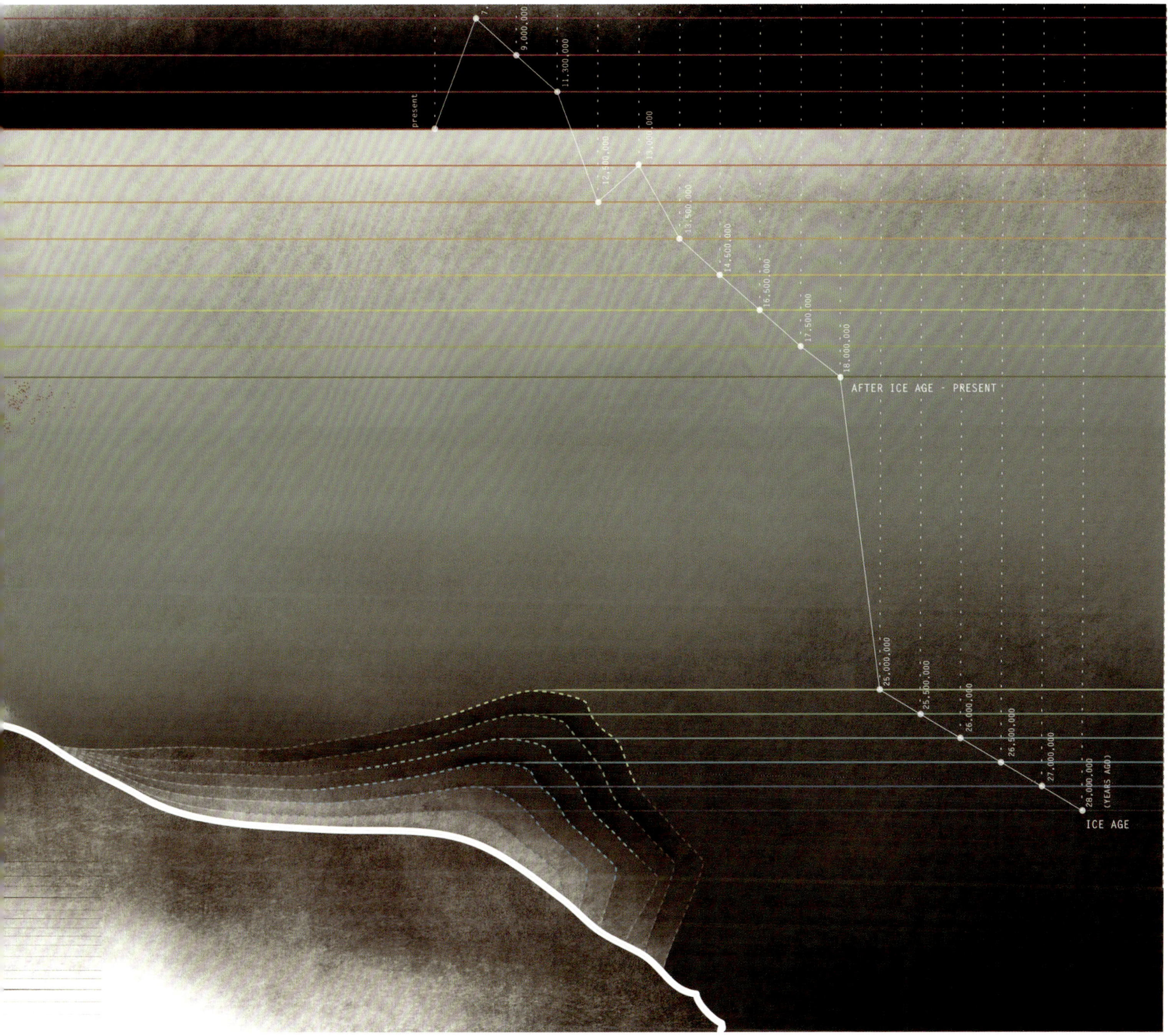
present
9,000,000
11,300,000
12,500,000
13,000,000
13,500,000
14,500,000
16,500,000
17,500,000
18,000,000
AFTER ICE AGE - PRESENT
25,000,000
25,500,000
26,000,000
26,500,000
27,000,000
28,000,000
(YEARS AGO)
ICE AGE

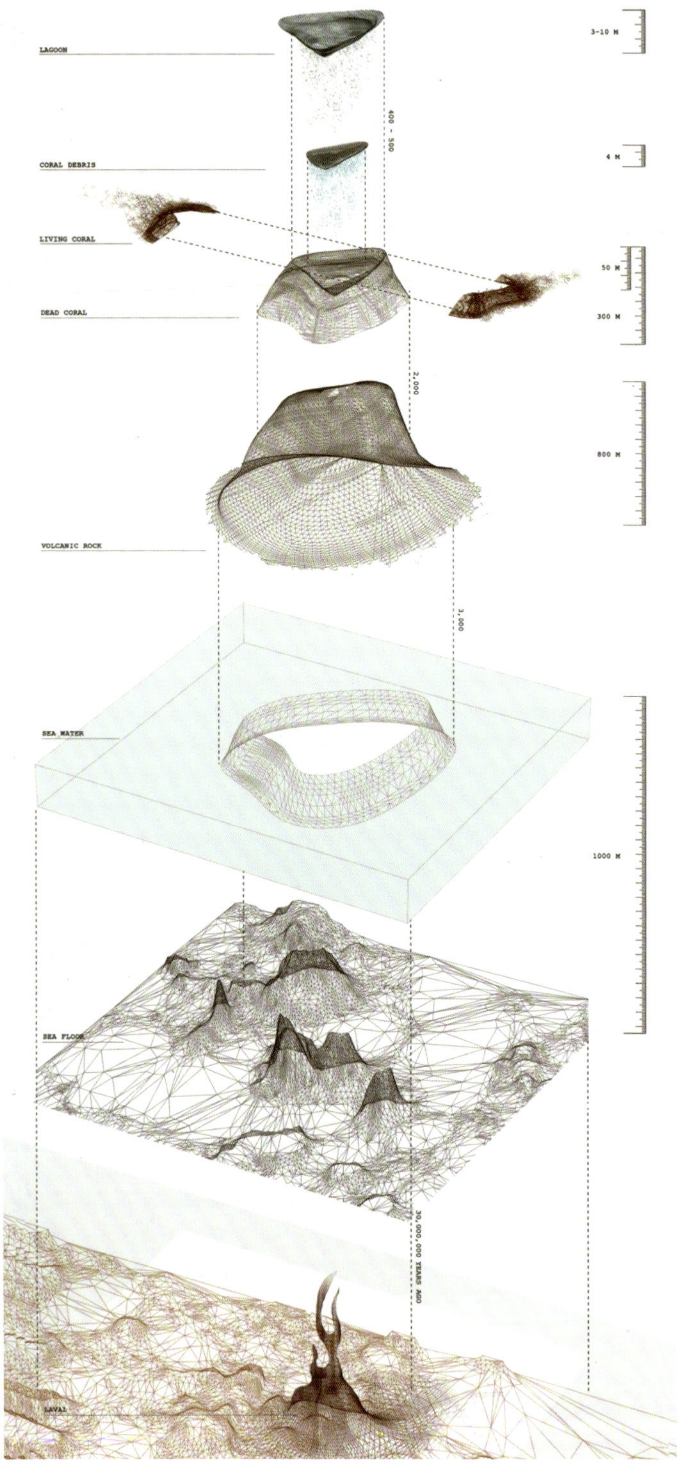

Above: Exploded view of an atoll (Majuro), also indicating a thirty million year timeline of its formation. From bottom to top: the hot spot erupted around thirty million years ago, creating the volcanic island (second layer). The coral polyps attached to the island's periphery, creating a fringing reef. When the sea level increased during the Ice Age, the coral polyps climbed higher creating a lagoon.

Opposite top and bottom: Water temperature in the Marshall Islands. On the windward side, the current hits the islands and air passes the islands, bringing moisture and cooling the temperature. On the leeward side, air rides downhill, becoming warmer and dryer. In this condition the water becomes warmer. Data from NOAA's coral reef ecosystem division. Von Kármán Vortex street in the Marshall Islands. Mapped with data from NOAA.

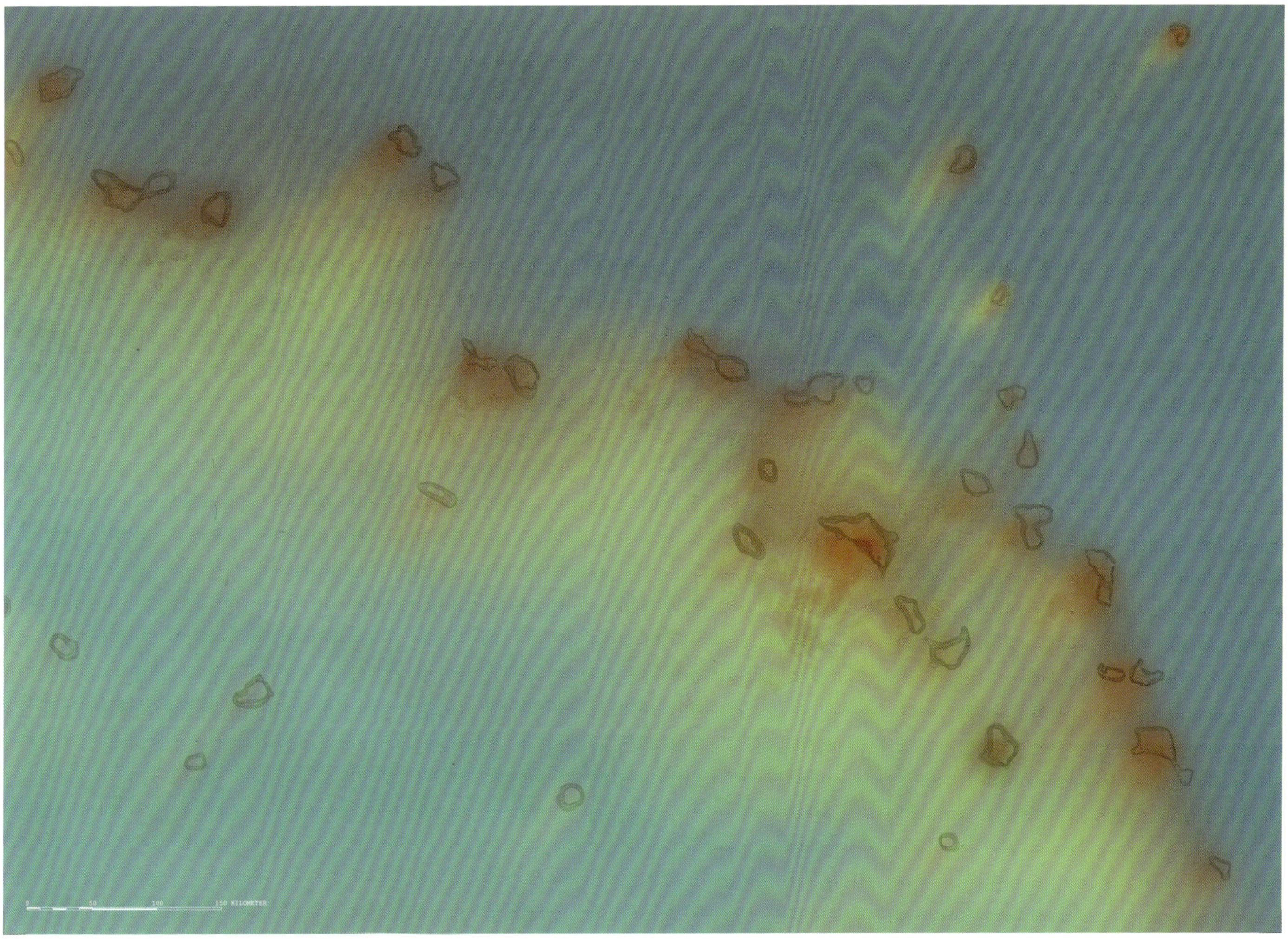
0
50
100
150 KILOMETER

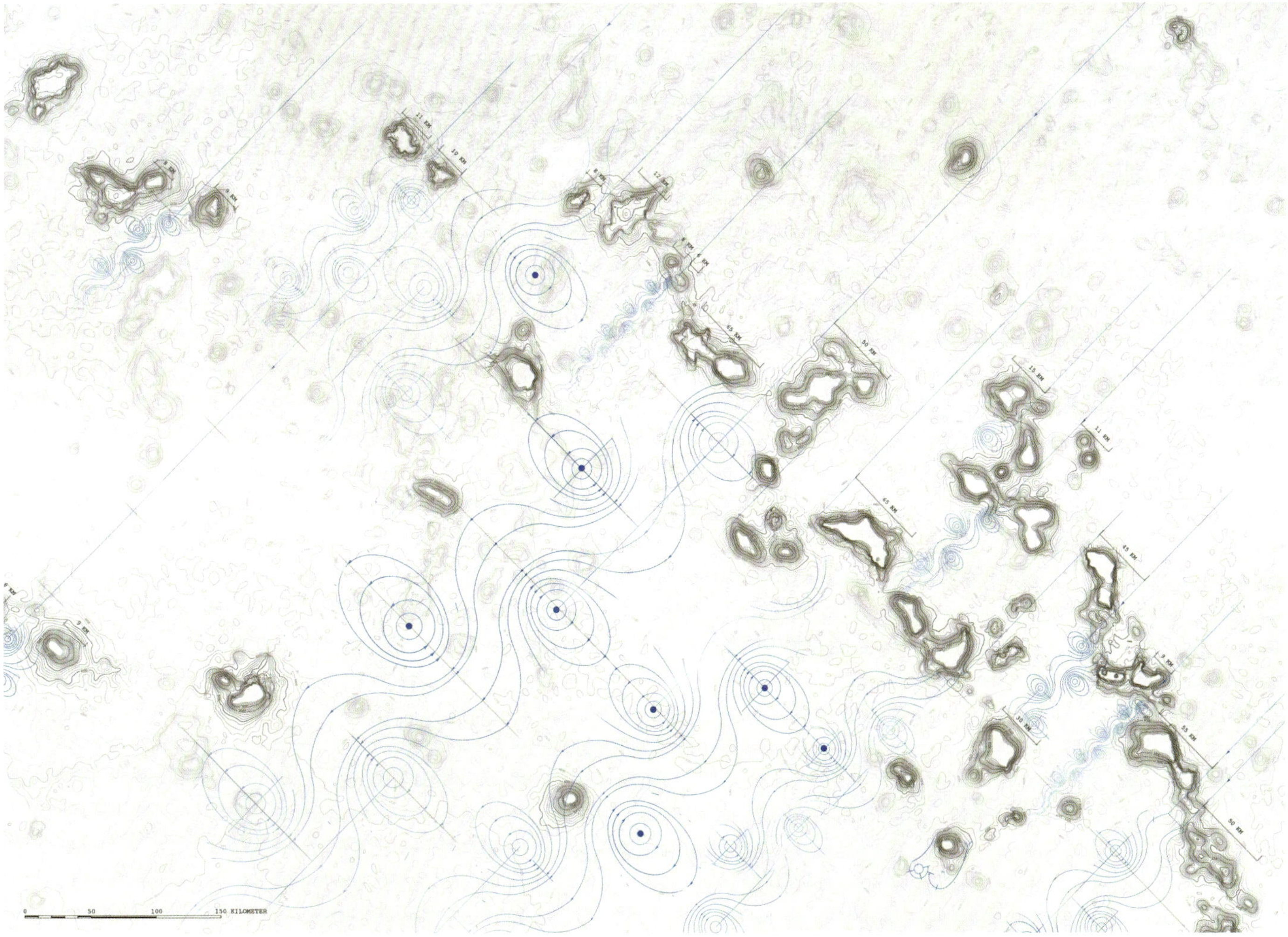
0
50
100
150 KILOMETER

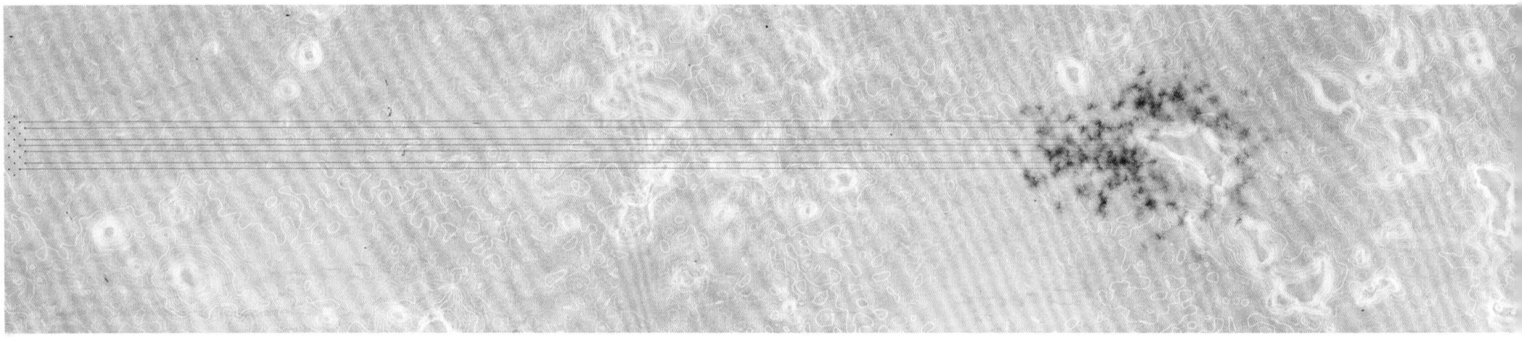

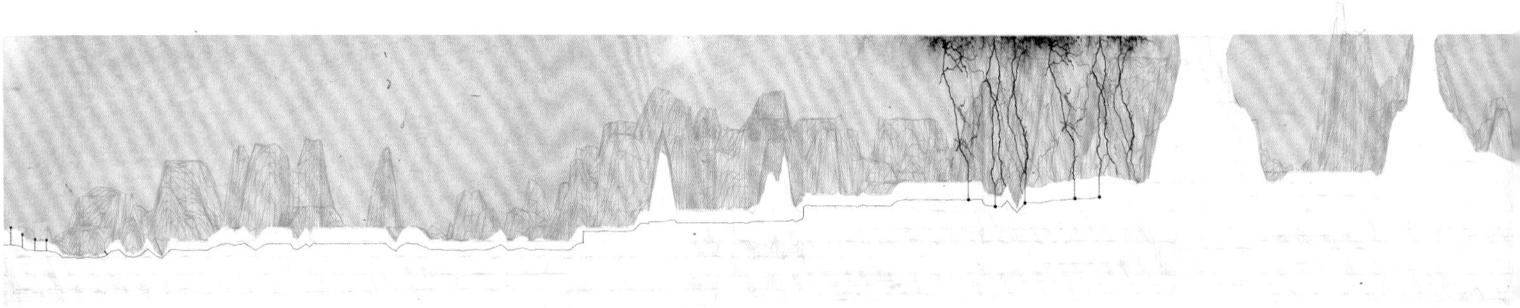

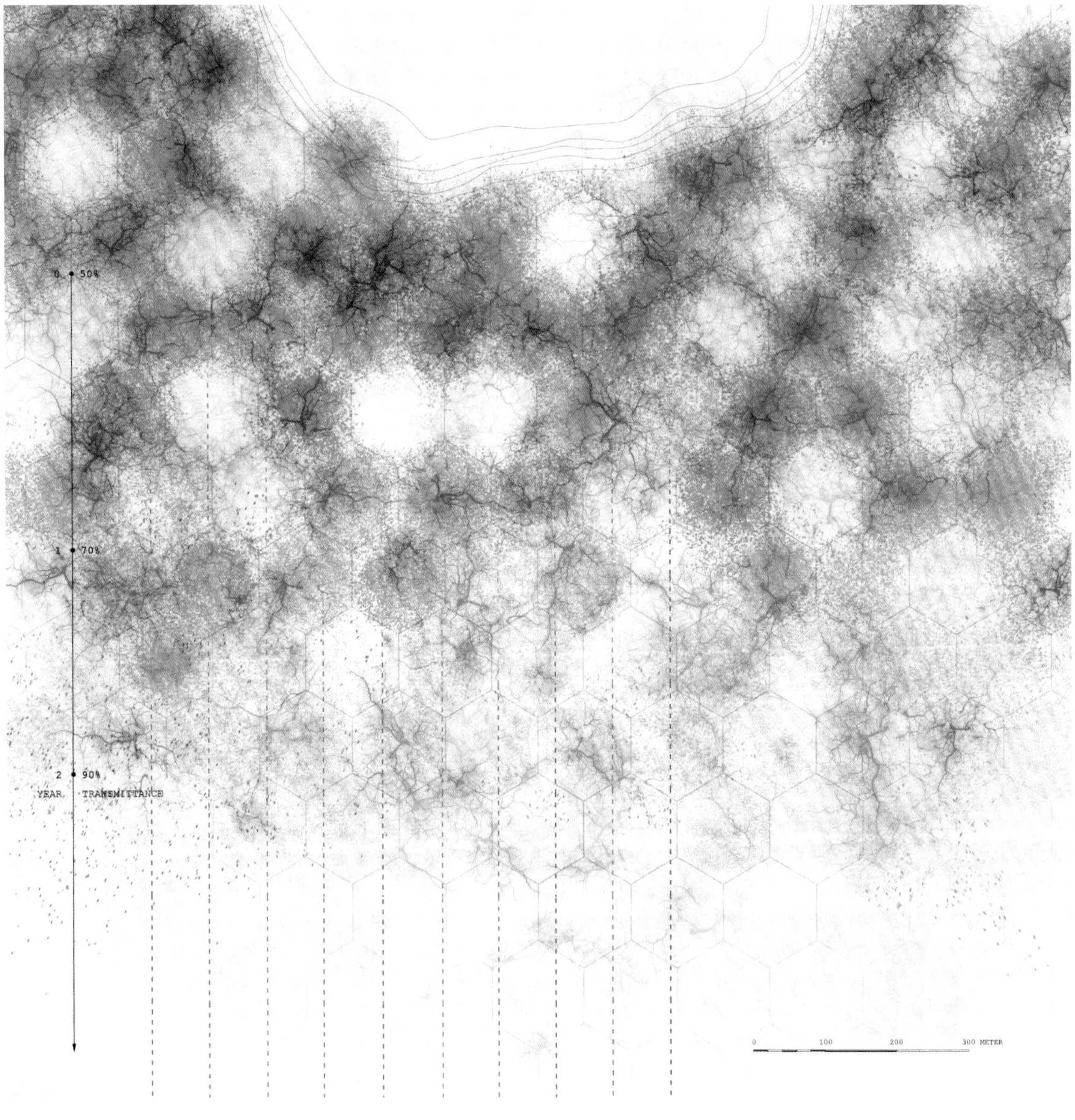
0 50%
1 70%
2 90%
YEAR TRANSMITTANCE
0 100 200 300 METER

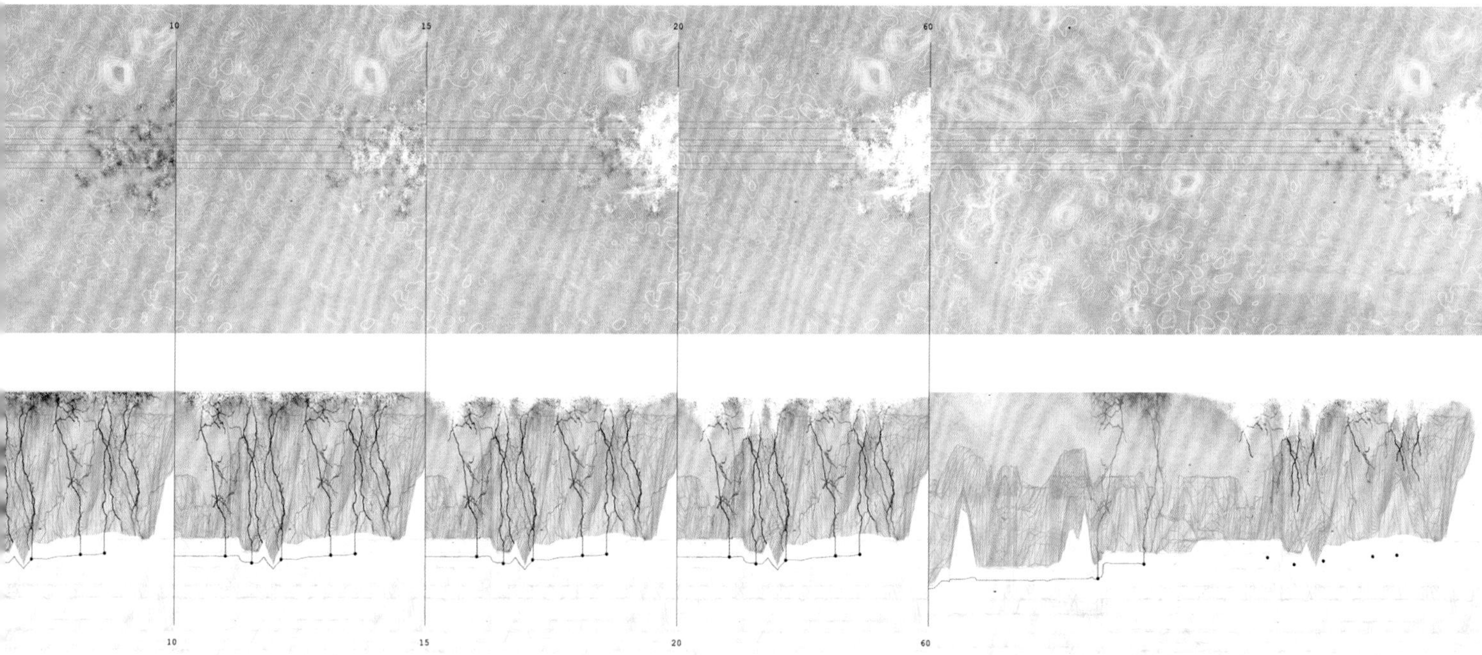

Top: The array of the floating units. The density of the units is higher near the island's periphery and becomes lower away from the island.

Opposite bottom: Plan and section showing the 100-year acceleration process of coral growing. From left to right, generators and electricity conducting cables for the floating wire units, which become larger and stronger as coral continues growing. They will be gradually swallowed up by the coral to become a skeletal structure from which a new reef will detach and be part of its natural habitat.

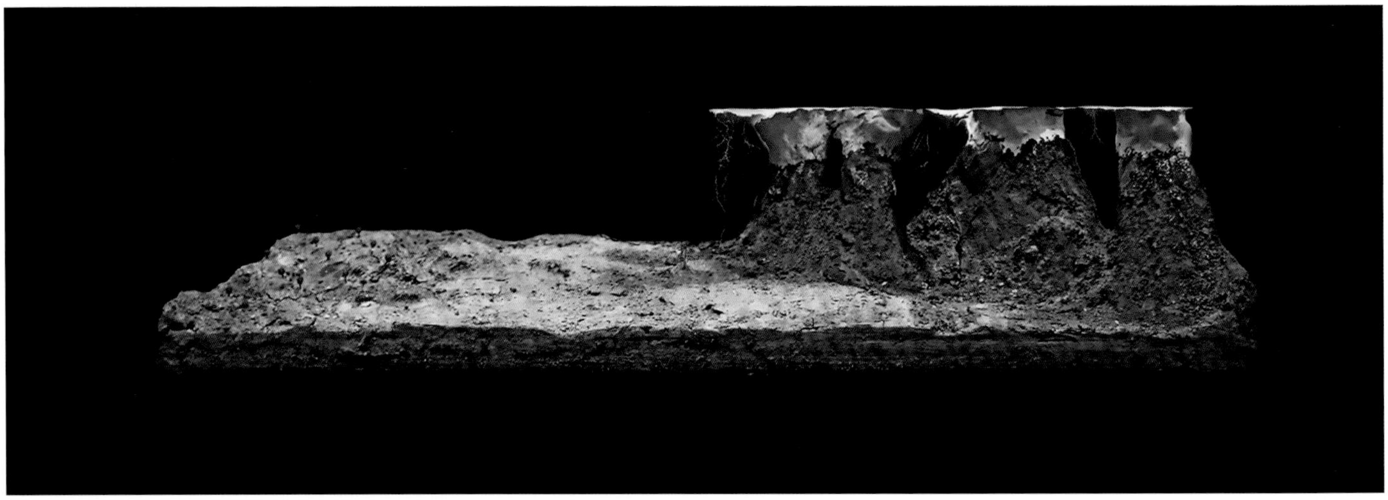

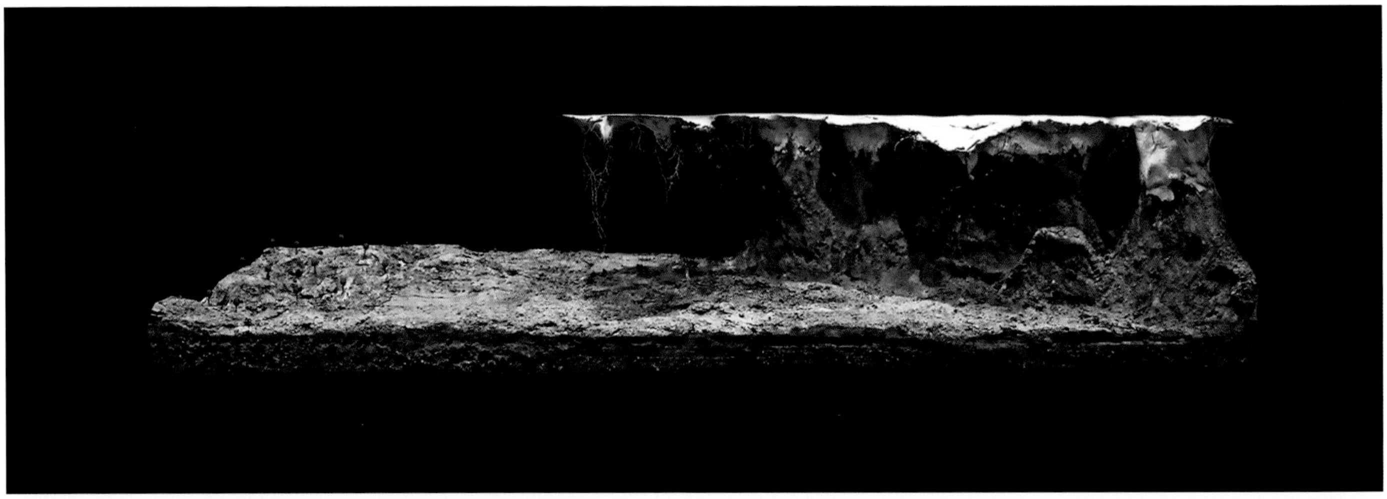

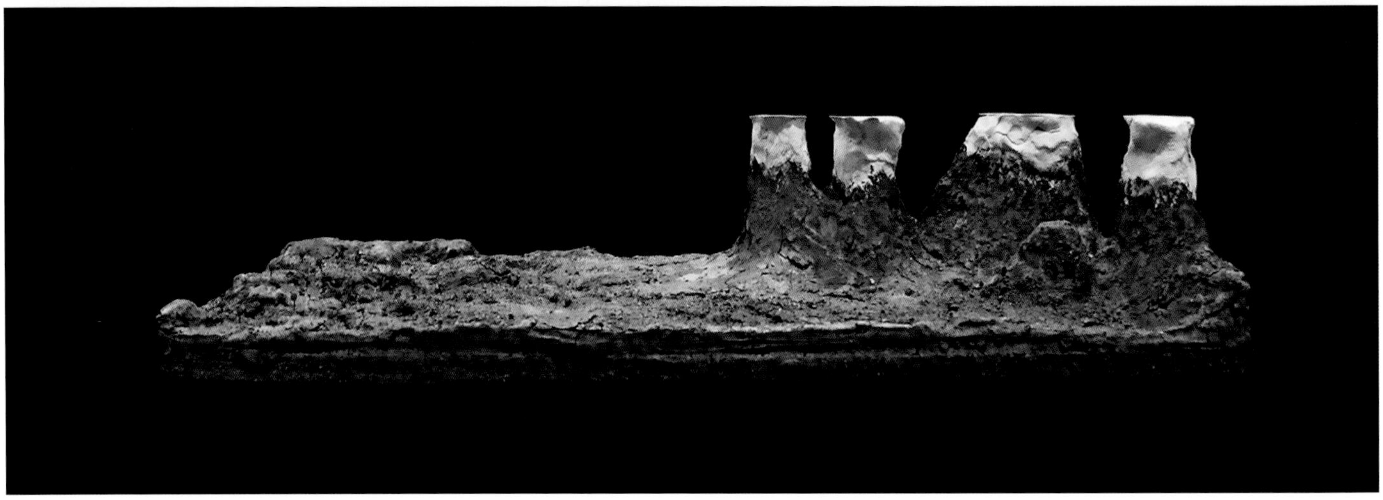

Above: Model showing the expansion of coral reef. The floating wire units spread over the islands' periphery, creating a new coral layer on the ocean surface. The space between floating reefs and the seafloor will become a new habitat for marine animals.

CONSTRUCTIONS OF NATURE: REPRESENTATION AS PRODUCTION

Peter Galison and Caroline A. Jones interviewed by Diana Agrest

AGREST: In the introduction to your book *Picturing Science, Producing Art* you write: "What much of this focus on art and science as discrete products ignores are the commonalities in the practices that produce them. Both are regimes of knowledge, embedded in, but also constitutive of the broader cultures they inhabit."[1]

The relationship you establish between art and science in terms of the development of scientific knowledge opens the discourse on representation as it relates to the study of natural phenomena. As we focus on nature as the object of study from the field of architecture, the question of representation is essential in the exploration of natural phenomena; an exploration based on scientific research. One could say, in relation to the opposition between art and science, that writing about architecture has historically been defined as the combination of art and science or art and technique—there is no opposition in qualifying the work as one or the other. In fact, we try to operate through representation on the overlap between both. Does this make any sense from your perspective?

GALISON: Sure—perhaps Caroline could comment first.

JONES: That's an interesting framing, because to my knowledge the representations of architecture don't traditionally include "nature" at all. This might be a way of bridging our introduction from the 1998 volume and the concerns of your current project. It may be that the very concept of nature is about representation, and this can be where architecture, or at least architecture's representation of nature, enters. Perhaps, somehow, this thing we call "nature" is precisely that world external to our bodies, which we represent to ourselves. That can be some kind of segue between our concerns and yours.

Neither one of us is going to have strong opinions about architecture as an art and/or a science. In my visual memory, the closest architectural representation gets to nature is Laugier's primitive hut, which is of course simply a representation. Did anyone build Laugier's hut? This was an imaginary representation of the human in nature. Marie Antoinette built the Petite Hameau [*Hameau de la Reine*, 1783] with completely simulated rock "grottoes"—but for the most part, when the art of architecture meets nature as concept rather than "field condition," its *techne* is in the realm of representation. Once form is built, as landscape, we designate it as a human construction, epistemically distinct from "nature."

One would have to ask, is the human, for you, a part of nature? When Alberti writes about commodiousness and the open window that allows the air to come in, I always feel that this humanist man is quite distinct from nature. Albertian (or Vitruvian) man is a figure for god, which of course subsumes nature, includes nature in the body of man, but is subject to his dominion (and the gender is intentional).

So what's interesting about the drawings produced in your studio is that there are no figures, there is no proportion indicated by the Vitruvian man, or the Corbusian "modulor," for that matter. The measure of man is in the metrics: abstract, scientific indicators of units at the bottom of the drawings. My first observation would be that it is quite interesting in these drawings that the body, the humanist body, has completely given way to this Cartesian measuring mechanism. There's no human presence other than this mastering metric. It is a sort of nature without us, except that the drawing is completely human in the way it is conceived.

AGREST: I agree, and this is a subject of great interest to me. I link this to the three stages of epistemic values in *relation to the role of visual representations in science* as developed by you, Peter (with Lorraine Daston) in your work on objectivity.[2] Could you perhaps begin with a brief summary of the three stages—from truth to nature, trough mechanical objectivity, and to trained judgment and the role of the self in these three epistemic moments as it relates to representation?

PETER GALISON: With a very exaggerated periodization, one might encapsulate the argument Lorraine Daston and I presented this way. In the 18th century, the systematic scientific depiction of bodies and objects aimed to show things as they should be, in their ideal form, not in their individual peculiarity—the right kind of self for the job was a sage or genius who could part the curtain of experience and reveal the purity of form that was otherwise unseen. Though idealization continues (and continues to the present time) in certain arenas, the 19th century came to embrace a mechanical, almost algorithmic transfer of objects to the page—the goal was to achieve a kind of self-abnegation in which artist-scientists removed themselves as much as possible from the process of representation. This too continues in certain ways even now—but the 20th century held yet a further twist, as the now more confident scientific community began to use their apprenticed vision to make what they hailed as skilled judgments in the correction of instrument-produced images. This was a scientific sight of *trained judgment* in which doctors or chemists or geologists could correct an image not because they were geniuses, not to achieve an ideal behind appearances, but because they believed through training they could find and repair artifacts of the apparatus or procedures. This newer scientific self of the 20th century was neither genius nor self-restrained worker—instead, she or he was a trained expert.

When we (Lorraine Daston and I) were looking at the transition in the early 19th century to "objectivity," so named, we realized that this

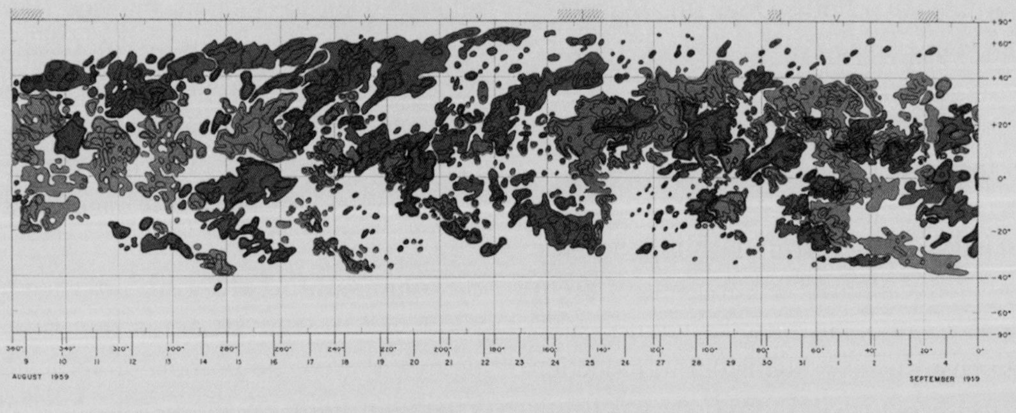

Objectivity, corrected. Plate 6.10 from Lorraine Daston and Peter Galison, *Objectivity* (New York: Zone 2007). The image is from Robert Howard, V. Bumba, and Sara F. Smith, *Atlas of Solar Magnetic Fields*, August 1959-June 1966 (Washington, D.C.: Carnegie Institute of Washington Publication 626, 1967). Courtesy of the Observatories of the Carnegie Institution of Washington, D.C. In this magnetogram, the authors actively modified the image itself as it emerged from their apparatus in order to remove artifacts of the instrument and procedure (that which was not "real"). But this "smoothing," as the authors dubbed it, was not in any way to claim for the atlas images an ideal (meta-physical) status—Howard et alia still aimed their chart to be an image not of the Sun's fields in abstract, but instead the particular rotation of the sun measured in the late summer of 1959—minus artifacts.

emerged from the big break that comes when you begin to distinguish a subjective from an objective account of the world and its representation. Subjectivity is an intrinsic part of the story. Objectivity required this new concept of the self as "subjective" before it could become possible in opposition.

For Kant, and the will-based psychology that followed him in the early 19th century, you see a self driven by will or controlled by will—together with the will to will-lessness—an ability to create a kind of quiet inner-self that allows nature to speak through us. This became a prerequisite for a new concept of what it meant to know the world. That was Schopenhauer's great ambition in *The World as Will and Representation* (1818—19).[3] Schopenhauer's aims were partly theological—we could only hear God speak if we willed the will to sufficient silence so that God could speak through us. But it is significant that nature, and an understanding of the natural world also required a kind of quieting of the will based on the will's suppression of the will. So you had to learn to quiet the self from the opacity of the will-based center.

Of course the faculty of the will is not new in the 18th century. The will exists in 17th and even earlier centuries in Europe with their concepts of the self, but in those earlier epochs, will is just one of many faculties. In fact, in the 17th century the dominant faculty of the self is reason. Reason is the king serving to control other passions that stand as subjects, will among them. But in an unruly soul, reason could be overturned by rebellious passions and desires, their movements hauling the self this way and that.

A well-ordered self was like a well-ordered society and was based on the king, Reason, subordinating these other things and keeping them in just proportion. Nature was part of this well-ordered kingdom.

But during the end of the 18th and early 19th century you begin to have a different notion, an idea of a forceful will that was actually the center of the self. And as I said above, this was a will that had to be willed to quiet in order to hear the divine. Here, then, you had the beginning of the talk about a forceful subjectivity that had to be restrained in order to allow an object world to present itself, whether it's theological or natural. And so, that separation between subjective and objective became crucial. On the one side you had the natural philosopher, who would become the scientist in the 19th century, who felt that in order to really know the world, we had to quiet this subjective will-based self. Yet on the other hand you had the artist, who saw in the imposition of will on the world actually the salient feature of art. So, what was interesting to me in this moment was that really for the first time you had this radical division between science and art.

To see how novel this division of objective and subjective (science and art) was, imagine this absurdly counter-factual scene: if we had asked Leonardo da Vinci about his drawings of turbulent water, and ask him if a specific drawing was art or natural philosophy, he surely would have found the question utterly uninterpretable. He wouldn't have any idea what you were

Art, or natural philosophy? The question had no meaning in the 16th century. Leonardo da Vinci, A Deluge, ca. 1517-18, pen and black ink with wash. Royal Collection of her Majesty Queen Elizabeth II of England.

talking about—were his studies of turbulent water science? Art?

They were one and the same. It is not until this turning point in the 1820s or 1830s that you begin to see this separation between the domains of art and science in Europe, and the notion that they actually require different kinds of subjects. In 1859, Baudelaire underscored this art/science division when he deplored the "invasion of photography" as part and parcel of the "great industrial madness" that was overtaking the world. For Baudelaire and many others, photography could not really be called an art because it was too mechanical, too divorced from the imposition of creative will.

AGREST: Would that begin the third stage, which you call trained judgment?

GALISON: Trained judgment is that stage (beginning in the 1920s and '30s) when scientists began to question, began to limit the rule of *mechanical objectivity.* This next, third epoch of the story is one where scientists began to say they needed to go beyond the purely rule-bound transfer of objects to the page. Instead, or in supplement to mechanical means, they needed to exercise *trained judgment*—marking the beginning of distance being drawn between the "merely" mechanical (formerly highly valued), and an explicitly celebrated imposition of expert judgment about a wide range of technologically-produced images. Trained judgment in the 20th century became what you wanted to produce in the student. You wanted to train an expert (not a self-abnegating, rule-following worker) who knew how to *interpret* and when necessary to adjust and modify the mechanical image. Without such trained intervention, it was thought there would be a risk of operating on the basis of a quirk of X-ray photography, or a glitch in the telescope leading the untrained observer to see an oddity of reflectivity on the moon as a mountain.

AGREST: Is objectivity necessarily a bad thing in the history of science and the representation of nature?

GALISON: There are all sorts of things that are potentially dangerous about objectivity (as Lorraine Daston and I see it), but there are tremendous epistemic virtues to objectivity as well. The great advantage, epistemologically, is that objectivity separated my (possibly arbitrary) imposition of will onto the world from yours. Prior to this production of objectivity—as long as you were in the earlier periods—it was only remarkable figures such as Goethe or Vesalius who could show their contemporaries how the world really was, behind appearances. When rarities like these were imposing their vision on things, the scientific community could hold that truth that was revealed only by this genial self.

In that early stage of Western representations of nature, there's not even a pretense that you or I could be trained to be a genius—there are just geniuses, they are given to us, sports of nature as it were. They have the ability to part the curtains of ordinary experience and see a reality

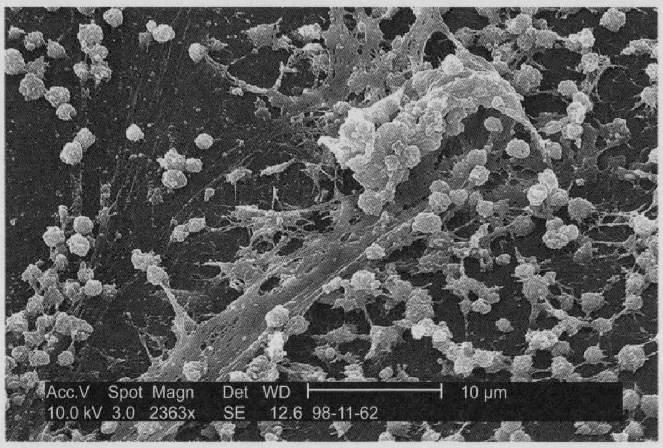

Bacterial Biomes. Scanning Electron Microscope image of a simple biofilm; on the upper surface can be seen the round, sessile forms of Staphylococcus, which has extruded a smooth substrate or "conditioning layer" that performs both adhesive and nutritive functions—future growth is enabled by migrating planktonic microbial cells that further colonize the conditioning layer. More complex biofilms consisting of multiple layers formed cooperatively by different microorganisms are called "microbial mats." (Magnification 2363X) Credit: Janice Haney Carr, photographer; Dr. Rodney M. Donlan, Centers for Disease Control, US Government.

that's behind it. But the idea of a mechanical objectivity is that it is something available to anyone behind that machine. And then, in the judgment phase, you could definitely train to become an expert in the sorting out of different kinds of images, whether leg fractures, cloud types, or electroencephalograms.

These phases are not crisply demarcated; one doesn't stop just because another begins. In mechanical objectivity, you could learn to restrain the self like just quieting your desire to impose your vision on the world. We're not all Goethes, we shouldn't aspire to be Goethe, but we could learn to tend the machine, to allow nature to speak without interference, without idealization or even the ambition to confirm our own theories. We should just let nature speak or write itself to the page, through the machine.

JONES: The drawings that Diana showed us are somewhere between that position and the trained judgment position. These images have an interesting look of the mechanically objective and yet of course, there's plenty of trained judgment embedded in the interpretation of the data, the rendering of the sections, the decisions to place wires in the ocean to harvest certain kinds of information. I mean, it's a very particular hybridization of the look of one and the practice of the other which I think is interesting.

AGREST: In our case you have a creative subject articulating with all of the information out there through our tools, our eyes, and our hands in order to produce a particular mode of seeing.

We don't research like scientists, we work with pre-existing material. Scientists in their research went into the field, they drew what they saw there, as in the early 19th-century production of the scientific Atlases, but we don't start from the real—we start from somebody else's work on the particular subject being explored. Would this be considered a sort of simulacrum? How do you see this from your perspective?

JONES: There is no "direct access" to nature. And scientists, too, will work with "pre-existing" material, analyzing other scientists' data. That is built into the much-vaunted "scientific method": replication. Scientists will do meta-analyses; they will compile 58 biology papers about the metabolism of coral. Even field biologists amalgamate data from others. This is part of the cumulative strategy of empirical science. Similarly, not all biologists are field biologists, and not all physicists are experimental physicists. Theorizing requires returning to pre-existing findings to account for as much of what we know as we can.

GALISON: I would say that the kind of thing that your students and studio are doing, to me, isn't so much between mechanical objectivity and trained judgment, but something that comes to be quite common after trained judgment, and it's a shift that I've come to think of as *presentation* rather than representation.

This came from the "trained judgment" phase after the 1920s. In preparing for an operation, the surgeon will often use MRIs (Magnetic Resonance Imaging). In the early days, and in certain cases, the technology would produce very dramatic artifacts—and because they were in the grips of mechanical objectivity, they were doing back surgeries where there, in fact, were no problems with people's backs. You needed to be able to say that that hole in the spine is not a real hole, it's actually an artifact of the mathematics of the way the image is being produced. That kind of judgment can only come with a lot of familiarity with the machine, the computer programs it employed, and their problems.

When this, in turn, shifts to what I call *presentation,* there is an embrace of the constructed nature of the image and how it comes into being. You might say that "nature" is nowhere to be found in these images: the objects being imaged are not simply being "found" in nature—molecular sized transistors and nanotubes are not generally speaking floating by while we capture them on our devices. Instead, we are making these objects and the images help us in that process—more like using a screen image to help re-attach a subvisible nerve in microsurgery. In cases of the building of new things in nanoscience, the goal is not so much to use images to *re-present* nature but instead to *present* things as they are coming into being: presentation rather than representation.

Perhaps your group's images were actually trying to bring out a salient feature that mixes politics, values, ecological reasoning, and so on, so that's why I think of these not so much as a representation of the sort of the object-and-representation dichotomy of the world, but in fact as presentations. That is, there isn't a thing already in the world or scene that answers to some of these drawings.

JONES: Are you saying there isn't a "Real" alluded to in these works (to use Lacan's registers of the "Imaginary," the "Symbolic," and the Real to which they refer)? Because Diana was talking about the real. That the scientist is the only one who is relating to the Real, while what she fears is producing only a simulacrum. Are you saying: there is a presentation here that is itself a reality? That even the scientist has no direct access to the real beyond his or her representations?

GALISON: I see in the presentational a compositional part of the Real, not a split between a flower and a picture of a flower. In other words, there's a line that says either you're a realist or a constructivist and the constructivist is a kind of epistemic relativist—you have your reality and I have my reality, they are both copies. But I don't think that the picture where there's a given nature and then a representative nature is the right way of understanding how these presentational images work. There are haptic forms of knowing, like physical modeling or simulations that are not "representations" in the conventional sense. The important point is that a simulation is not a copy of something. A lot of the objects that are being made in science are not copies; the goal of them is not exactly to represent something that exists already. It is to present something, to make something new, more akin to engineering than classical photography. When you make circuits the size of a molecule, those don't exist in nature, you're not copying nature, you're making something new. And it is this more engineering kind of ethos that I think becomes very dominant in synthetic biology and the experimental neurosciences. In these and other arenas people are making things of scientific interest, not so much imaging the already-there.

JONES: And that's where the architecture of nature can be properly spoken of.

AGREST: For us, when we are working with pre-existent material, be it drawings, texts, diagrams, or charts, it is like raw material on which a transformation is produced, and that is where I think our tools of representation play an important role—in that transformational process. I feel that this is close to the concept of presentation as you explain it as opposed to just representation.

GALISON: There's an old conception from the history of art, when people say something is *drawn from nature,* they don't necessarily mean that it's "realistic." What they mean is that in front of the person making the drawing stood the person or the thing being drawn. Life, not another drawing, was being drawn. Similarly, in science you'll hear people say, "this is highly idealized." Now, if it is drawn from nature but people say that it is idealized, isn't that an oxymoron? But of course it's very clear: it can be simpler than nature but still drawn from nature. We are talking about procedure, like asking if you are drawing from this cup or from a picture of the cup. Procedure is an independent question of whether it's accurate or not accurate or idealized or not idealized or simplified or not simplified.

JONES: There's also a vernacular understanding that the representational is a regime of vision—it appeals to vision. "It looked like this," whether it's the real cup or picture of the cup, you're making a representation of how it *looked.* "Drawn from nature" vouchsafes a moment when the renderer's eyes saw it just this way, and then your eyes can see how it looked. This is the contract of representation.

For me, this vernacular understanding can extend to the presentational. It can still be visual, but it needs to be understood as being an image that *hasn't existed before,* rather than one "before the eyes" of the renderer. (This same epistemic shift had to happen with photography, by the way. Etienne Jules Marey's chronophotographs were like nothing that had ever come before human eyes!) The presentational is an image that visually produces a new reality or a new relation to reality: perhaps something that is mathematical or something that is based on heat, or something that is based on tectonic forces, or something that is based on forces five miles under the Earth's surface—in other words it's another form of visualization that is distinct from simple representation. Perhaps this is a less precise, less scientific, but nonetheless accurate way of understanding these terms of presentation, versus representation. Representation is announcing: it looked like this when I saw it. I am faithfully representing that which presented itself to my vision, whereas presentation is a new thing. Presentation announces: there is nothing that looked exactly like this! These were abstract numbers, these were sonic traces that I have made into an image. When the drawing of the volcano erupting shows the eruption as a series of expanding sound waves, yes, on the one hand, it's a representation; technically, you're representing data—but you can also argue that it's a presentation of information that doesn't exist otherwise in this *visual* register.

But I want to introduce a completely new question to you, Diana. The question would be whether you ever want to challenge the ancient view of nature as being other than us. Nature is the dichotomy I opened with: nature is precisely that which is *other* than the human. Is this a view we must now abandon? Is there a new emerging order? This is what Donna Harraway is now arguing for, the "withness" as opposed to the witness of nature.[4] In place of objectivity, we have entanglement. We are part of a crustal life formation on the surface of a living entity. The images produced by your studio don't seem to have a way of reflecting this embedded entangled episteme.

GALISON: You mean because there are no people in these drawings?

JONES: A: no people, but also B: how do you reflect on the scale of the Anthropocene, or the dynamism of a whole planet? How do you visualize something that isn't still, that isn't fixed in some sense? While some projects, such as those on the mangroves or coral reefs, attempt at dealing with a biology of entanglement, of circulation of bacteria from one biome to another, we still have few ways to render the entangled symbiotic flow of whatever life is. The very scientific precision of the project's drawings, their very constructed beauty seems a different regime, perhaps "objective." This is a collective challenge. How do we convey the sense of our smallness, at the same time as our embeddedness in this vast symbiotic mesh? On the one hand, even though we have done unspeakable damage to the ecosystem we have evolved in, it will also continue to evolve without us. Different life forms will thrive, anaerobic bacteria will take over the dead oceans, just not *us.* So, it seems to me that any project on nature has to now address this conundrum. It's no longer possible to argue that nature is "out there" and we can just measure the sound waves or the rate of coral growth or the exact temperature and "fix" the picture. It's just much messier.

AGREST: You are making a very important point. I agree, as we consider the earth as a whole living organism. In terms of human presence and scale, I always point to the size of a volcano as an example, which in sections goes to the center of the earth; we are nothing next to it, so when we approach this type of natural phenomena there is another scale of space and time where many have taken millions of years to be formed and therefore, the human absence is premeditated. We do, however, incorporate living organisms in some of these projects, as an essential part of nature, in ways that present very different types of "entanglements" or complex ecological systems, as in the projects you mentioned above and others: particularly the algae and sequoia. In each case we aim to address from the micro scale of bacteria or cell reproduction to the macro scale of the overall phenomena, such as ocean currents or tectonic plates. And I have to admit that to represent this in terms of the entanglements that you describe so well using our tools and modes of seeing and adapting them to think and present that complexity is a real challenge, but that type of challenge is integral to the research in this studio.

JONES: This sounds very interesting. This is far beyond inserting a human figure for scale. I'm trying to imagine a regime of the image, where the human would not be adored, the human would not be figured as a heroic Corbusier modulor. How could we envision the human as, instead, a virus or contagion? What if the human were a kind of scum that was spreading in a certain way? What if the human were a termite?

AGREST: Following up on another aspect of scale and representation, one of the challenges in this work is to bring time into the equation—the space-time continuum (as in the theory of relativity) as a concept that opens a different understanding of parameters than those usual in architectural representation. I'm trying to incorporate this to bring that way of thinking of space and time into our mode of seeing and representing, which is very difficult because we're now talking about the fabric of the universe.

GALISON: Well, the great philosophical transformation of the space-time continuum through relativity deals not so much with Newton's physics and Einstein's first special relativity, but with special relativity and general relativity. That difference in some ways is where space-time becomes essential rather than an optional way of re-describing physics. At first, when Hermann Minkowski invented the idea of space-time around 1908, Einstein thought Minkowski's idea was just a mathematical re-description of what he had already done in 1905. But very soon he realized that if he was going to carry his special relativity theory further to be able to account not just for things moving at constant speed but also for accelerating objects, and eventually for gravity itself, he needed the idea of Minkowski's four-dimensional space-time.

In Einstein's general relativity (1915) space-time was neither a theater stage on which events took place, nor a neutral void around the objects that interest us. In Newtonian physics and also in special relativity you can have space without mass or energy—an empty theater so to speak. But in general relativity, without matter or energy there is no space-time. In fact (this was part of what was so revolutionary about general relativity), space-time is produced and shaped by mass and energy; and in turn, space-time tells the mass and energy how to move. So there's this famous phrase of John Wheeler (an American physicist of the mid-20th century) who said: "matter tells spacetime how to curve and spacetime tells matter how to move."

Space and time, mass and energy are inextricably bound together. There's not an independent theater of space and time in which objects come on stage, do their actions and then leave. Without the actors there would be no theater—but in this case, neither would there be a building nor a stage. That's really fundamental, as is the fact that space-time is shaped by the sun that curves space-time through gravity, and then objects like the earth simply travel along the straightest lines they can (the shortest paths) in that curved space-time.

Recently, this great new discovery was made about gravity waves. Two black holes, more than a billion light-years away from us, fell into each other and changed space-time with their huge gravitational waves, which emanated out from their collision and eventually reached observatories in Louisiana and Washington State. Those waves squished and expanded space-time along these several-mile-long evacuated tubes fitted with mirrors at the end—the waves displaced a beam of light by a distance thousands of times smaller than a proton, and that displacement was measured *in both detectors a continent apart*. The slight difference in when it was detected in both of them gave the observatories the direction the wave was coming from, and the pattern of the squish/expansion linked what they saw to the colliding black holes. Almost like a sound wave, (not a sound wave but almost, because the compression and rarefaction of waves in a medium such as air or water is here like the compression and expansion of space-time itself), this wave was registered, and that's really the echo in a very deep sense of what Einstein theorized in 1914—15. This is a new form of observing, one not based on light or radio waves but instead on the contractions and expansions of space-time. By converting these space-time vibrations to the electromagnetic spectrum in which we are tuned to hear sound, you can hear the black holes collide. It is matter of listening rather than looking at the universe around us, putting the verb "observing" under pressure.

AGREST: Do you think there is a way in which that could be reflected in the type of things we are doing at this scale?

GALISON: What's amazing about this event is that these waves are *different*. They are structurally unlike anything we've been able to measure before. All of our astronomy, all of our measurements are in some ways measurements of electricity and magnetism, the same electromagnetic spectrum we have evolved to sense (even if some frequencies are beyond our unaided human senses). The light that we see, the gamma rays, the X-rays, radio waves, all of that is on the electro-magnetic spectrum. *The gravity waves are something completely different.* Our being able to sense them—almost like *hearing* that collision (and in fact "hearing" it with the right transduction)—is transformative, as if everything before was seeing and now we can hear and that is a completely different sense of the universe around us and our relationship to it. If I were to suggest (metaphorically) an analogy with what we are doing, drawing, building perhaps, very speculatively, we could say we should be attentive not just to the architecture of the visible but to the architecture of what we gain access to through our other senses—through feeling and hearing, for example.

JONES: Peter's suggesting an extraordinary challenge: what if architecture could get to a place where its own participation in space-time, those gravitational fluctuations, could be haptically sensed in this way? In other words, we're humans; we have to work with the equipment we have. But that equipment and its technological extensions give us a large repertoire of electro-magnetic, chemical, acoustic, and haptic senses. We actually have a pretty robust range of scales and abilities in our extended apparatus. We have disproportionately relied on the electro-magnetic in our scientific and visual communication, privileging sight. Certainly these beautiful drawings are well within that tradition. But other models are possible.

GALISON: If you wanted to question the norms, for instance, when you're in studio with your students, and under your supervision they make these three-dimensional models, what if you learned about them just with your eyes closed? Or let's take the phenomena themselves; just touching them would be a profoundly different way of coming to know those geysers, that underground steam and water movement. Coming to the knowledge through a different sense produces different knowledge of nature—perhaps getting to that embedded, entangled relation Caroline was speaking about earlier.

AGREST: What interests me in this respect is how we can incorporate such dimension, the understanding and visualizing of space-time, not falling into just the metaphoric representation.

GALISON: You were worried about the simulacrum, but for science there is a very strong engagement with *simulations*. The role of simulations is very much a part of the way science, or many parts of science, work these days. We can't *be* in a black hole, but we can use our knowledge of its mass, rotation, boundary, and so forth to simulate the black hole at another scale—a human perceptual scale. This is how we can "hear" the ancient collision of the two black holes. Simulations are interesting because they're not necessarily a copy of something. We try to say, what happens when a super-massive black hole encounters a little black hole? What happens if a star comes near a super massive black hole and is shredded into bits and pieces by the tidal forces there?

A lot of science has used simulations for these kinds of exploratory questions that aren't of a copying sort. Simulation is a kind of modeling. But sometimes when we say model, we implicitly think that it's a model faithful to the *appearance* of something else, that it's a copy. (The sculptor "models" clay to make a copy of the "life model.") Simulation forces us to recognize that our entities can be models without copying. With these simulated models, you can study things statistically, you can try 100 different volcanoes with different initial conditions; or you can imagine 1,000 different bacterial interactions.

JONES: Scientists and artists also work with analogical comparatives that may be physical models, materializing the metaphors we use to understand the original "natural condition," which then radically shifts the initial simulation. The example I'm thinking of is in the book project I'm co-editing titled *Experience* (MIT Press, 2016). It contains documentation of the millennial simulation of the filamentary matter condensing in the early universe. The model is hilarious for a lay person, because the visual image has a scale bar indicator of 125 million parsecs per centimeter—you can't really get your head around that. A common metaphor is that these early stages of the universe (before the complex structures of stars and galaxies) look like a web—but the interesting development happens when the architecturally-trained artist Tomás Saraceno takes that seriously, asking: "what if it were a physical analogue, could the material model teach you something you didn't know?" These filamentary structures of cosmological condensation visually resemble and can be analogized to things like spider silk, which can then be analyzed for its tensile properties and torque; another model uses the analogue of mathematical network theory to calculate the spider web's connectivity, bringing that same abstract calculus to the cosmic web's nodes and connections.

What began as a metaphor gets physical and computational, functioning as a robust and manipulable analogy that can be measured at various scales to explore scale itself as a factor in the behavior of physical matter in space-time. How are the tensile properties of spider silk, with its complex protein strings, related to early strings of matter? Does this analogical model give useful insights or is this irrelevant? I mean, at this scale, do the physical properties in question even scale up? I think Peter has very appropriately landed on this point—that our sensory capacities are embedded in nature, because we've evolved to sense this nature in which we're embedded. This is not just a tautology. It doesn't mean that sensing space-time haptically couldn't give you a profoundly new access to the "nature" of the universe.

The paradox is this: whatever "nature" is, we're part of it, made of it, embedded in it. We've necessarily evolved to resonate with its harmonic frequencies. Yet we can only "get to it"—that is, produce it as some kind of object for contemplation, for sharing, for culture—by modeling, by presenting, by analogy, by metaphor, by externalization, by speculating on it as "*what is not us*." We are of course a part of it all. But we have to pretend we aren't, just to be able to think about it. So, is it an abstraction? Must we utilize an abstracting operation? It can't be anything but that—still, different forms of abstraction matter. They communicate differently to us and others; they set different parameters for what they're looking at: they make different points, they might be about the warming ocean, or they might be about the acidifying ocean or they might be about the salinity changes that have been introduced, or they might be about any one or all of these things simultaneously. If you were to taste that model rather than look at its data, you would rapidly have a very different relation to that knowledge. These are all powerful forms of abstracting from existing, complex dynamic systems: what is it we want to talk about when we talk about this thing called nature?

GALISON: The one other thing about nature that I've been thinking a lot about in the last years is that we have this radical distinction that we make between whether we control nature or whether we are its servants. For a very long time there was a kind of theologically based understanding of the relationship of the human to the natural. In God's image, Adam named the creatures, etc. These Abrahamic religions produced origin myths that in their most extreme form informed the concept of "wilderness," especially in the American cultural imagination. This kind of nature was there *for us*; a Promised Land. Our relation to land in the US went through a process that was economic, but also driven by religion.

There was, in this country, something salvific about the Wilderness—out of the darkest swamp comes the redeemer. The Wilderness was the raw material out of which humans were formed in the kind of repetition of Genesis not just at the beginning of time but even in our own historical epoch, in our understanding of this world. But in this back and forth, whether thinking that God made us to control nature or that God made us to be servants of nature, it turns out that both have theological foundations. And both, again, return to the paradox Caroline outlined—we are of nature, but find ourselves mythologically placed outside it (to serve or dominate). One of the things that I've been interested in recently is the instability or even crisis of that theologically propelled idea of the human as master or servant of nature. Increasingly, people are beginning to speak in a very different way, either because of powerful new philosophies (Haraway's "withness") or simply because of very practical concerns.

To give an example. There are these big areas I've been interested in, of nuclear contaminated zones: whether around Fukushima, whether the Nevada (nuclear) test site or the Ukrainian contaminated zone around Chernobyl (and there are many other sites like this). Because humans have been excluded from these "sacrifice zones," these toxic territories, they become sites of great biological diversity. Since people conceive

After Fukushima. "Mrs. S," a former homeowner, visits the devastated and abandoned town of Namie, Futaba district, Fukushima Prefecture, Japan, May 2013. Severely impacted by a triple disaster (Tohoku earthquake, tsunami, and nuclear meltdown), the town was evacuated on 12 March 2011. Still from Peter Galison and Robb Moss, *Containment* (2015), 81 min. documentary, HD video.

of biodiversity as actually a stand in for the Wilderness concept now, there is a new kind of Wilderness *closed to us* and hence without the theological foundations we have imposed on lands we inhabit, use, mine, farm, and so forth. With these toxic wildernesses, we have a very different relationship.

Although we do sometimes come to these places as nuclear tourists, we don't stay (we can't stay), we're just looking. (This builds on a long tradition of dark tourism or disaster tourism that goes back into the 19th century.) The new nuclear tourism is given a very specific relationship to these territories, a new kind of concept that the most natural nature, the wildest, are the most biologically diverse—and the most bio-diverse are the places where people are forbidden to go for safety reasons. And so we begin to think of these areas as human zones of exclusion. I've become very interested in what happens when the theological begins to fall away in endorsing our relationship to nature. We begin to try to formulate it around something like biodiversity reserves and these "sacrifice zones" are, again, nature because we are not.

In my film *Containment*, there's a site like this that I've filmed at and written about—the Savannah River nuclear site. Highly contaminated, this is where nuclear weapons were made, and in some cases the waste was just shoved in cardboard boxes and shoveled into a shallow landfill on the site.[1] Yet, for certain kinds of things like water bugs and other things it's the most bio-diverse reserve in the United States. It comes as a surprise that the most biodiverse site has the greatest concentration of radiological waste.

Sublime Visibilities. This aerial view of the BP oil "spill" in the Gulf of Mexico, made by the National Oceanographic and Atmospheric Agency, is considered a "close-up," since it is photographed from an airplane rather than a satellite. Yet it still connotes the sublime detachment of a removed, surface view. NOAA caption: "A heavy band of oil seen during an overflight of the Deepwater Horizon spill on May 12, 2010." Credit: NOAA

AGREST: Would that fall within the realm of the sublime, as you both wrote in your article "Unknown Quantities" on imaging the oil spill in the Gulf of Mexico? Where there is the horror of the nuclear explosion and then the image of this natural disaster enters the realm of the sublime in representing as a phenomena the two essential aspects of the sublime: horror and beauty.

JONES: Absolutely. And the sublime is a rhetorical device, generated in response to a set of experiences—it's not the thing. And what I'm proposing as this sort of polemical thought condition is that nature, too, is a rhetorical relationship and not a thing. I began by saying nature is precisely what is *not us*; I then staged a paradox by noting that we are in nature but constantly eject it in order to think about it. Now I want to begin to conclude by suggesting that "the natural" is precisely this paradoxical relationship. (It is not *out there*, but how we imagine our relation to this world, and how we produce it *as* external while we are embedded in it. That "both/and" is nature.) And, you know, I think the space-time conversation was very powerful because the tangle of these concepts is like that—nature is constituted through this rhetoric and through these modes of representation, *and thus, so are we.*

AGREST: To me it is sublime because of the power of the forces that are at play there.

JONES: Of course, the sublime is a register we reserve for speaking to the scale that you're working at. As to my own relation to the sublime, I find I have completely schizophrenic and alternating positions. One is prompted by something like Robert Smithson's *Spiral Jetty.* Smithson's relationship with time was extremely post-apocalyptic; he drew comfort from thinking 10,000 years into the future, envisioning a world without us, we're extinct, fine. It's a comfort to him to conceive of this sublime annihilation, to accept that there's really nothing we can do to stave off this inevitable future. (As a result, he was often opposed to environmental groups, who seemed naïve to him. Yet he was willing to accept the 18th-century version of the sublime.) And then the other position is anti-sublime; it's in the trenches, it's fiercely activist. Motivated by the existence on earth of our granddaughter, this position calls to our responsibility to get in there and clean things up a bit. These positions either alternate or just co-exist in my muddled mind. And your book in progress is clearly more like Smithson's. It's a look at a very long term at a very large scale, potentially post-human in its sublimity.

GALISON: I want to return to my earlier comments about waste wilderness and about presentation as it differs from representation. I want to make it clear that the theological foundation of wilderness has begun to fall away, even among people defending the idea of wilderness—increasingly activists say, more and more, that it's the biodiversity that we should care about. And humans are not divinely separated from that.

And once you're in that domain, you no longer have the sanction that somehow you're dealing with the primeval, untouched nature of wilderness. In turn, that puts us in a different human position in relationship to nature. The old idea of primeval wilderness seems to me, in many ways, a kind of romantic fantasy and a danger.

JONES: The word primeval implies an origin point that was unchanging or at least a steady-state. Biological homeostasis is, in fact, very short-term. So "primeval" is a very strange word. So is "sublime."

GALISON: There is an important essay by William Cronon called "The Trouble with Wilderness."[5] He's a scholar I very much admire, and in this essay he suggests that environmentalists have gotten themselves into all sorts of trouble by having an ideal concept of wilderness that doesn't make contact with people's interaction with the world around them.

I think Cronon is right. The idea that somehow the only pure, true nature is without people ("the forest primeval") and that this is the way things were then, it authorizes an oddly dominating point of view. It makes it possible to sort of look over at this rainforest or arctic tundra or evergreen forest and say, "what's important about this is that it was never touched by humans." Apart from being biologically naïve (there are no parts of the planet that have been "untouched" by human agency), this kind of statement is becoming increasingly strange. Moreover, it can lead you to all sorts of disasters like trying to drive people off the land to capture its primeval truth.

JONES: And the ones being driven out to produce the primeval are most often native peoples, that's another necessary part of the story.

AGREST: I have a question about the disciplines that take care of the different areas of the study of nature defined in terms of its materiality, physical causes and effects, etc. It appears as though the division is still made in terms of natural elements such as earth, water, atmosphere, living organism, etc. There are so many specialized fields within the environmental sciences that it is hard to decide in relation to the complex phenomena we look into in this work whether they should be grouped under the rubric of a certain disciplinary umbrella when there are so many overlaps.

GALISON: Well, back in the 1920s and '30s

when the sociologist and philosopher Otto Neurath was thinking about the nature of science, he used forest fires as an example of how the disciplines separately couldn't produce the kind of knowledge that we needed.[6] His point was that a forest fire is of course a chemical reaction, but it's much more than that. It also has to do with the land and the wind; it has an economic dimension and a human dimension—so we need to think about understanding, said Neurath, as a kind of orchestration of the disciplines. Like an orchestral composition that is only achieved when the different sections, the wind section and the string section and the percussion section, are brought together into some kind of harmony.

His metaphor was necessarily embedded in high German-speaking culture of the moment. But the point is very important: there really isn't an understanding of something as basic as a forest fire without interdisciplinary coordination. It is only when these are orchestrated and brought together that you can have an understanding of what is going on. Who will be the conductor? This is the political issue of implementation, and here we see the struggle with achieving coordination in response to climate change.

A lot has happened since the 1920s and 1930s in our understanding of knowledge, but I think that Neurath's image is helpful. We need the different disciplines: chemistry, biology, physics, etc. But we also need the orchestration of the disciplines rather than looking for a primordial or "kingpin" discipline that really will explain everything about something as simple as a fire.

AGREST: I call what we do trans-discursive, which I like as a term, that refers to the construction of or articulation between discourses. This is important from my perspective because we are expanding the very discourse of architecture in this work by articulating it with other discourses: scientific, philosophical, historical, etc. So following up with the question of disciplinary boundaries, it seems that philosophy or history of science are more general in scope, but when considering the specific disciplines dealing with the environmental sciences, such as applied science, problems are set in a very specific framework. How do you negotiate this difference? Or is it at all relevant?

GALISON: Science studies—of which history of science figures as a part—looks at how something such as oceanographic knowledge is put together, assembled, and deployed. Well, oceanography is already a hybrid discipline and not because I think that there's a radical distinction between pure and applied, but because even at the present time oceanography still bears the very visible concatenation of different nineteenth- and even eighteenth-century disciplines within it. So you have oceanographers who are mainly interested in heat flow; you have oceanographers who are interested in macro biological or micro biological structures of the oceans; you have scientists affiliated with oceanography who are interested in sea water rising, models of global warming, and things like that. But it doesn't have the character, at this point, of a single discipline. It very much looks like an assembly of disciplines that are trying to learn how to talk to each other.

I think that some things like particle physics or fluid dynamics have a kind of consensual, integrated structure, but not because they were always that way, but because at this point they have worked out a coordinated program. So, I think disciplines do come to have that kind of first order coherence. The purest part of mathematics, the part of it that most mathematicians would identify as "the center of our discipline, the pure part" would now be called algebraic geometry, but even the name tells you something about its historical origins as a combination of two things. It took a lot of work to produce the thing that now counts as pure. So, the hybrid can become integrated in that way and maybe one day nano-science or neuroscience or things that still bear this concatenated function will begin to look pure or integrated in a more complete way. So, one distinction is between disciplines like organic chemistry or particle physics or fluid dynamics or those disciplines that are recognized as single integrated disciplines (despite their hybrid names), and more concatenated structures that still are working out how to talk to each other. Fields like oceanography or nanoscience or neuroscience are still working out their common language; you can see this even in the motley nature of their visualizations. There is also a question of what related disciplines, such as science studies, history of science, or philosophy of science, will do; will they amalgamate or break apart? They are not looking directly to try to resolve questions of science so much as to understand how the knowledge system comes to function.

AGREST: An important part of the approach to this work as done within the framework of architecture is the production of knowledge. So, in taking nature as an object of study, I find that an interdisciplinary, or rather an interdiscursive approach is intrinsic to the exploration and understanding of the concepts of knowledge that bear upon our own understanding of nature.

GALISON: Much of my work has been trying to get away from talking about interdisciplinary or symbiotic discourses, while trying to look at what happens when disciplines try to talk to one another.

The idea of trading zones and interlanguages that get formed at these boundaries have motivated much of my work in the history and philosophy of science. I'm most interested in historical moments when algebra and geometry, or biology and chemistry, or physics and engineering begin to have contact. I study how they need to create terms and then effective jargons, pidgins, creoles at the boundary between them. So, to me a term like "transdiscursive" might name the problem, but I want to know how the trading of ideas actually works. And so, a lot of my work has been about how we might get at the process by which knowledge builds at the boundary. It is analogous to the way an anthropological linguist would study the way German and French began to navigate in the terrain of Alsace—on the ground, and among people. And so I think that that process of the elaboration, articulation, and the creation of metadiscursive ways of moving is very important and revealing. The pidgin is ad hoc until people "grow up" in it, disciplinarily speaking—then it becomes what creole is for the anthropological linguists, a fully functional language.

AGREST: So, we may have a chance here with this architecture of nature in terms of architecture to explore those boundaries.

GALISON: That would be a great launching point for our inquiries both about architecture and about nature.

JONES: Then maybe you could define where the discipline (as *techne*, as producer of knowledge, as representational practice) stands in relation to "nature."

Endnotes

1. Caroline A. Jones and Peter Galison, "Introduction, Picturing Science Producing Art," in *Picturing Science, Producing Art*, ed. Caroline A. Jones and Peter Galison (New York and London: Routledge, 1998).
2. Lorraine Daston and Peter Galison, *Objectivity* (New York: Zone Books, 2010).
3. Arthur Schopenhauer's great ambition in *The World as Will and Representation* (1818-19).
4. Donna Haraway, *When Species Meet* (Minneapolis: University of Minnesota Press, 2007).
5. William Cronon, "The Trouble with Wilderness," in *Uncommon Ground: Rethinking the Human Place in Nature*, ed. William Cronon (New York: W. W. Norton & Co., 1995), 69-90.
6. Otto Neurath, "Unified Science as Encyclopedic Integration," in *International Encyclopedia of Unified Science: Foundations of Unity of Science* (Chicago: University of Chicago Press 1938), I, 20-22, 26n1.

Invisible Clouds: Nuclear Testing and Radioactive Spaces

The Marshall Islands, Pacific Ocean
Daniel Meridor

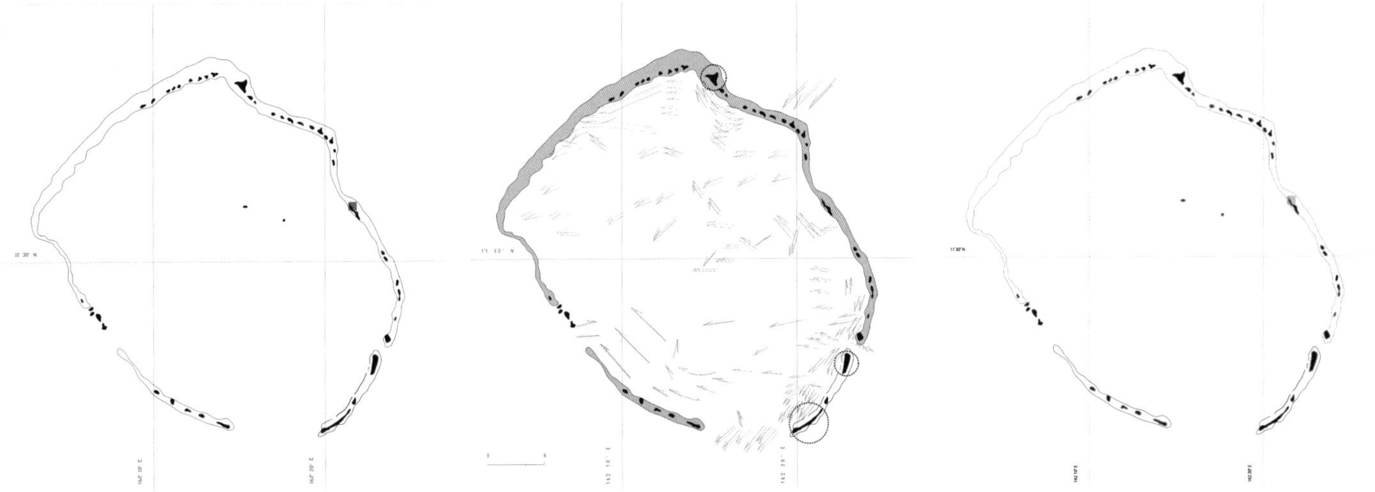

From 1945—1980 the estimated total yield of nuclear atmospheric testing was 428 megatons (MT), the equivalent of approximately 29,000 Hiroshima bombs. Between 1946 and 1958, sixty-seven nuclear atmospheric and underwater tests were carried out by the US in the Marshall Islands, yielding about 78.5 MT. The Castle Bravo test was the most powerful nuclear device ever detonated by the US (1,000 times larger than Hiroshima), and created a fallout of more than 11,000 square km, spreading traces of radioactive material as far as Australia, Japan, India, the United States, and even Europe. Continued testing resulted in the unrestrained global release of radioactivity.

This project focuses on revealing the non-visible radioactive spaces generated by nuclear tests, tracing their evolution, pointing at their potential accumulative effects on the environment, and showing the effects of each detonation by looking at the radioactive debris in the ground and water, and from there to radioactive clouds in the atmosphere and in space. Transcending the local effects such as contaminated fish, burnt coconut trees, or contaminated ground and water, each impact interacted with external forces, expanding in scale and scope as wind carried radioactive debris traversing hemispheres. Following the dropping of nuclear bombs on Hiroshima and Nagasaki, President Truman, in a speech on August 9, 1945, assigned external meaning to human-made destruction, allocating the control of this powerful weapon to God, exonerating humans from the responsibility of their destructive tendencies. The frenzy of nuclear testing reflects the paradoxical claim of both impotence and omnipotence to irreversibly change, evolve, and alter the environment. Nature is not a separate entity from human existence; our actions affect a system in constant flux, which evolves and transforms without prioritizing our species within it.

Top: Location of nuclear testing in the Enewetak Atoll, a testing ground for forty-three tests ranging from 9 kt (the size of the bomb detonated in Hiroshima) to a hydrogen bomb of 15 m (1,500 times bigger), completely vaporizing the island of Elugelab. Center: Enewetak water currents. Right: Enewetak Atoll.

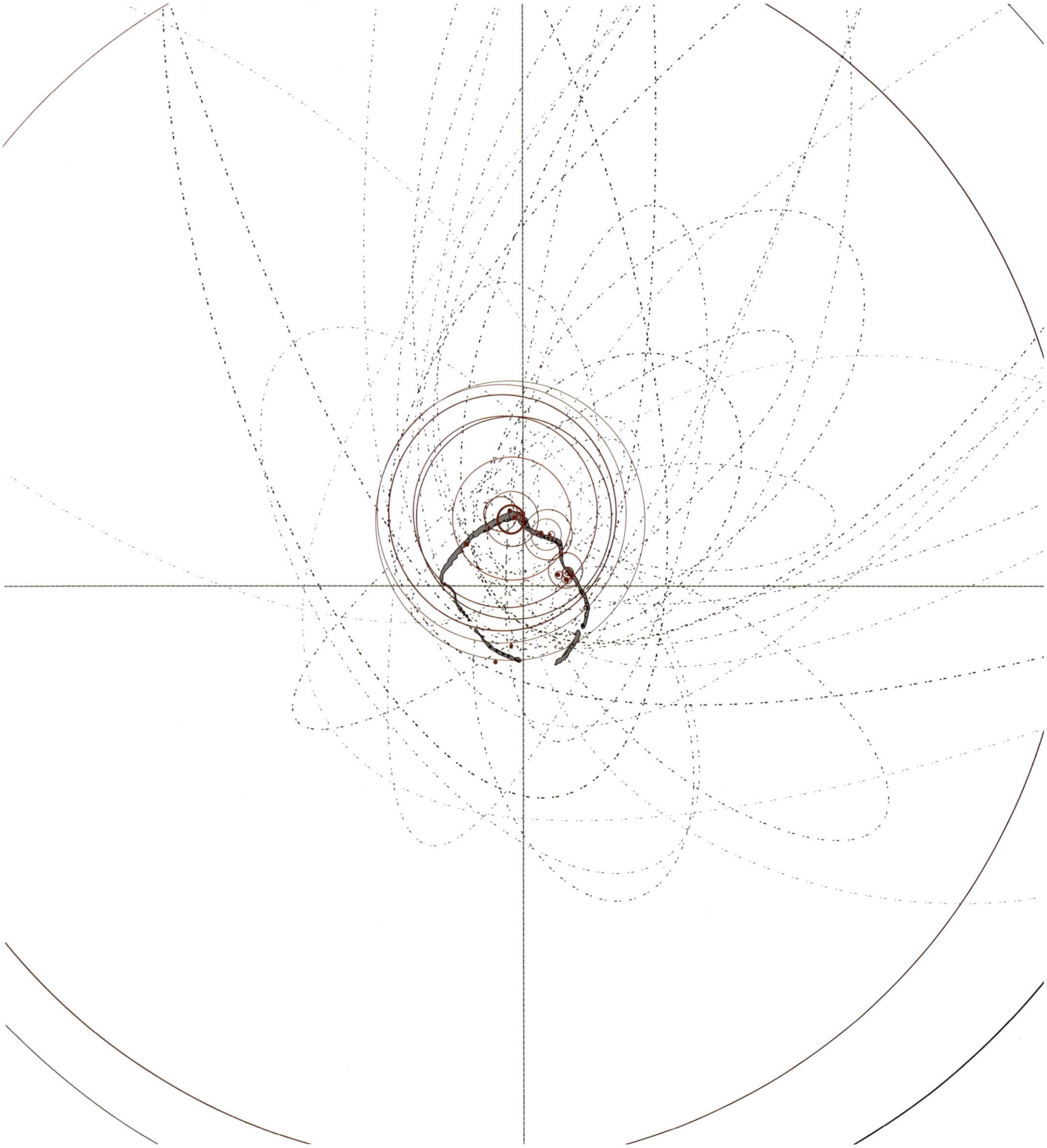

Above: The worldwide fallout from Ivy Mike, detonated on the island of Elugelab and completely obliterating it into the atmosphere in November 1952. Detonated in the Enewetak Atoll, this test generated a 6,250-feet-wide, 165-feet-deep crater where the island once stood. Its yield was estimated in the range of 10—12 MT of TNT.

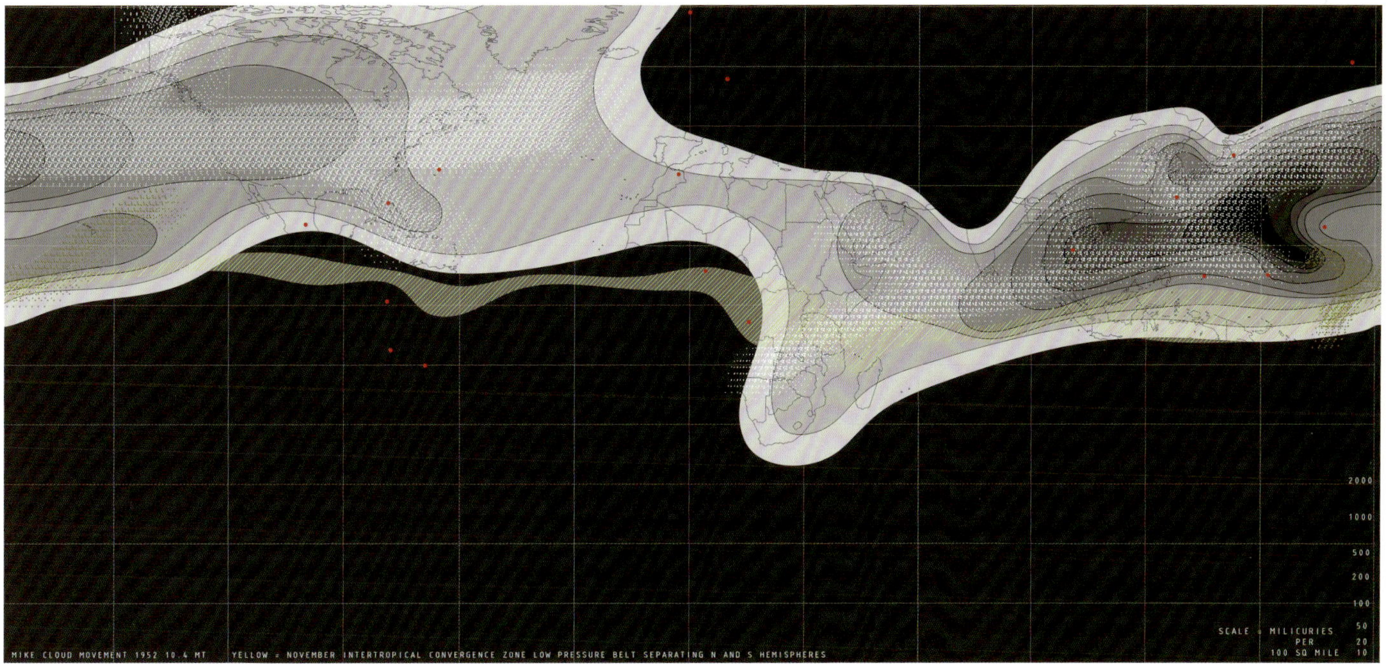

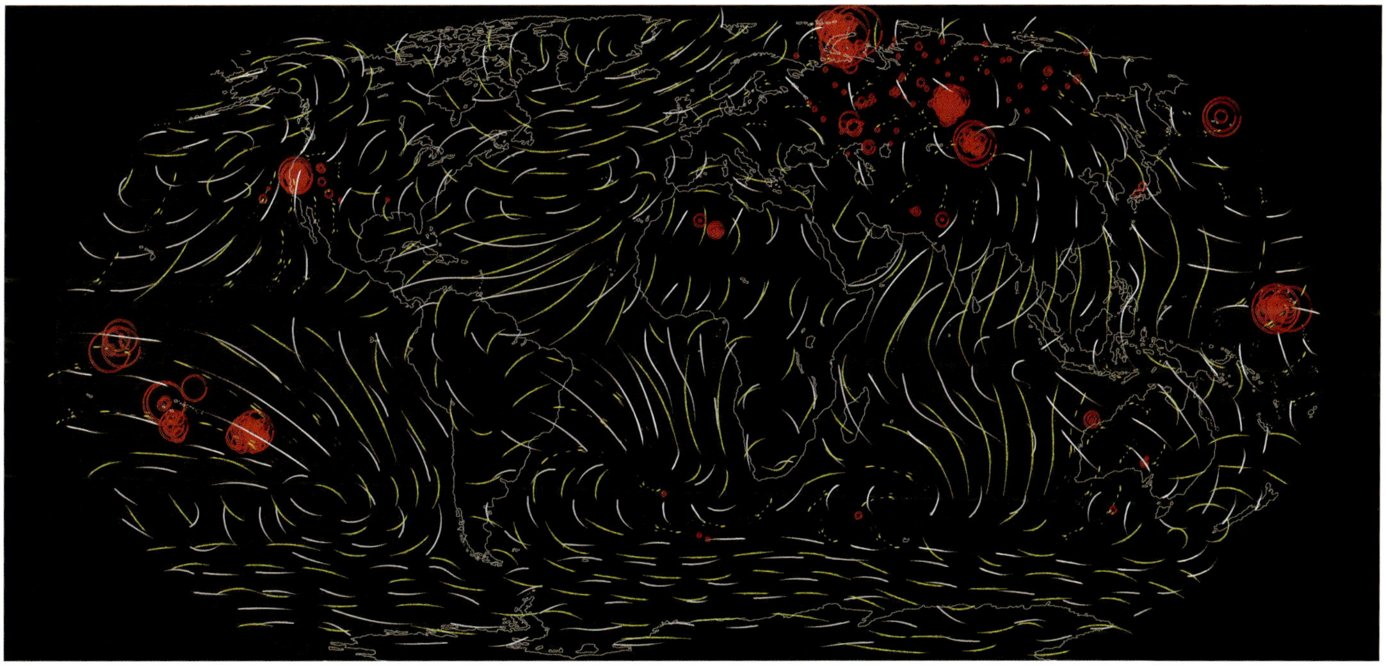

Top: Drawing following the cloud during the month of November. The yellow zone marks the inter-tropical convergence zone where the northeast and southeast trade winds come together. The cloud's gradient represents the number of millicuries per 100 square miles from dark to light gray.

Bottom: Map overlaying the nuclear atmospheric detonations from 1946 through 1980 and global wind patterns, showing the patterns of radioactive debris spread beyond geopolitical or continental boundaries.

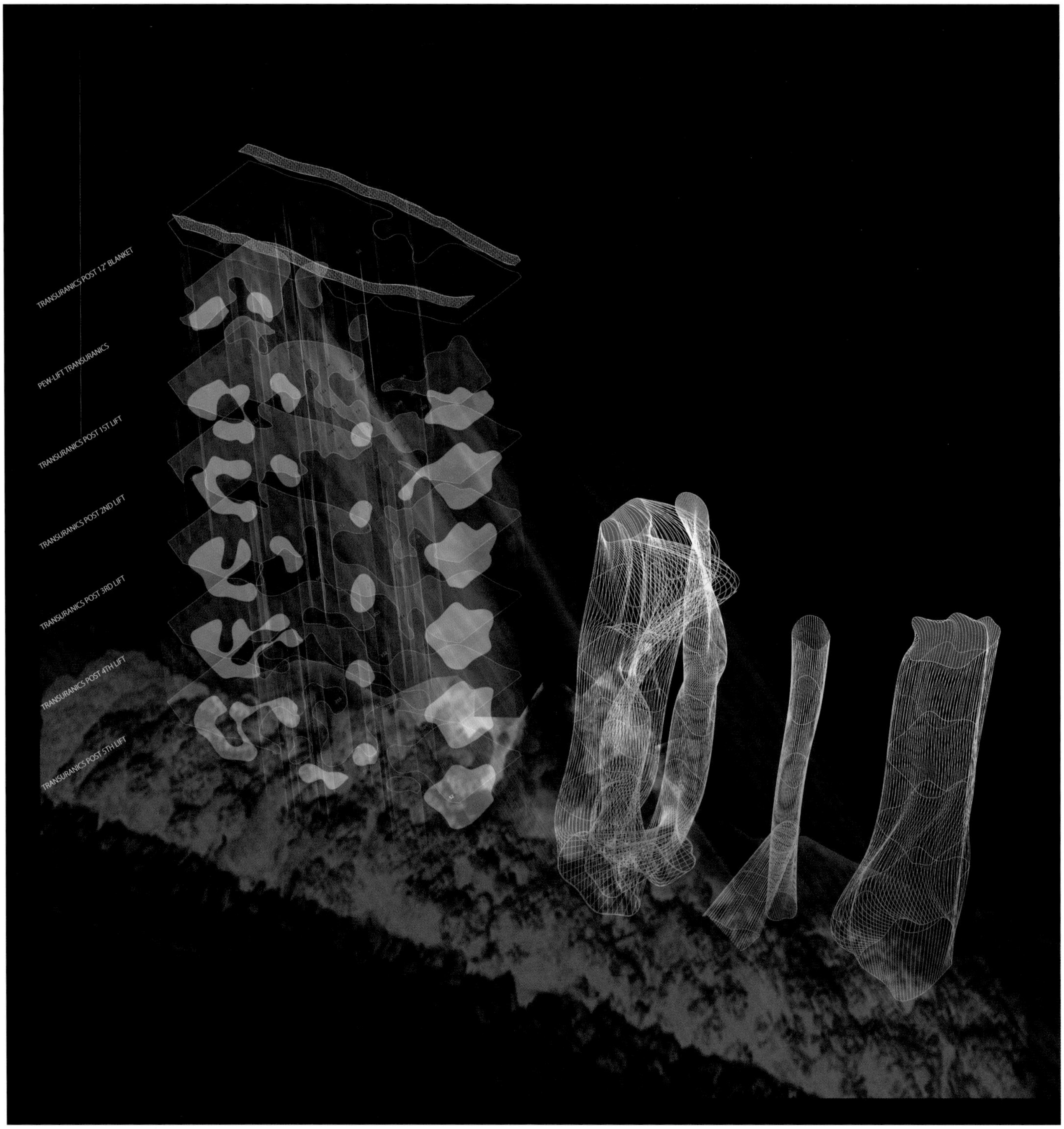

Above: Inversion drawing comparing plans of the contaminated nuclear debris and the atmospheric plume on Runit Island, and comparing the three-dimensional space of contaminated debris underground to the nuclear plume.

Opposite: Axonometric view of the radioactive topography in the lagoon, overlaid with water currents present prior to the explosions as well as the locations of the nuclear detonations on the Atoll.

A2
B2
C2
D2
E2
F2
G2
H2
12
12
K2

A Dissolving Landscape

Mammoth Cave Region, Kentucky, USA
Chih-Wei Hsu

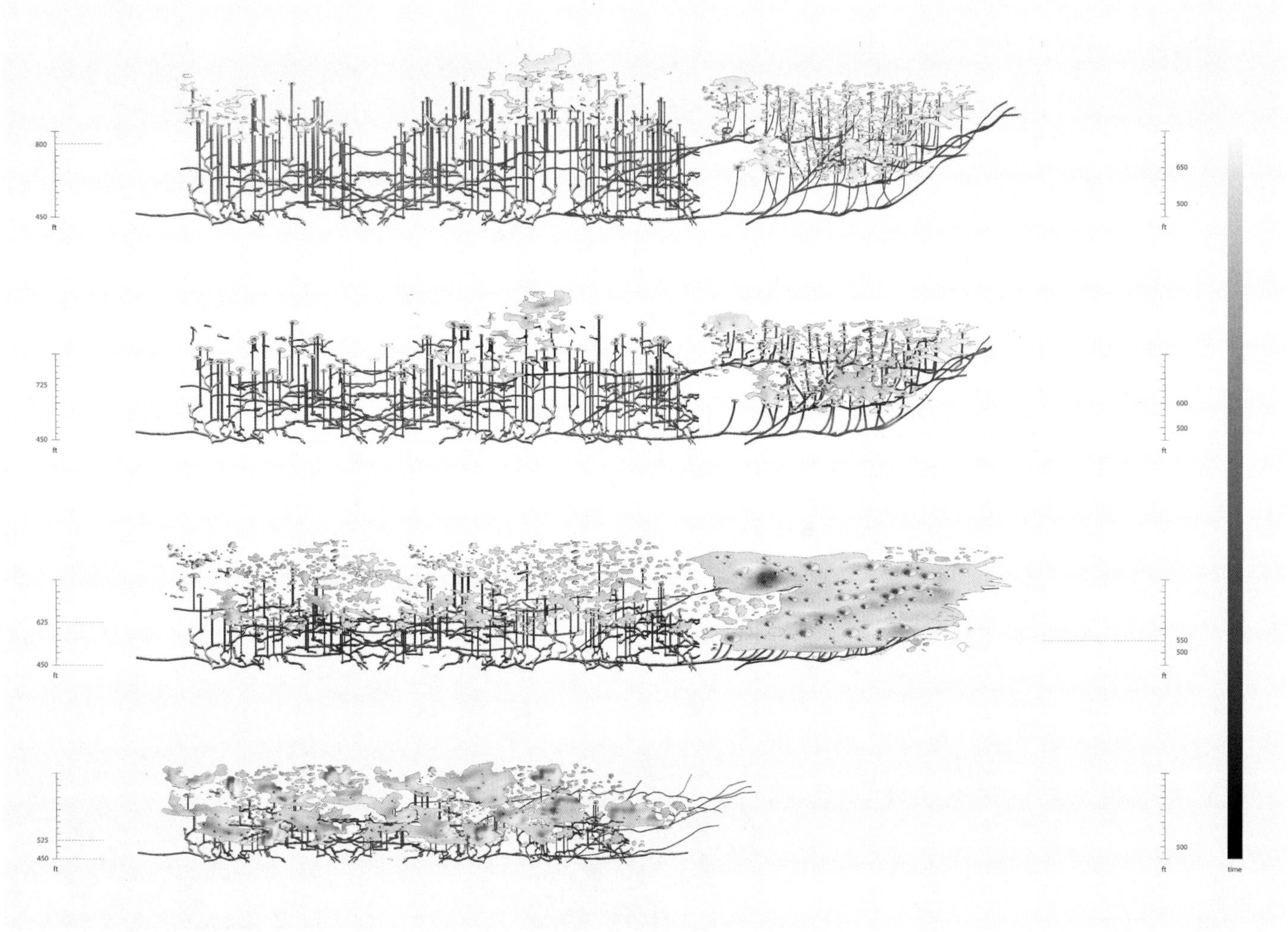

Under a layer of sandstone, acidic water dissolves the thick Mississipian Period limestone strata making the Mammoth Cave region in Kentucky the longest cave system in the world. This project is a reading of the process through which acidic water gradually dissolves into the earth, transforming the cave landscape into a sinkhole plain. Erosion in a top layer of sandstone exposes the limestone strata beneath, which reaches a depth of 379 feet. As gravity draws water down towards the underground water table the water dissolves the acidic layer of limestone and develops the interconnected cave networks of the Mammoth Cave system—a relatively young karst landscape dating back 15 million years in an area that is comparable to the sinkhole plain in south Florida.

As water flow continually descends from the mountains through the boundary between sandstone and limestone, it dissolves the limestone at certain points, creating vertical shafts that connect the ground flow and the underground water system and creating a sinkhole. After one sinkhole is formed, the transformation process affects the geomorphology of the whole region. As this process repeats itself, new vertical sinkholes are created in the shrinking sandstone and more water flows underground, turning a solid landscape into a porous, crumbling territory.

Taking advantage of these conditions, we propose an irrigation system as a transformative process connecting sinkhole areas and using the natural, underground water systems.

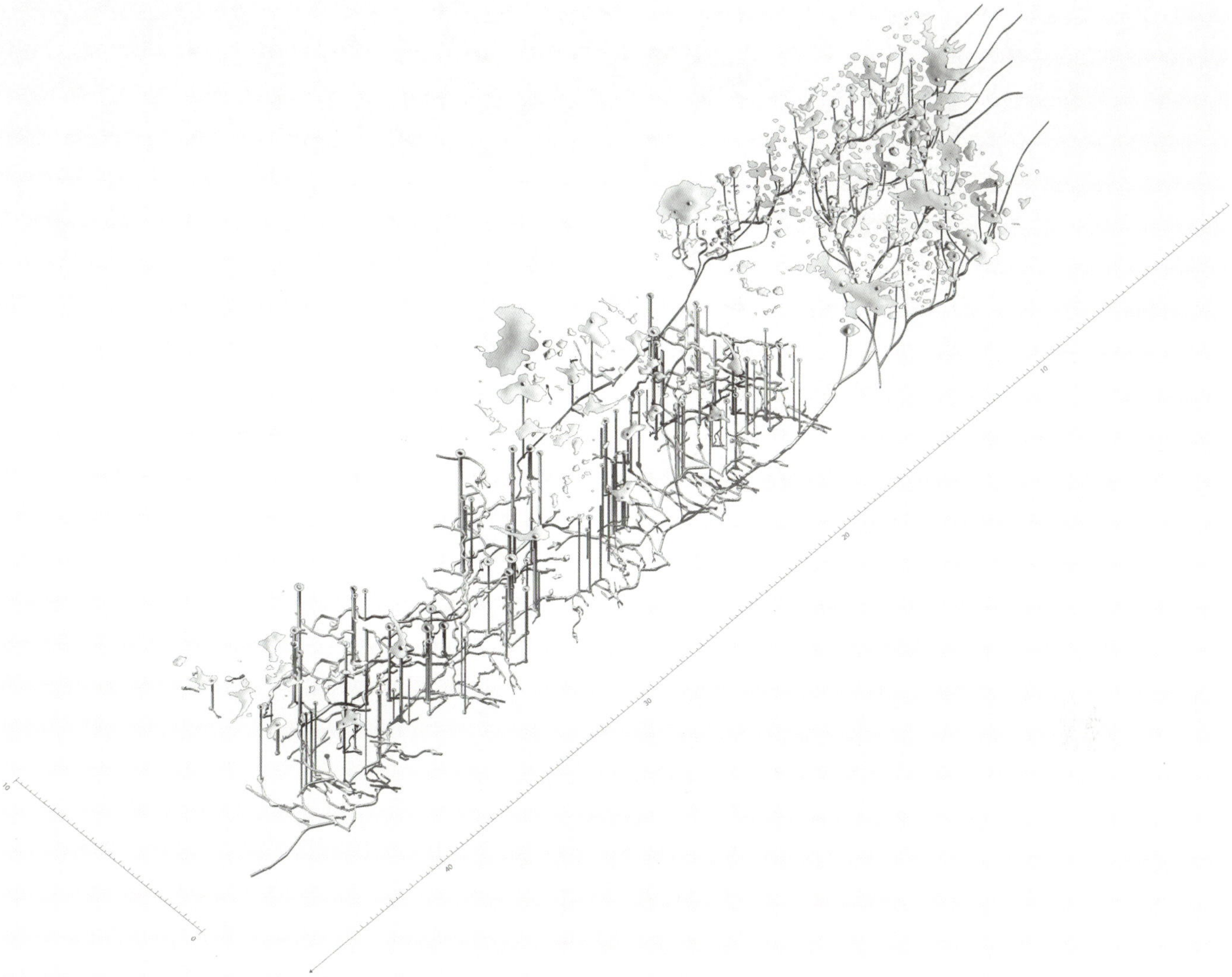

Opposite top: Axonometric view of the development of the connected drainage system in the Mammoth Cave region over an area of 400 square miles.

Above: Axonometric view of a conceptual model of the connected drainage system, from the mountain region to the plains region over an area of 400 square miles.

Right: Potential for an irrigation system as a transformative process connecting sinkhole areas and using the natural, underground water systems in the surrounding agricultural area.

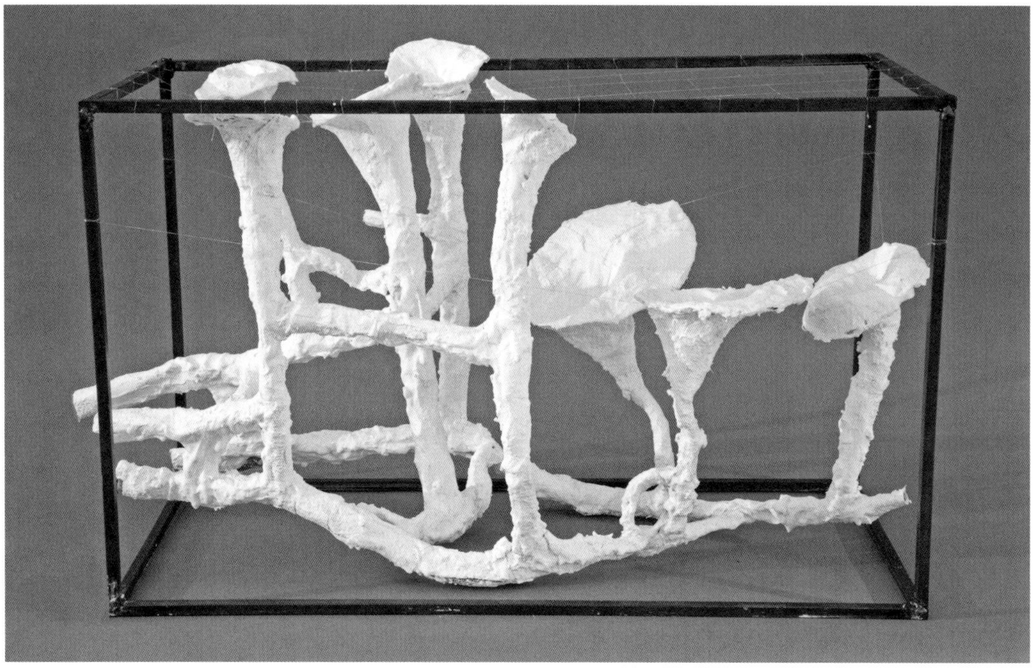

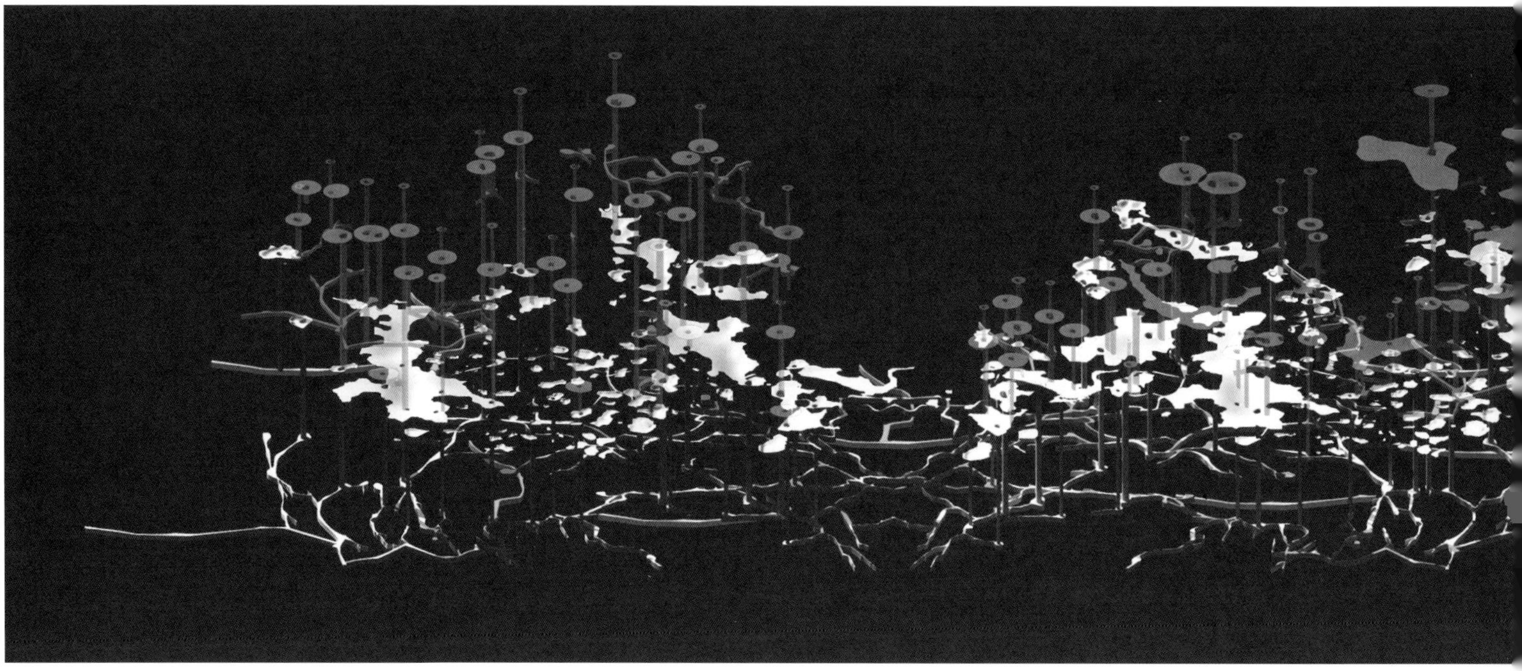

Top: Model of the connected drainage system with dissolving topography.

Bottom: Axonometric view of the connected drainage system during four different time periods.

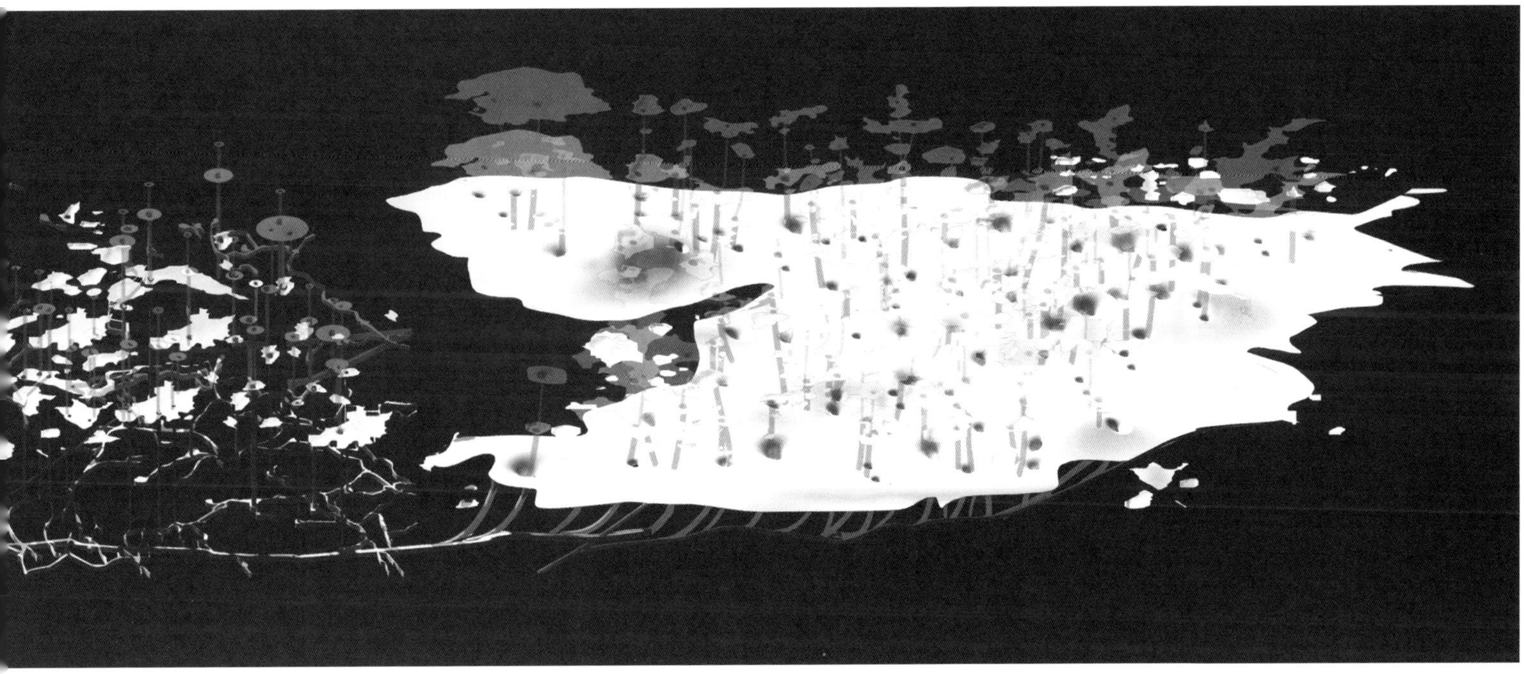

Traces of Choreography of Fractures

Lechuguilla Cave, New Mexico
Bahar Avanoglu

Lechugilla Cave is 138 miles long, 1,604 feet deep, and six million years old. Its boundaries, however, reveal the traces of 255 million year old tectonic fractures that are the result of geologic events dating to the late Permian Period (255-251 Ma) and determine the configuration of the cave configuring its external topographical section. These forces have allowed for the interaction of water and sulfuric acid; the chemical exchange between these two elements during the Miocene (12-5 Ma) and Pliocene (5-2 Ma) epochs determine the configuration of the cave. This project focuses on the forces at play at two different scales and time frames on the formation of the cave's morphological structure and the process of formation of its boundaries. At a large scale the topography of the Guadalupe mountains, above, reveals the major forces correlated with the location of the cave in the mountain system. These forces generate smaller scale fractures that allow the water and sulfuric acid rich water to penetrate and interact, thus generating the cave's boundaries.

Top: Plan showing the correlation between the tectonic system of the Guadalupe Mountains region and the location of the cave. The arrangement of stratigraphic units, joint patterns, and folds, which are among the most decisive control mechanisms for the cave development, took place in the late Permian Period (≈255—251 Ma).

Opposite: Plan of fractures at the Guadalupe Mountains in New Mexico. The area bounded by the Capitan Reef Escarpment is approximately 40 miles long. Hand drawing, charcoal.

1 2 3 4 5 10 miles

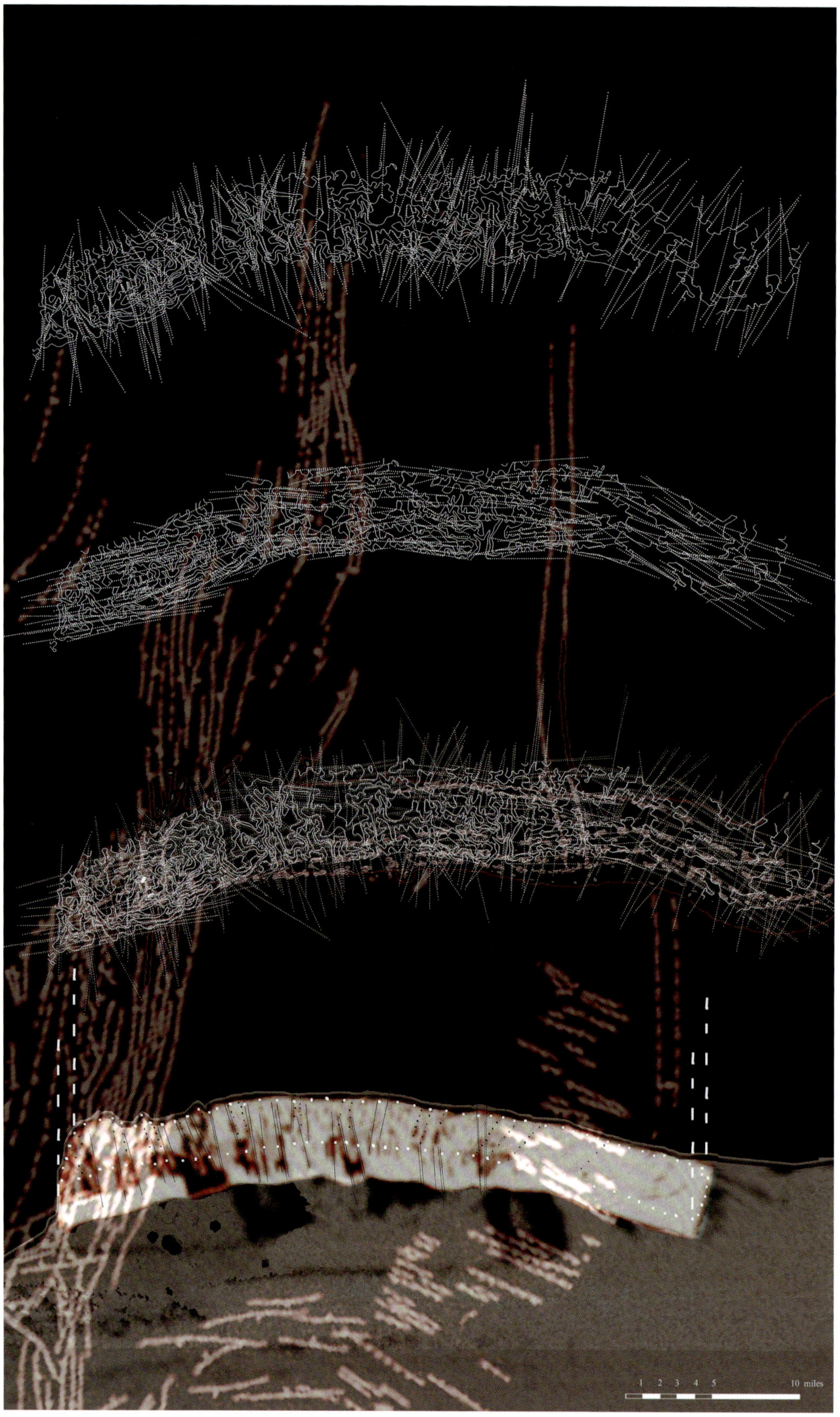

Above: Reading of the tangents to the topographical contour lines of the Guadalupe Mountains in detail: parallel and perpendicular trajectories reveal the fracture pattern and the impact of the erosion during the last 12 Ma, exposing some parts of the cave-bearing strata as present-day canyons.

Opposite: Axonometric drawing revealing the traces of perpendicular intersecting fractures based on the cave pattern composed of rooms and narrow passages.

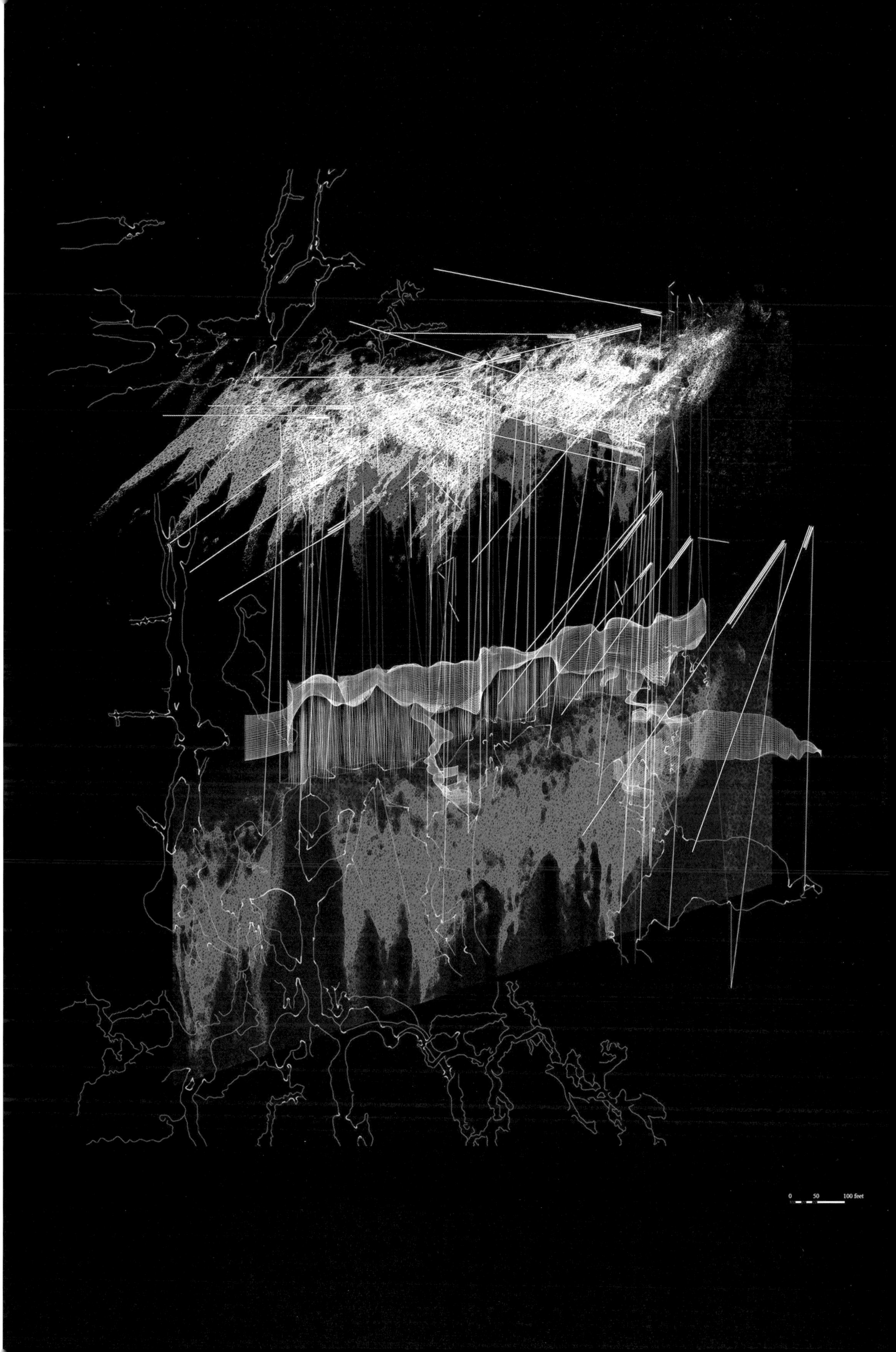
0 50 100 feet

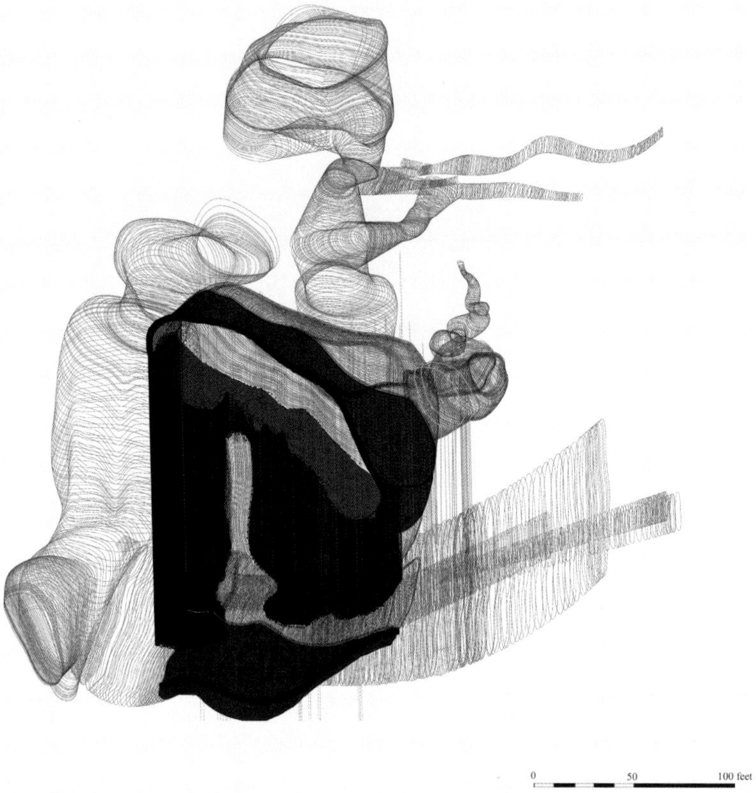

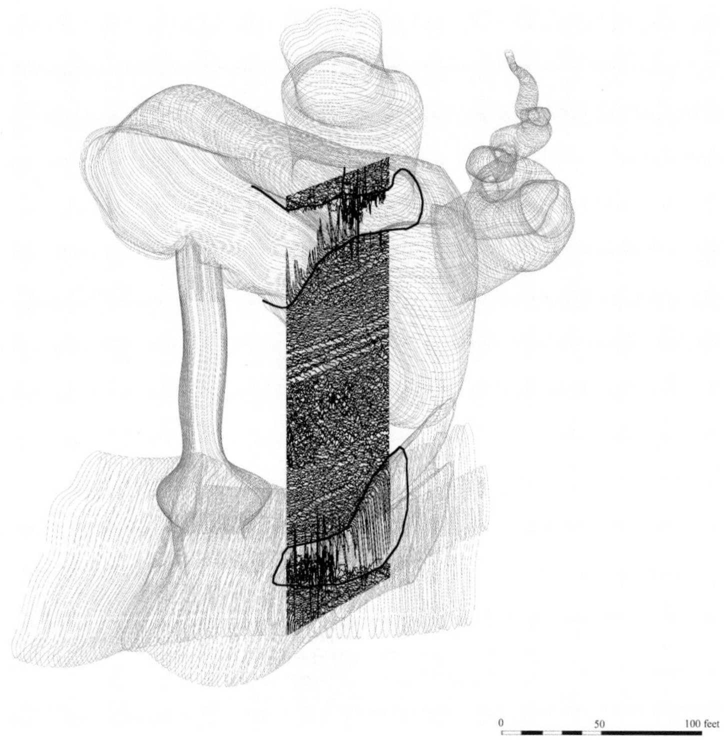

Top and above: Sectional perspective showing the vertical interactions between two rooms located within 100 feet of each other. The chandelier formations are generated by the convective atmospheric conditions and an evaporation and condensation cycle within the caves. The "Chandelier Ballroom" samples a specific case. 1: two separate rooms; 2: penetration between the rooms; 3: dissolution of the gypsum floor.

Opposite: Sectional perspective showing the potential for vertical interaction between two rooms located one above the other. Fissures can generate formations and consequently alter the atmospheric conditions at the lower level. The resulting formations at the lower level slowly block the passage, which changes the atmospheric conditions in the lower level, thus altering the entire airflow system in the cave.

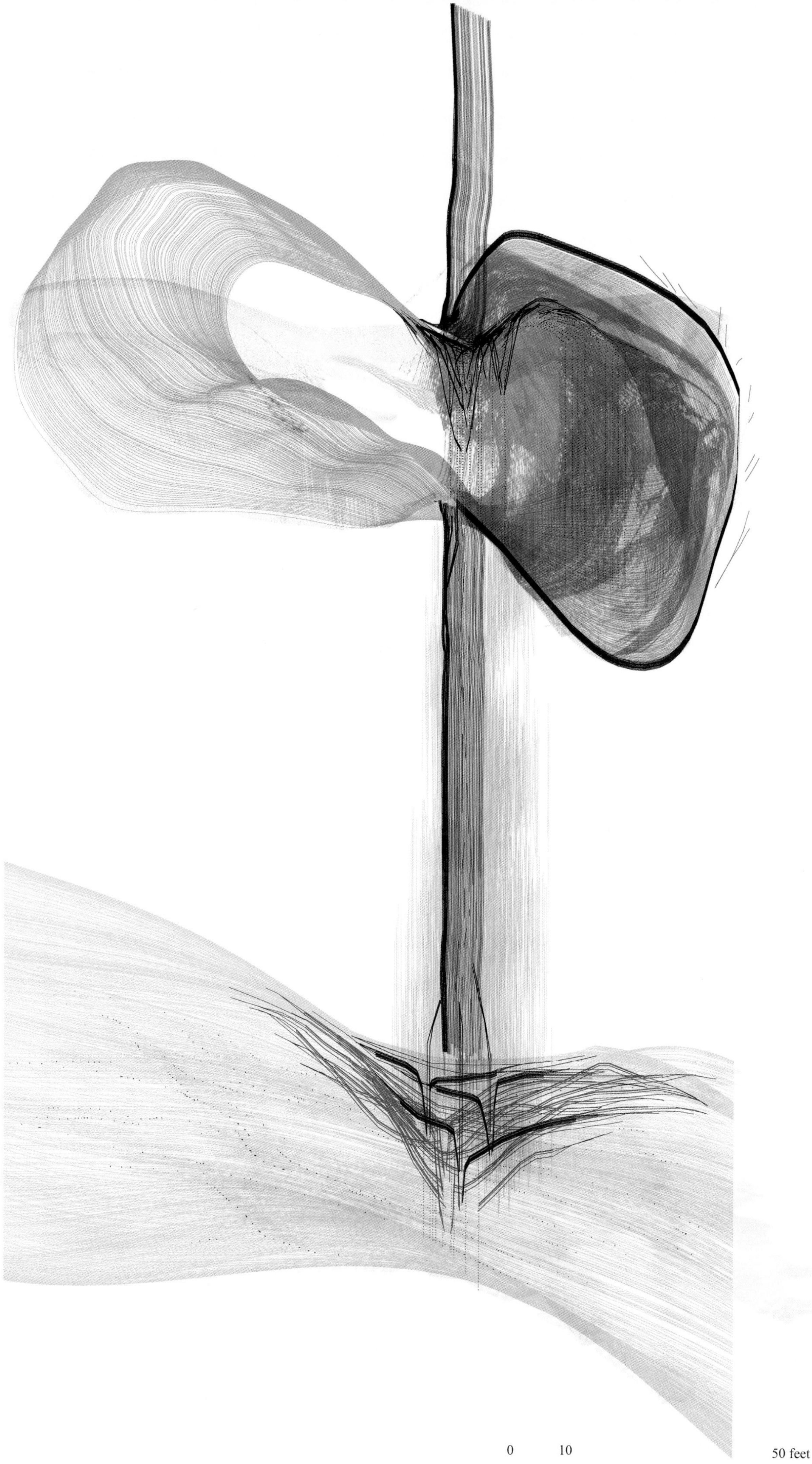
0
10
50 feet

Above: Elevation of a calcite "column," showing its formation in relation to axial dripping through fissures at the ceiling. Calcite columns can reach up to 50 feet in Lechuguilla Cave. A column is the name given to a formation which results from the meeting of stalactites and stalagmites, or when stalactites reach the floor.

Residual Surface

Mammoth Hot Springs, Yellowstone National Park, Wyoming, United States
Betty F. Bluvshtein

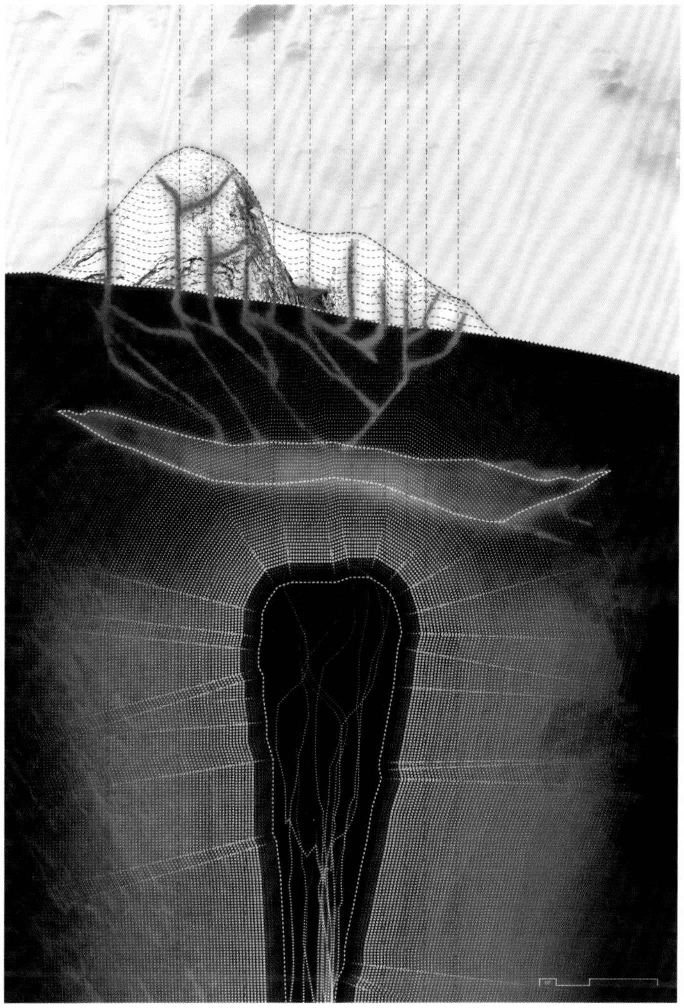

Residual Surface explores the process through which an underground, masked condition can leave a mark upon the Earth's surface. Yellowstone's geothermal landscape is fueled by an active caldera that spreads heat throughout the landscape. Below the ground, fault lines transport heat and water through the terrain. One of these fault lines, the Norris-Mammoth, spans over 20 miles, linking the Yellowstone Caldera, the Norris Geyser Basin, and Mammoth Hot Springs, and creates a serendipitous relationship between heat, water, and air. As heat at an approximate depth of 1,500 feet warms groundwater, it combines with minerals at an intense pressure, eventually puncturing the Earth's surface. Minerals, hot water, air, and thermophile bacteria interact in a combination of biotic and abiotic conditions resulting in the formation of travertine or hot spring limestone. These are now known as the Travertine Terraces, a complex spanning nearly one mile and comprised of more than 20 springs and the residue of this process, making the Mammoth Hot Springs an impressive representation of a temporal narrative on a grand scale. This project proposes a series of additional punctures following the natural Norris-Mammoth fault line. The new interventions would allow water to form new travertine terraces and springs. Through the enactment of a narrative over time, a representational investigation becomes a geological exploration.

Top left: Section showing the water runoff from the nearby Gardner Mountain as it interacts with the system of heat transfer fueling the hot springs.

Top right: Section displaying the underground river as it intersects with the Norris-Mammoth fault line and creates hot springs.

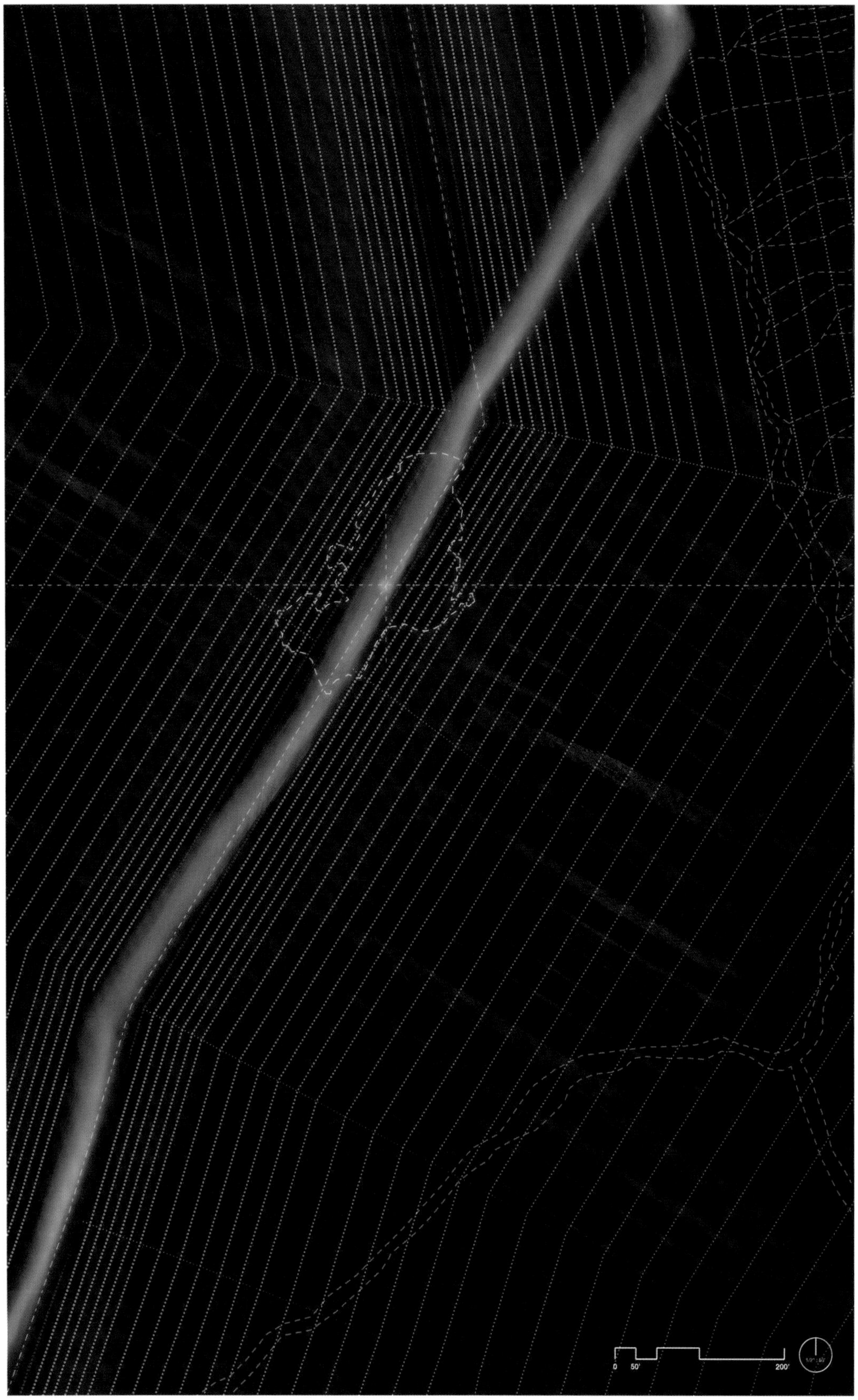

Above: Underground map showing the flow of heat and water along the Norris-Mammoth fault line as it appears directly under the Mammoth Hot Springs. Due to the change in directionality of the fault line against the river flow, the location of the hot springs is determined by water's exposure to air.

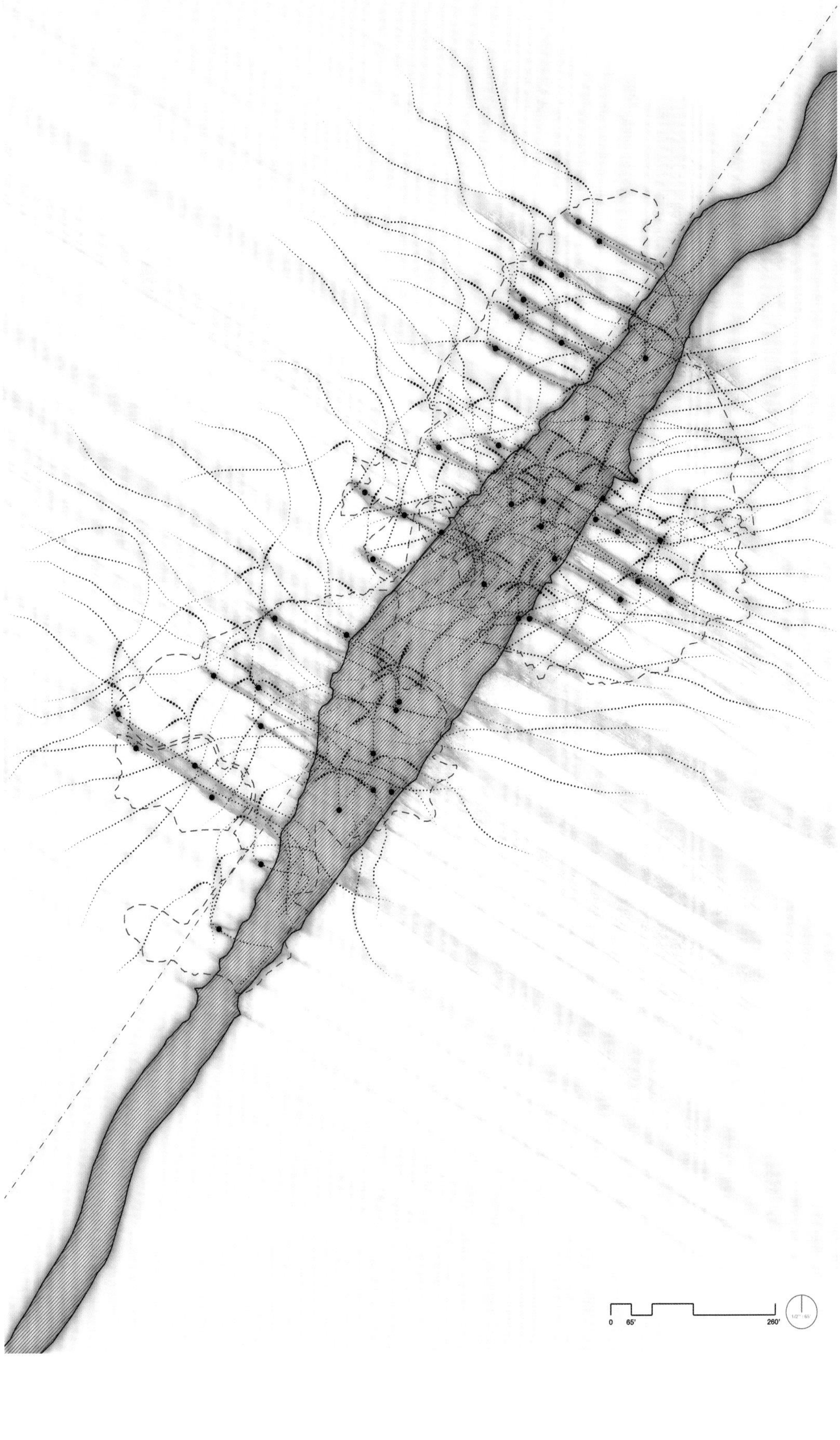

Above: Infrared drawing showing the puncture points where water meets air and disperses in multiple directions to create the travertine springs.

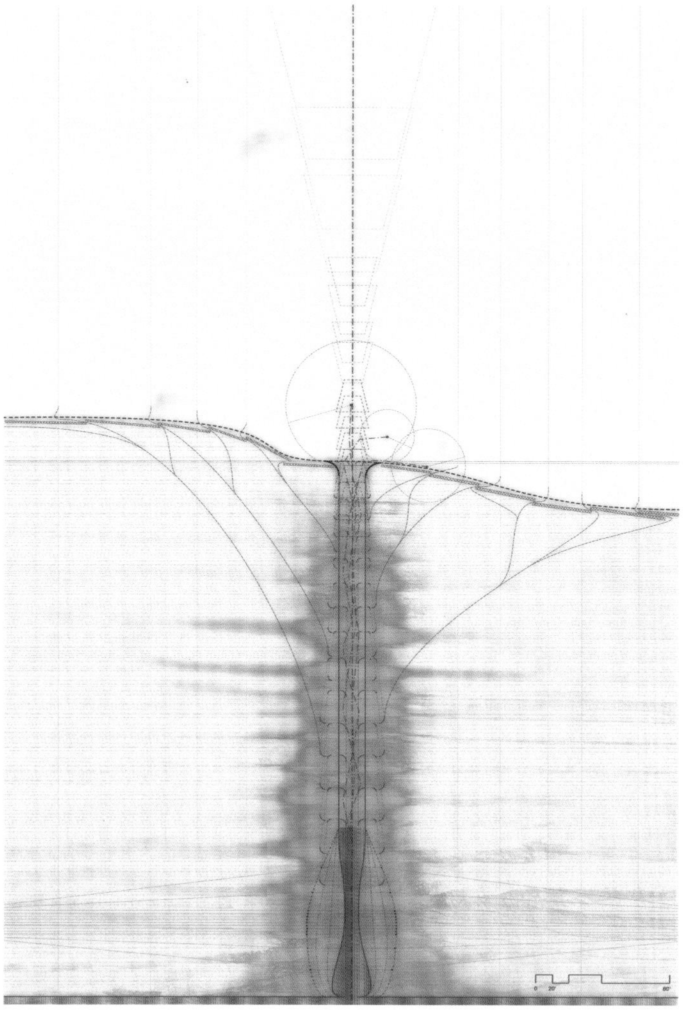

Top left: Section depicting the interaction of the narrative processes that together create the travertine hot springs.

Top right: Axonometric view showing multiple springs and their trajectory as the water travels through the ground to meet the surface.

Opposite: Mammoth composite plan illustrating the flow and direction of water from each spring.

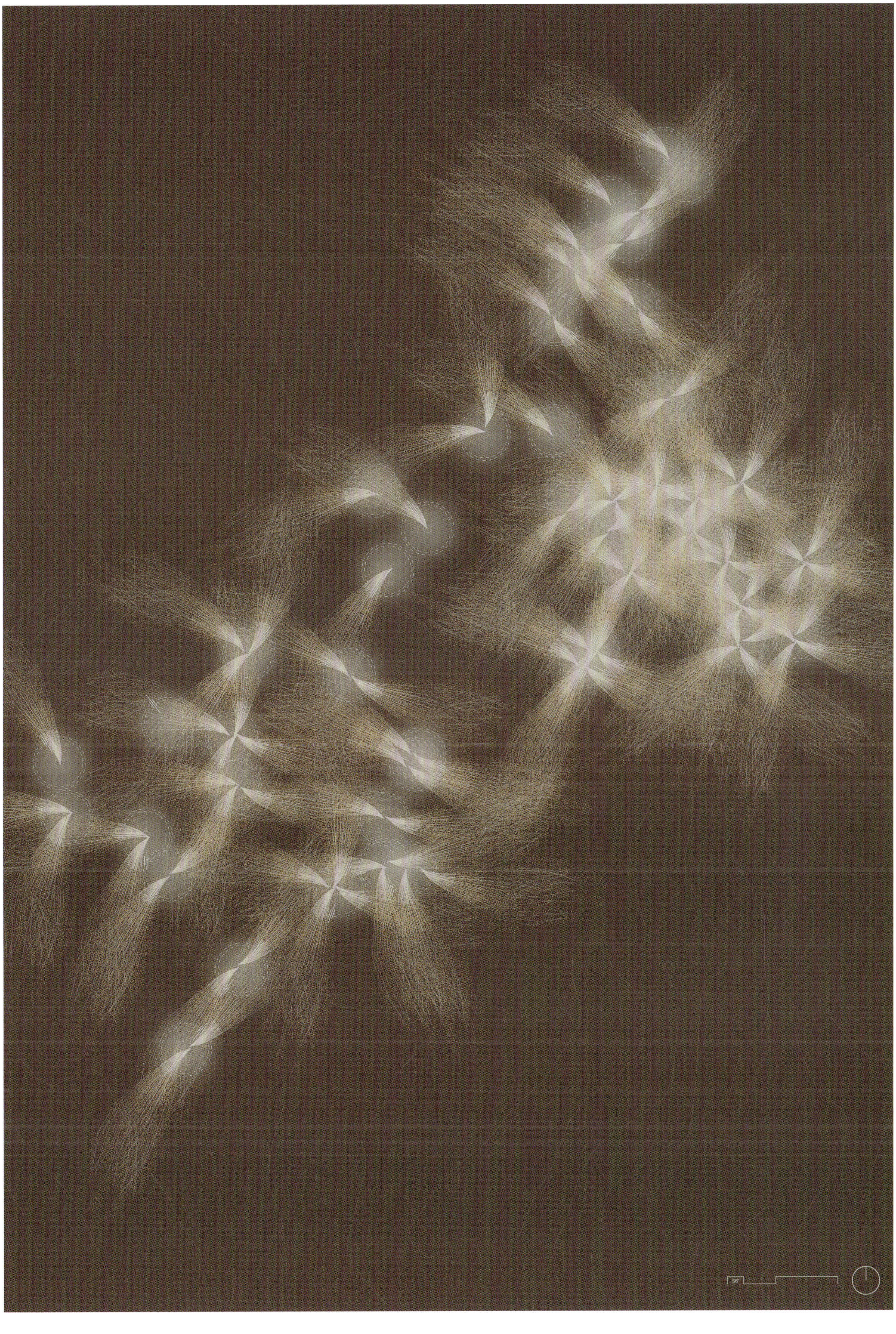

Between Erosion and Sedimentation: Water Flow and Land Mass

The Mississippi River Delta, Gulf of Mexico, Louisiana
Ja-Sheng Chen

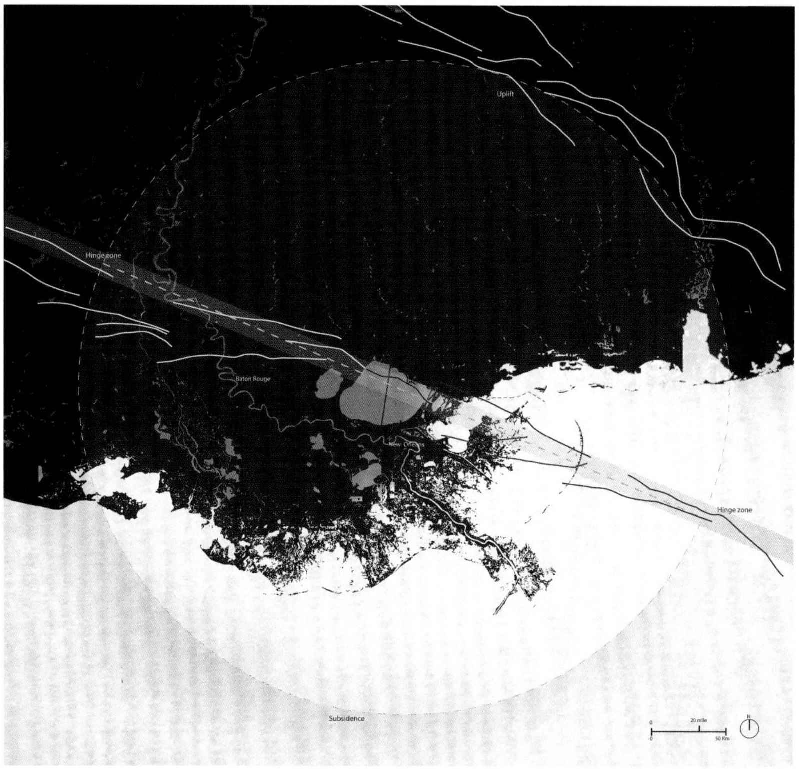

Part of the Louisiana Coastal Plain, the Mississippi River Delta extends over a 12,000 km^2 land area and contains 4,000 square miles of coastal wetlands, one of the largest in the US. Furthermore, it is the largest drainage basin in the US, draining 470,000 cubic feet per second. Two opposing forces are at play in the process of erosion of the Mississippi River Delta: the sediment from river floods that cannot follow its natural flow due to infrastructural interventions and the eroding forces of ocean tides and the salt water it brings.

Within the context of these general conditions this project focuses on the forces at play in the severe land loss of the Mississippi River Delta, exploring the relationships between sediment and flows, and the potentials in manipulating this dynamic by directing water flow through the reconfiguration of the land mass in an attempt to reverse the effects of the built infrastructure to prevent further erosion. A particular area of the Delta has been used as the locus for this exploration, considering its ecological conditions and potential enhancement.

The reuse and reposition of dredged material through fresh water diversion and flow could offer an opportunity to reconfigure the coastal delta by creatively manipulating natural forces and natural materials that would grow and also eventually disintegrate, including water flow, sediment deposition, and plant growth. It is possible to create new animated landforms that will in turn deter erosion.

Top: The Mississippi River carries 200 million tons of sediment every year. The accumulation of sediment over thousands of years has had a geological impact manifested in the tilting of the tectonic plates. Like a seesaw, the fault line in the eastern portion of the state of Mississippi has emerged due to these forces.

Opposite: Plan and Sections showing the relationship between the Mississippi River's sediment and tectonic plates.

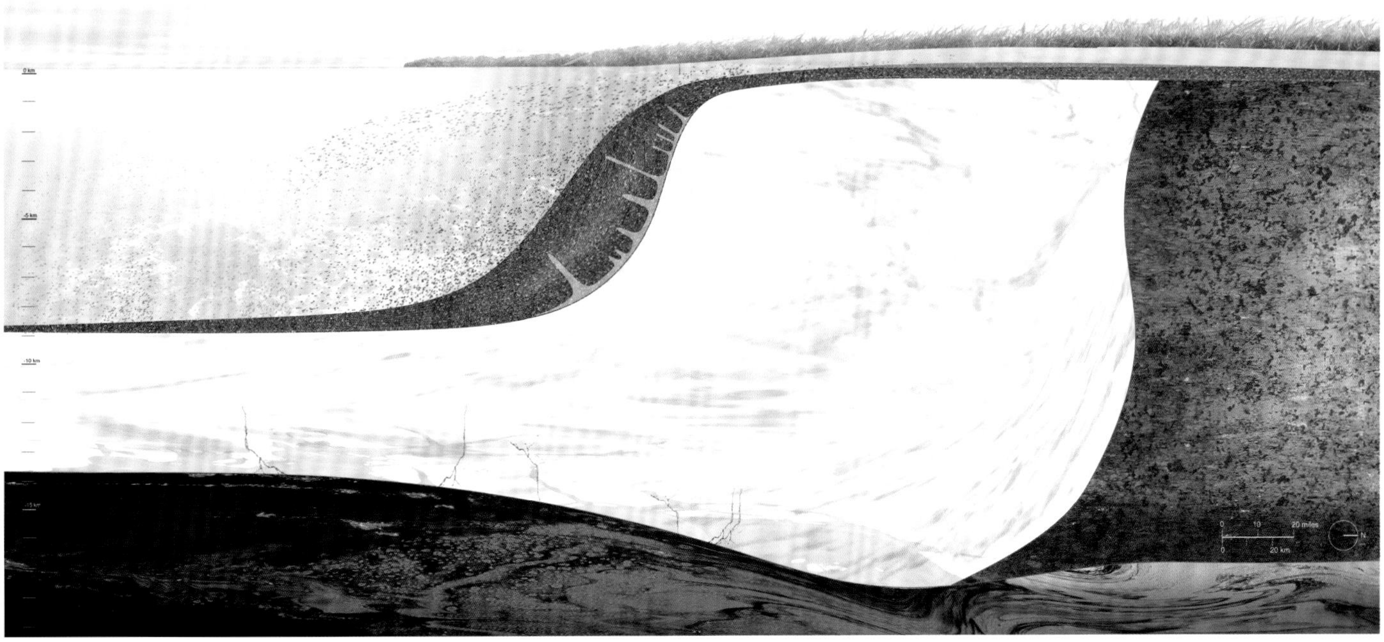

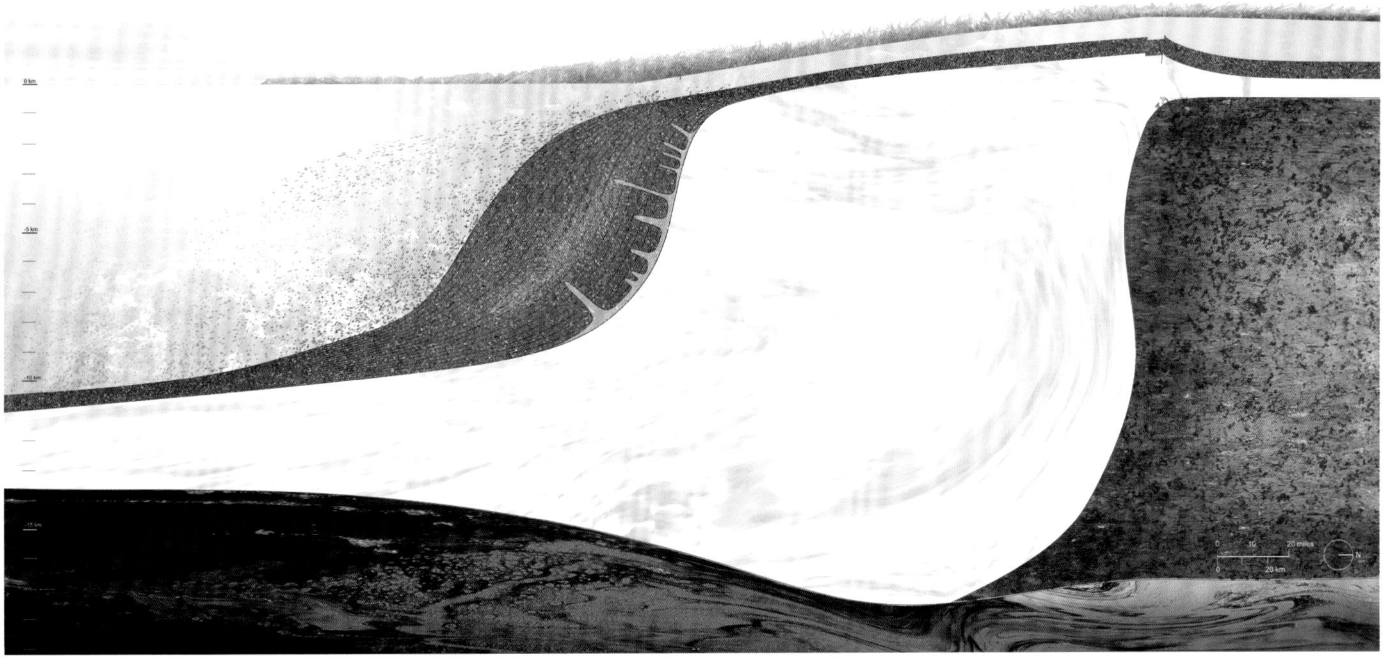

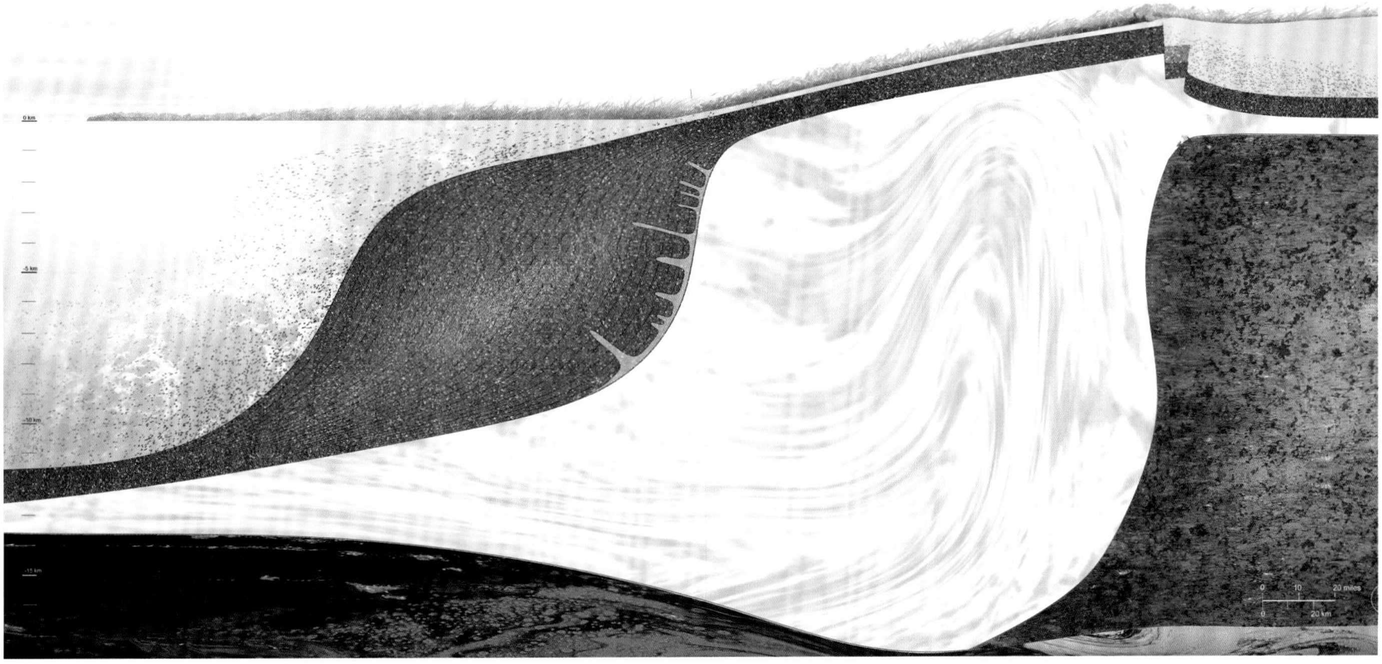

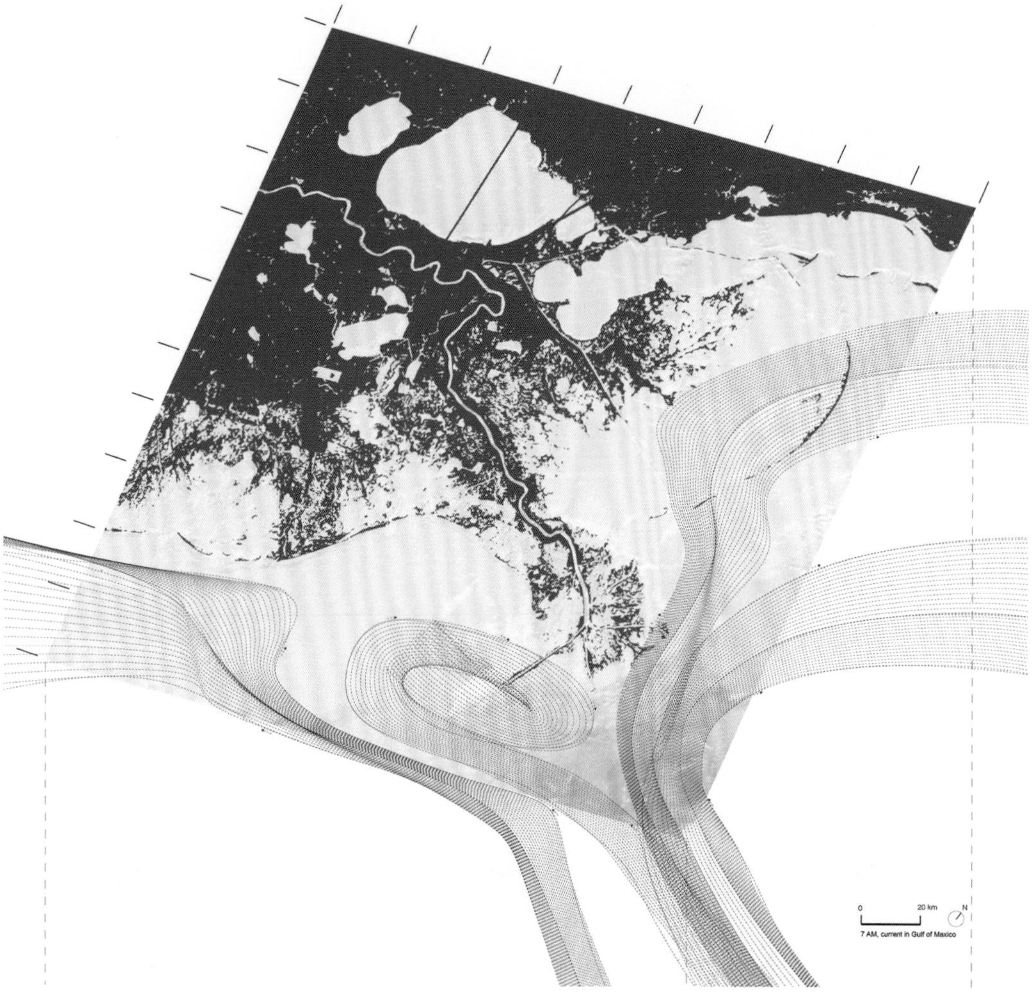
0
20 km
N
7 AM, current in Gulf of Maxico

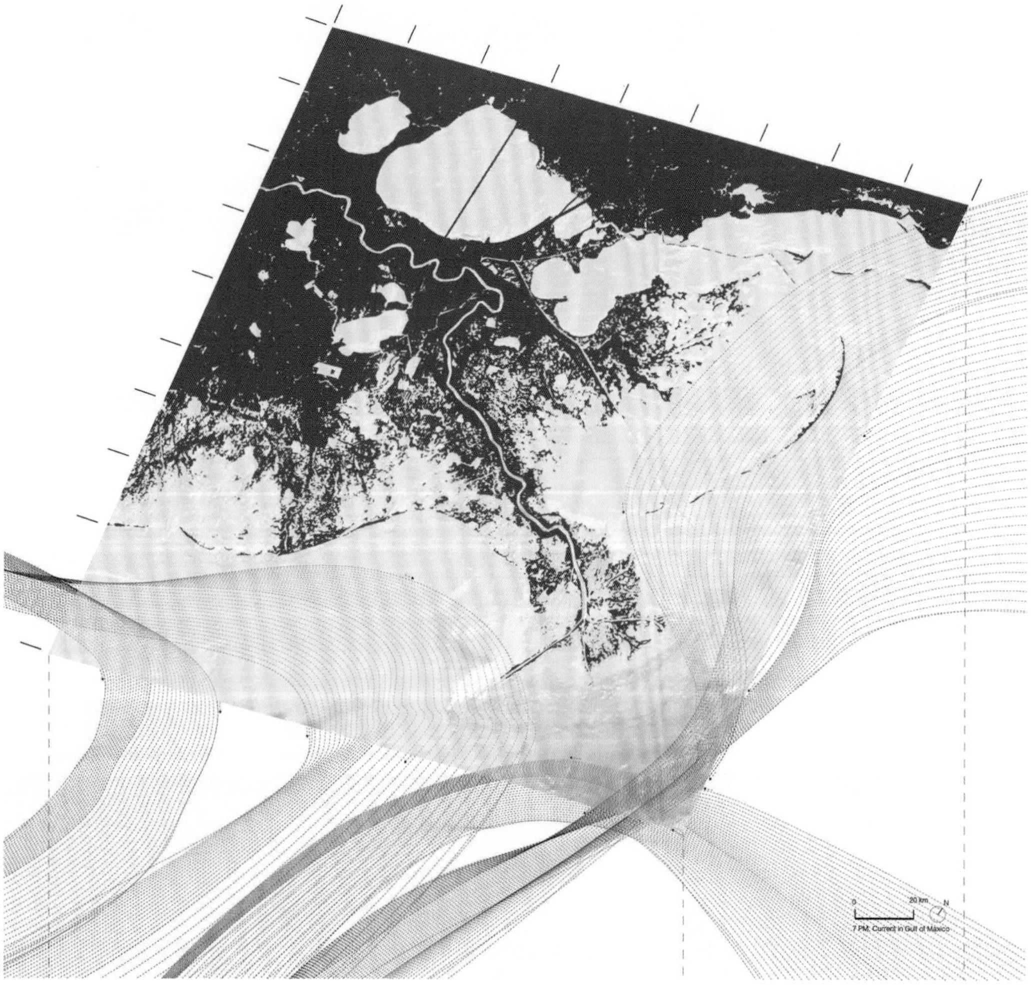
0
20 km
N
7 PM, Current in Gulf of México

Opposite: Plans depicting different orientations of currents along the delta at 7AM and 7PM. Ocean currents are determinant in the formation and destruction of the Mississippi Delta. While land is eroded by ocean waves hitting the coast more than 10 times per minute, land is built up by waves hitting the coast fewer than 10 times per minute.

Above: Plan of the West Bay counter proposal applying a mechanism using natural elements and materials to harness natural forces in order to facilitate land retention and to generate a landscape with the forces in play.

N
0
1 KM
2 KM
birds Migration route in delta area (fall)

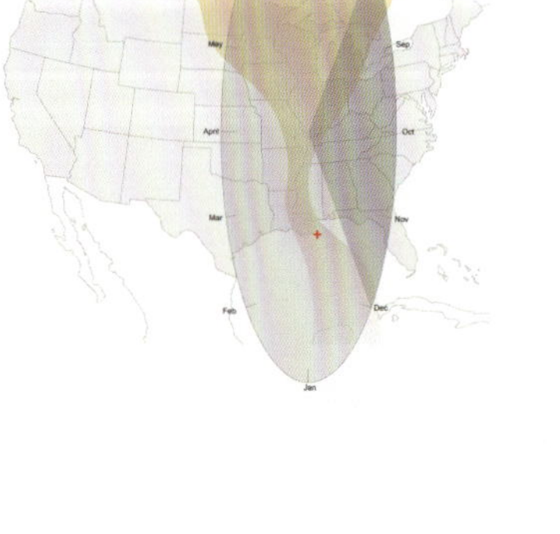
July
June
Aug
May
Sep
April
Oct
Mar
Nov
Feb
Dec
Jan

N
0
1 KM
2 KM
birds Migration route in delta area (spring)
July
June
Aug
May
Sep
April
Oct
Mar
Nov
Feb
Dec
Jan

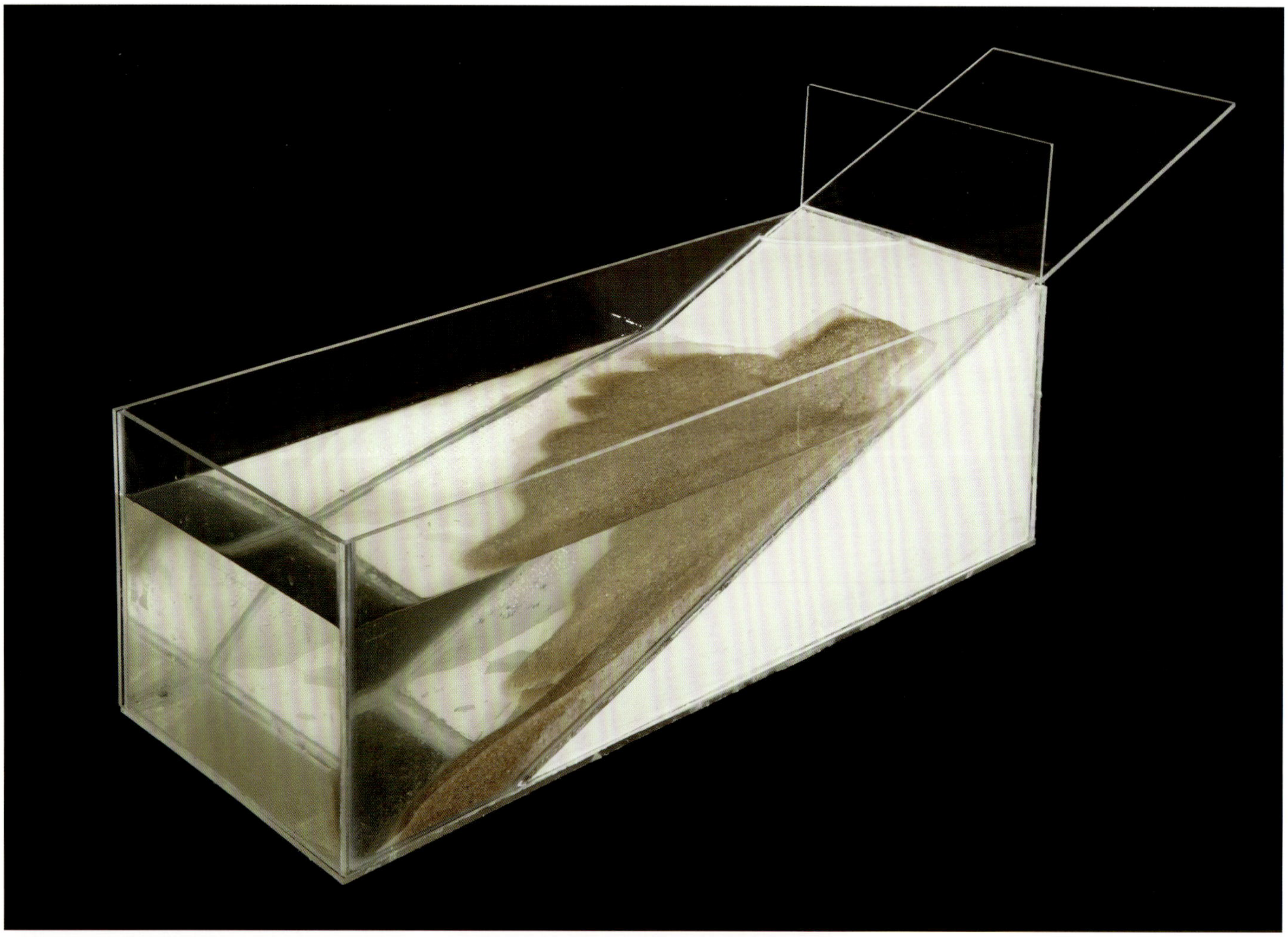

Previous: Plan of the West Bay landscape and bird migration in spring and autumn in the proposal to reshape the land through the deposition of dredged material by manipulating a large volume of sand in conjunction with water flow speed and the trunks of dead, bald cypress trees, abundant in the adjacent freshwater marshland. Site located on an important North American bird migration route.

Top: Model of sand accumulation was obtained by replicating the accumulation of sediment with sand and a water pump.

Bottom: Models of new interventions generated by manipulating natural forces and materials, including water flow, sediment deposition, and plant growth, creating new animated landforms that will in turn deter erosion.

Between Two Waters: Disaster as Opportunity

Lake County, Central Florida
Ling Li Tseng

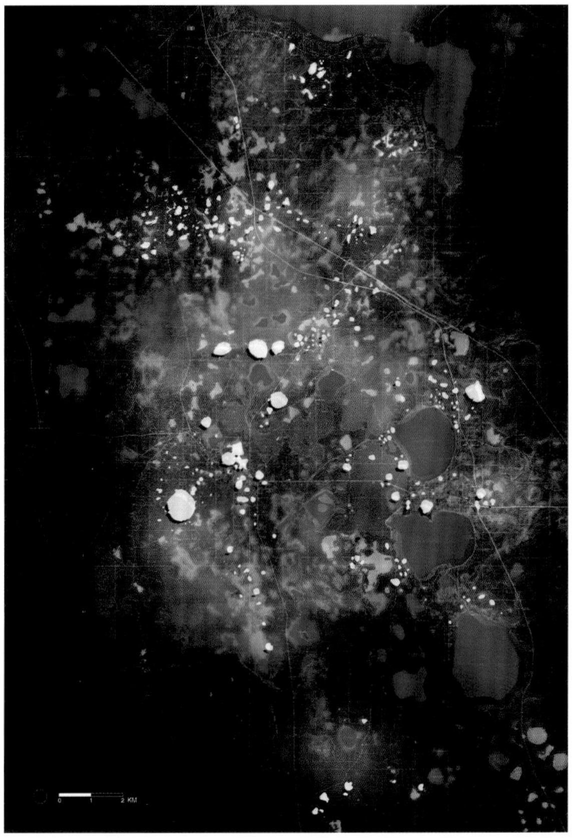

The Karst landscape of Lake County in central Florida is filled with sinkholes caused by the collapse of the ground into a vast system of underground limestone caves. This project, which focuses on this phenomenon over the past 300 years, is concerned with the formation of sinkholes and their relationship to the limestone caves beneath. The formation process of the large network of underground caves begins when falling rainwater absorbs carbon dioxide, becoming acidic, and then reacts chemically with the limestone bedrock, changing the ground water to a weaker form of carbonic acid ($H_2O + CO_2 = H_2CO_3$).

These sinkholes, whose formation processes go back 30 million years, cover an area over 900 square miles and can reach a depth of 6.2 miles, cause land subsidence and accelerate flooding. Geologists predict that seventy percent of central Florida will eventually become a huge wetland connected to the Everglades farther south. Sinkhole formation has accelerated during the past three decades, affecting both the ground and underground geology. Thus, this proposal looks to turn a disaster into an opportunity by materializing the traces of the eroding caves and reimagining an interaction between built form and the natural forces present in this extreme landform.

Above: Water mapping of Lake County, Florida, at 10 kilometers below grade. This negative section plan of Lake County shows the vast extension of the underground water, which causes an unstable ground structure and sinkhole activity.

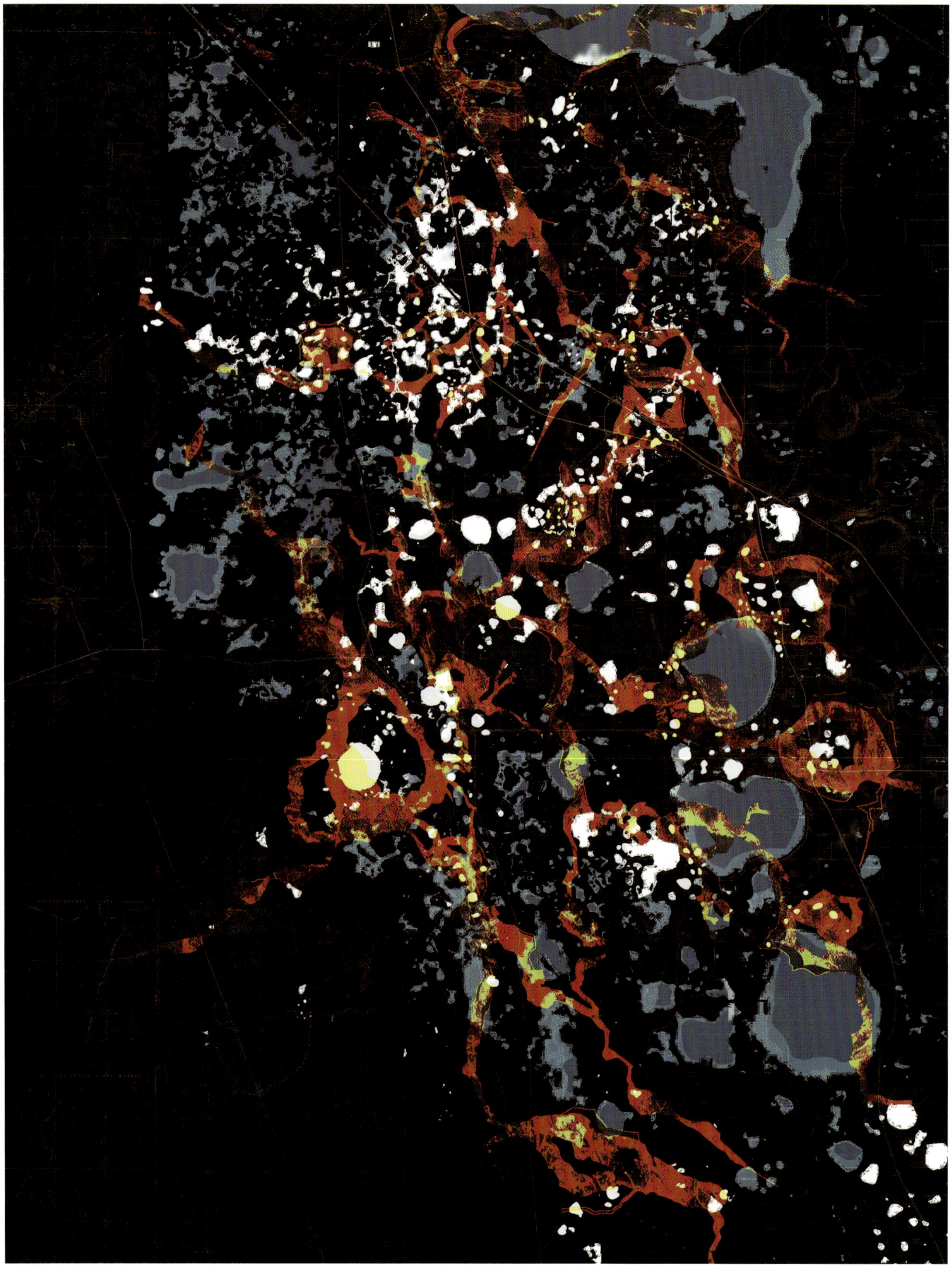

Above: The location of the sinkholes corresponds to the underground cave system. Since a chemical effect in limestone caves produces heat, scientists can use temperature mapping to determine the age of sinkholes and to reveal the underground system.

Opposite: Plan showing the location of the sinkholes relative to the large network of underground caves that form as permeating rainwater becomes acidic through absorption of carbon dioxide, which reacts with the limestone bedrock and changes the ground water to a weaker form of carbonic acid.

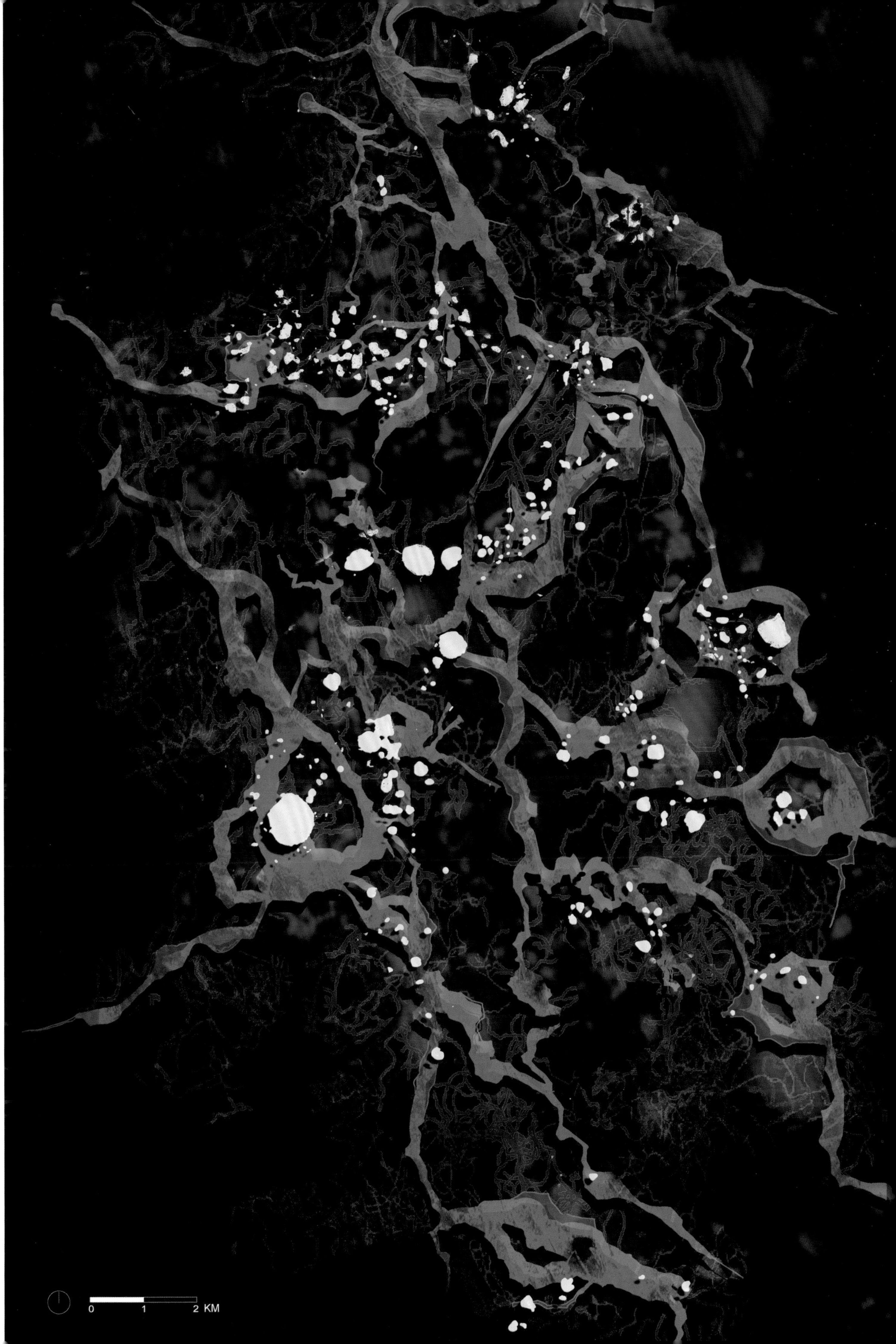
0 1 2 KM

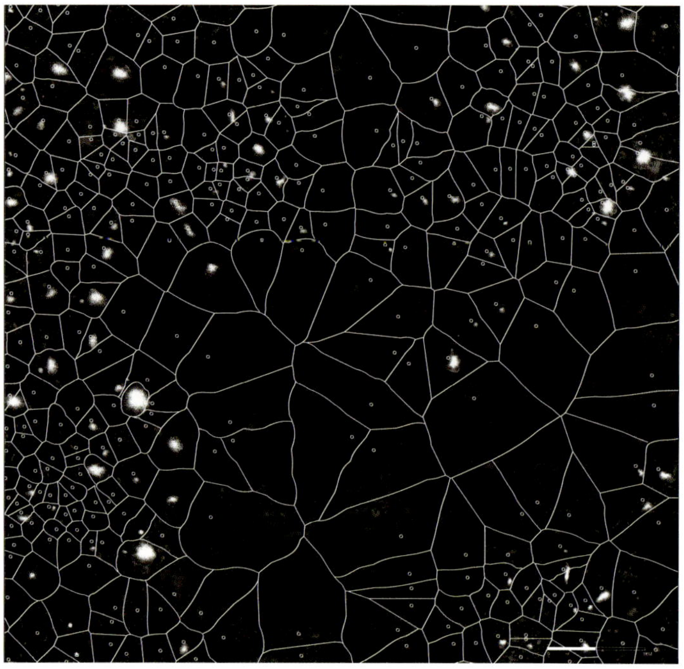

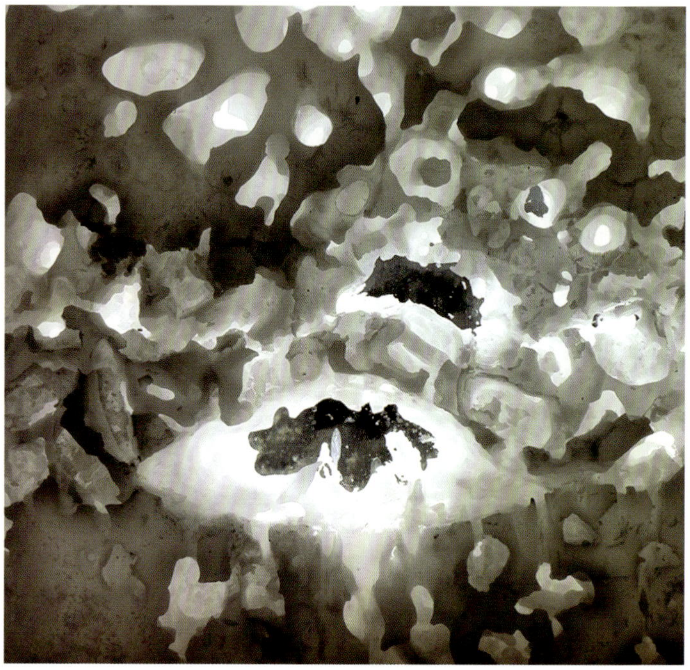

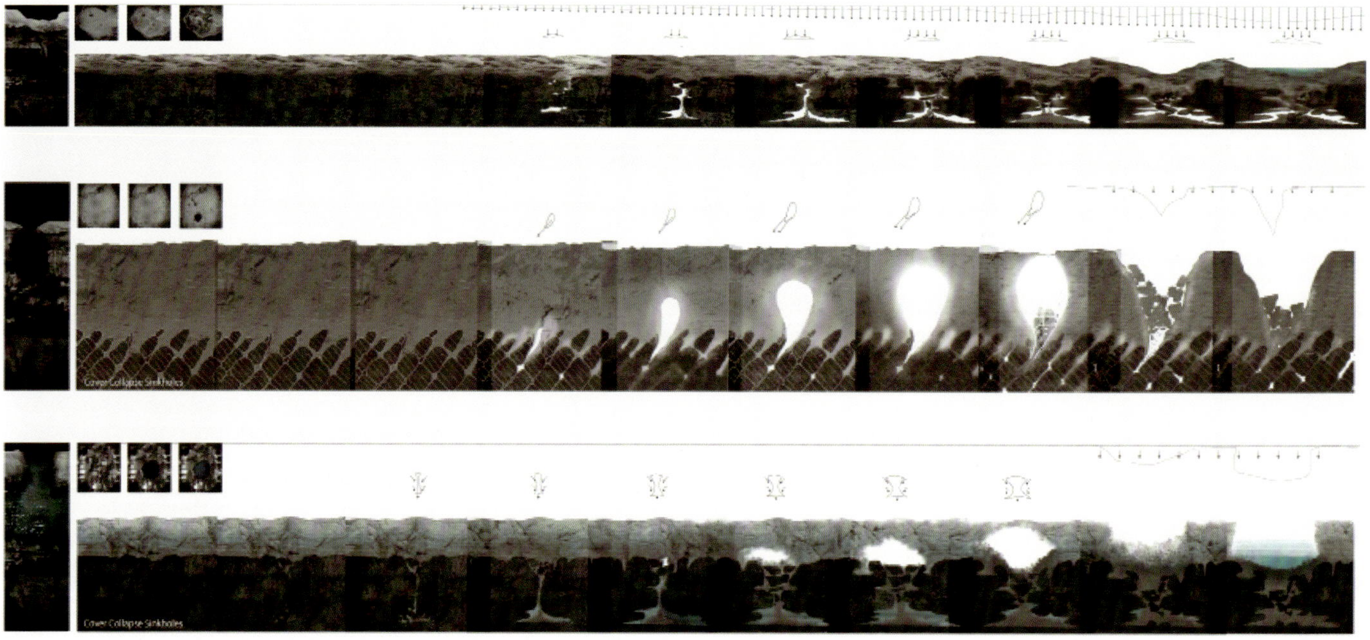

Top left: Morphological mapping of the sinking border. The underground water of the limestone landscape makes the ground structure pattern similar to the organic Voronoi pattern. This could indicate potential future sinkholes.

Top right: Physical model simulation showing the process of limestone erosion.

Above: Sinkhole typology. 1. Solution sinkholes: where limestone is exposed or covered by thin layers of soil and permeable sand. As the water first contacts the rock surface the dissolution of the limestone or dolomite intensifies. 2. Cover-subsidence sinkholes: develop gradually when covering sediments contain sand and are permeable. 3. Cover-collapse sinkholes: where the covering sediments contain a significant amount of clay and may develop abruptly. Constant air suction in caves can be a cause as well.

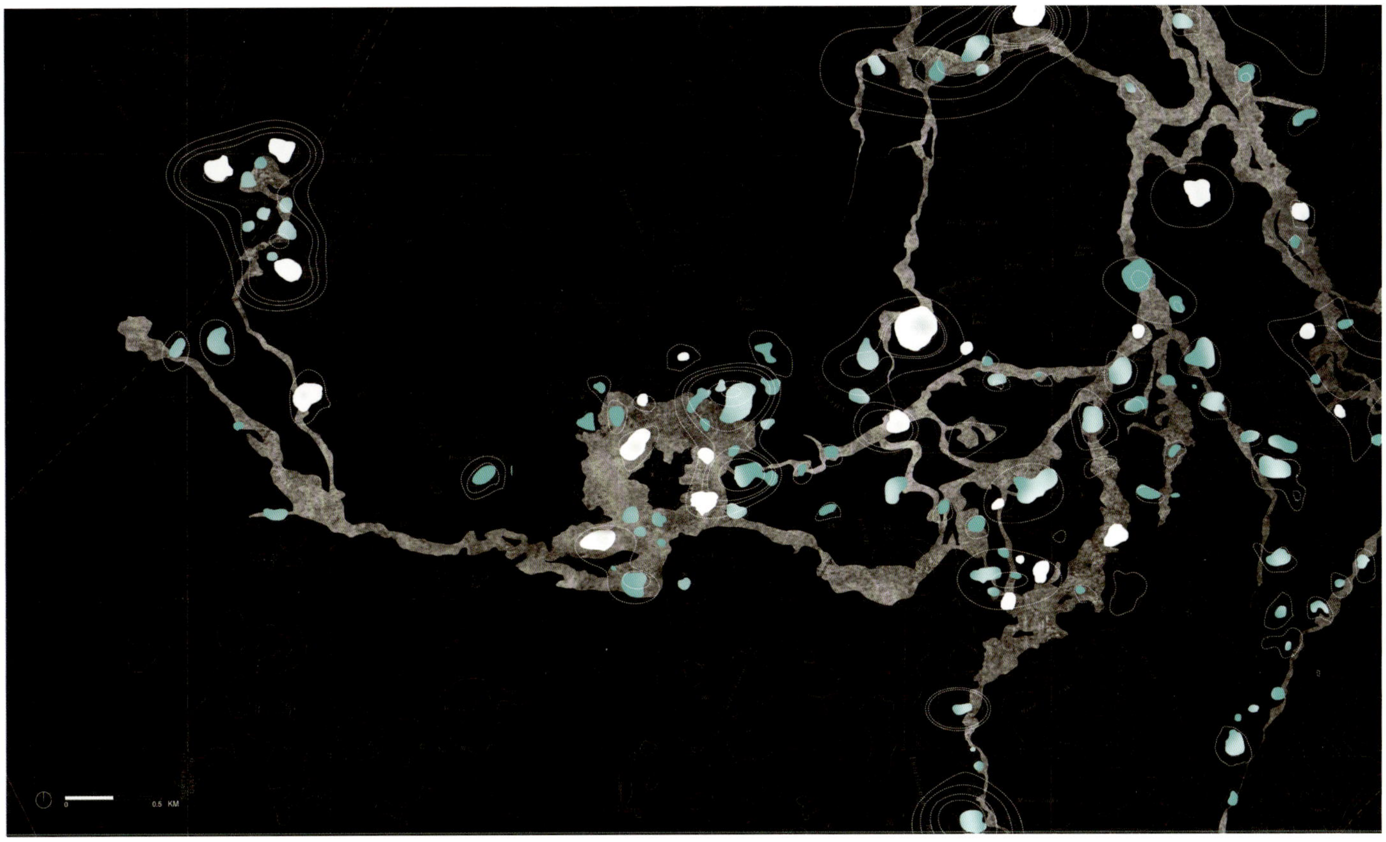

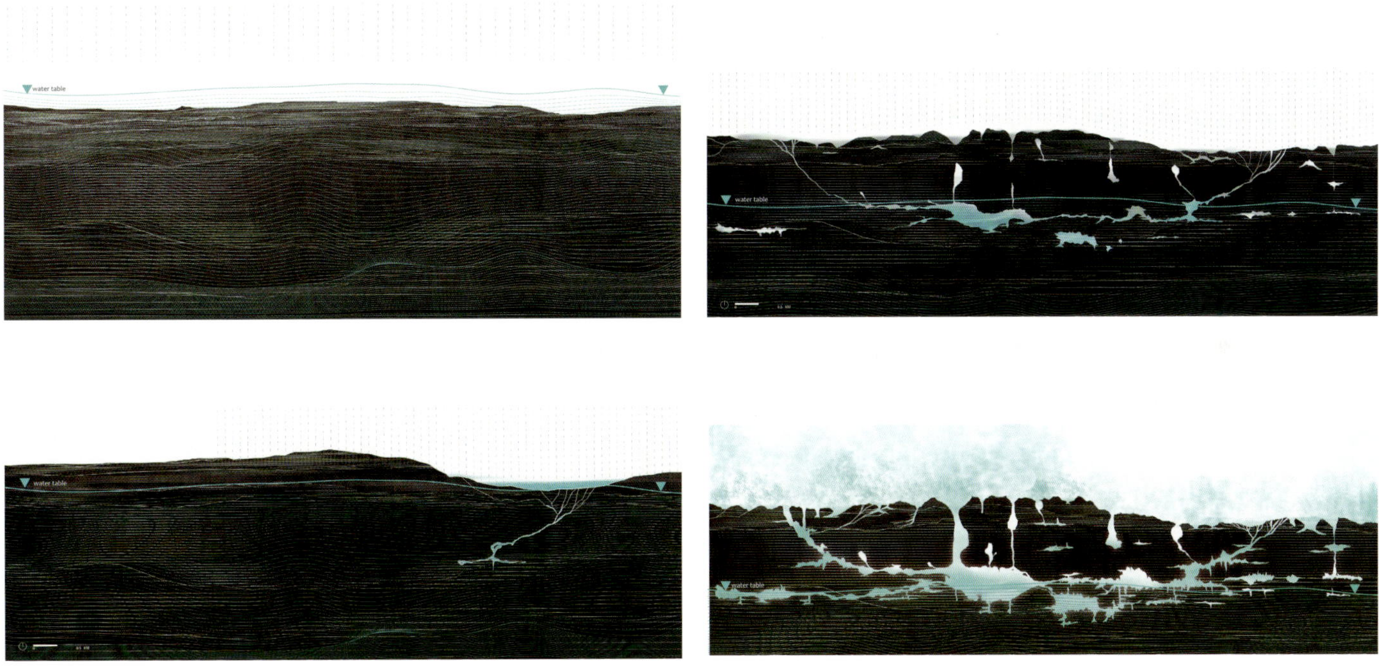

Top: Plan showing the physical and chemical processes present in the formation of sinkholes.

Above: Section diagrams showing physical and chemical processes in the formation of sinkholes. As carbonic acid, produced by acid rain, travels down through the ground it reaches solid rock.

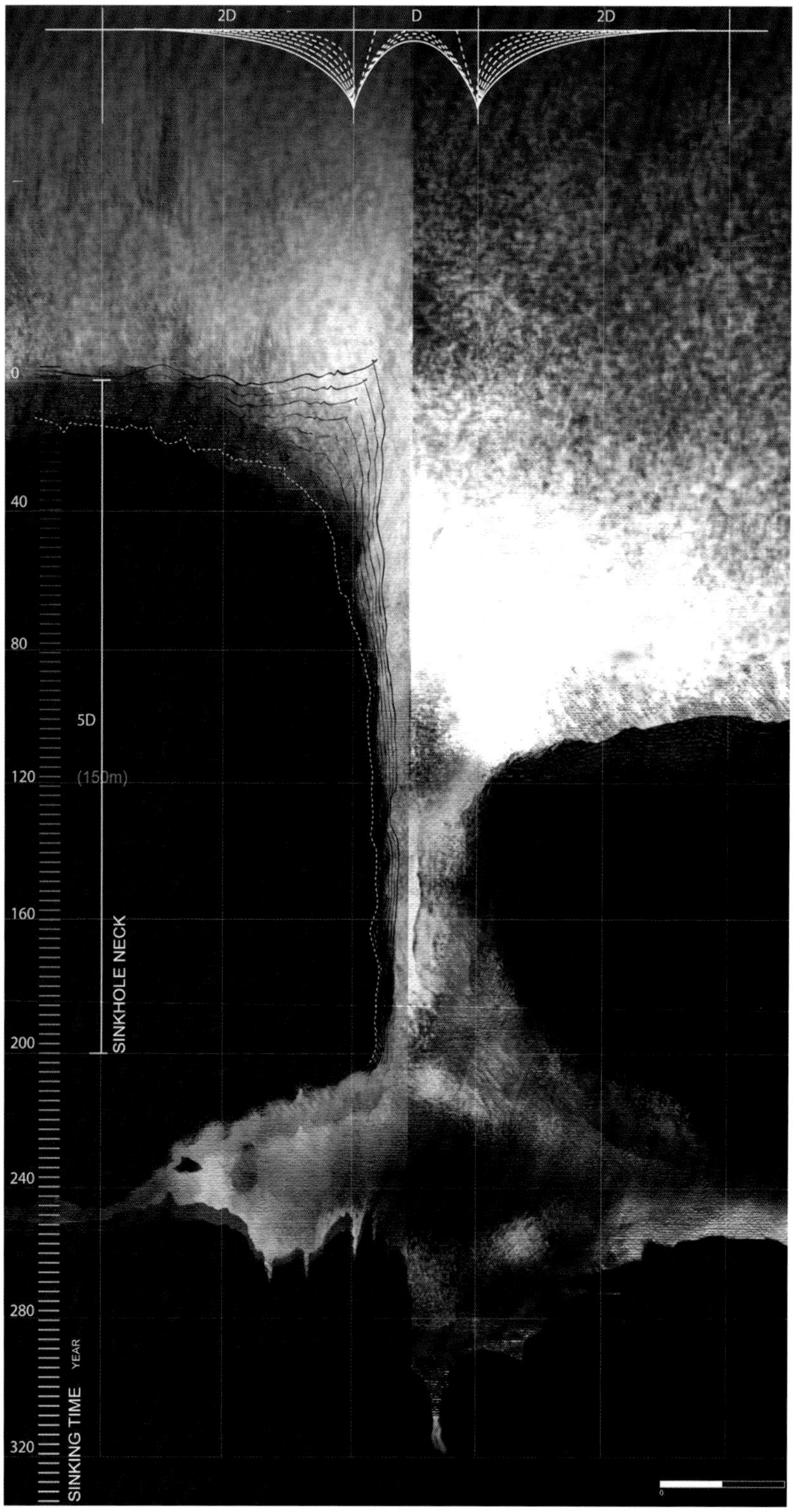

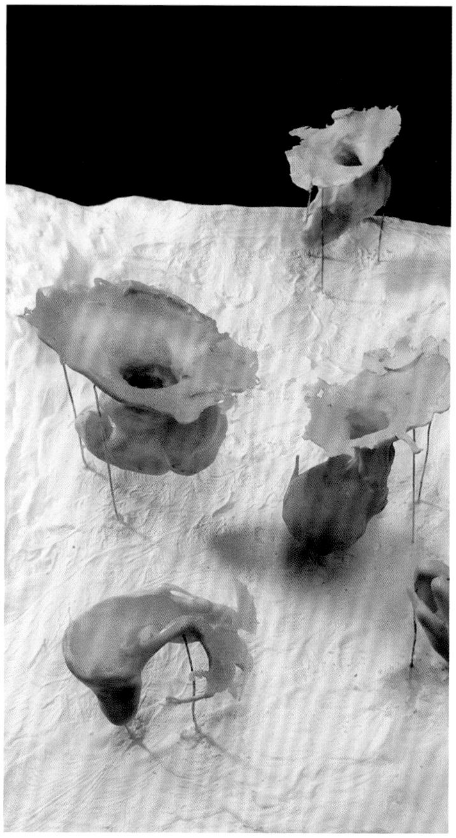

Top left: Section of a typical sinkhole. The ratio between an average sinkhole opening and the depth of its neck is 1:5. In the next 200 years, land subsidence in this area is projected to be about 100—150 meters.

Top right: Model of transformation of the sinkhole void into a vessel-like space, created with casting and material experimentation.

Opposite top: The cave systems resemble an organic creature—growing, expanding, and causing ground subsidence.

Opposite bottom: Model of the cave system as floating vessels when the area is completely covered with water.

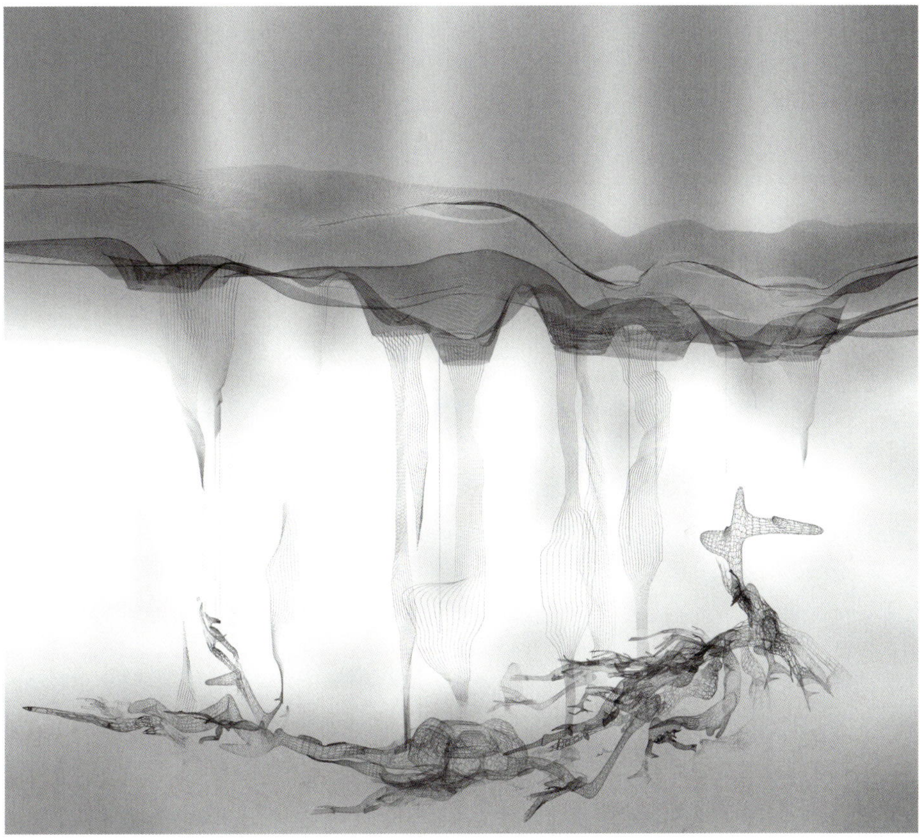

Growth in Anoxic Conditions

Mangroves in the Florida Wetlands, Southern Florida
Lenia Pachy

In the transitional wetland zone between dry land and water, mangroves play an important role in fostering ecosystems, which in turn provide a rich terrain for environmental change supporting life from microorganisms to algae, invertebrates, fish, reptiles, amphibians, birds, and mammals. Mangroves have an old history. Rhizopora and avicennia were widely spread 50—55 million years ago when the shallow equatorial Tethys Sea full of coral reefs and islands was closing with the continental drift, which may account for their global distribution.

The Red Mangrove Rhizophora mangle grows in both oxygenated and anoxic environments. It reaches 82—125 feet high in deltas and 26—33 feet along the shoreline. This capability depends upon systems that act at multiple scales, from the scale of a forest to that of a single tree, and even at microscopic levels. In particular, the airflow between roots above ground and those underground allows for growth in anoxic conditions by providing gas exchange. In order to access sufficient oxygen, the Black Mangrove Avicennia germinans grow to an average height of 66 feet and can reach up to 133 feet. It develops a linear underground root structure, which comes out of the ground and serves as a networked respiratory organ through (pneumatophores) vertical aerating branches that extend up to eight inches above the soil.

While the scale of one mangrove root system may seem small, when aggregated, a mangrove forest can alter tidal currents and capture sediment, ultimately transforming the landscape. This project examines how red and black mangrove tree species adapt and expand, challenging established notions of environmental boundaries and permanence.

Above: Red Mangroves propagules are dispersed through the water as they detach from the tree in different degrees of embryonic development, remaining in the water as this development continues.

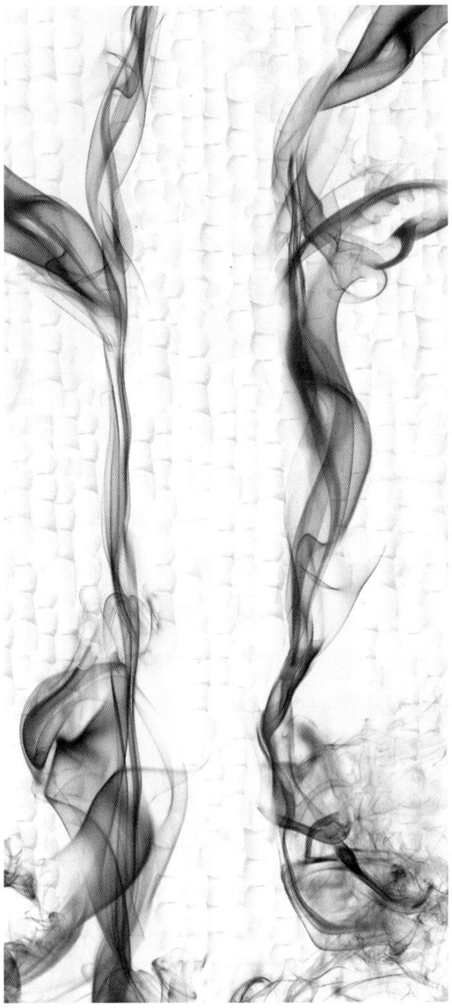

Above: Collage of the Red Mangrove's aerial root system and vertical section of the Red Mangrove's underground root system. The tree's "prop roots" provide a physical structure and allow the tree to survive in hypoxia, without oxygen.

Above: Gas exchange in the roots of the Red Mangrove.

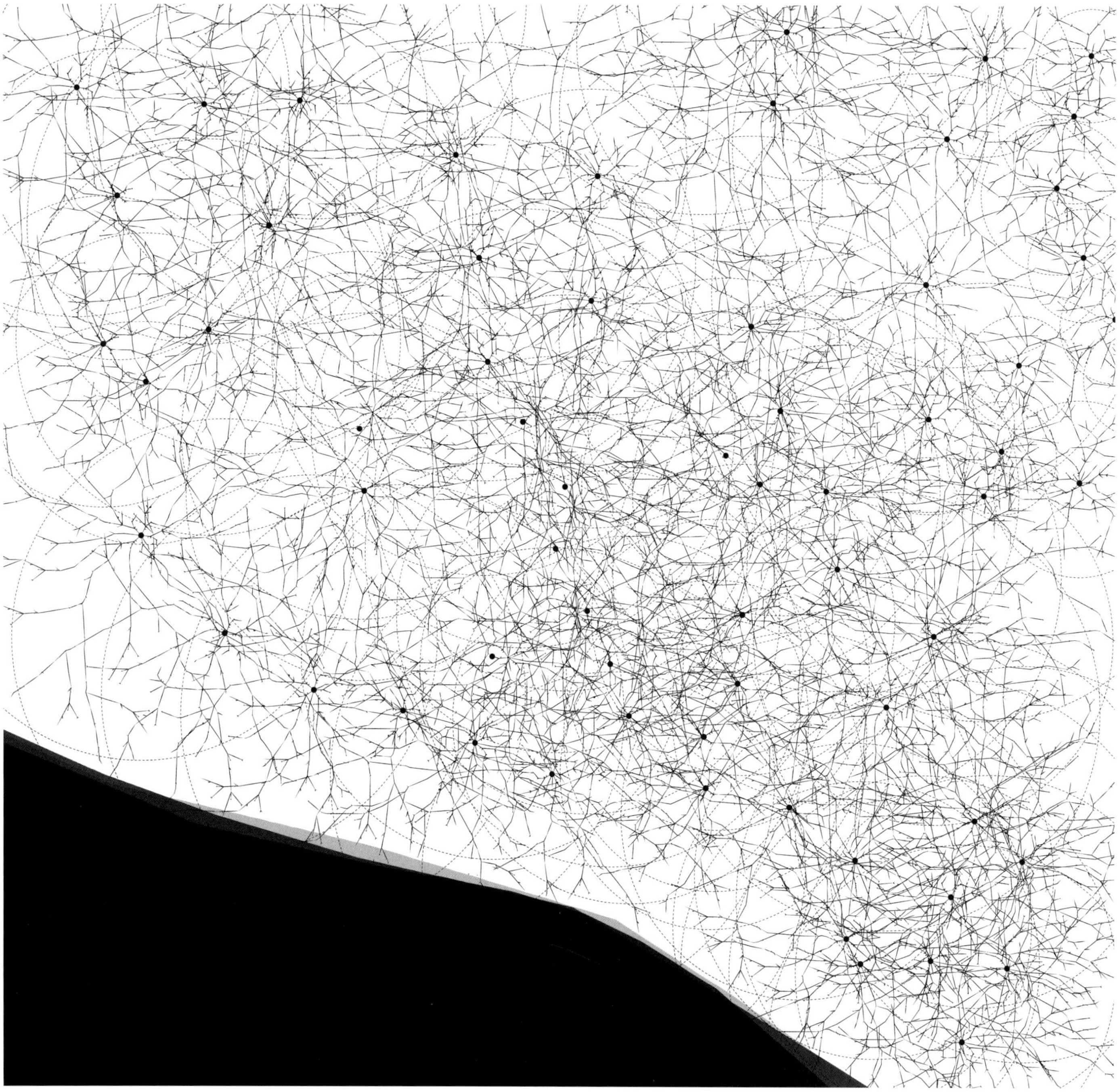

Above: Plan above ground of a Red Mangrove forest
in formation during the first 10 years.

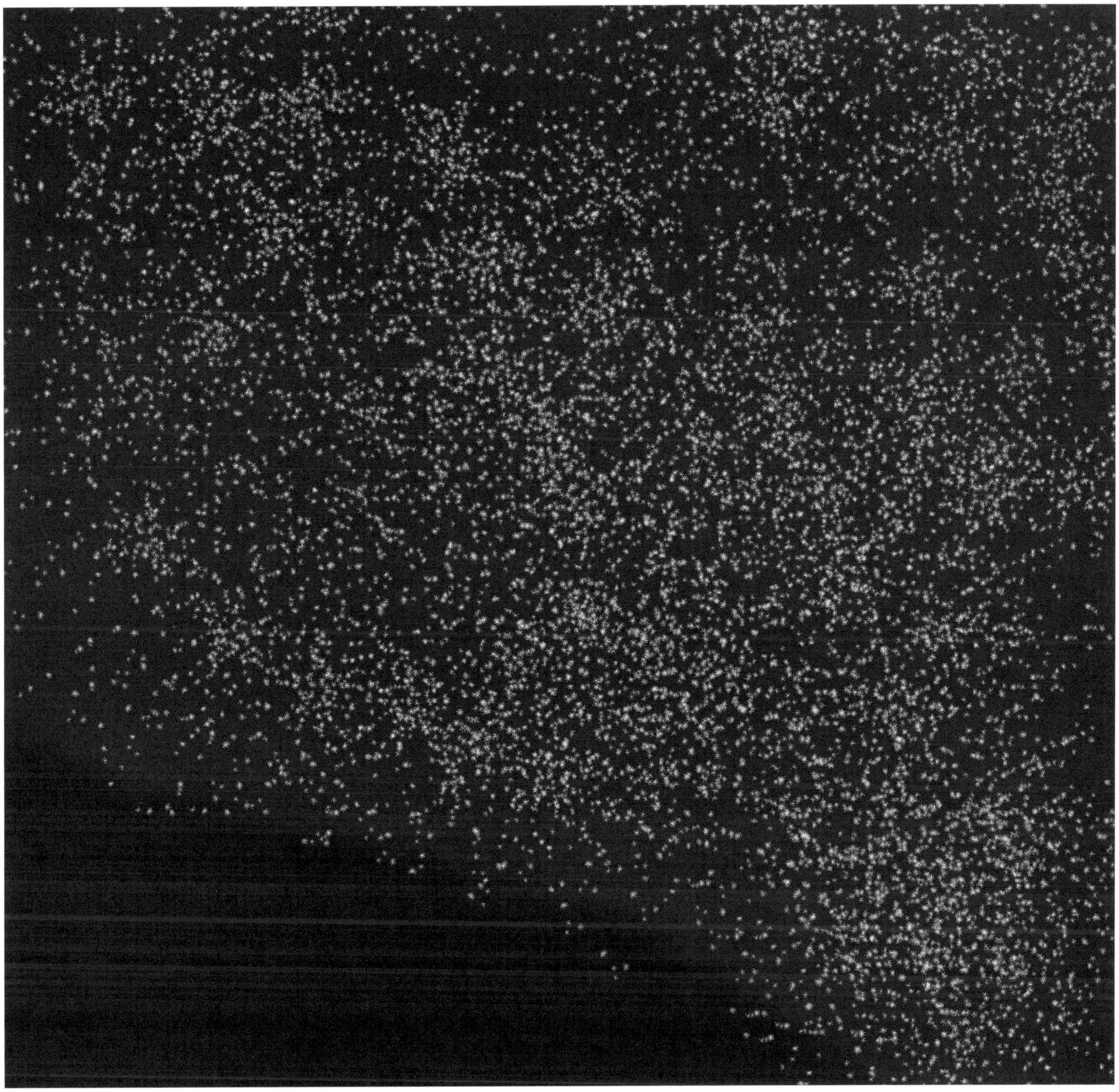

Above: Plotted horizontal section at 12 inches below ground level, showing the Red Mangrove's underground root system.

Above: Model of the Red Mangrove root system above- and under-ground. The prop roots originate from the trunk with and grow downward from the branches. Prop roots increase stability of the tree and provide oxygen supply to underground roots.

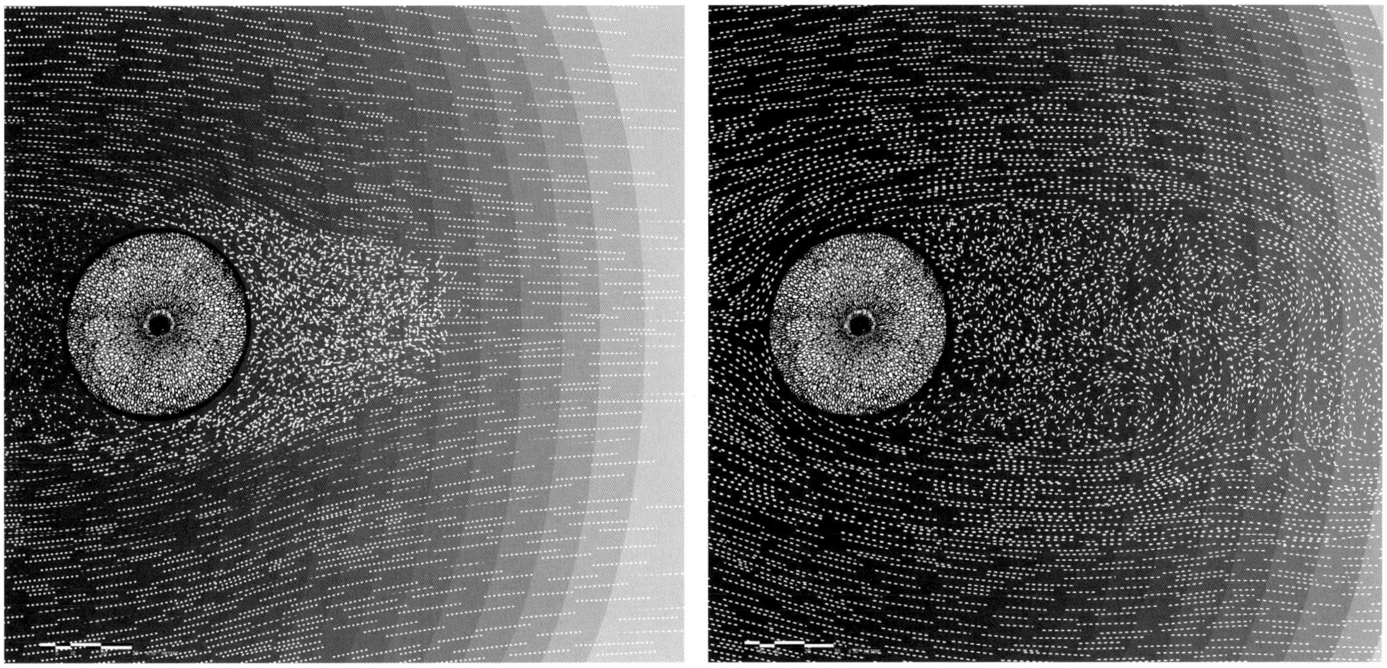

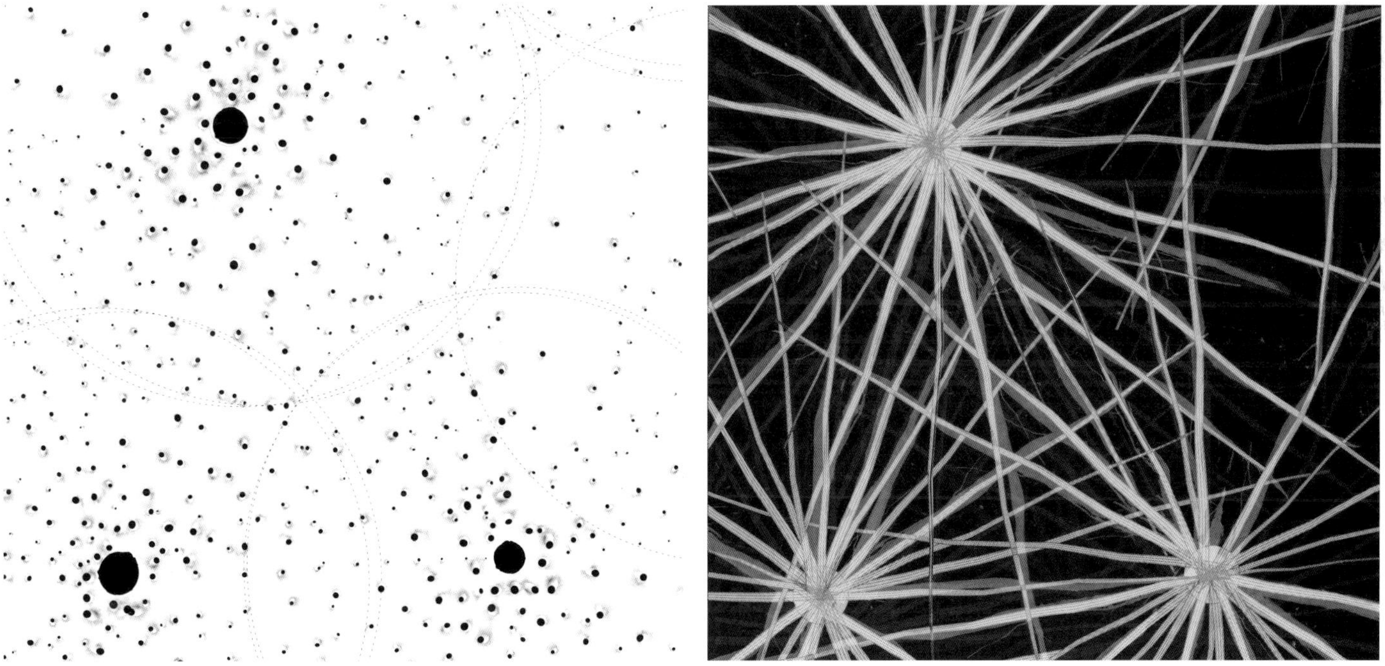

Top: Detail drawing of Black Mangrove reproduction system. The pneumatophores of the Black Mangrove act as a barrier for sand carried in by the tide, creating turbulence around each "chimney." When the tide returns, debris and detritus are trapped around the pneumatophore.

Bottom: Diagrammatic horizontal section of area "x" covered by Black Mangroves.

Above: Section of the black mangrove through its root system. This tree is characterized by long horizontal or cable roots with short vertical aerating branches (pneumatophores) that penetrate the ground substrate.

Above: Model of the Black Mangrove root system above- and below-ground. Underground: long horizontal roots. Aboveground: root projections (pneumatophores). Pneumatophores originate from underground horizontal roots and project from the soil, providing oxygen to the underground and underwater root systems.

SEA CLIFFS AND THE SUBLIME: A CONVERSATION

D. Graham Burnett and Diana Agrest

AGREST: Graham, it is a pleasure to have this chance to sit down together and talk. I have the clearest memory of your visit to my studio at Cooper a few years ago, when you presented on the sea. I remember how struck I was by your decision to open that vast subject with the students by means of a close reading of the Wallace Stevens's poem "The Comedian as the Letter C." We centered on that text, and across the time of our collective reading, you brought us to a contemplation of the sea as something like the antithesis of human being. An anti-mirror. The failure of language, rooted in the failure of an I-Thou relationship. It was an affecting seminar.

BURNETT: Thank you, Diana. Now you have presented me with the chance to review the work that came out of your studio, *Architecture of Nature/Nature of Architecture*, over the years, and I see how powerfully those same themes—the challenge of scale, the drama of extremes, the limits of the human—inform every page of this book.

AGREST: The aim of this research, as you say, was *exactly* to look at extreme natural phenomena, and from there to focus on the materiality and forces at play in them, using the tools and ways of seeing of the architect. I believe that in architecture, as in other fields, one only learns from extremes. Focusing on the extreme, one can understand conditions that prevail in less extreme forms in other phenomena.

BURNETT: Understanding and extremity. Ah, well, yes. And also no, of course. You remind me of a story. Just last week, my daughters and I were on a small, open boat making a slow turn around the island of Capri. The magnificent rock formations loomed up before us: natural arches and precipitous cliffs that drop into the sea; the caves high up in sheer faces of stone, and the caverns opening into the deep at the crashing waterline. As we quietly rounded the northeast corner of the island, Francesca, nine, sitting on the bow, looked up and said to me, anxiety clear in her eyes: "those cliffs are scary." And she was right, of course. Being at the bottom of a very high cliff that drops into the ocean *is* frightening, somehow. Now it *could* be "rationally" frightening because something might fall off the top and hit you. But we were way too far out in the water to have that be a real possibility. She was not afraid of that. Indeed, there was nothing to be afraid of in any rational way. And she sensed this. Hence, the puzzle—the queerness of the occasion. Its heightened air.

What she was noticing, of course, is a phenomenon that has been of great interest to philosophers for a long time. She was experiencing the queasy power of an encounter with the "sublime"—the affective-cognitive shiver Kant dissected so closely in the *Critique of Judgement*. It was very interesting to take a moment with

Experiencing the sublime. View from the water of two Promontories in Capri emerging from the Tyrrhenian Sea on the south side of the Gulf of Naples. Photo: Diana Agrest, 1982, personal collection.

her, there on the bow, and to ask her (and myself) why it is that this kind of situation—an inhuman thing, large and close—touches us so deeply. Kant, of course, thinks he has figured out why this happens, and his answer remains, for me, extraordinary. But put his answer aside for a moment. In looking at the images prepared for your studio, in considering the projects that the studio took up, I am reminded of the problem of the sublime: extremity of scale; absence of the human.

AGREST: But the sublime is an aesthetic category, and, as I conceive of this project, the intention here is not an "aestheticizing" of nature. These drawings are tools for understanding. The aim is expanding knowledge about natural phenomena and the Earth in the field of architecture. It is not about representing natural phenomena as art.

BURNETT: That may be so, but the sublime sits right at the conjunction of understanding and extremity, and the understanding is very much in play in any aesthetic experience, at least as far as Kant is concerned. By invoking the sublime, I am hoping to lay the groundwork for a clarification that I think you might offer to a certain kind of possible critique: this book presents explorations of big things in nature. The scales are vast and there are no people.

View from the water of three promontories from opposite side. Photo: Diana Agrest, 1982, personal collection.

AGREST: The question of the absence of people, which I would call the human figure as this is about representation as a tool for thought, is not about considering nature as such, separate from humans. It is rather related to the actual scale of the phenomena we are working with. Just as this is not about trying to make art from nature, it is not looking at it from a social science perspective. We are developing these explorations from architecture, and in this sense, the presence of a human means something entirely different. The human can be understood, from my perspective, in different ways, such as the place of "man" in architectural theory or the presence of the user through program and function.

BURNETT: To be sure. And yet, it is also the case that architecture has long been driven by a double consciousness in relation to the human. On the one hand, there is that Vitruvian man at the heart of each built space, each architectural form. On the other hand, however, there is that Promethean-*cum*-Faustian reflex that repeatedly traduces the human in the direction of the monumental. The works in this book could be understood to participate in the latter program, no?

AGREST: Not at all. Not as I understand them. Approaching these explorations of nature the way we do here is an implied *criticism* of the prevailing approach to architecture that indeed focuses almost exclusively on "expressive" monuments—those centered on the architect or on the client, king, pope, corporation, or other institution, and in a way the absence of the human figure is not to monumentalize nature as such but rather is done to avoid placing man at the center of it all.

BURNETT: Interesting. Let's go back to Capri for a moment. And to what Kant has to say about Francesca's heart-shiver beneath the cliffs. What he offers is an account of that shiver that exquisitely suspends a simple-minded distinction between thought and feeling, cognition and affect. Recall how a judgment of the sublime works, according to the Third Critique. It is a kind of heart-beat of thought, and consists, like a pulse contraction, of a systolic evacuation followed by a kind of diastolic swelling. First, the naked, overwhelming *magnitude* of the object produces a harrowing realization: "My god! That's so gigantic that, before it, I am reduced to a speck of insignificance in the cosmos." I think your own interest in the extremity of many of the projects in this book participates in that posture of humility—not to say humiliation—before the grandeur of nature at its largest, deepest, and oldest. But the sublime as such requires that a diastole follow hard on the heels of that first trigger in the cycle. The systole, again: "Oh, that cliff, tsunami, volcano, supersedes me nearly infinitely, and by doing so, leaves me approaching naught in my nature, reduces me to a sense of myself as nearly nothing, sets me winging on course the trajectory of which recedes asymptotically to the zero line." But then, all of that merely sets up the crack-back that births the true terror-exhilaration of the sublime: "Wait! However big that thing is, *I am bigger*—since I am a rational agent and *that thing has no mind*."

We can think of that second component as something like the narcissistic self-salvage by which we bounce back to ourselves from the nihilistic negation occasioned by a real reckoning with our impotent fragility.

My point in reviewing all this is not to inquire of you whether you are in fact sympathetic to such a metaphysically robust treatment of the human. Rather, I want to set up a reading of the project presented in this book of yours. Since, in my view, what you are up to here is really best understood as a kind of cataloging of contemporary gestures in the direction of a recognizable program—call it the "neo-sublime."

This new program trades heavily on the *aesthetics of information*. In these cases, what we stand before that occasions a moment of nugatory vertigo is not a big cliff or a deep cave but a colossal mass of *data*. And the work of figuring out how to recover a sense of what we are as human beings *before the data* is very much the aesthetico-political challenge of our times. In much the same way that the Kantian sublime managed the question of who we were supposed to be *before a "godless" nature*—the dominant aesthetico-political challenge of the early nineteenth century. The question then becomes, what is the diastole by which we "recover" ourselves (in some form) from the terror-shadow *of the data*. I think it is something like this problem that unifies the projects in this book. The best of them demonstrate *both* an unhinging brush with the magnitude of the data sets, *and* a program for achieving a point-of-view adequate to that (immanently devastating) encounter—a "perspective" capable of "withstanding" it. Indeed, perhaps even "transcending" it—through form.

AGREST: It is possible that something like this is what is at issue when, in the studio, we talk about "potentials." I often try to emphasize in the process that underlying all the complexity, the data, everything we deal with as architects—through all of this, through a confrontation with all of this, it possible to reveal unseen aspects of the object of study. That is where the drawing and the work of representation come in. They are tools that in terms of dealing with this kind of subject afford powerful and different ways of approaching scale and magnitude and mass. We're not trying to replicate the data "faithfully" or at least not "literally." One could use triple curvatures and topological geometry, but then it would result in an attempt to emulate natural forms stylistically. On the contrary, I encourage the work with physical models produced as part of their readings of natural phenomena. These incorporate a haptic dimension, through a lot of experimentation with actual materials, from plastic to metal, plaster, wax, or rubber mixtures. These models are not replicating their referents but rather reinterpreting them. These activities may create or suggest the kind of "perspective" you are invoking. They may make more than the models themselves; they may make the "point of view" as well.

BURNETT: Yes, exactly! I can see exactly how that might work. It puts me in mind of that powerful line at the end of Heidegger's essay "The Thing," the moment where he calls for a "step back" from the modes of thought that represent and explain, in order to begin the work of recovering the thinking that "responds and recalls." The work of recovering ourselves from the data-terror may involve exactly this. And it may begin with human hands on a lump of clay—exactly like Heidegger's jug, which of course began in the same way.

AGREST: I sometimes insist on sketching by hand—as in the study of tornadoes—where the forces that are at play are so complex. Looking at the renderings done by means of data-intensive computation, I realized that this was totally inadequate. They needed to be drawn by hand with a soft pencil or brush where the hand and the mind, where the gestural and the body, partake in this exploration echoing, in a way, the dynamic complexity of the tornado itself.

BURNETT: This juxtaposition—the data armature versus the free-hand image—recalls a central tension in the history of science that I have worked on quite a bit: the history of cartography. Map making. I think that many of the images in this volume can be productively considered in relation to the history of cartographic representation. This is a key locus for thinking of data in relation to earth forms and earth processes.

From the fifteenth to the early nineteenth century the terraquous globe was significantly "apprehended" by the expanding program of

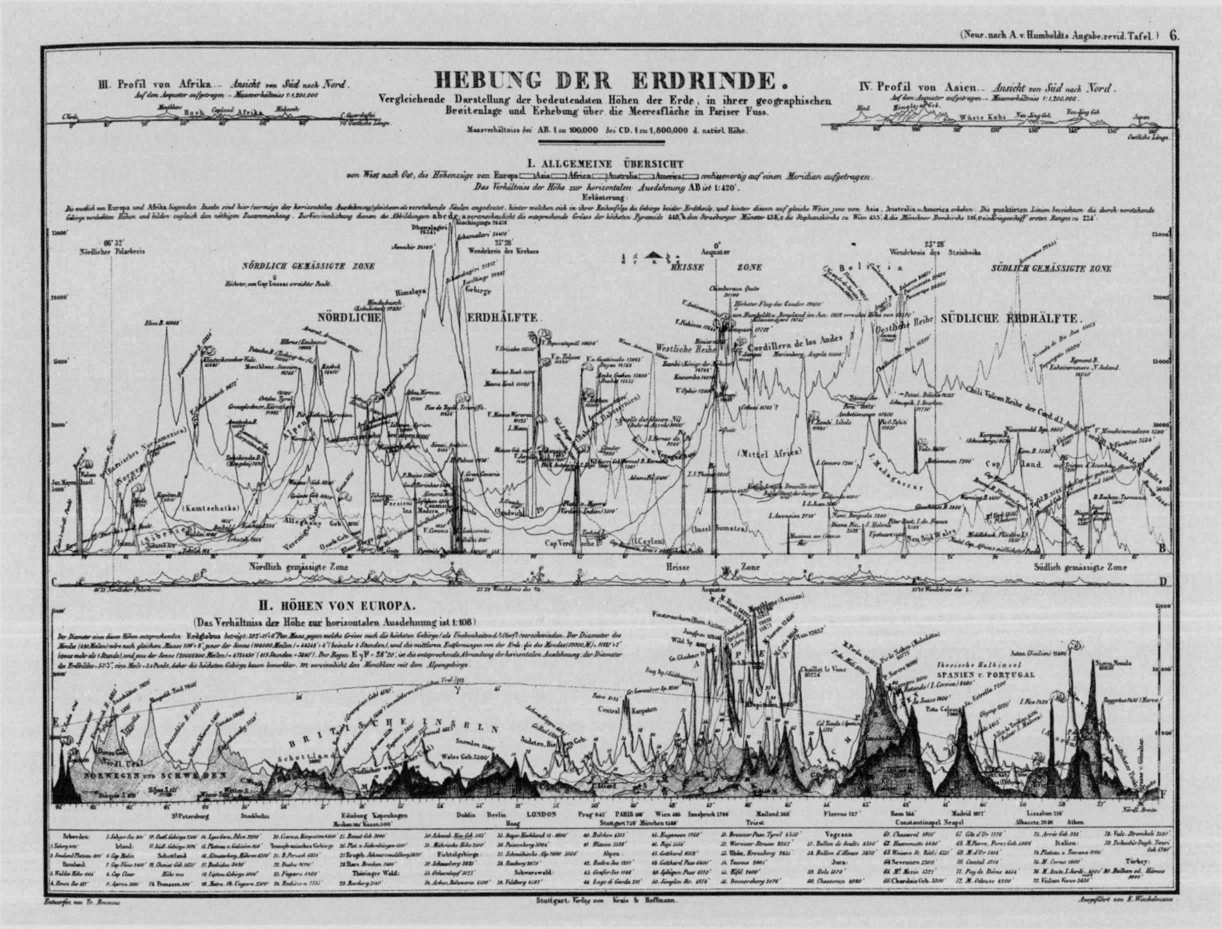

Elevation of the Crust of the Earth. Comparative rendering of the most prominent heights on Earth placed according to their geographical latitude and elevation relative to Paris at sea level. From the Atlas in Alexander von Humboldt's *Kosmos: Draft of the Physical Description of the World Volume V*, ed. Bromme Traugott (Stuttgart: Krais & Hoffman, 1851).

European natural science by means of twinned processes: on the one hand, you had a program of "global inventory," the collection and collation of the *stuff* of the planet (plants, animals, minerals, etc.); on the other hand, you had a continuous enterprise of "mathematical cosmography," the intersecting work of surveying and wayfinding and positional astronomy that produced increasingly extensive and reliable geographical representations of the surface of the earth. My own argument is that the early nineteenth century saw a significant new intersection of these projects: by this point, the geographical armature of the Earth has been substantially fixed, and the vast abundance of natural phenomena substantially cataloged. In the early years of the century—paradigmatically in the work of Alexander von Humboldt—one sees a dramatic development: a preoccupation with the *spatialization of inventory*. Which is to say, a new interest in investigating the geographical distribution and geospatial configuration of plants, animals, rocks, and even human beings. Out of this work—biogeographical and structural-geological—comes many of the most important developments of nineteenth-century science: Darwin's theory of evolution by natural selection above all. I am here giving a very compressed account of a complicated story, but the gist of it holds: the early nineteenth century saw a revolutionary crossing of two world-knowing traditions, geography and natural history. Spatialized thinking about the stuff of the Earth proved revolutionary.

I rehearse all this because, as I look at the images in this book, I find myself tempted by an analogy to that early nineteenth-century moment.

Geography of Plants in the Tropics; A natural painting of the Andes, based on observations and measurements, which were made from the 10th degree north to the 10th degree south latitude, in the years 1799 to 1803, by Alexander von Humboldt and AG Bonpland. 36"x24" depiction of the Chimborazo extinct volcano in the Andes occidental Cordillera. From "Essay on the Geography of Plants" by Alexander von Humboldt and A. Bonpland, Tubingen-Paris 1807.

I wonder if it is possible that we are in the middle of a comparable transformation. The rise of GIS systems and the new computational and representational tools that are part of every architect's formation now, coupled with the wide availability of extraordinary data sets that bear on Earth environments and history would seem to afford conditions not unlike those that occasioned the "Humboldtian Turn" in the first decades of the nineteenth century. Are we in the midst of something similar? Do images like those that have come out of your studio represent a new crossing of geospatial frames and collatory Earth-data? It seems not-impossible to me. More work would need to be done to deliver on the suggestion, but it is an alluring notion. Not least because the intellectual and cultural consequences of the last time this happened were enormous! One is left to speculate as to what may follow on the heels of this iteration of a new geospatial-data complex.

AGREST: Humboldt is a very interesting reference: his studies of Chimborazo, his Romantic preoccupation with extremes, his interest in volcanism. Look at his images against the one in this book, the model of the Kilauea Volcano in Hawaii. This image works like X-ray vision, revealing the forces that produce the hundreds of daily mini-earthquakes that happen within. Other models depicted in this volume reveal the geological history of the structure of the salt domes found in the Gulf of Mexico, both on land and under water. This model is very interesting because in fact the salt dome formations, which are up to fifteen kilometers in height, are very irregular. But by making drawings in both horizontal and vertical sections the configurations could be generated by planes made with a laser cutter—the planes were then manipulated afterwards by hand. That is a wonderful example of how you use architecture tools in this kind of work. It would have been impossible to do this sort of model any other way.

BURNETT: Yes. And what we have here are these images. Images that use an architectural idiom to try to understand the dynamics and forms of the natural world. I had not thought of it before, but looking at it this way, I recall one of the key moments in the history of nineteenth-century science: Lyell's writings on the Temple of Pozzuoli in the *Principles of Geology*. As you may know, this classical-era temple presented a profound geological puzzle to the naturalists of the late eighteenth and early nineteenth centuries. The story goes roughly this way: when the temple was excavated, it was noted that the columns had been bored by marine snails in a region that began about nine feet off the temple floor, and extended to a height of about fifteen feet. Not above. Not below. How the heck could *that* have happened? A mystery!

Temple of Serapis at Pozzuoli Frontispiece of Charles Lyell's *Principles of Geology* of 1830. "This representation of the Temple of Serapis is a reproduction of that by Canonico Andrea de Jorio in his 'Ricerche sul Tempio di Serapide, in Puzzuoli.' Napoli, 1820." The ruins of the temple's columns were seen by Lyell as an indication of former sea level differing from that of 1820.

The resolution of that mystery (short answer: volcanic ash, compacted to a height of nine feet, protected the lower part of the columns when subsidence drew the whole temple under water to a depth of fifteen feet; subsequent uplift pushed the whole thing above sea level) had tremendous implications for understanding of the physics of nature. That the whole temple had been subjected to such forces *and the stacked marble column-blocks had not collapsed* powerfully indicated that these large-scale changes had occurred very slowly and smoothly—gradually. This afforded key support for those defending gradualist and "uniformitarian" accounts of geology—and even biology. Charles Darwin, after all, was hugely affected by Lyell's account of the Temple of Pozzuoli.

My point here is that the work of interpreting the dynamics of nature in this episode hinged on specifically architectural forms and specifically architectural representational techniques. In that sense, your project here, Diana, can cite a distinguished precedent.

AGREST: You have brought us back around to Naples I see—from the cliffs of Capri to the Temple of Pozzuoli.

BURNETT: Yes! Quite right. The Temple is just a little northeast of the island. And maybe full circle in another way: back to the sublime. Since the discovery of "deep time"—a central consequence of Lyell's uniformitarianism—afforded a vertigo from which, one might argue, humanity has never really recovered. Deep time was too deep. It was, we might say, the final half-heartbeat in the Kantian sublime, in that the diastolic conceit of human transcendence has never quite thumped back against the systolic evacuation occasioned by the discovery of the empty eons of geological time.

AGREST: So we come back to fear.

BURNETT: Yes. And to the human held at naught by the vast—by the mere magnitude of what obtains. My own view is that every effort to cognize this "absence of us" must be activated dialectically—must be used to bring us back to some new formulation of the basic work. And that basic work, for me, as a humanist, is the "singing of the we"—the project of not merely trying to "define" or "account for" the relevant first-person-plural, but actually trying to *generate* and *perform* it, as in the choral occasion of joined voices. Let us hope that this book of yours, so apparently people-less, returns those who read it to the central problem of "us." Of us now.

Salt Domes

The Gulf of Mexico
Yu-Chen Lin

This project focuses on the formation of the 9.3-mile-high salt structure that lies under the sea floor in the Gulf of Mexico, a process beginning 250 million years ago, by which sea water is transformed into solid salt rock and finally into a highly viscous fluid structure: the salt dome. Salt domes can be found throughout the coastal area of the Gulf of Mexico, covering an area over 150,000 square miles.

As dense sediment above a layer of salt increases in quantity and weight, It compresses the salt layer, which, as a result, pushes upward folding rock. Heat is an important element in this process. Transmitted from magma through two aquifers above and below the salt structure, it is in constant interaction with the cold ocean water. This contact produces vertical oscillation that generates landslides offshore, weakening the salt structure. At the shoreline, the salt formations are fingerlike, while offshore they become a double layer structure due to the changing density of the sediment. This project reveals the three-dimensional structure of the salt domes, which have developed both horizontally and vertically, by "detaching" them from their physical context in order to expose their extraordinary formation resulting from the interaction of multiple forces and transformations originating over 150 million years ago.

Top: Axonometric view showing three types of salt domes found in and around the Gulf of Mexico—the ellipse, circle, and "two-layer structure." The two-layer structure forms a topography that is likely to cause landslides.

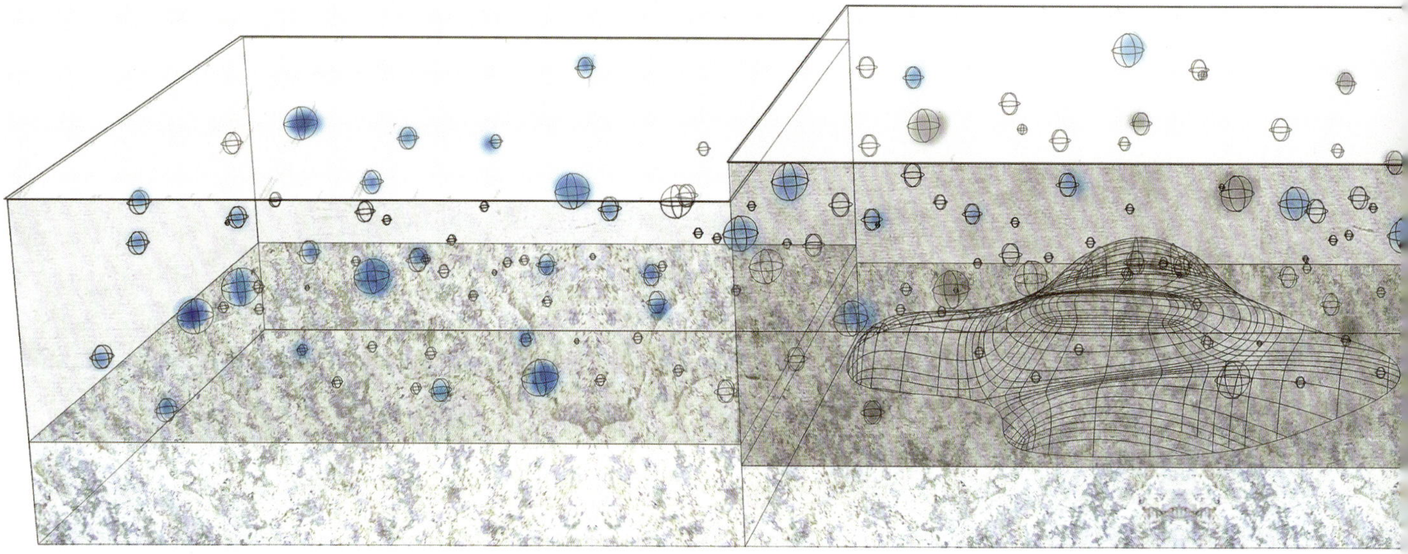

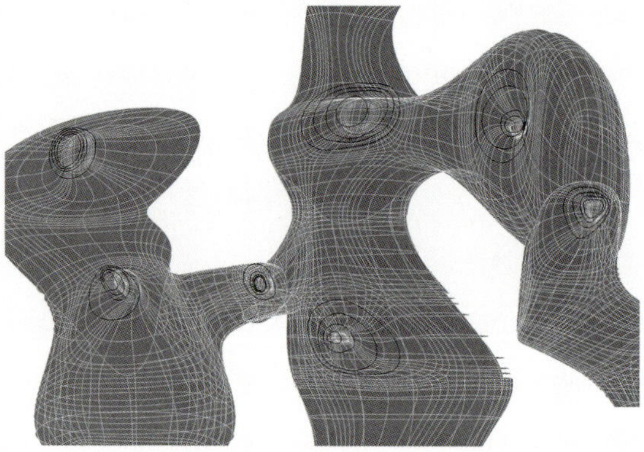

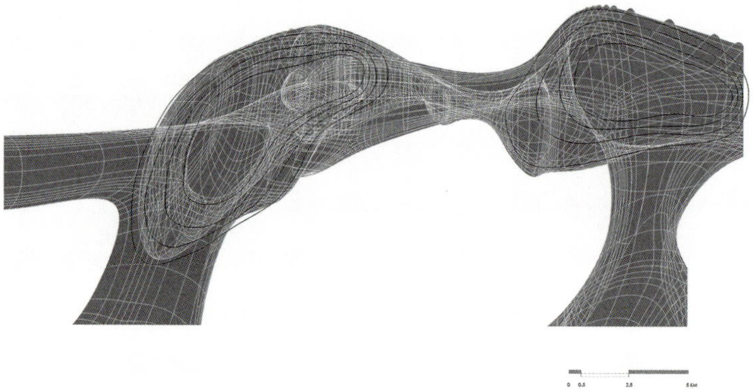

Top: Isometric view showing water flow through the sediment, increasing its density and squeezing the rock salt, which is thus transformed into a viscous fluid. As this fluid flows upward, salt domes are formed underground.

Bottom and Opposite: Three-dimensional views, plan, and section of salt domes depicting the difference between onshore and offshore salt domes.

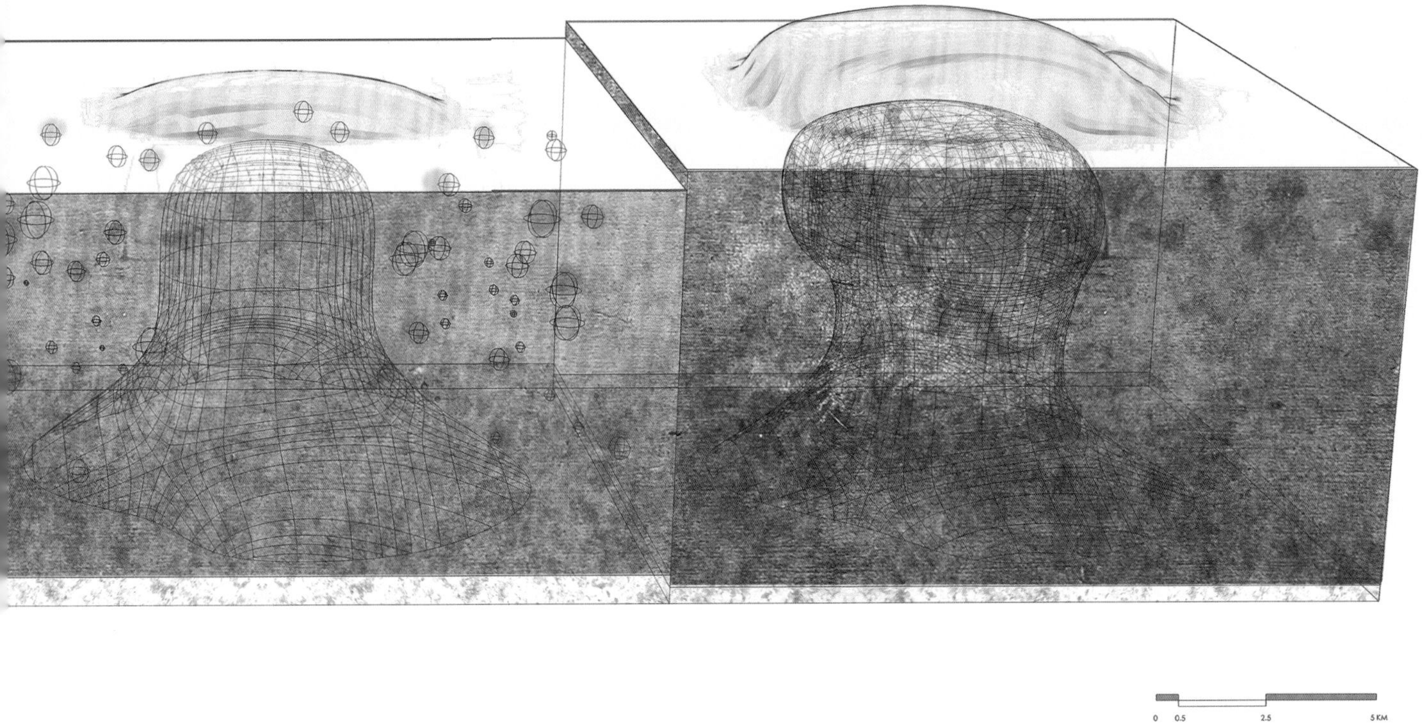
0 0.5 2.5 5 KM

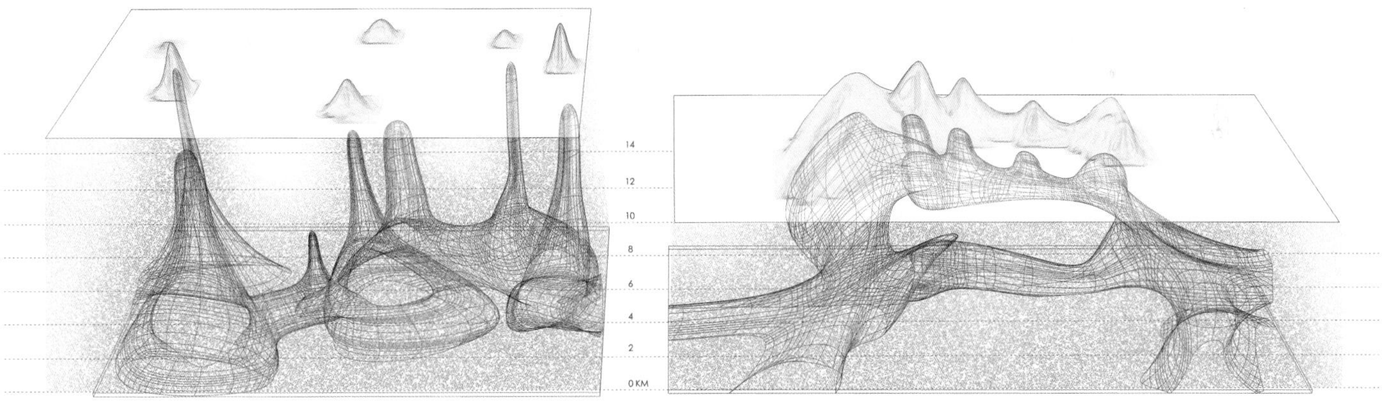
14
12
10
8
6
4
2
0 KM

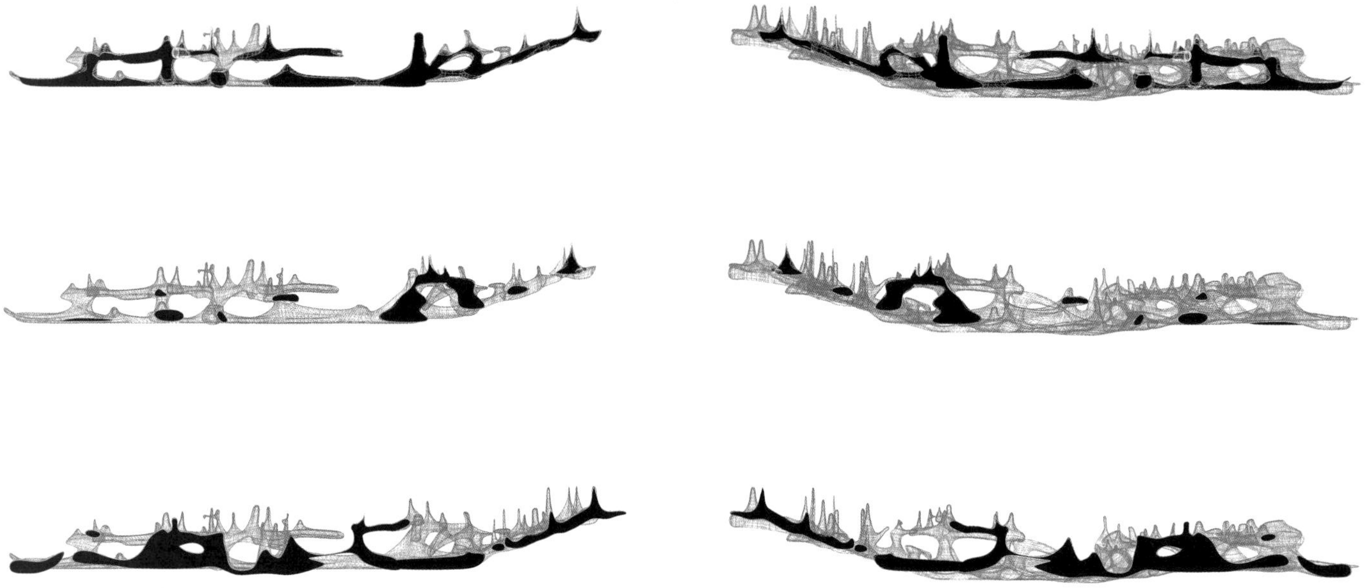

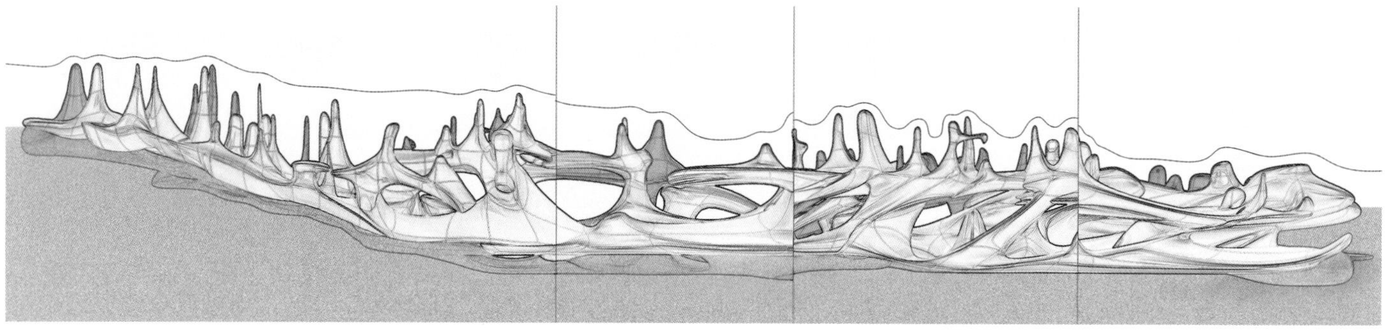

Top: Sections of salt dome at different levels showing the spatial organization of the salt structure.

Bottom: Three-dimensional reconstruction of a section of the nine-mile-high salt domes' structure.

Opposite: Plans of salt dome structure at different levels showing its spatial configuration.

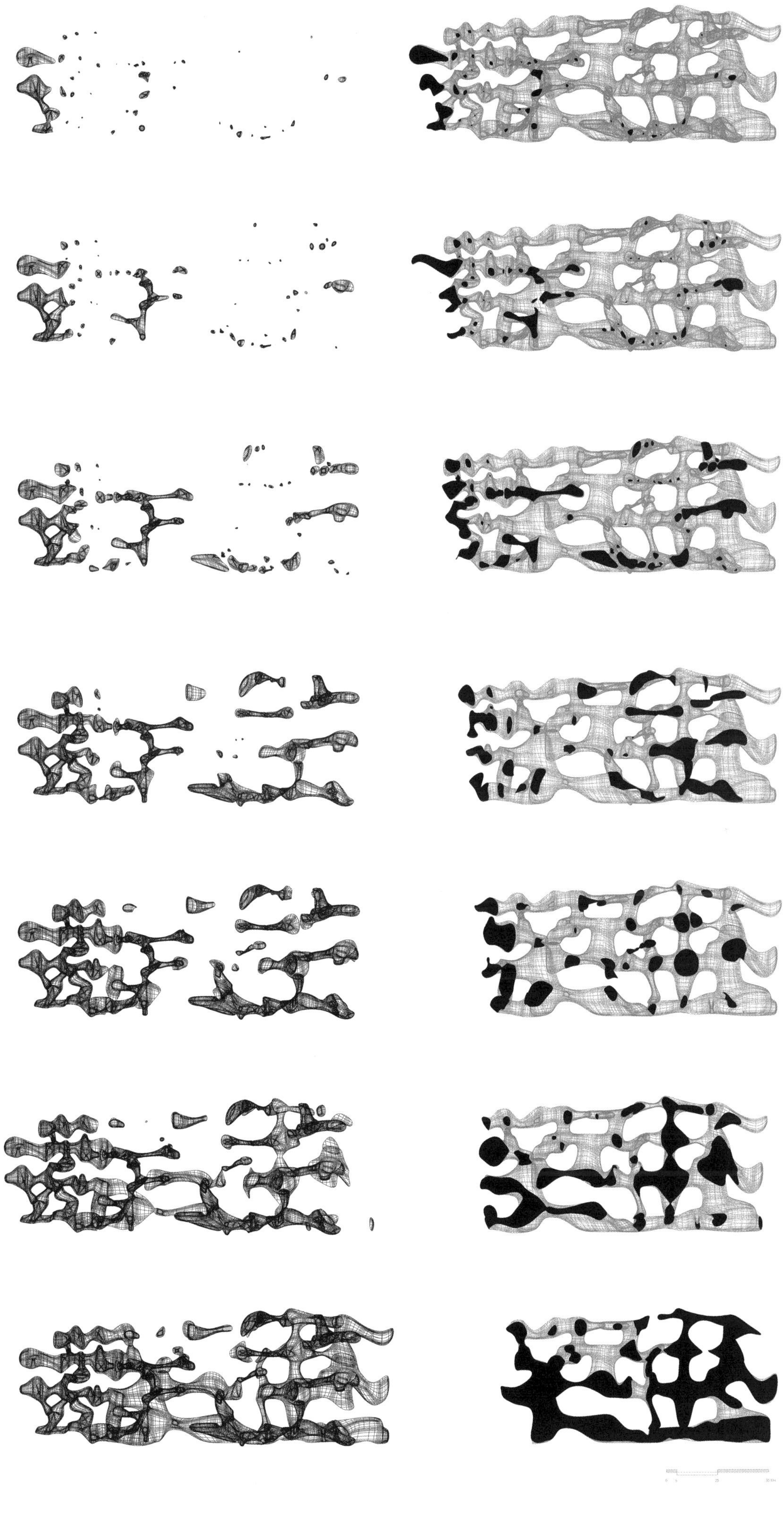

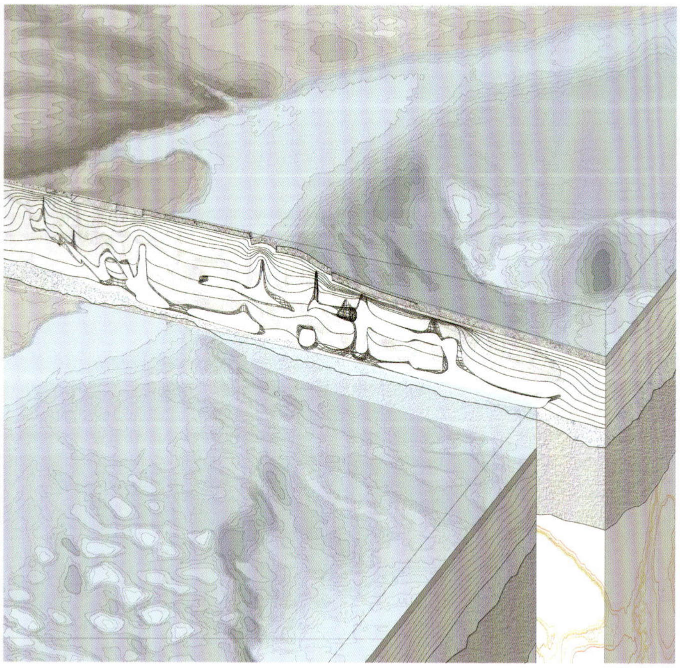

Top: Model showing the salt domes extracted as a freestanding structure.

Left: Axonometric section showing the salt domes' structural oscillation that is the cause of collapse and landslides.

Opposite: Model showing the relationship of the salt structure to sediment layers below.

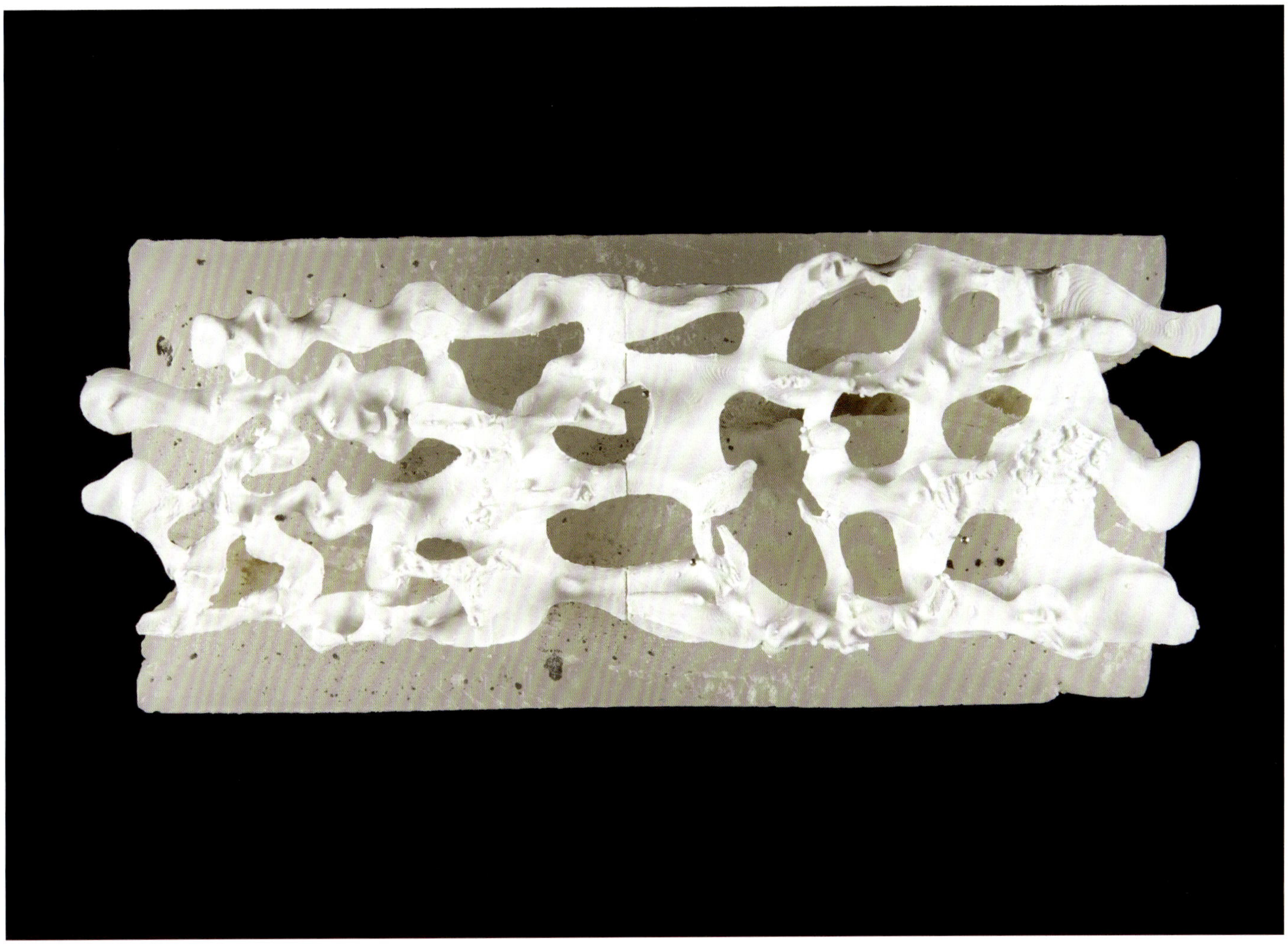

Chronicle of Eroding Forces

Apostle Islands, Bayfield Peninsula, Wisconsin
Boreum Lee

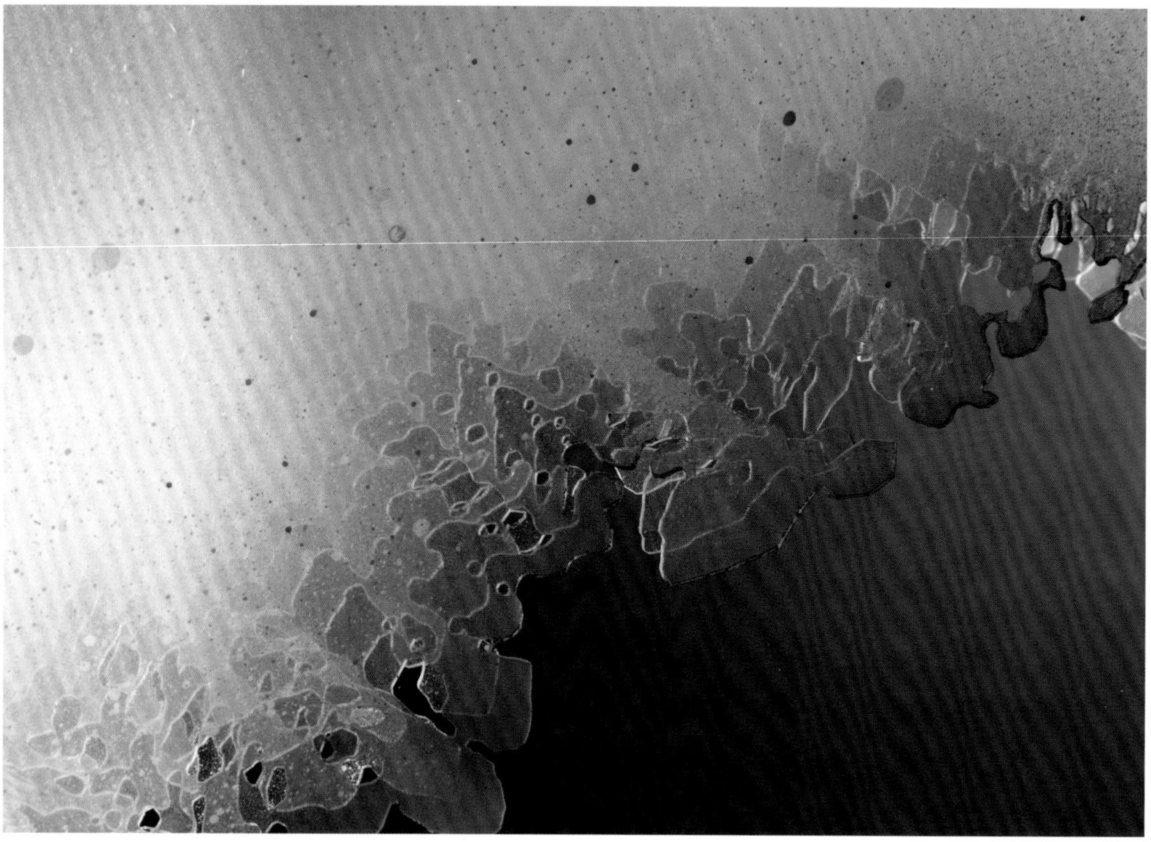

The Apostle Islands, a group of islands in Lake Superior's Bayfield Peninsula that covers an area of close to 32,000 square miles, are the result of glaciers and several glaciations, the last one being about 12,000 years ago. The erosion caused by the melting, the increase in the volume of water, and the waves of Lake Superior resulted in the formation of the islands. Sandstone sea caves, which surround their edges and have average depths ranging from about 500 to 1,300 feet, were also a result of erosion caused by the compounded effect of various forces: wind, tides, waves, ice, and water currents. The erosion process must be considered at different spatial scales, from the Great Lakes region as a whole to the microscopic scale of the sandstone, in order to reveal the simultaneous action of distinct forces working in different timeframes.

The shape of the sea caves acts as a register of various points in time, ranging from one billion years ago with the beginning of Devil's Island to the end of the last ice age 12,000 years ago to seasonal and daily process of transformation that are simultaneous, instantaneous, and continuous. The structures of the caves become a living timeline.

In order to understand the process of erosion and cave formation, this project visualizes the eroding forces as volumes. Their voids become the figures in a figure-ground relationship study.

Top: Model showing the record of erosion, created using a water jet.

Opposite: Plans of three moments in the erosion process resulting from water currents.

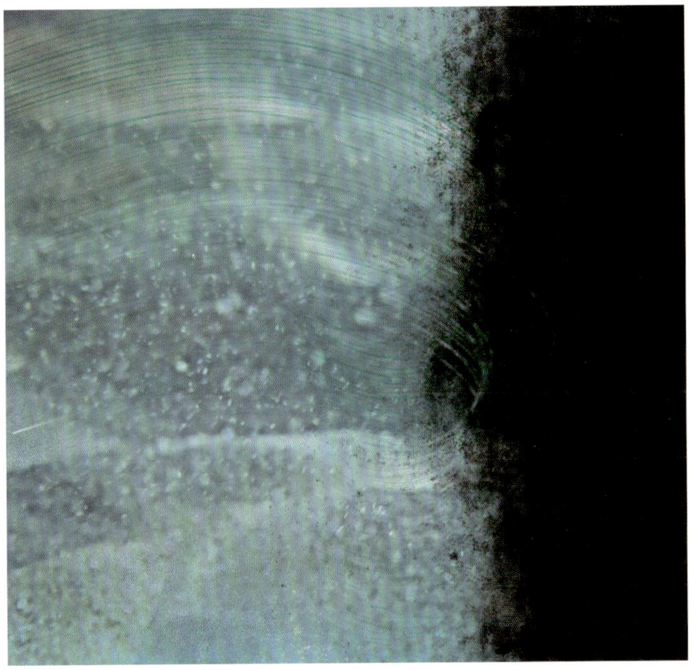

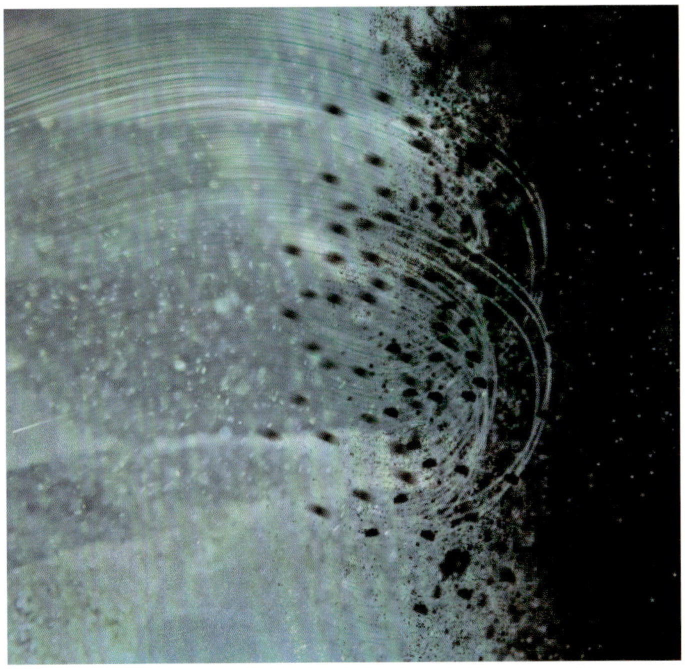

100
200μm=0.02mm
0.001inch

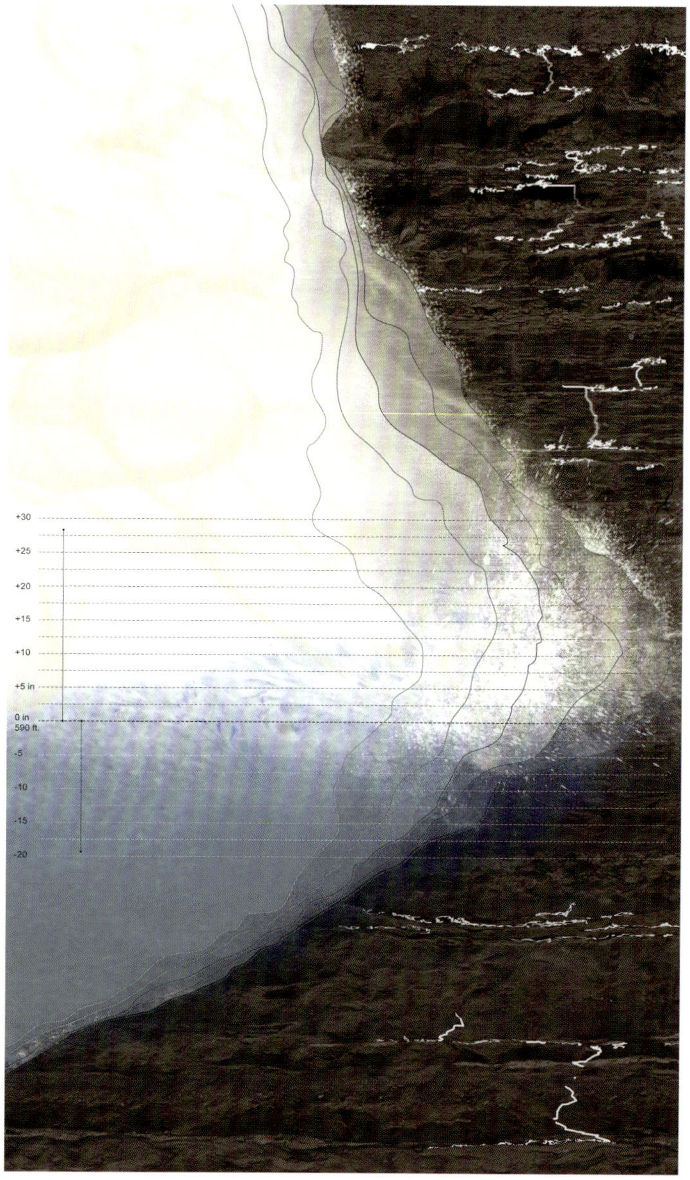

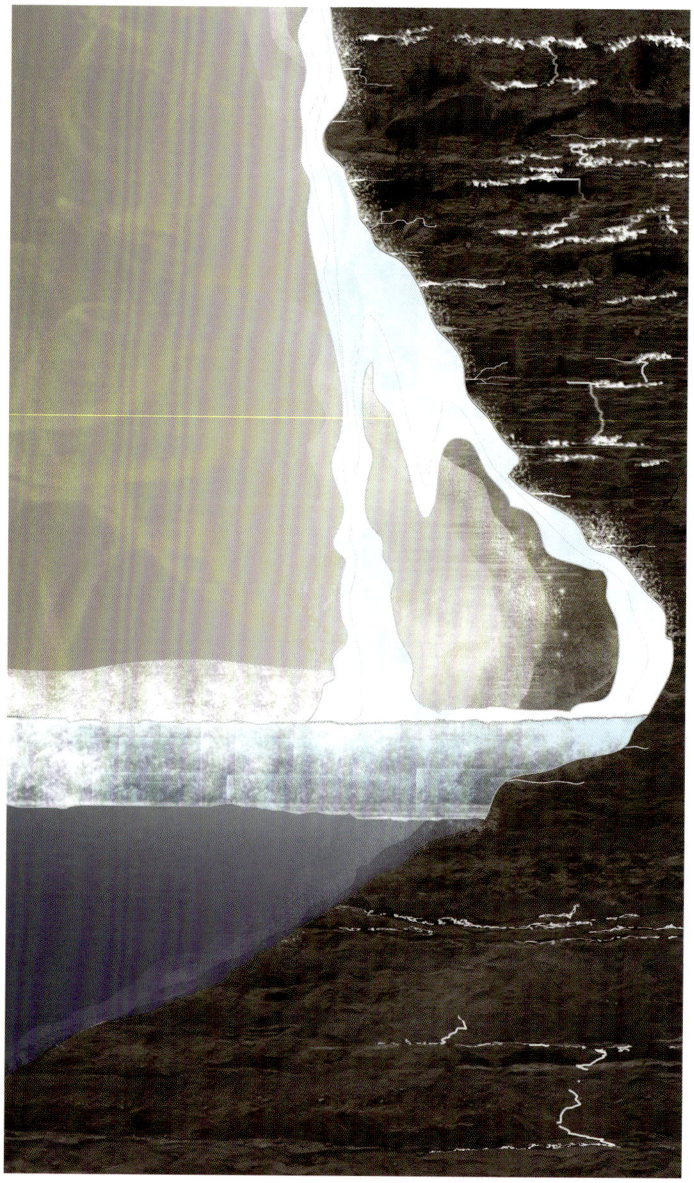

Top left: Section of transformations during a 10,000-year period.

Top right: Section of transformations during one winter season.

Left: Section of ice formations within the rock through a winter season. The expansion and compression of the rock accelerates the cave formation.

Above: Model of three moments in the erosion process resulting from water currents.

An Aeolian Sense: Configuring Power of an Invisible Force Field

Great Sand Dunes of Colorado
Katerina Kourkoula

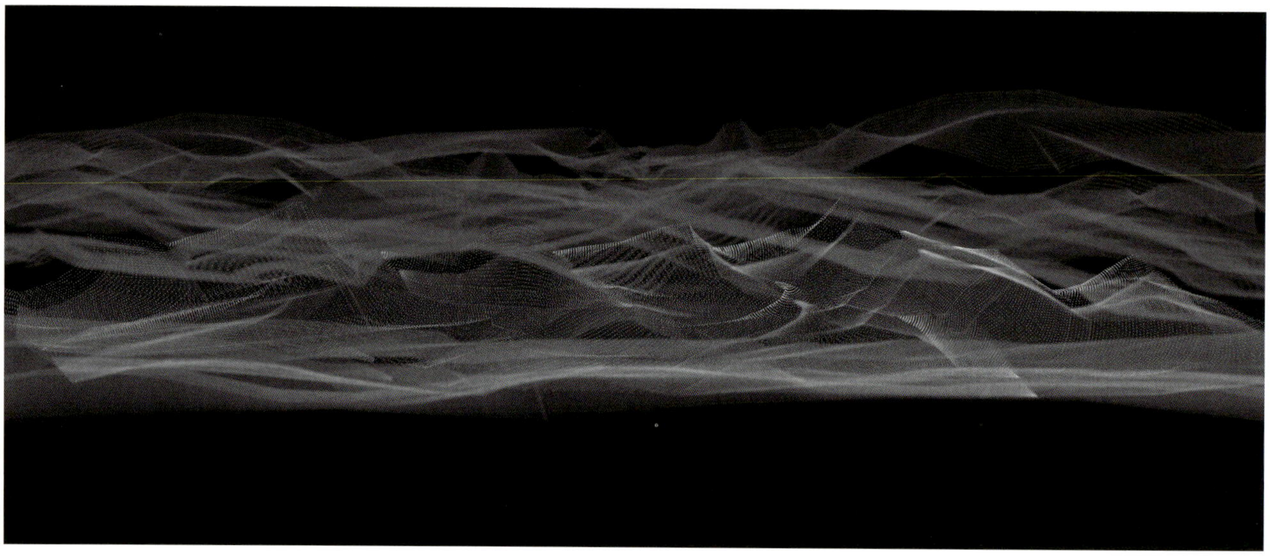

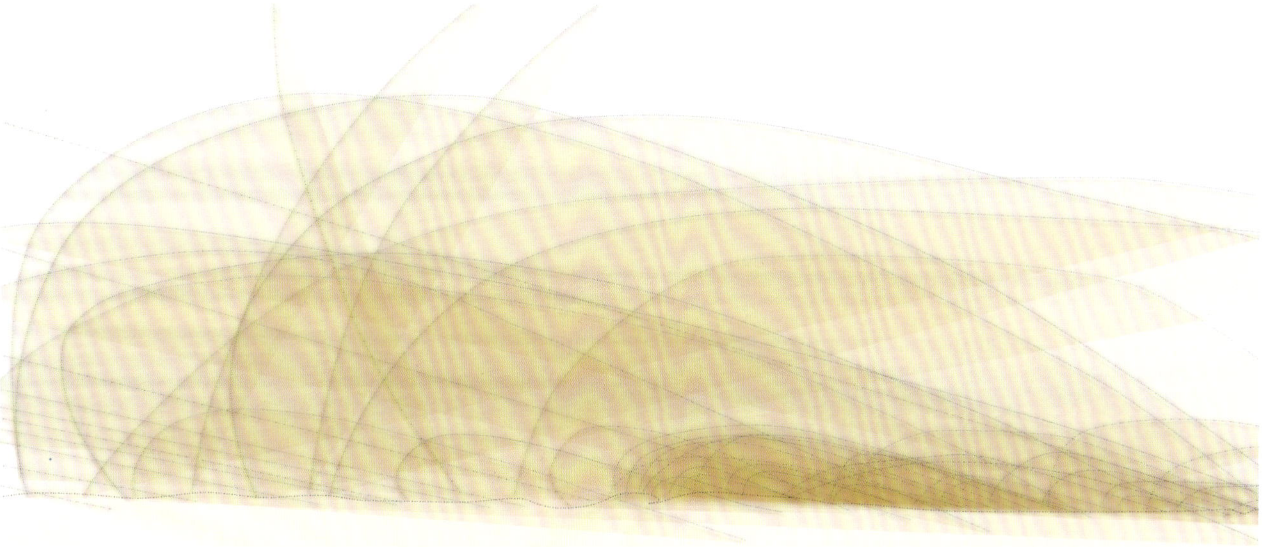

As the physical and visual manifestation of wind forces, the sand dunes, formed 440,000 years ago, stretching over 130 square miles and reaching a height of 750 feet, are molded through the aggregate movement of sand grains transported by wind. Aeolian sand, sand constantly kept in motion by wind, gets its name from the mythological ruler of the winds: Aeolus.

Through the tools of architectural representation, this project reads, re-presents, and utilizes the natural laws that characterize the Great Sand Dunes landscape in order to produce space. The accumulative sand-particle movement that has been induced by the wind generates a fluid and dynamic landscape. The placement of physical objects on dune surfaces, which work as probes along the wind paths that alter the direction of sand movement and forces the sand to accumulate in differing dune configurations, is an exploration into the potential for generating new, controlled spaces that are formed within the geophysical context of landscapes shaped by their material conditions and active forces.

Opposite top: Elevational view of sand dunes. A sand dune, though materially consistent, is composed of a core that is stable and a surface that is constantly affected by the wind. The surface sand grains are in continuous motion. Within a period of a few weeks a dune oscillates back and forth, perpendicular to its length. During a yearly cycle, a dune gains and loses height due to accumulation and loss of sand grains moving forward and backward, leaving it roughly in the same position.

Opposite bottom: Movement of sand grains on the surface of dunes at a microscopic scale. A single grain is picked up by the wind and dropped farther down the slope of the dune, impacting other grains that are, in turn, relocated. The movement of a single grain translates into the movement of a whole landscape.

Above: Cross section of a single dune, showing the movement of a sand dune in three time frames—weekly, monthly, and seasonally—and in different directions in each of these time frames. This drawing depicts the complexity of that movement.

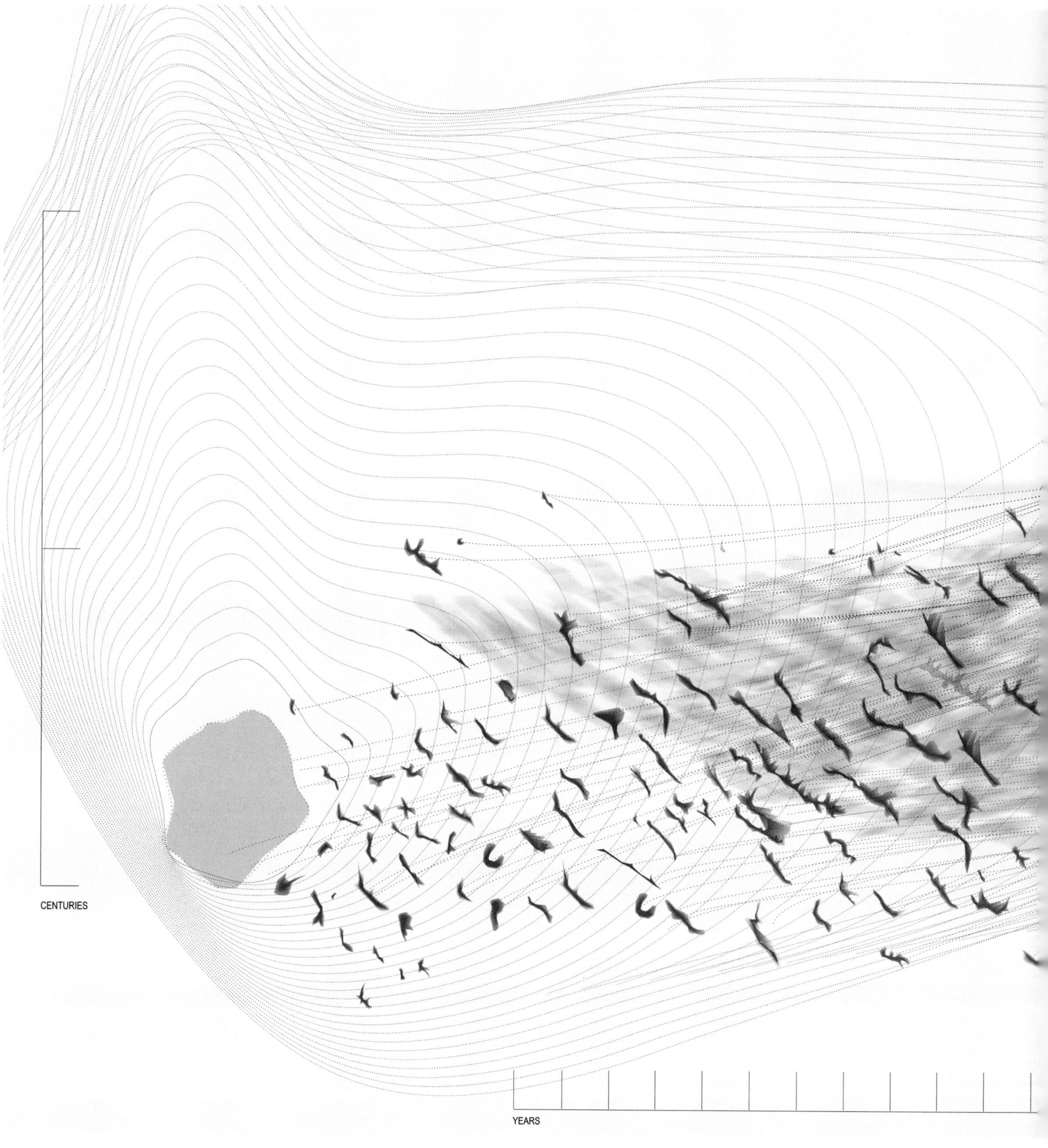

Above: Axonometric view of the creation of the Great Sand Dunes of Colorado. Over 400,000 years ago, a lake evaporated and the lake sediment travelled, following the winds until it hit the natural obstacle of the Rocky Mountains. The dunes oscillate daily and increase and decrease in height within their yearly cycles.

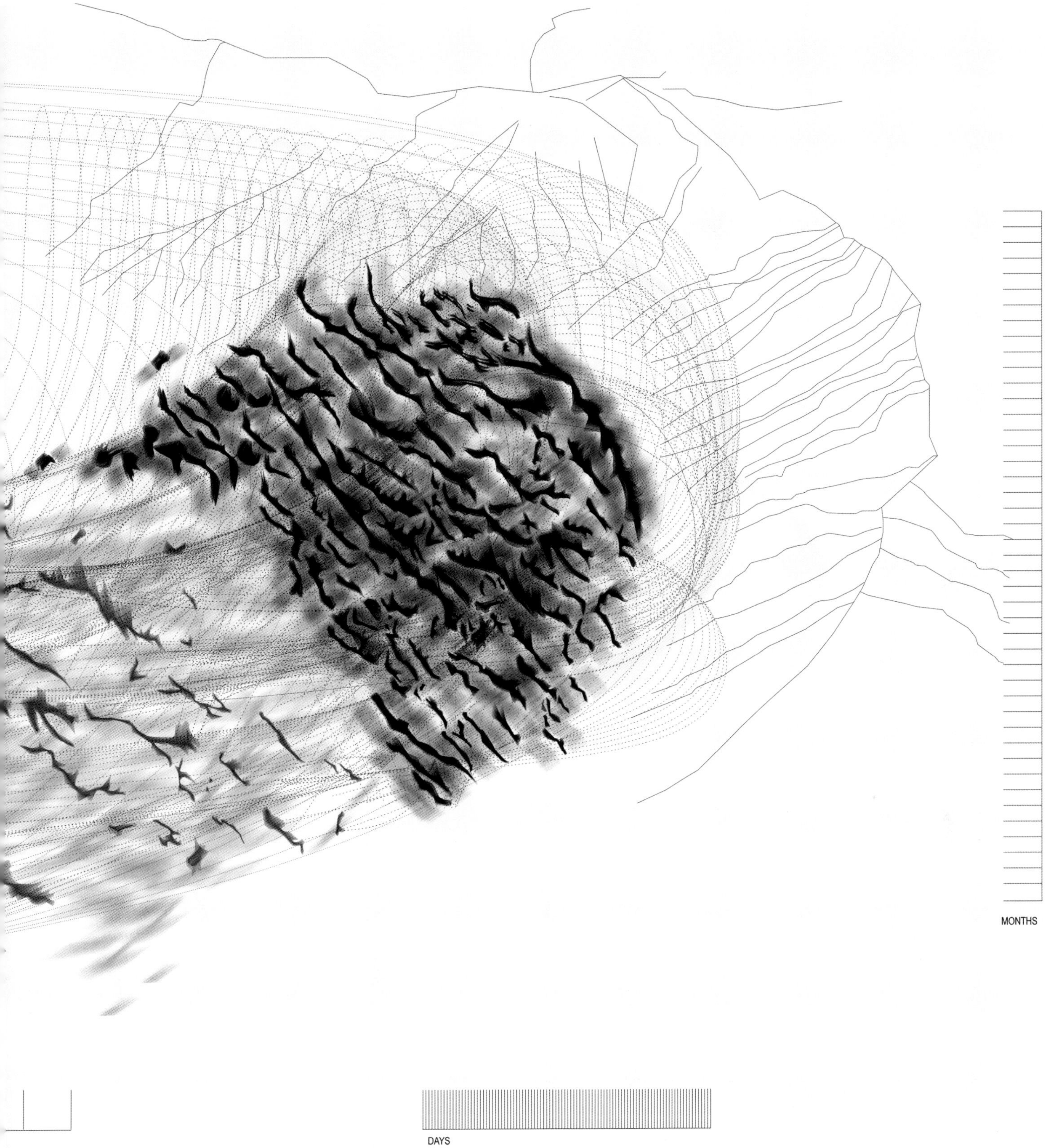
MONTHS
DAYS

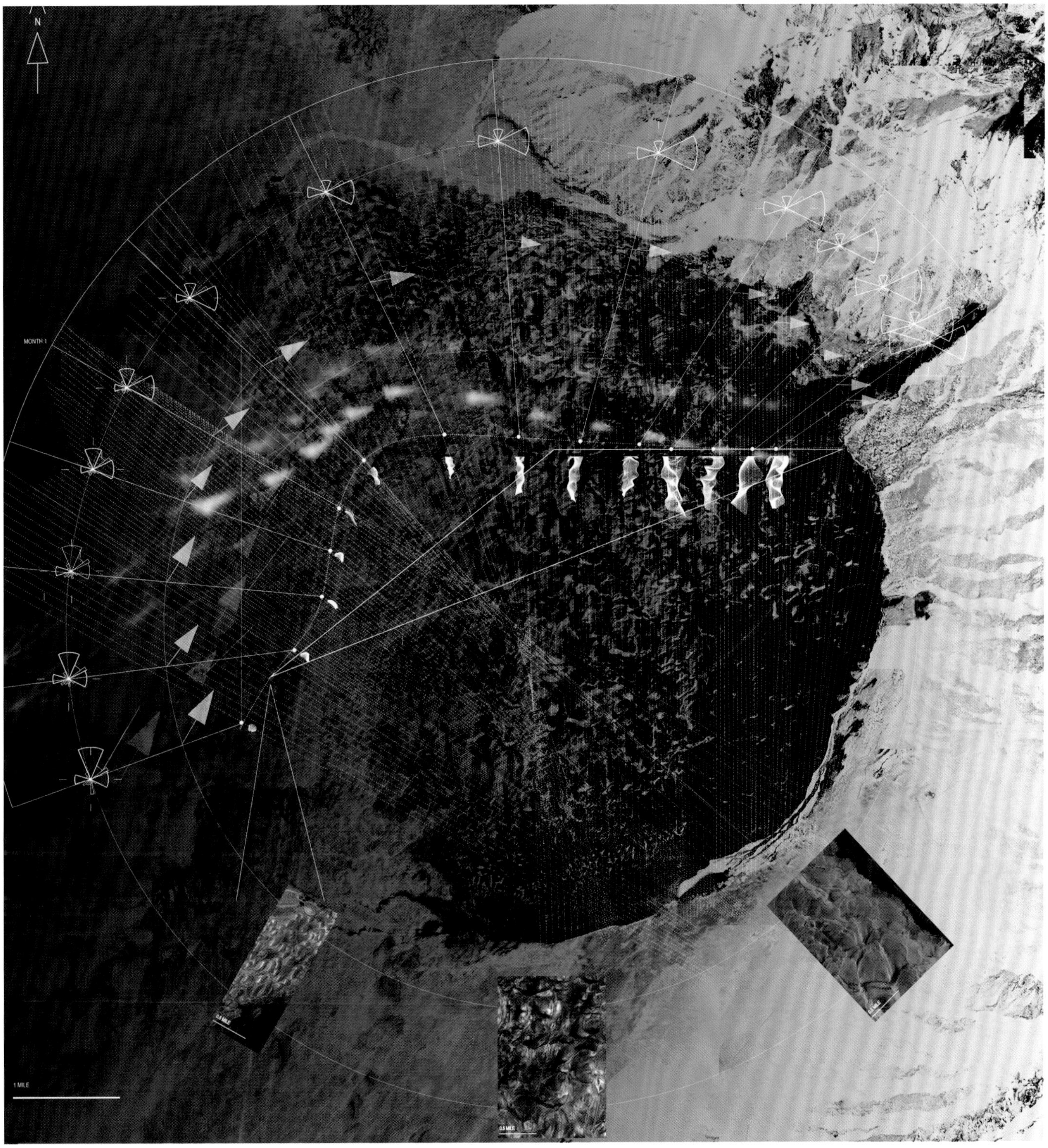

Opposite top and bottom: Model showing the wind forces at play in the formation of dunes. 1 and 2 cast plated steel wire and nails.

Above: Probing the effect of wind on the dune configuration by tracing the movement of a single sand grain. The sand grain can start from the edges of the dune and travel, solely by wind forces, through the whole topography of the dunes. The depicted routes reflect existing wind patterns illustrated by the wind rose diagram.

Water Motion in a Topographical Vessel

Bay of Fundy, Canada
Mando Fytou

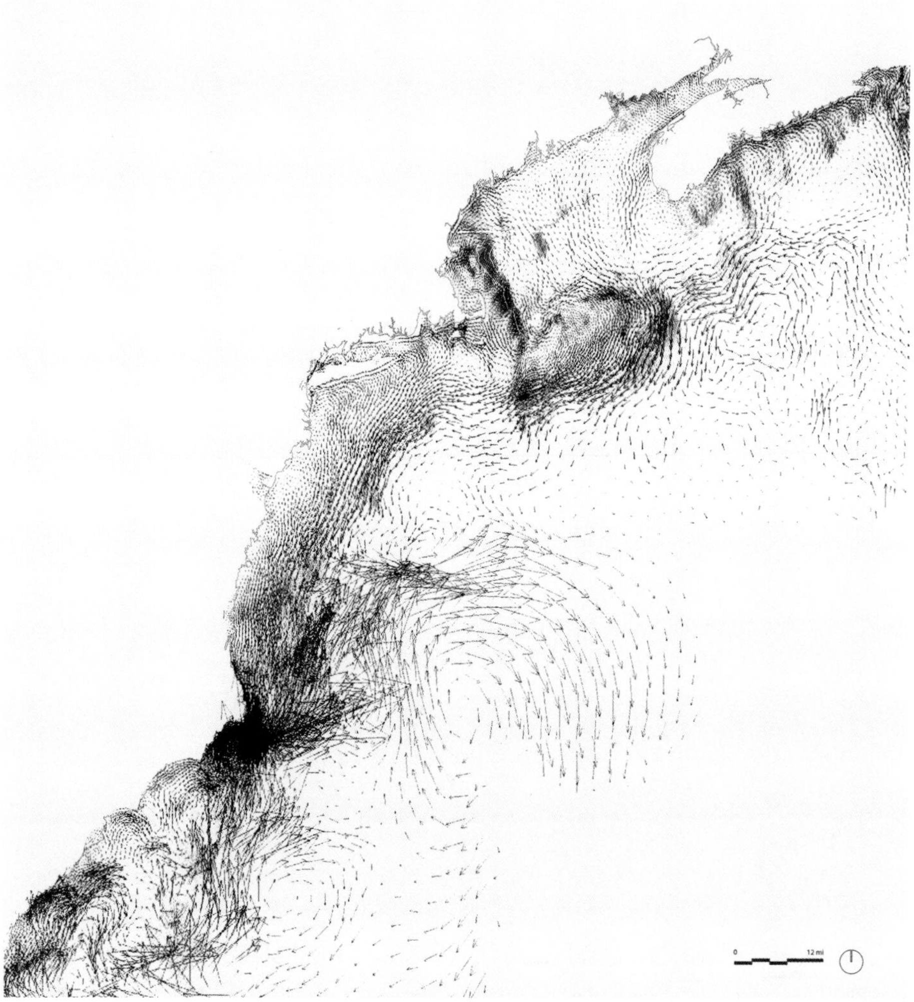

The Bay of Fundy, which stretches for 170 miles at the northeast end of the Gulf of Maine, is home to the greatest tidal variations on Earth. One hundred and sixty billion tons of seawater flow in and out of the bay during a single tidal cycle. This is more than the combined flow of all of the world's fresh-water rivers. As is the case with other natural sites animated by movement, the Bay of Fundy exhibits a causal relationship between the perpetual motion of seawater and the topographical cavity that hosts it. Complex underwater topography fosters perpetual and intense tidal movement.

The bay is comprised of a long series of vast and violently changing altitudes, ranging from deep wells, ruptures, and narrow portholes to flatlands, which serve as a formative vessel, violently affecting the shifting water masses that move among them.

An examination of the colliding forces that drive tidal motion in the Bay of Fundy reveals the site to be not only a place but also a mechanism.

This exploration proposes a scenario whereby a complementary mechanism unfolds across the bay in the mode of a deconstructed watermill that while harvesting energy animates the exchange between the moving water mass and the resting cavity.

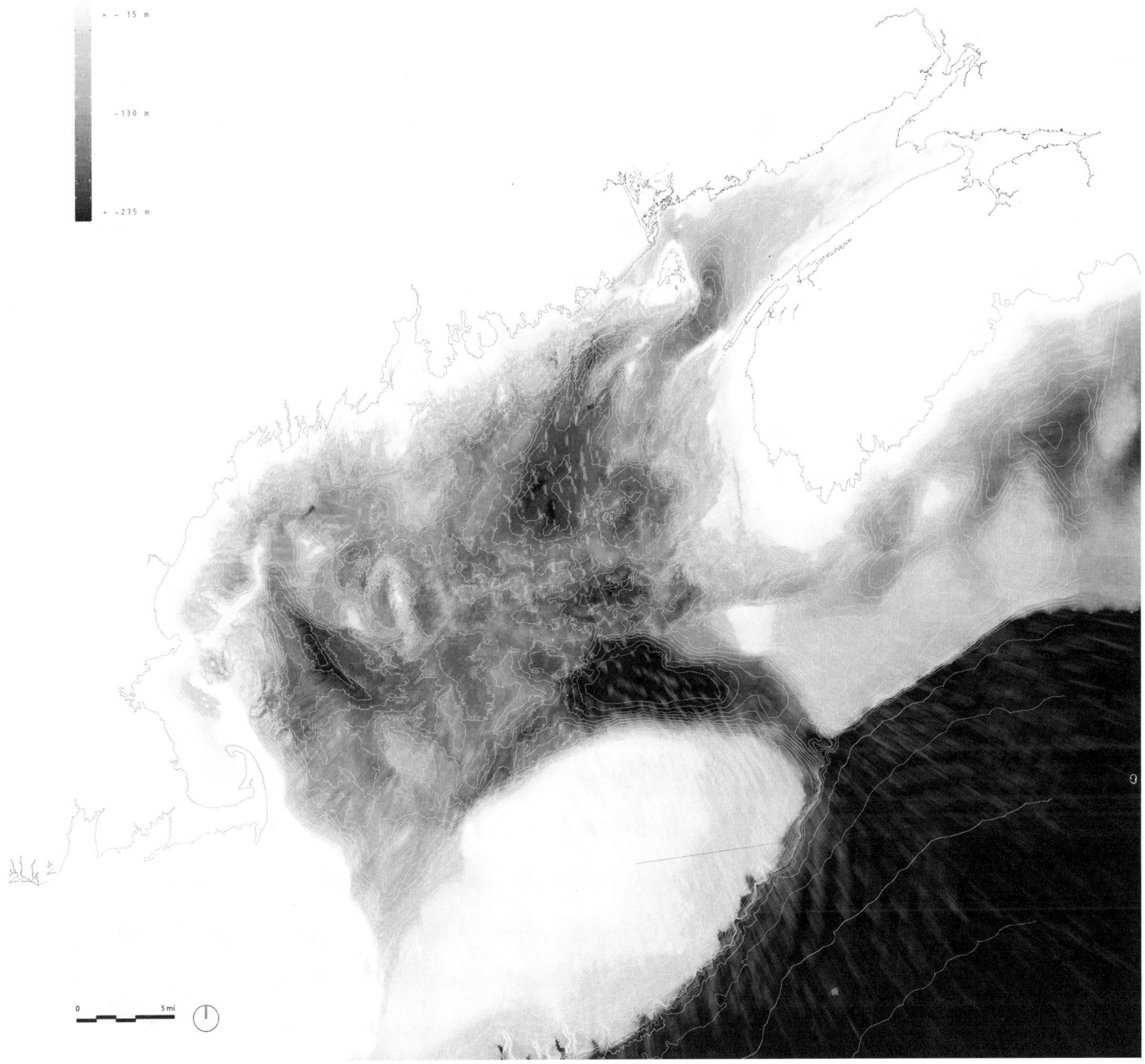

Opposite: Plan of drawing the Gulf of Maine system showing its complex geography uniquely suited to sustaining colliding, turbulent currents along the coastal edge.

Above: The perceptible tidal waves are the result of underwater topography.

Above: Analytical plan of tidal cycles showing that each tidal wave enters the bay as the preceding one exits it.

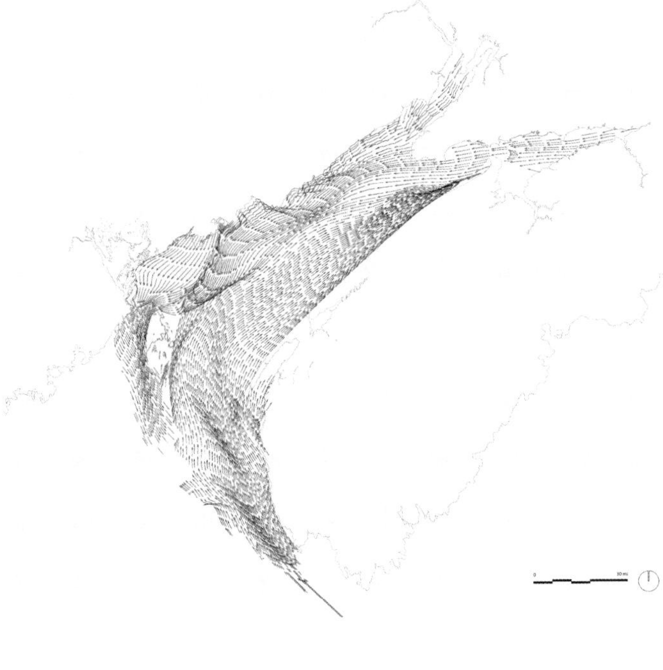

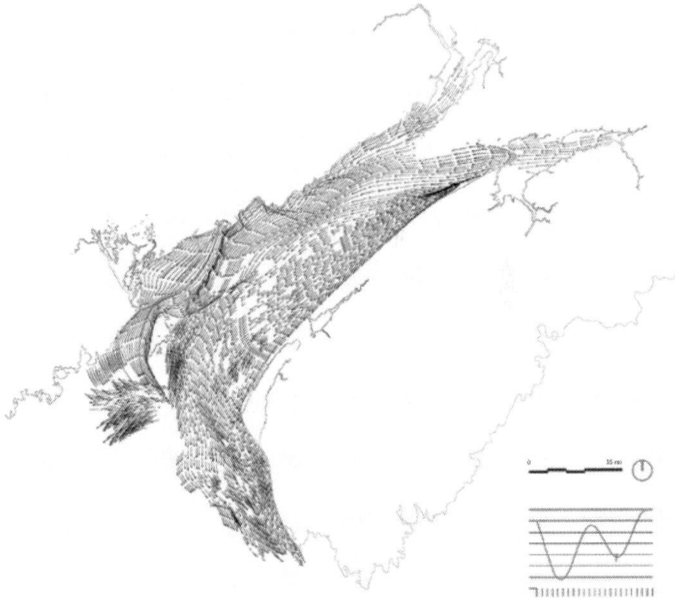

Top: Plan of the Minas Channel, a passage 3.5 miles wide and 66 miles deep, that lies at the easternmost side of the bay. The Minas Basin has the highest tidal range within the Bay of Fundy due to its underwater geography and a basin size that allows for the tidal waves to resonate.

Bottom left and right: Analytical plans depicting the currents through the maximum and minimum levels of two tidal cycles during the time of the month when the tidal range is most extreme. As the two opposing currents resonate, the tidal effect is magnified.

Impact and Flow

Lituya Bay Megatsunami, July 9, 1958
Yeqing Cao

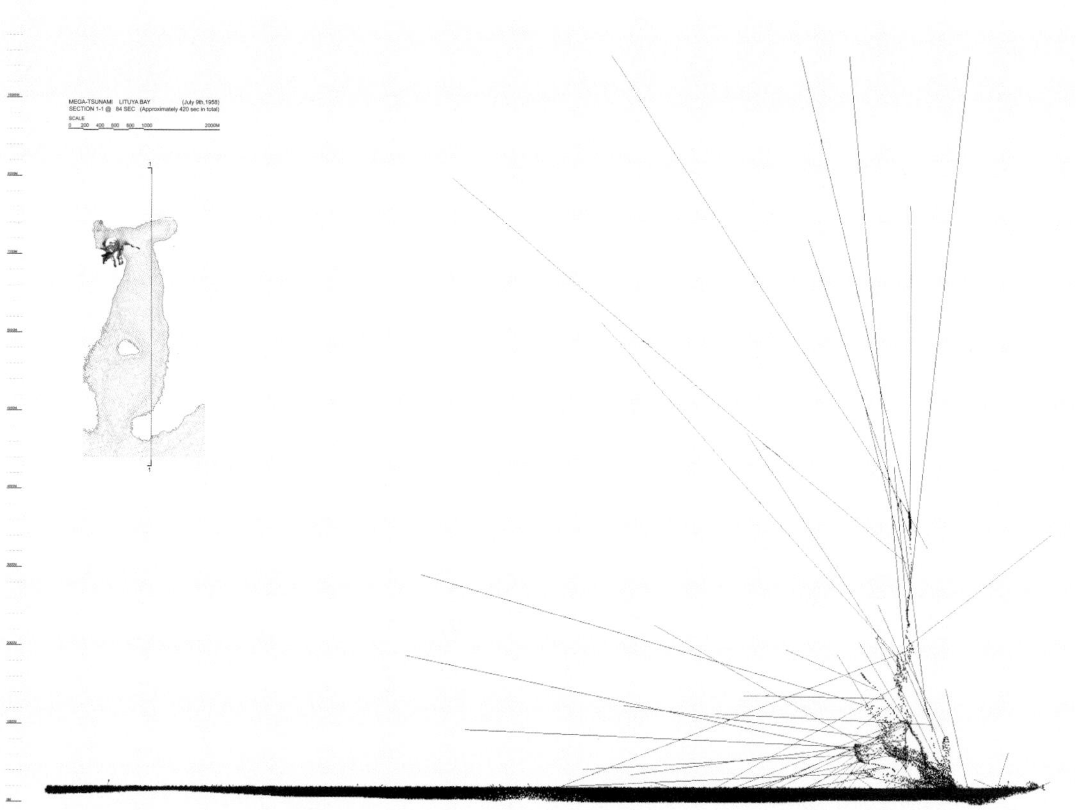

Most tsunamis are precipitated by movement of a fault between two tectonic plates in the ocean. The Lituya Bay megatsunami, however, was triggered by a giant stone approximately 16 times the size of the Empire State Building that slid into the 500-foot-deep Lituya Bay Fjord in Alaska from about 5,000 feet above sea level. The impact was tremendous, and it blew a large volume of water out of Lituya Bay into the north Pacific Ocean. Occurring on July 9, 1958, the megatsunami lasted just seven minutes but generated a swell 3.2 kilometers wide and 14.5 kilometers long.

This project focuses on the representation of the extraordinary force generated by gravity, transferred to the flow of water and absorbed by the earth, through the reconstruction of the morphology of the main force carrier—the water body in the bay. A point cloud computational method fed with verified tsunami data was applied to simulate the entire seven minutes, divided into 100 frames. Each dot in the computational drawings represents a seven-meter-in-diameter giant "water molecule" in real scale. The interdependent behavior of all the molecules under the control of fluid dynamics and algorithmic gravity illustrates the time and space embodied in the tsunami.

Top: Longitudinal section of Lituya Bay Alaska showing the impact of the megatsunami on the water surface 84 seconds after the tsunami took place using point cloud simulation. The vector attached to each point represents its speed.

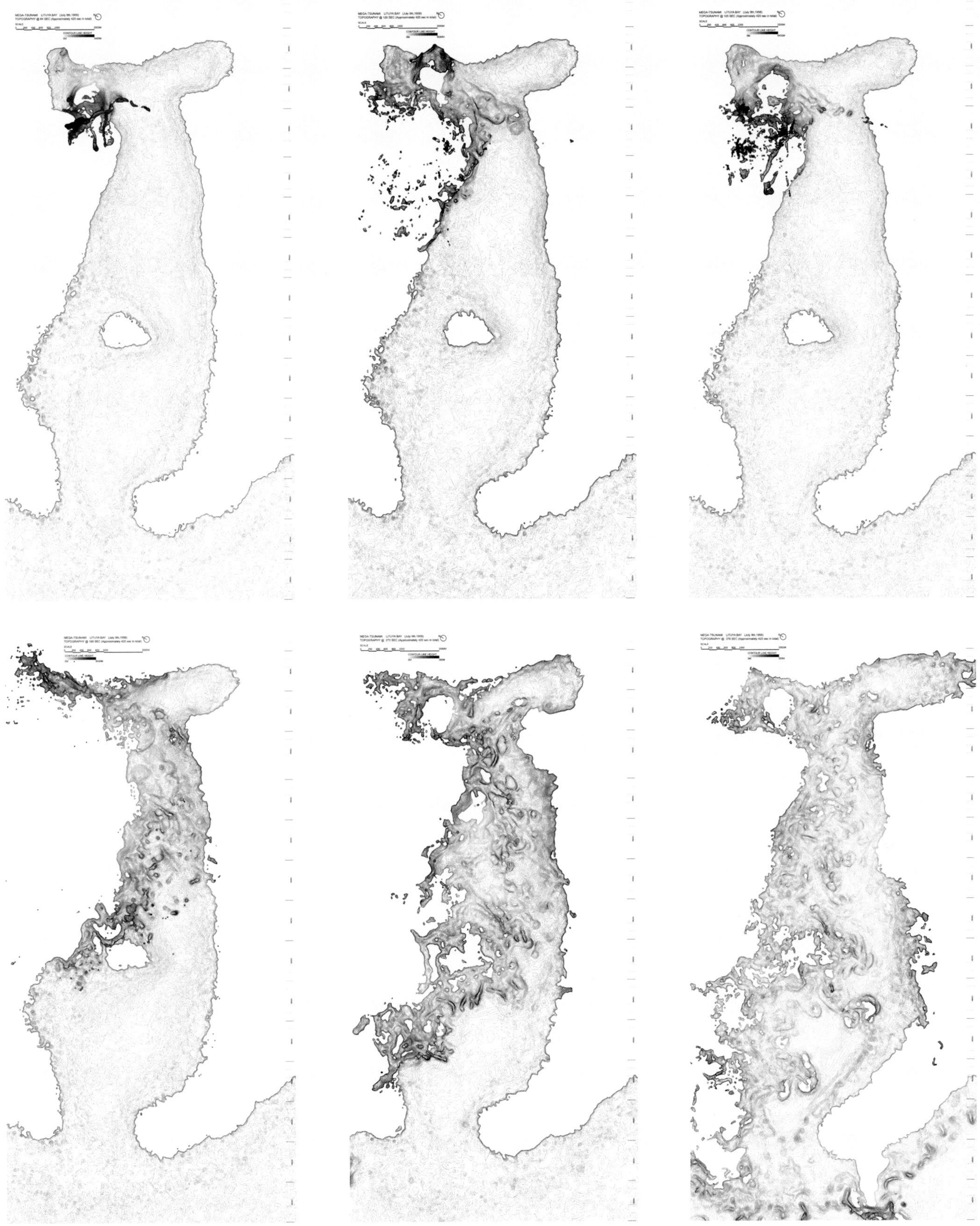

Above: Plan of Lituya Bay Alaska, showing the impact of the megatsunami on the water's surface 126 seconds after the tsunami took place, 189 seconds, 273 seconds, 315 seconds, 357 seconds and 378 seconds, respectively.

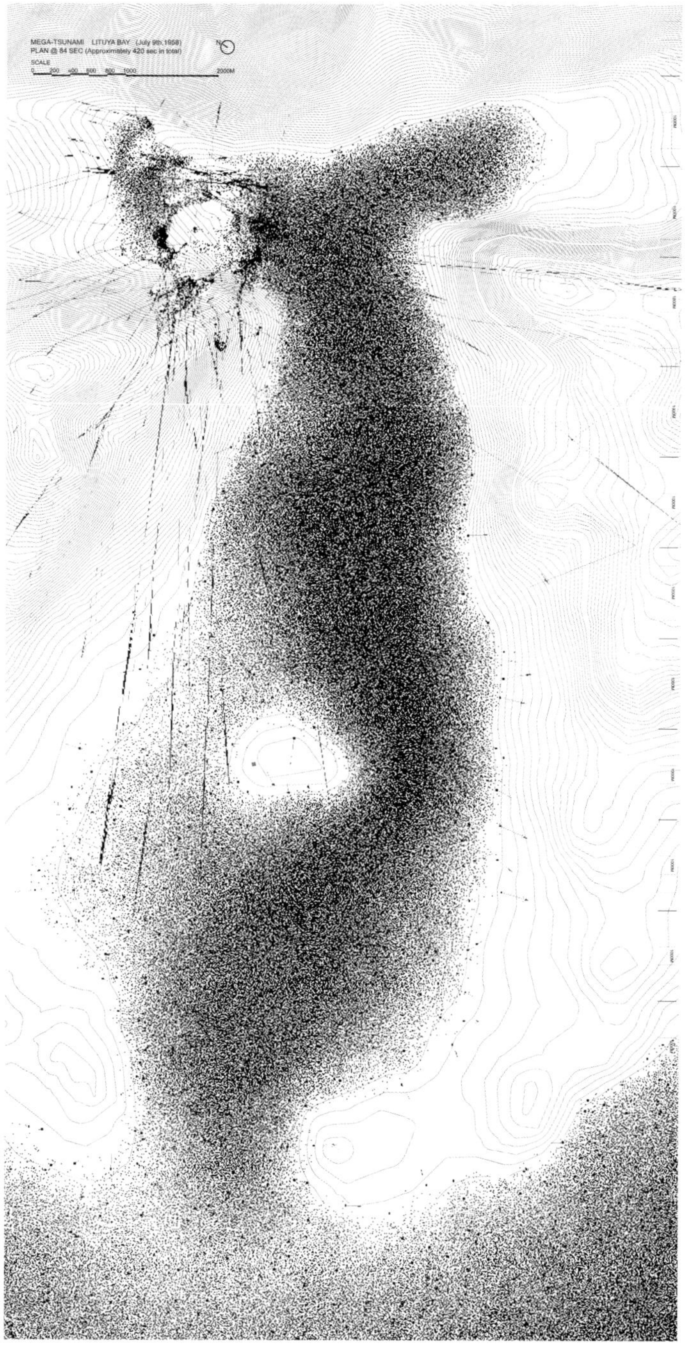

Above left: Plan of Lituya Bay, Alaska showing the impact of the megatsunami on the water's surface 84 seconds after the tsunami took place using point cloud simulation. The vector attached to each point represents its speed.

Above right: Plan of Lituya Bay Alaska showing the impact of the megatsunami on the water surface 105 seconds after the tsunami took place.

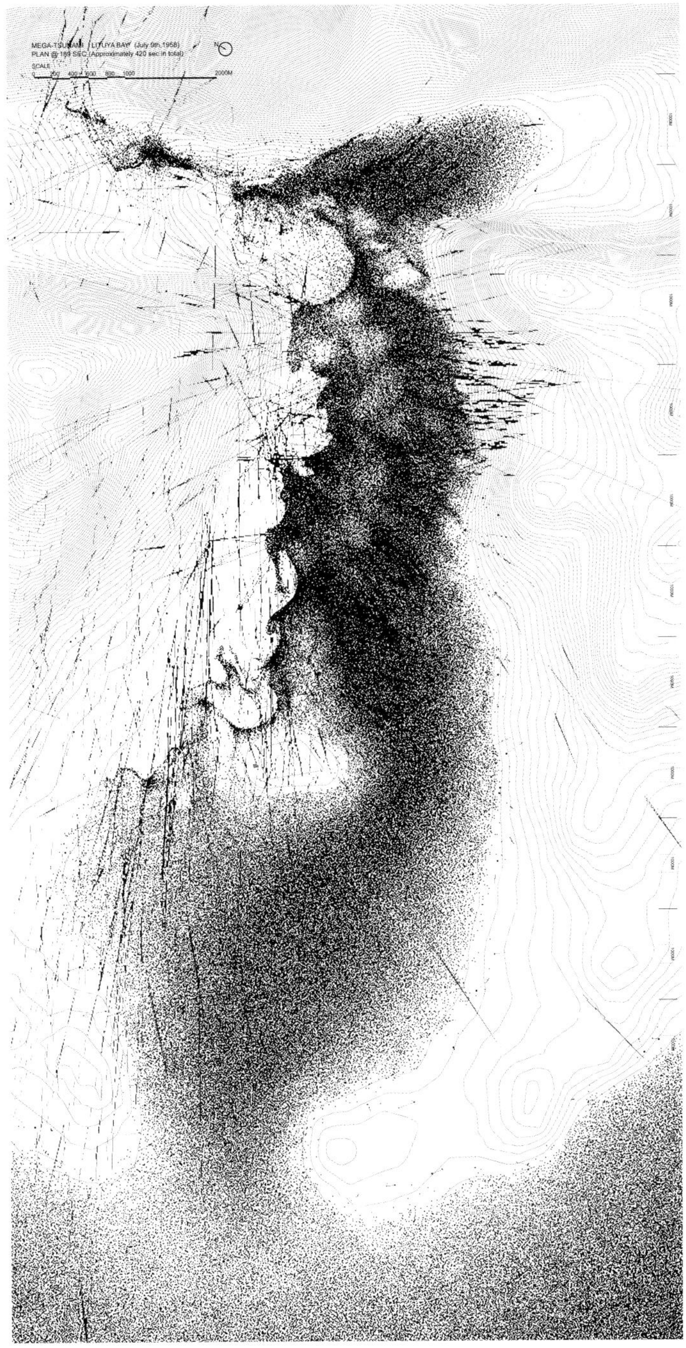

Above left: Plan of Lituya Bay Alaska, showing the impact of the mega tsunami on the water surface 126 seconds after the tsunami took place.

Above right: 189 seconds.

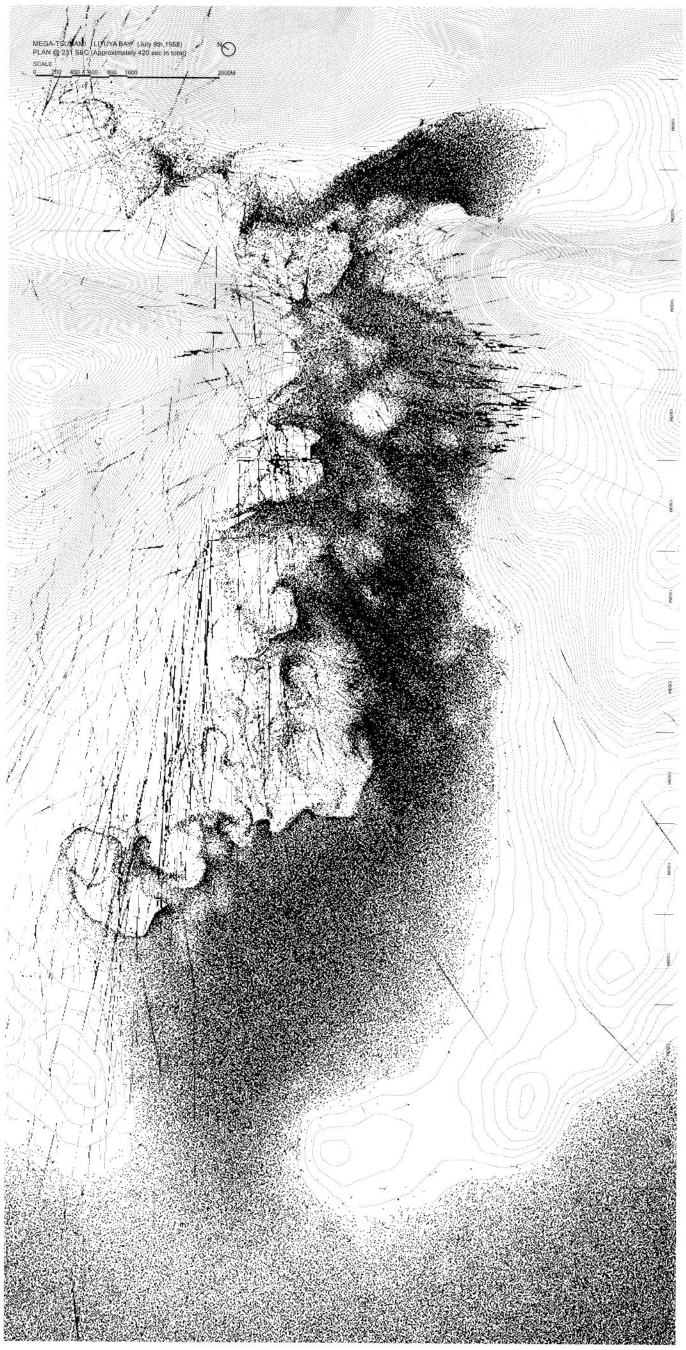

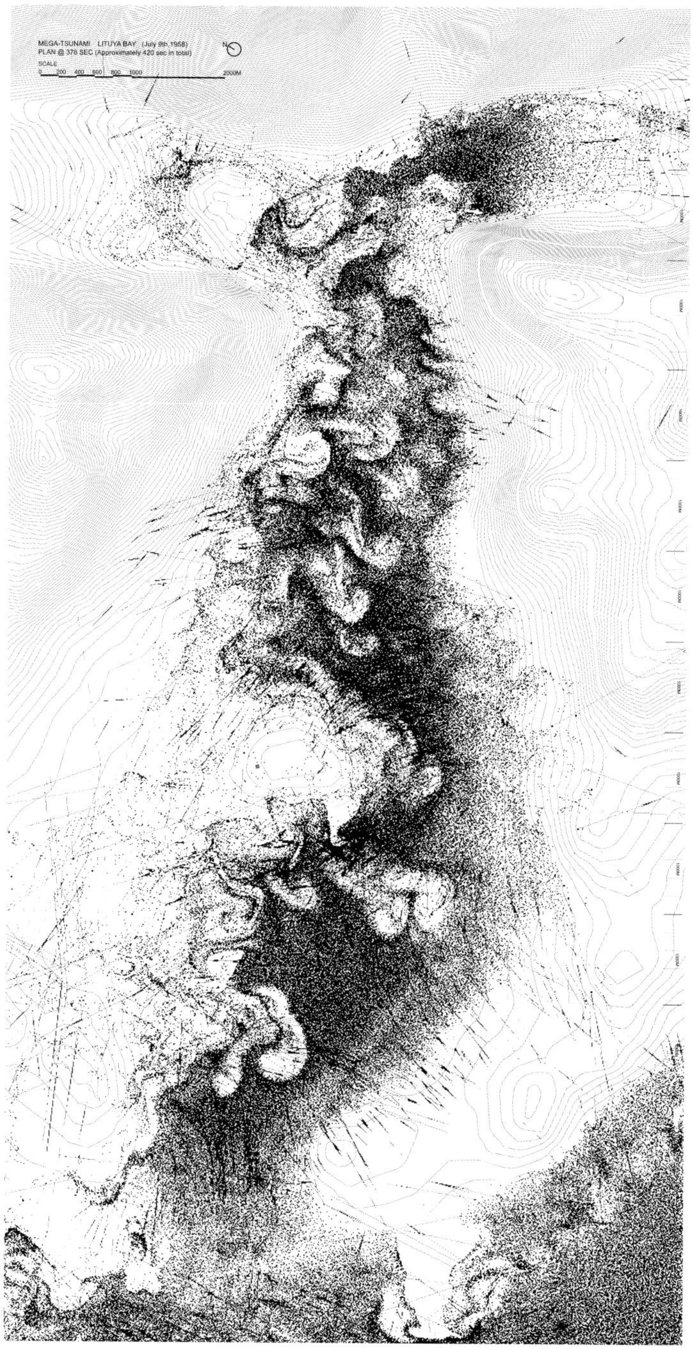

Above left: 273 seconds.

Above right: 315 seconds.

Opposite: Plan of water volume topography of Lituya Bay Alaska 84 seconds after the megatsunami took place.

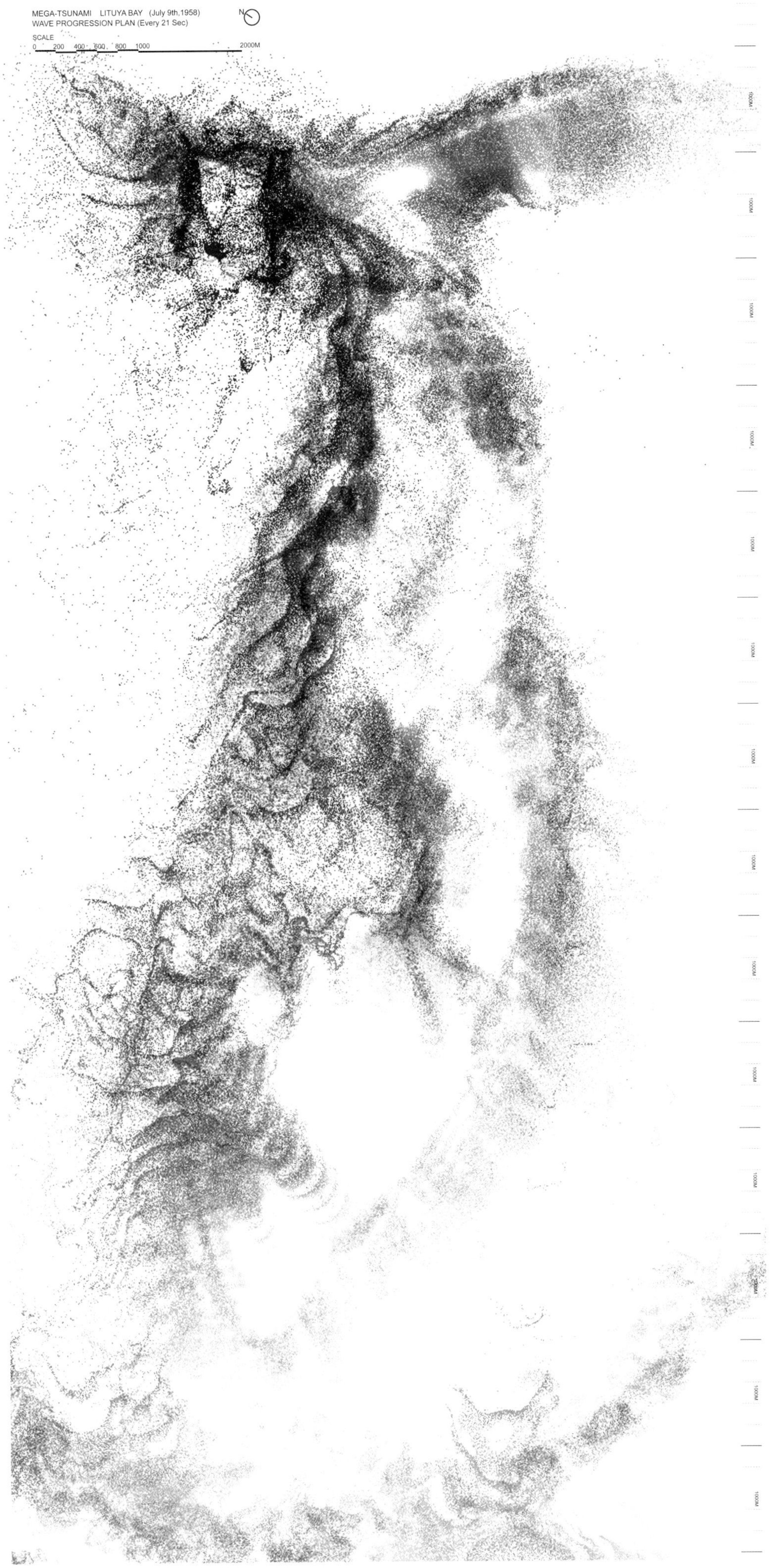
MEGA-TSUNAMI LITUYA BAY (July 9th,1958)
WAVE PROGRESSION PLAN (Every 21 Sec)
SCALE
0 200 400 600 800 1000 2000M
N

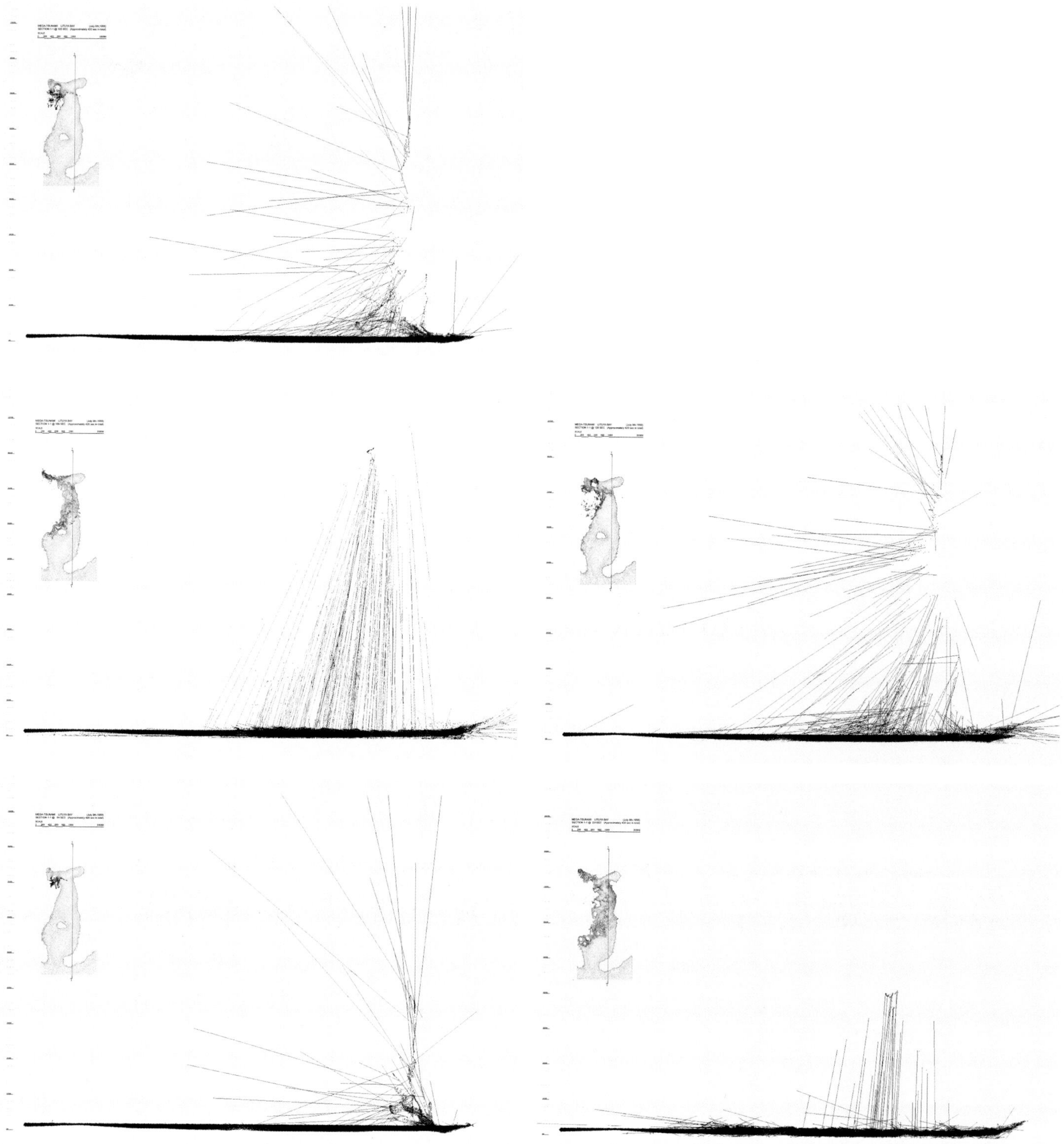

Above: Longitudinal section of Lituya Bay, Alaska showing the impact of the megatsunami on the water surface at 84 seconds after the tsunami took place using point cloud simulation. The vector attached to each point represents its speed.

Top: Model of water volume in the megatsunami's impact area 84 seconds after the tsunami took place.

Bottom: Model of water volume of the megatsunami's impact area 126 seconds after the tsunami took place creating a dramatic rain. (Acrylic)

Manipulated Life Cycles

Bering Strait, Alaska
Melanie Fessel

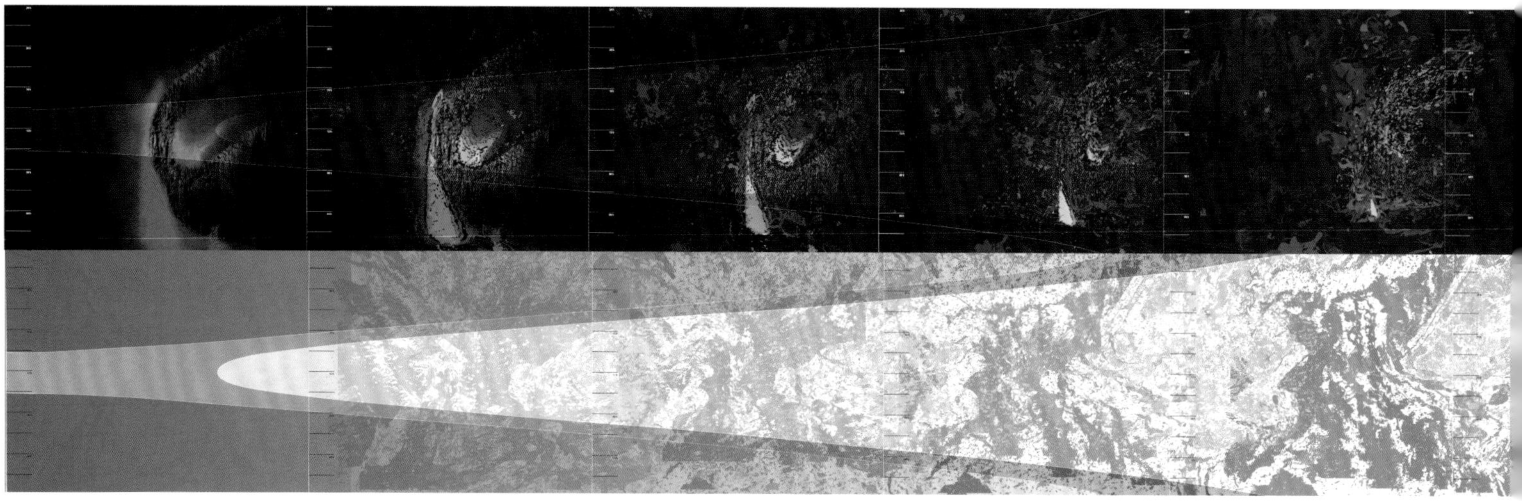

The Bering Strait is where today changes into tomorrow, where the westernmost point of the North American is only 2.4 miles away from the easternmost point of the Asian continent, and where the Arctic and Pacific Oceans meet. Sea ice, which fully covers its landscapes for ten months, has an essential function in keeping the balance of the ecosystem, along with phytoplankton, which accounts for about 90 percent of ocean life. With global warming, the Arctic summer sea ice is rapidly disappearing, affecting the production cycles of phytoplankton and endangering the whole ecological system.

Furthermore, during summer months, the Bering Strait is used as a commercial shipping route by container ships, which largely affect the seasonal sea ice cycles and the bloom season for the phytoplankton. The rapid retreat of the sea ice is affecting the life, habitat, and traditions of the Inuit population as well.

Manipulated Life Cycles envisions a way for local natives to use an interconnected network that empowers them to counteract the accelerating process of environmental change and take control of their homeland through the use of traditional weaving techniques. Vast fishing nets created out of local materials are released in the open ocean. This would provide closure of the Strait through a surface on the upper layer, stopping commercial shipping, while maintaining aquatic migration routes beneath. The net will create a platform for sea ice to return to a natural cycle and permit phytoplankton to maintain their unique form. The feedback loop, created by the intertwining components of the net, invites collaboration with the Inuit to map out a future for the Arctic and our global climate. Their homeland is no longer strategically insignificant or isolated, and we have to recognize that their region is an integral part within our planet's ecosystem with significant influence on our global climate, wildlife, and indigenous groups in the Arctic region.

Top: Lifecycle analysis of seasonal differences. The natural cycle of sea ice is influencing organism patterns. Microorganisms thrive from the water rich in nutrients that are released during the springtime melting of the sea ice. This supports the growth of phytoplankton and forms the basis for organisms higher in the food chain.

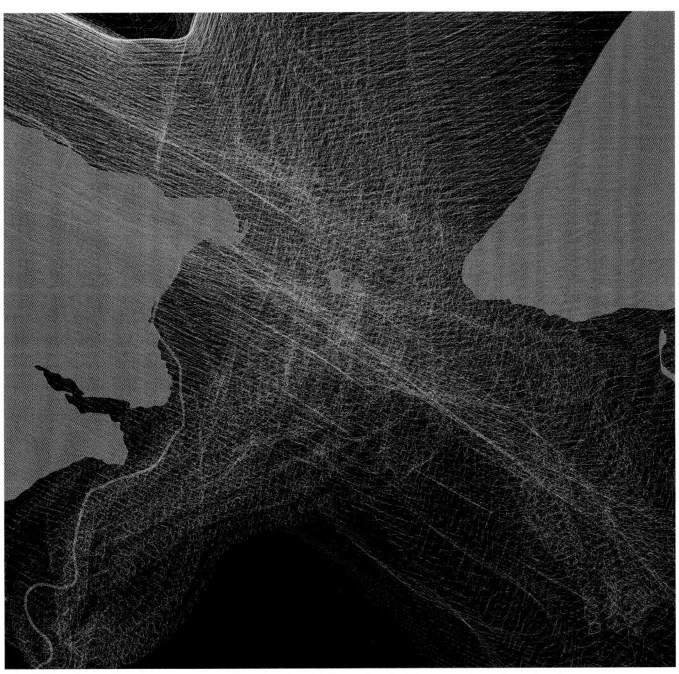

Above left and right: Forces in the Bering Strait are defined by wind patterns, water migration routes, ocean currents, and sea ice migration.

Above: Plan—Winter: sea ice fully covers its landscapes for a solid ten months of the year.

Above: Plan—Summer: permafrost lakes and Inuit woven net systems.

Top: Longitudinal section depicting sea ice. When sea ice freezes not all the salt in the sea water (brine) can be incorporated and falls to the ocean under the ice. This is called brine rejection. Sea ice thus becomes less salty than the saltier underlying water. As the ice melts, it creates a layer of fresher water on the ocean surface, which has all the nutrients essential to the ecosystem, and in particular to phytoplankton.

Bottom: Sectional view of Inuit woven nets that prevent commercial traffic affecting the local ecosystem during summer months, allowing sea ice to recover and thus preserve the natural cycle of microorganisms, which is the basis of the marine food chain and life.

Frozen Flow

Hubbard and Columbia Glaciers, Alaska
Josefina Poroli

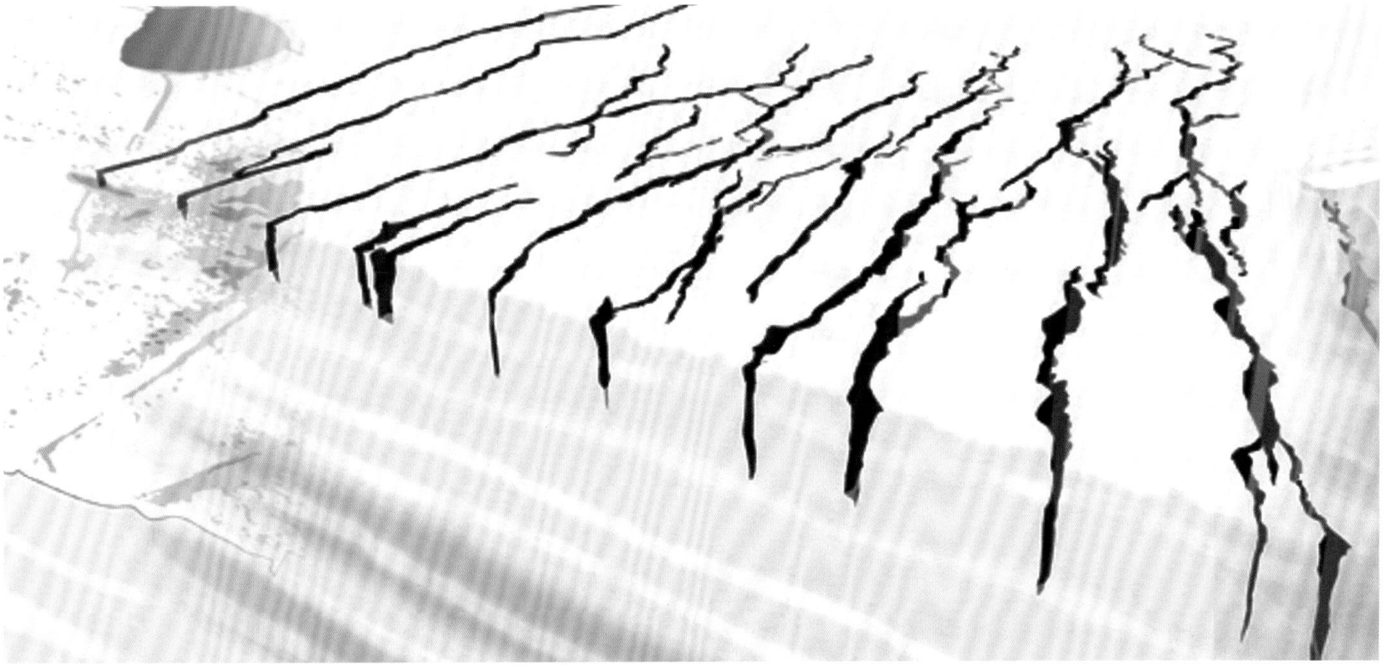

A glacier is a dynamic organism under constant transformation. It is not defined by a moment in time or by the influence of a single force but rather by its complex materiality and external physical forces, including climate change. A glacier emerges from the interaction and exchange of contrasting states of matter: a brittle exterior surface and a fluid interior, volatile snow and compact ice, freezing water and melting ice, slow accumulation and fast ablation, fresh water and salt water. Glaciers advance, retreat, grow or disappear, modifying the landscape and the earth's surface.

The simultaneous study of the Hubbard Glacier (which is advancing) and the nearby Columbia Glacier (which is retreating) shows that in this type of glacier terminus movement is the result of specific dynamic forces rather than climatic effects. It must be acknowledged, however, that there are a few glaciers advancing while most of them are retreating. From small and transitory particles of snow, glacial landscapes emerge at an extraordinary scale. Glaciers are fragile and provisional; they must lose mass in order to grow, reflecting, in turn, our own provisional nature.

Top: Axonometric view of the topography of a section of the glacier reflecting on the surface the plastic behavior of ice deep in the glacier.

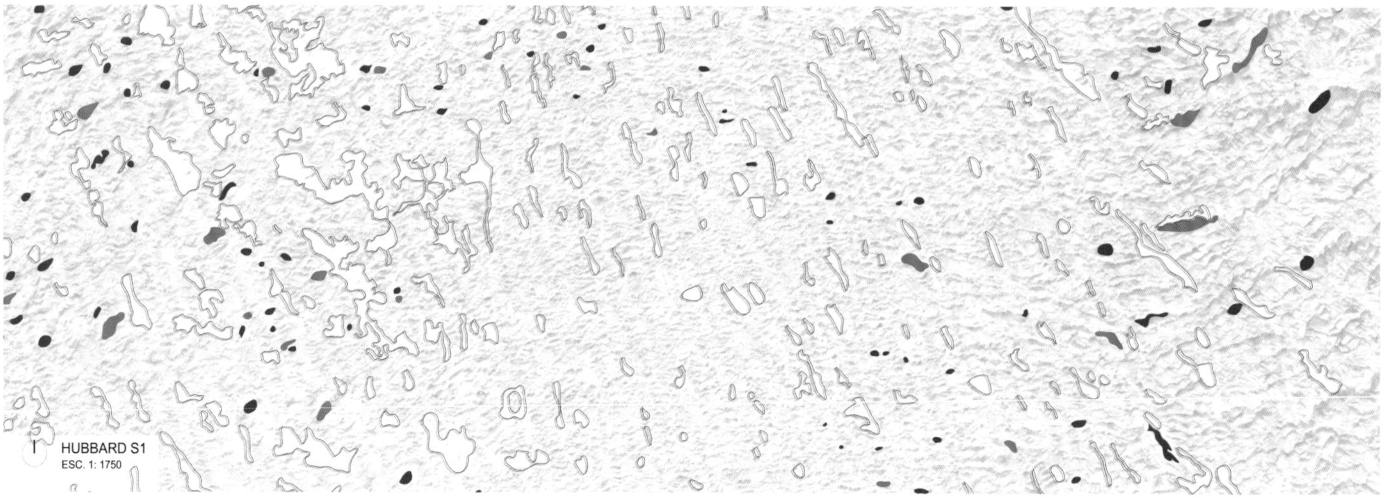

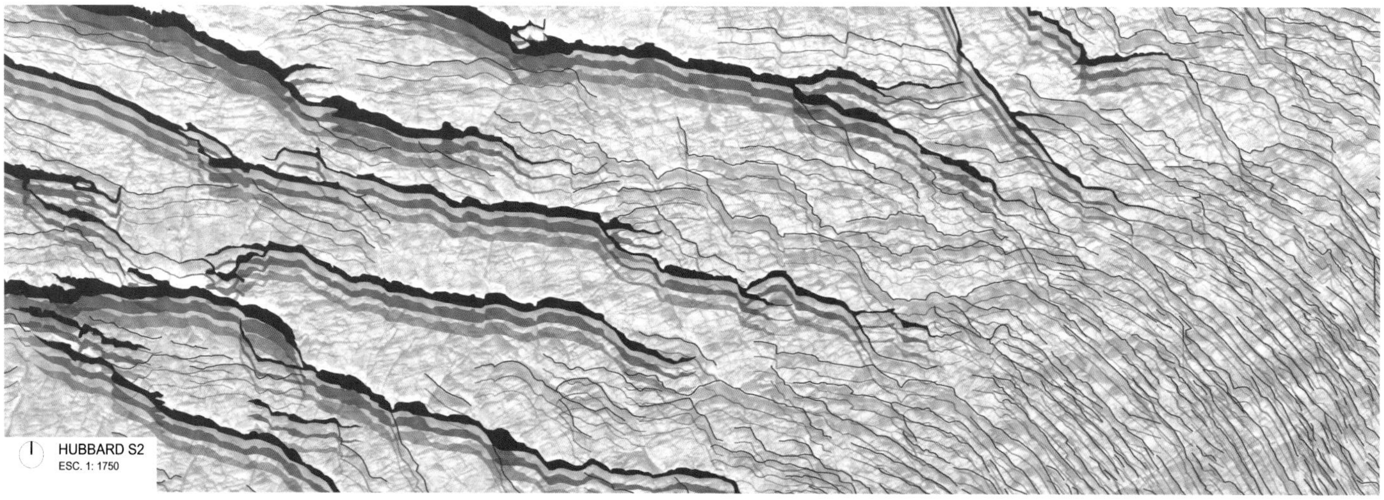

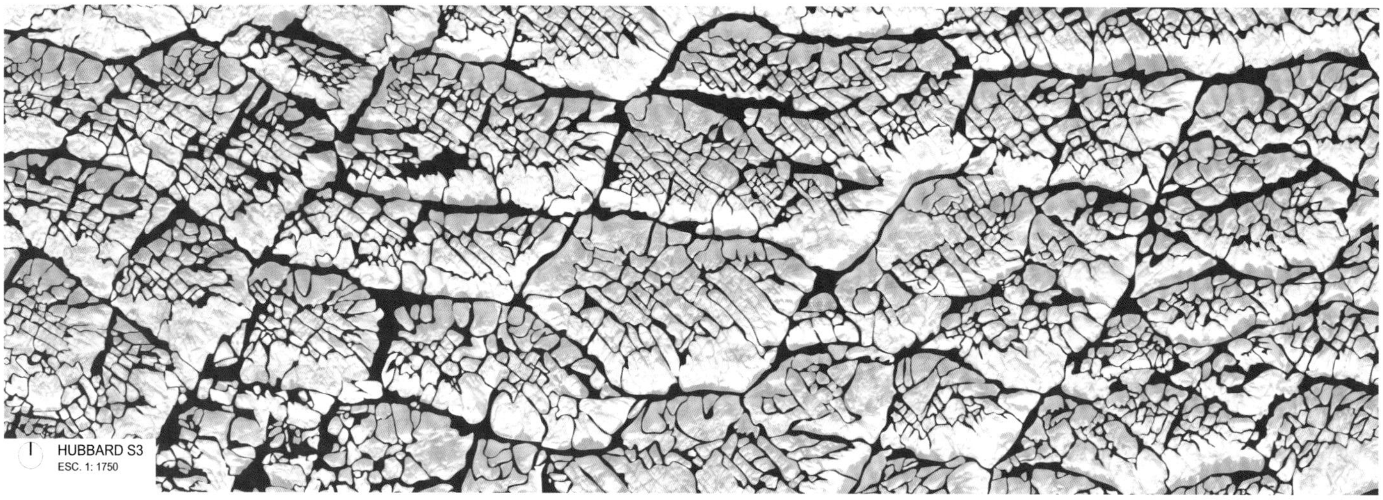

Top: Horizontal section of layers of sedimentary accumulation in the snow zone where snow transforms into granular ice.

Middle: Axonometric section of ablation zone with flowing ice and crevasses.

Bottom: Plan of the glacier at its terminus, where it vanishes into the sea by melting, evaporating, and calving.

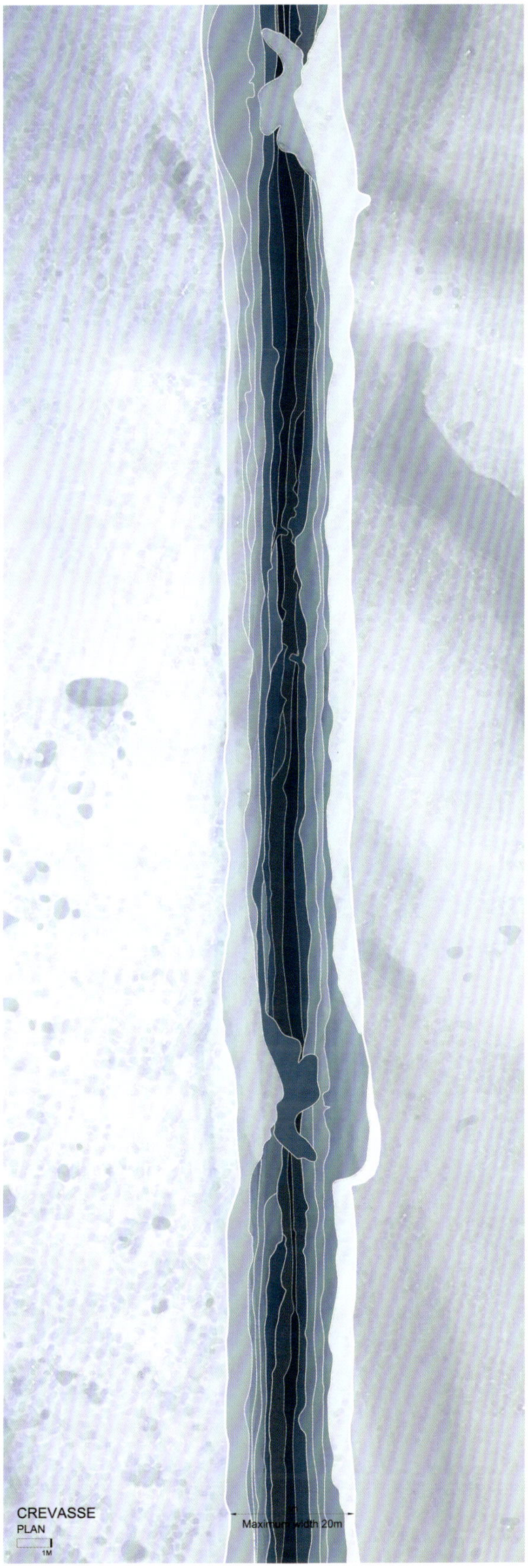

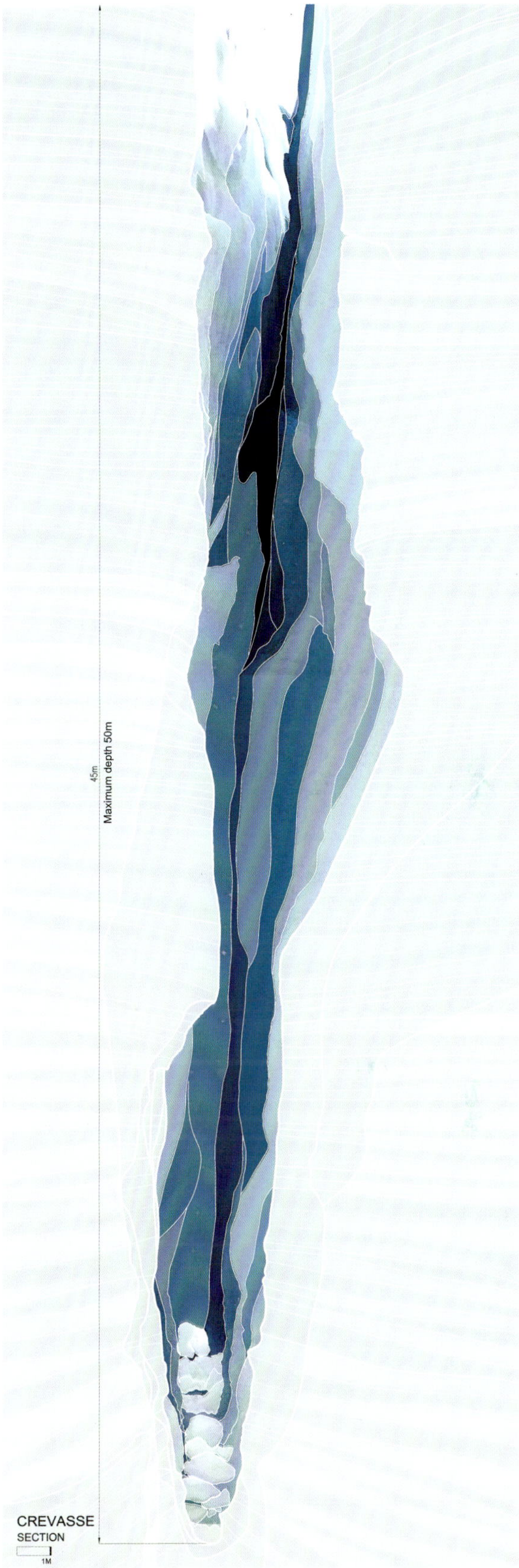

Above left: Crevasse plan: the bright white snow of the surface is a marked contrast to the deep, rich blue inside the glacier.

Above right: Crevasse section: a crevasse can expand up to 45 meters deep and 20 meters wide, up to several hundred meters long and in some cases, 300 meters deep or more.

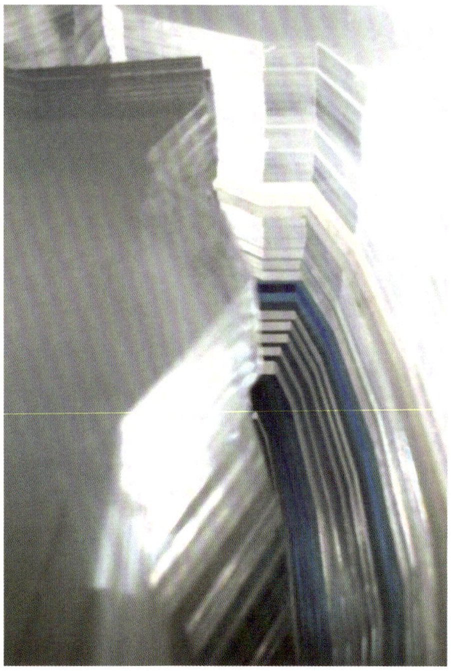

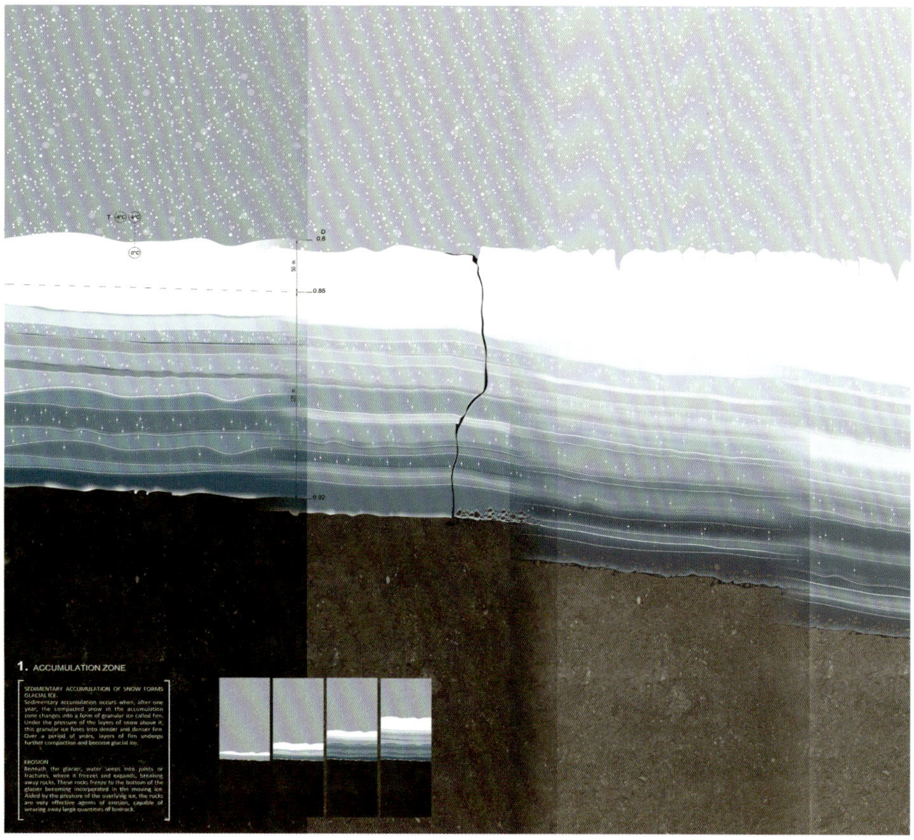

Above: Longitudinal cross sections of the Hubbard Glacier in the advance phase of the tidewater glacier cycle.

Above left: Accumulation Zone: as the glacier grows thicker through snow accumulation on the surface, increased pressure melts the ice within. Melted water that seeps into fractures expand, resulting in the rocks breaking away, eroding the earth's surface.

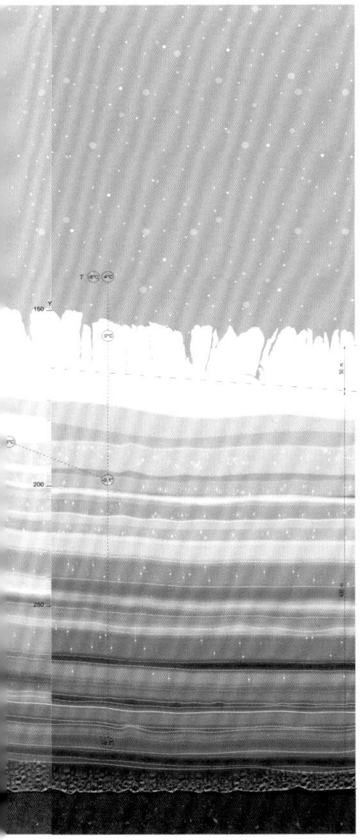

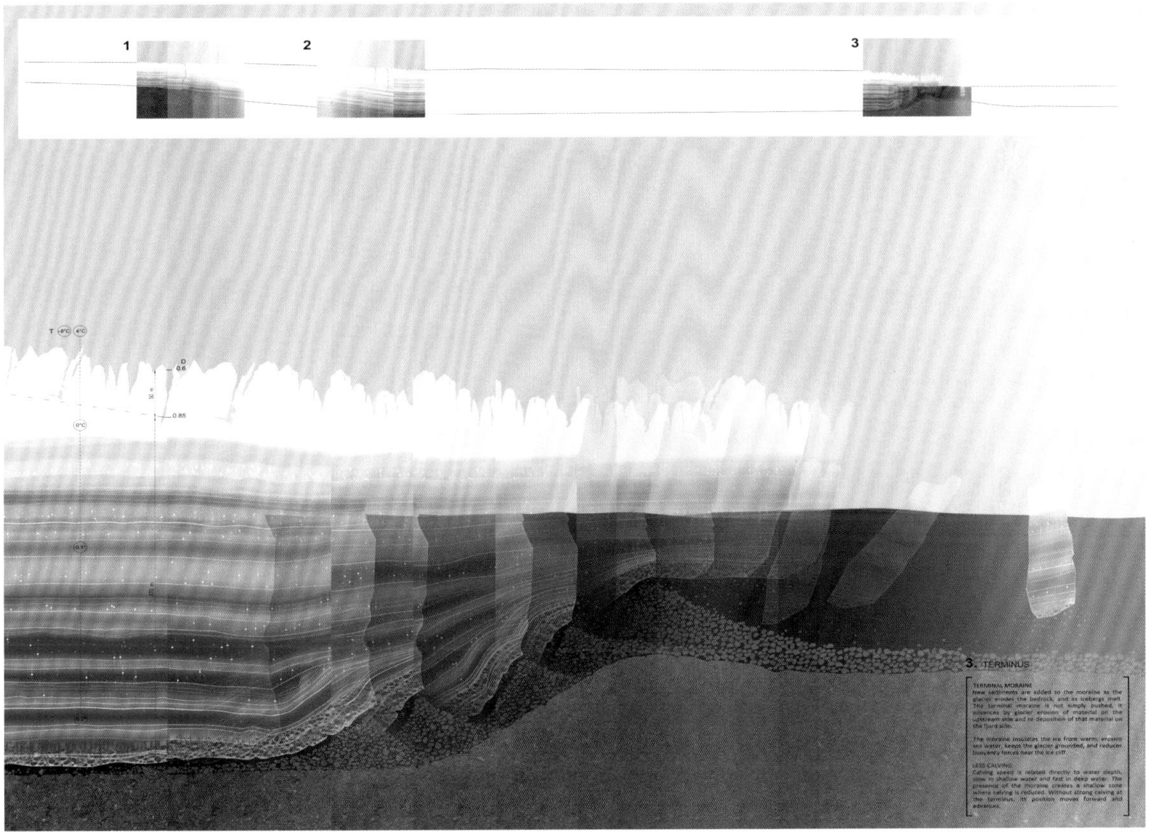

Above middle: Ablation Zone: in this section ice behaves like a brittle solid until its thickness exceeds about 50 meters, when the pressure within the ice causes plastic flow. As ice has a much higher viscosity than liquid water, the flow of the glacier is laminar and horizontal, transporting sediment.

Above right: Terminus: the end of a glacier at any given point in time. At the terminus, ancient ice leaves the system. A terminal moraine advances by glacier erosion of material on the upstream side and re-deposition of that material on the fjord side.

Transformative Materiality

Bering Glacier, Alaska
Jonathan Heckert

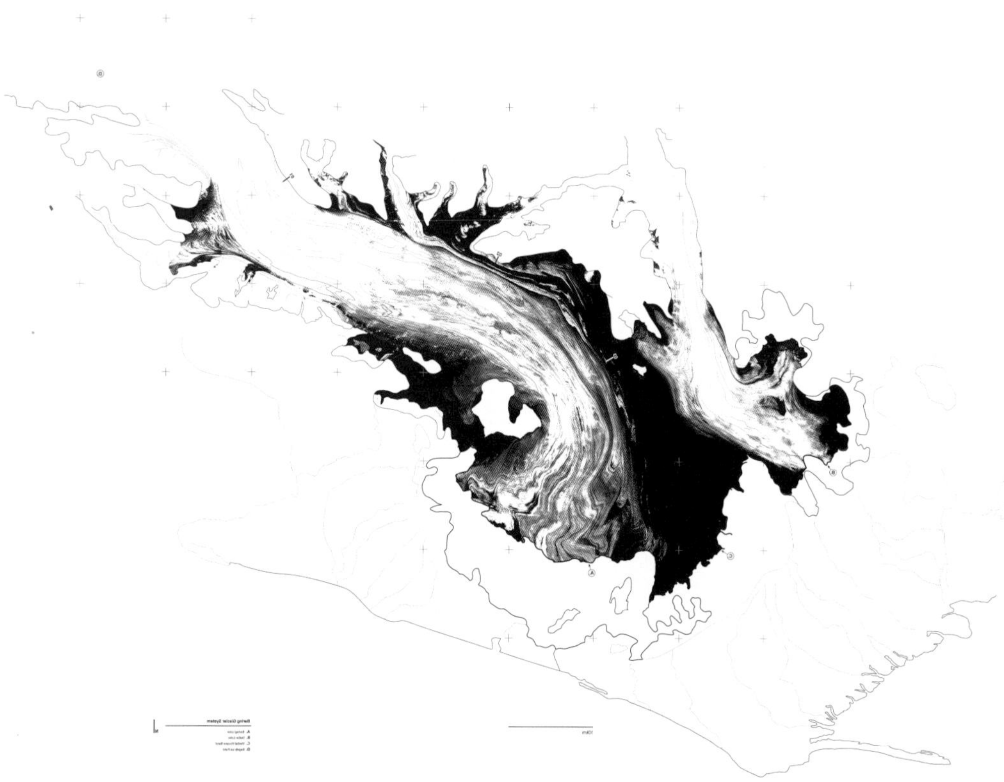

The 30,000-year-old Bering Glacier is located on the south central Alaskan coastline bordering the Gulf of Alaska. A study of the Bering Glacier offers an investigation of a landscape in continuous transformation, formed and re-formed under the shifting weight and pressure of physical material.

With an area of 5,200 square km and a total length of 190 km, it is the longest temperate surging glacier in the world. The Bering Glacier system is also located within an active environmental zone which includes a major subductive fault line and the Chucukula and St. Elias mountain ranges, which elevate from sea level to over 5,000 feet. In retreat, the glacier has had six major surges in the last 100 years. The 1993-95 surge totaled about 10 km from the advancement to final retreat location. The initial and most aggressive part of the surge displaced the ice nearly 100 m a day.

Duration, time, and scale are critically important to understanding the complex interactions that regulate and reform the site. Shifts between ice and water and parallel tensions between surface and subsurface movement are generated by the deformations of ice undergoing both plastic and elastic transformations. Sub-surface topography causes the deflection of flowing ice toward the surface of the glacier. Coupled with plastic to elastic divergence and the melting of ice into water, this deflection creates a site of continual motion and change. The Bering Glacier system displaces 1.3 gigatons of fresh water into the Gulf of Alaska every year. As the melt rate increases along with the upper limits of the ablation line, this number will only continue to increase.

Top: Plastic Bodies: Bering Glacial System seen on an area 50 km long.

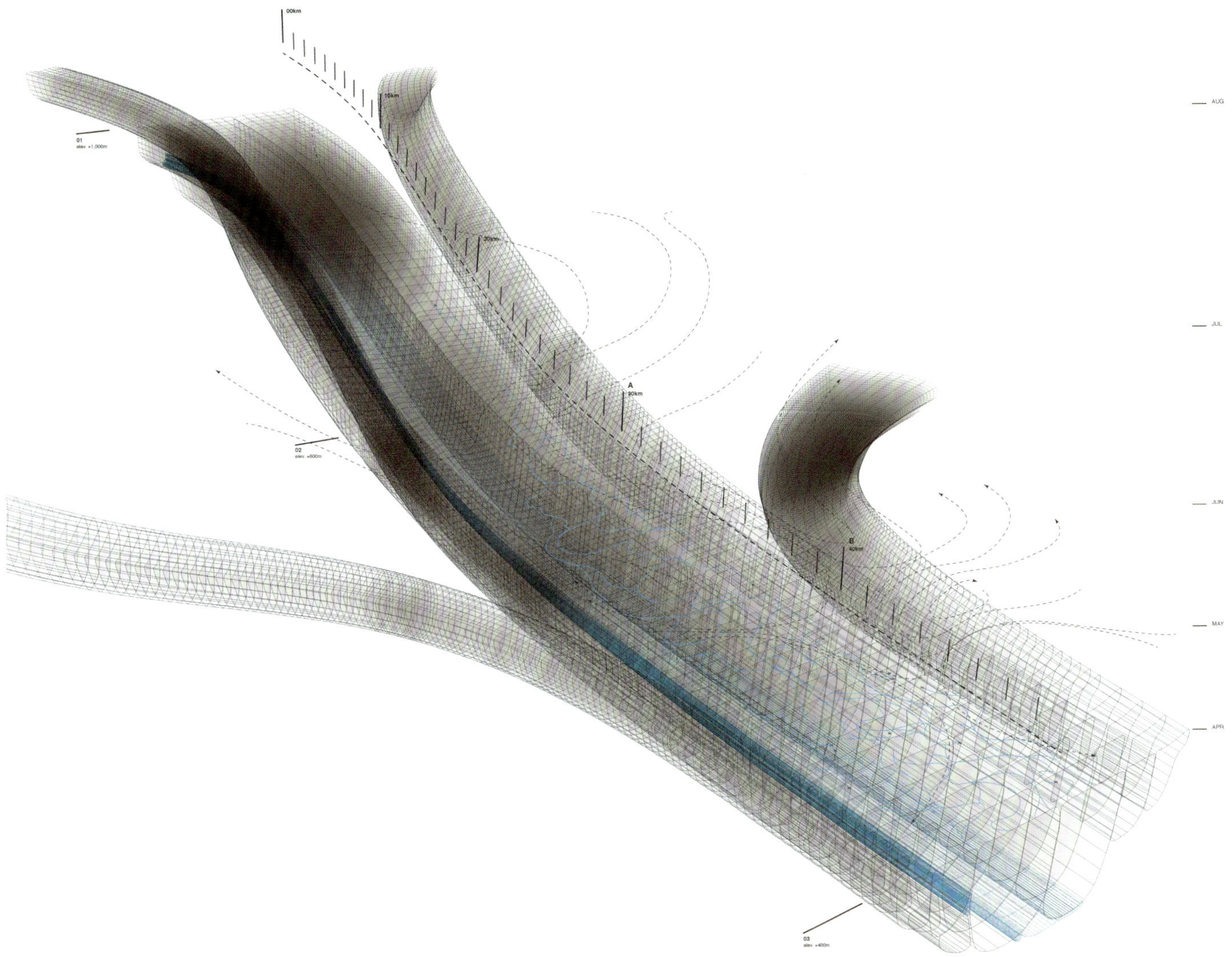

Above: Axonometric diagram of Covalent States-Bodies in Motion: Ablation Zone & Seasonal Flow Rates. Length: 30 km.

The fluidity of the ice at deeper sections alters the surface conditions of the glacier, breaking and splitting to form deep crevasses. These crevasses collect and distribute water along and through the glacial system until it reaches the terminus and eventually the Gulf of Alaska.

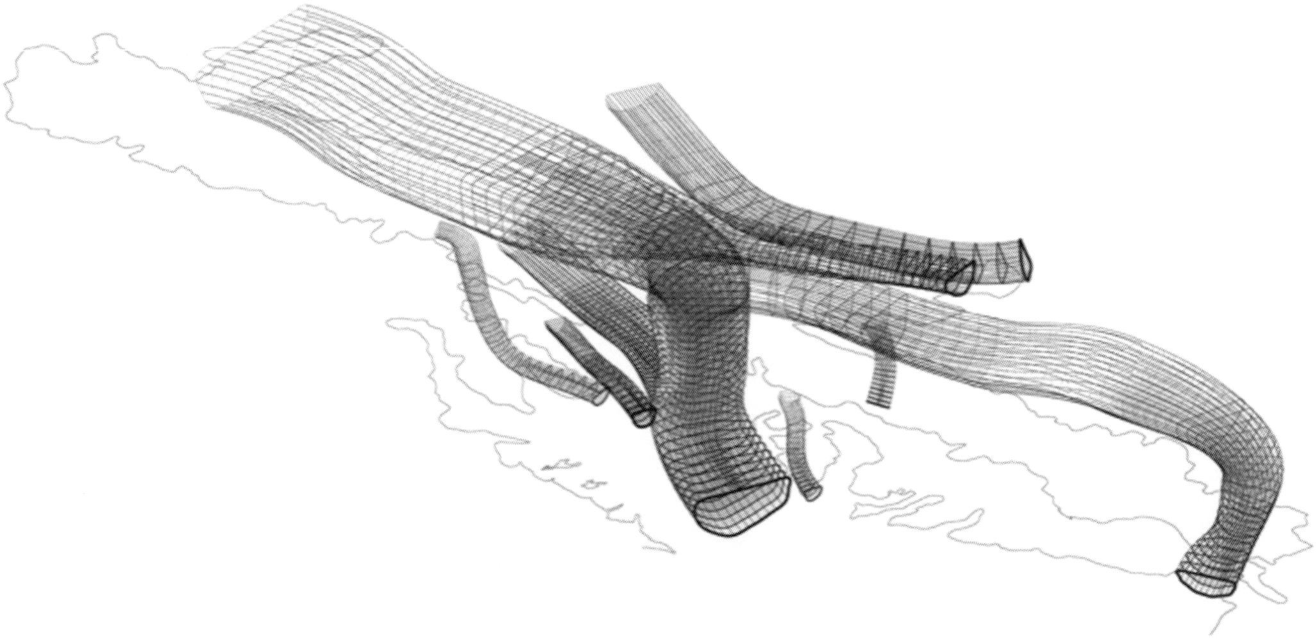

Above left and right: Diagrams reflecting the glacier's movement spatially. The time and speed as well as the mass of the displacement are variables that depend on climatic and topographic conditions, internal ice deformation and the interaction between the gravitational force driving the ice downward and the friction with its bed and edges. The glacier slides over the bed, enabled by the meltwater acting as a lubricant as well as the deformation of subglacial sediments.

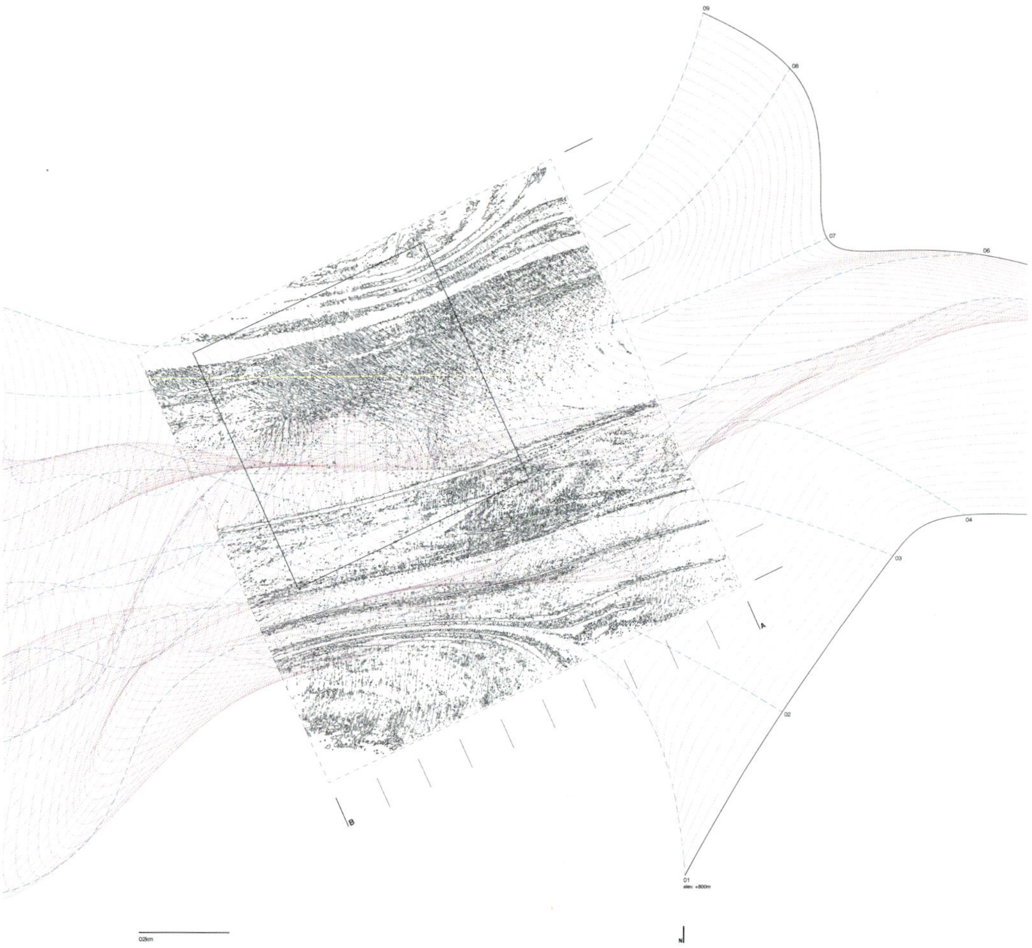

09
08
07
06
04
03
A
02
B
01
elev. +800m
02km
N

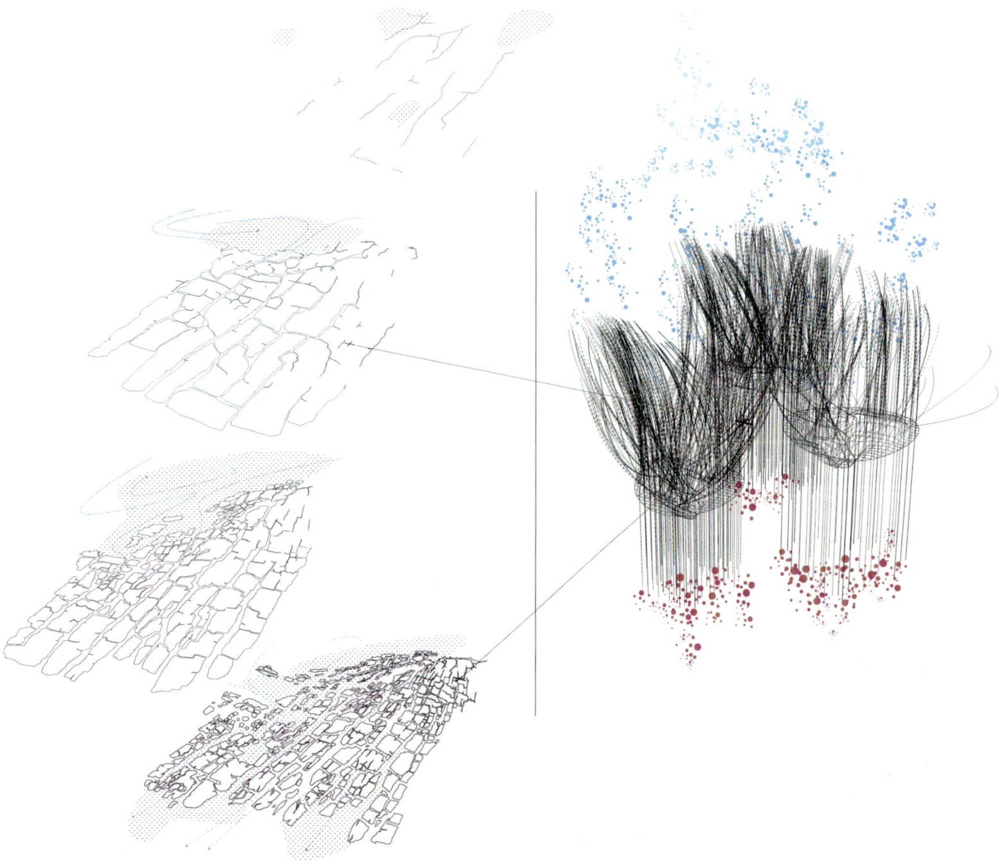

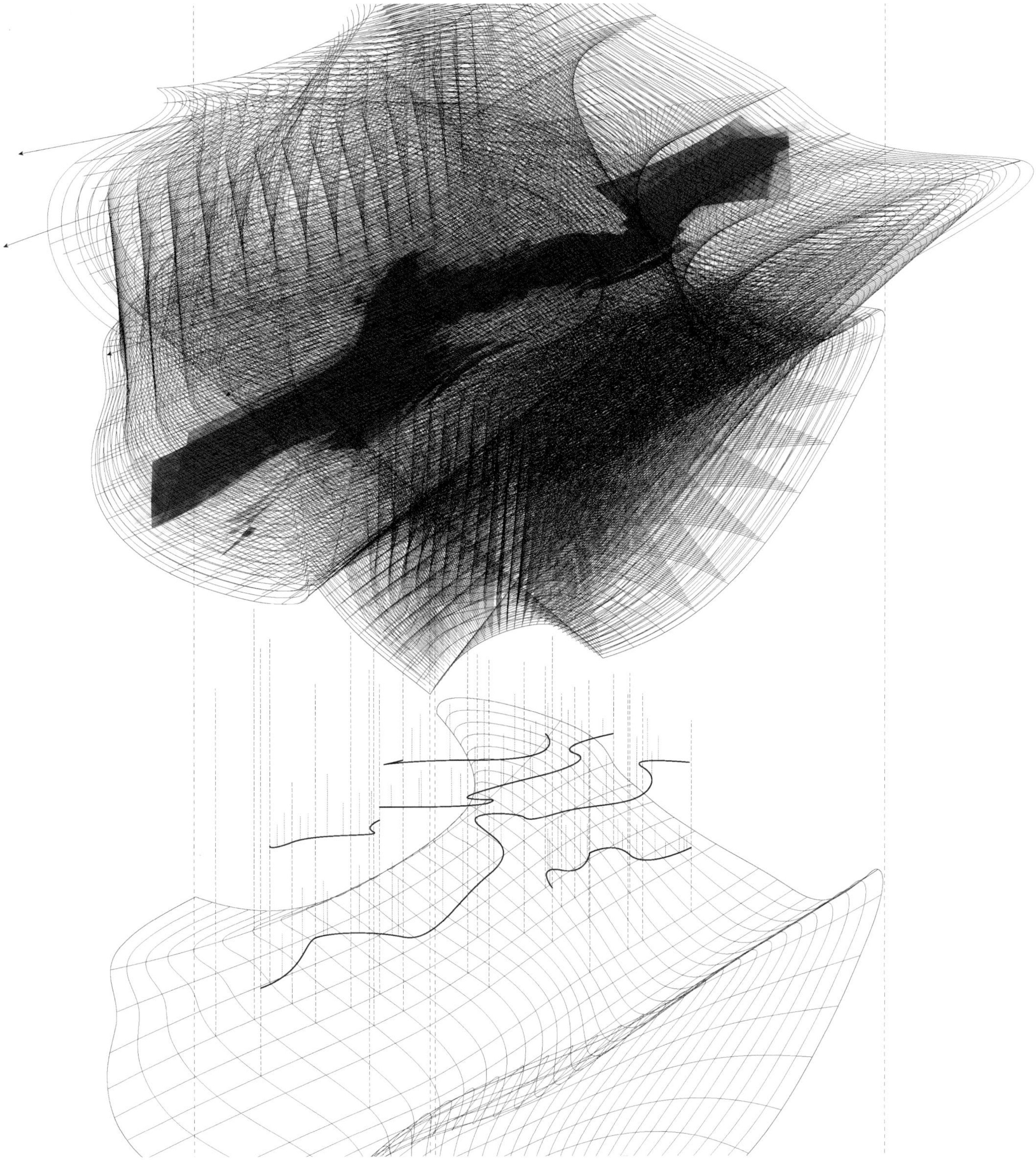

Opposite top and bottom: Shifting Ground: Surface pattern & volumetric displacement through ablation zone over an area of 10 square km. The ablation zone is where the material shift in the glacier is most expressive but is also sufficiently stable for scientific study.

Liminal Exchange: Ad-Hoc Networks (1 square km). Single individual "energy collectors" are placed along the ablation line of the glacier in groups. As the ice surges, or melts into water, the collectors move. At each point of transformation, energy is released from the material into the collectors for storage.

Above: Mass-Fluctuation: Surface Translation-Hydrologic Depressurization-(Re)Graft. Superimposed on an area of 5 square km. Axonometric view of the three layers involved in the phenomenon.

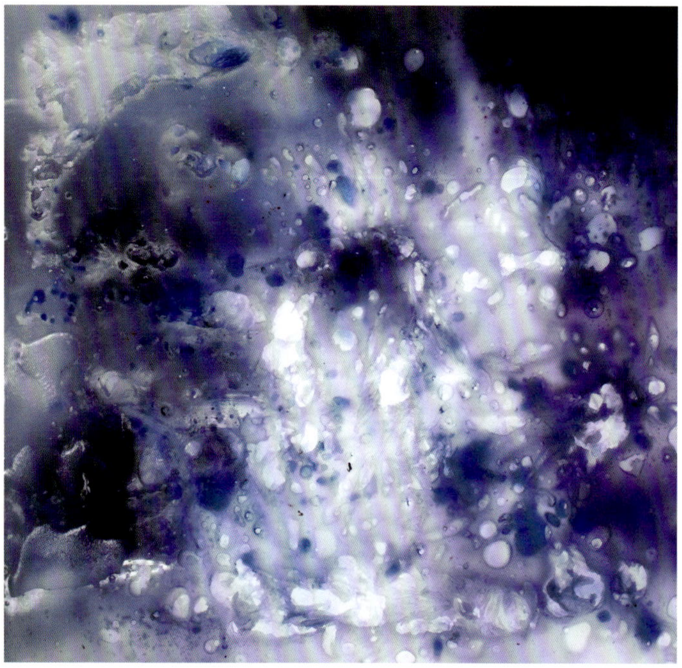

Top and left: Two Protectants: Plastic Bodies: The collectors are free to move as the glacier moves, congregating into areas of the highest potential energy within the glacial system. Once the ice melts, the collector moves down the glacier, absorbing energy along its path. The collectors transcribe the evolution of the landscape, remapping the glacial territory.

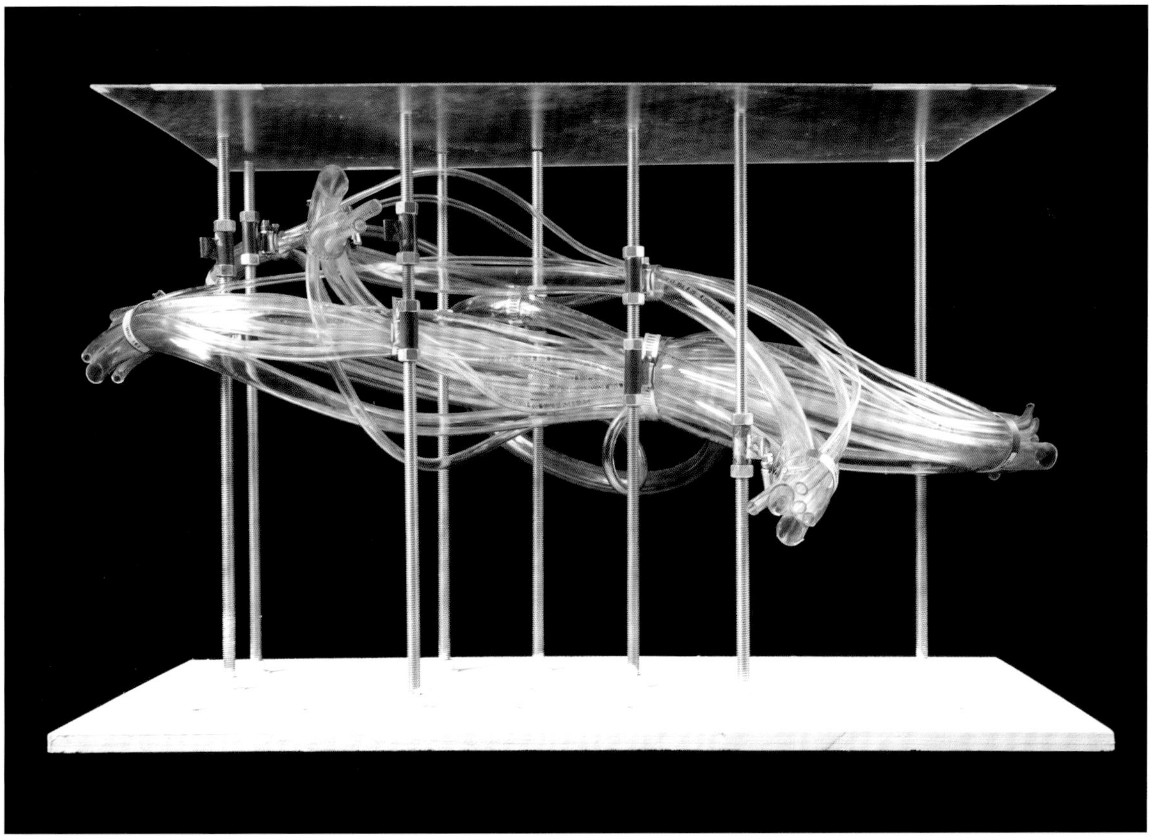

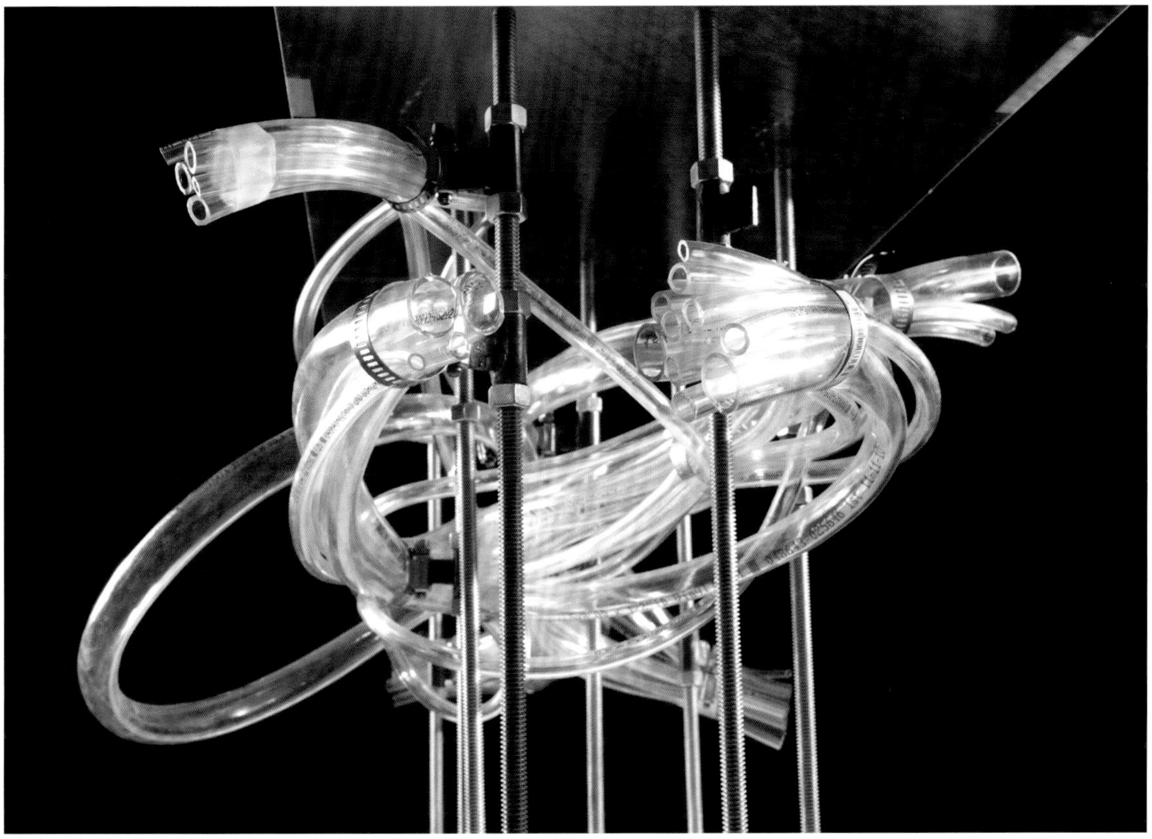

Top and bottom: Models showing glacial flow forces.
Hydrologic field analysis.

[Perma]Frost Landscape

Northern Alaska Currents
Seongmo Ahn

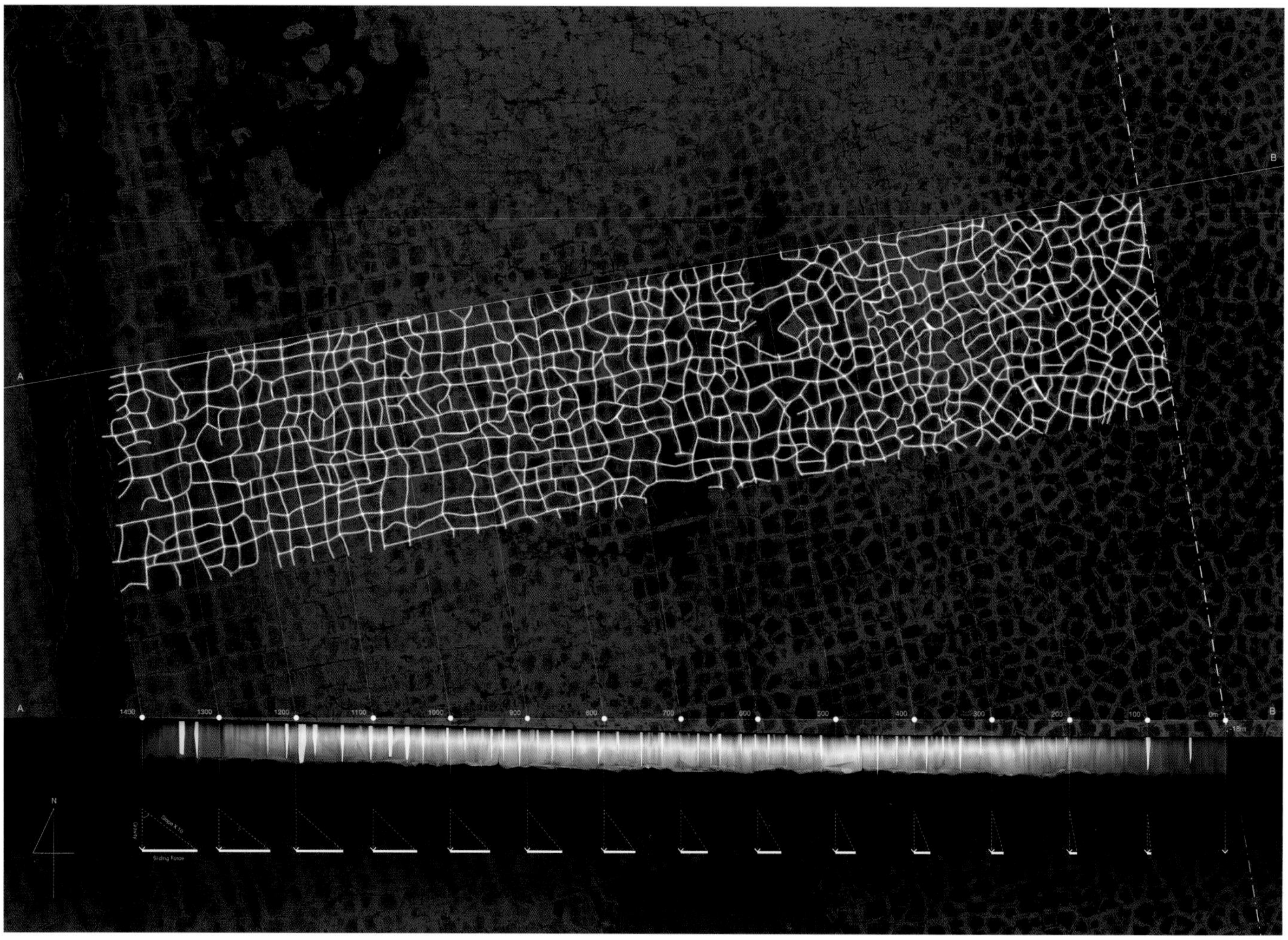

This project focuses on the permafrost covering a territory 20,000 square miles up to 2,256 feet deep on the North Slope of Alaska, which took its current form during the Quaternary period (about 775,000 years ago), revealing the morphological processes that formed the ice architecture beneath the Earth's surface, which in turn forms the cryonic soil or permafrost. These processes operate in a series of spatiotemporal scales, ranging from the scale of a molecule to that of the universe.

Seasonal weather changes and transformations create the specific structural systems that characterize permafrost. As the ground contracts due to the severe cold weather of the long Alaskan winter, it leaves polygonal cracks on the snow-covered surface of the earth. As the snow melts during the summer months, water permeates these cracks, but in winter, the water freezes again and expands. The recurring seasonal cycle of freezing and thawing produces permanent vibrations in the ice and water which result in the generation of a deep network of ice wedges. These ice wedges in turn create small ponds which merge and develop into thermostatic lakes, producing a unique landscape characterized by thousands of oval lakes.

When the lower limit of the permafrost surpasses 0°C, confined lake water begins to drain. The insulation provided by the lake is thus eliminated, and with exposure to the cold, the permafrost begins to freeze and harden, beginning a new cycle. Due to increasing pressure under the drained lake, water molecules migrate toward the center and generate a pingo, or ice volcano, with a pure water ice core.

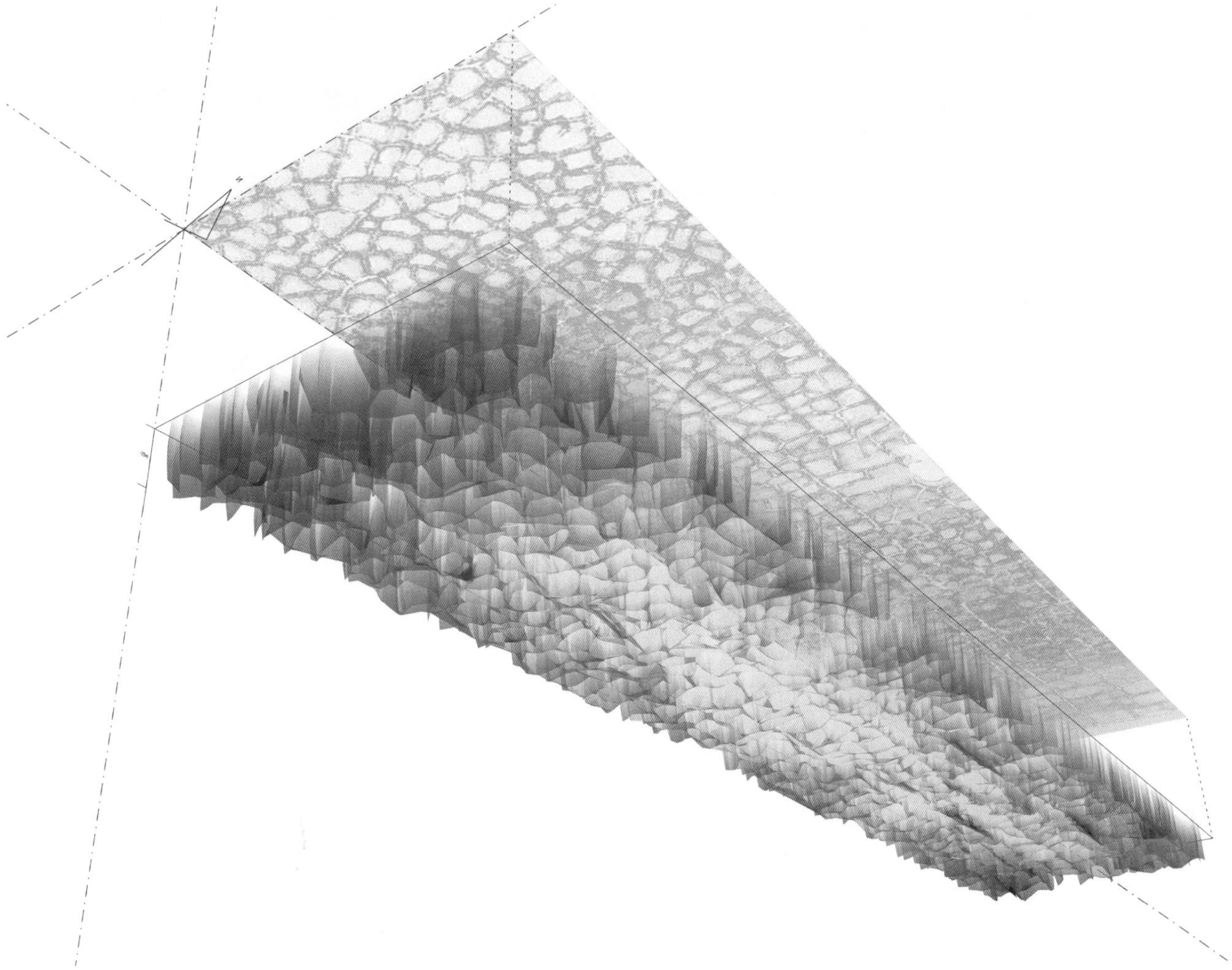

Opposite: Plan and section of network formation. Time and topographic configuration shape the complex ice networks. Gravity shapes the patterns on steep slopes, while, on flat ground, regular patterns gradually become irregular as more cracks develop.

Top: Axonometric view of the ice landscape as seen from below. Exposed ice wedges are just a small part of huge ice networks. Dormant complex ice networks lie below the earth's surface. This drawing shows the speculative architecture of a transparent ice void underground.

Bottom: Permafrost section from the surface to its lowest point, where the geothermal temperature is above freezing.

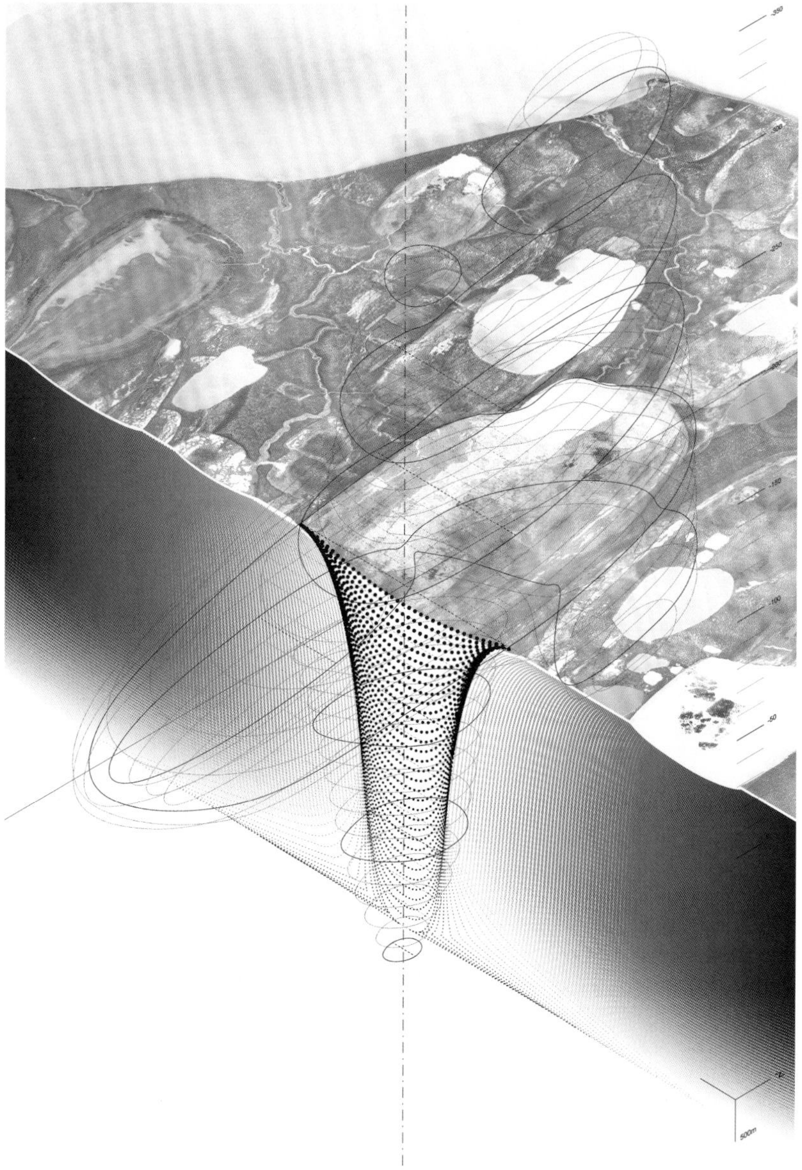

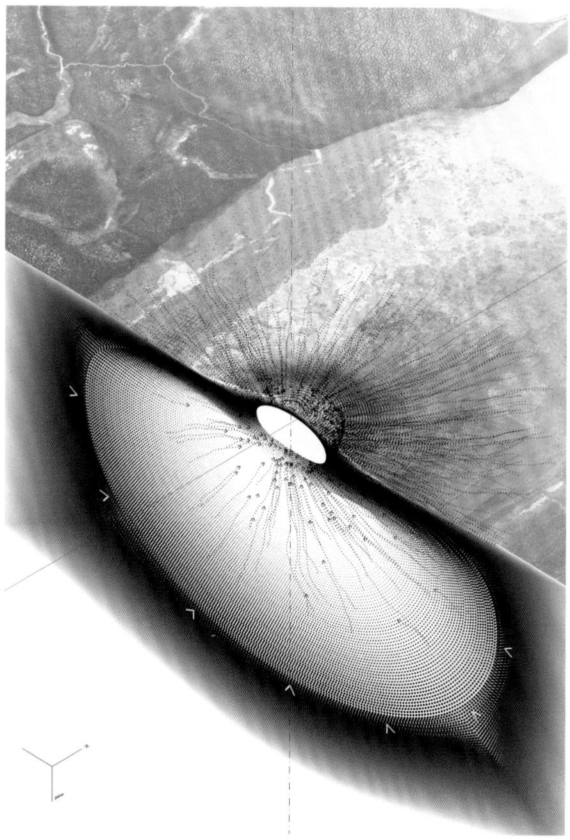

Top left: Sectional Axonometric of lake drainage. When the lake is created, it insulates the ground below. When the permafrost thaws to the base limit temperature, the lake water is drained all at once.

Top right: Sectional axonometric of a pingo, showing a drained lake as permafrost begins to develop toward the center of the lake. A pure ice core pushes the ground up, creating an ice volcano.

Opposite: Axonometric view of lake transformations and their traces on the North Slope of Alaska. Oval shaped lakes result from directional wind.

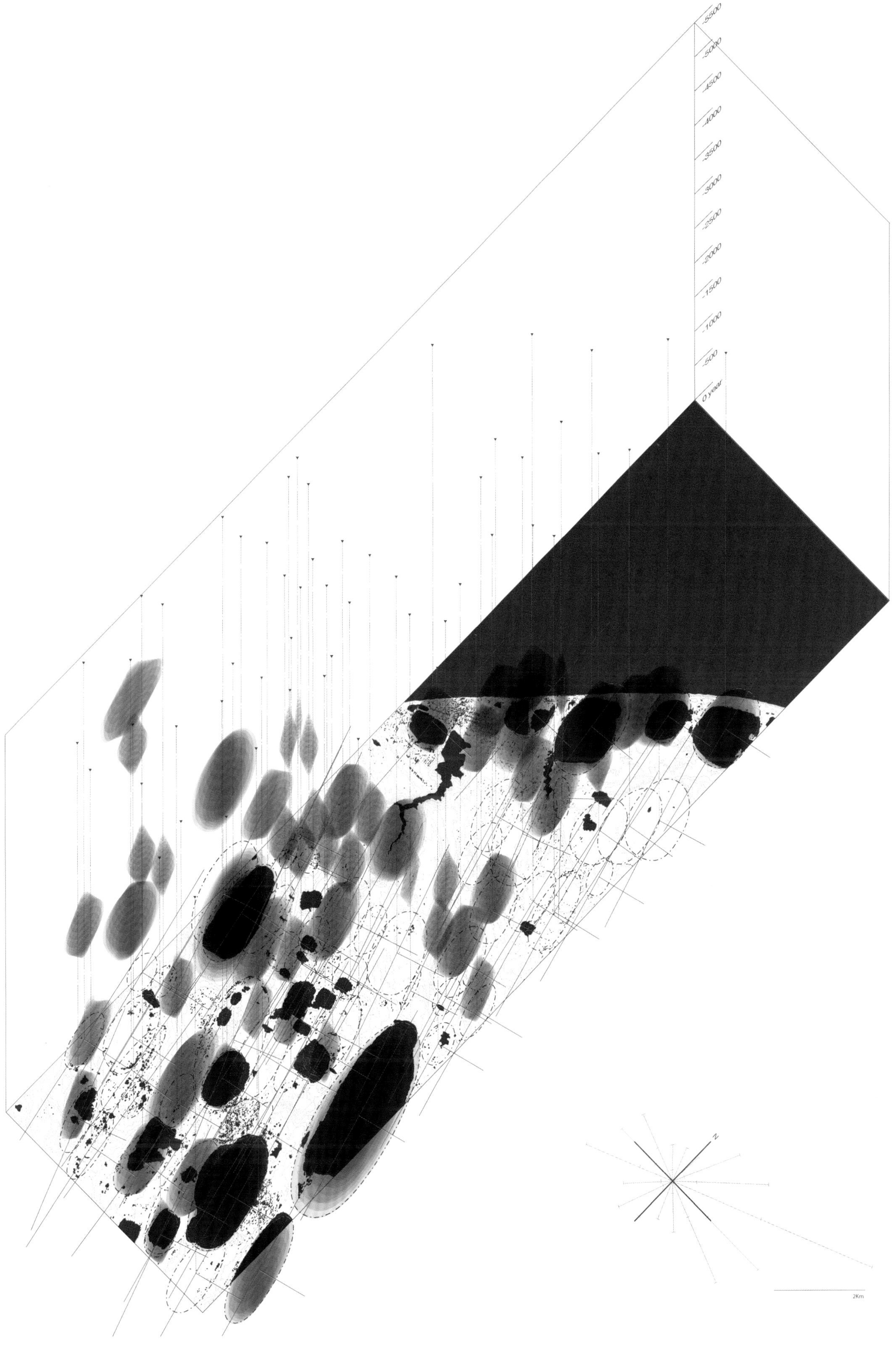
-5500
-5000
-4500
-4000
-3500
-3000
-2500
-2000
-1500
-1000
-500
0 year
N
2Km

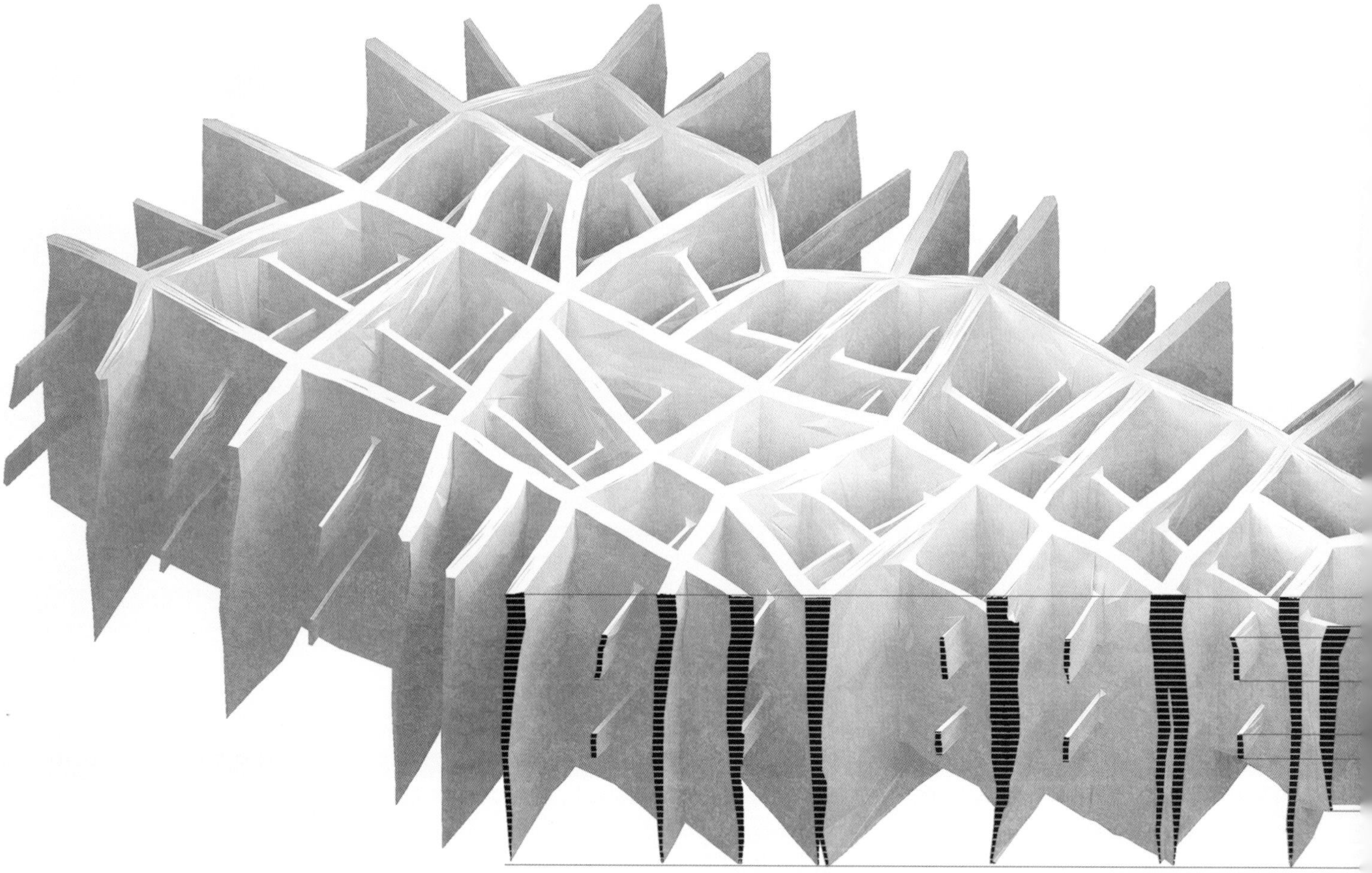

Top: Ice model experiment.

Bottom: Axonometric view of permafrost ice structure. This structure is formed by the seasonal cycle of soil cracking in winter and ice melting in summer, generating water that permeates these cracks and then refreezes, producing an even larger crack.

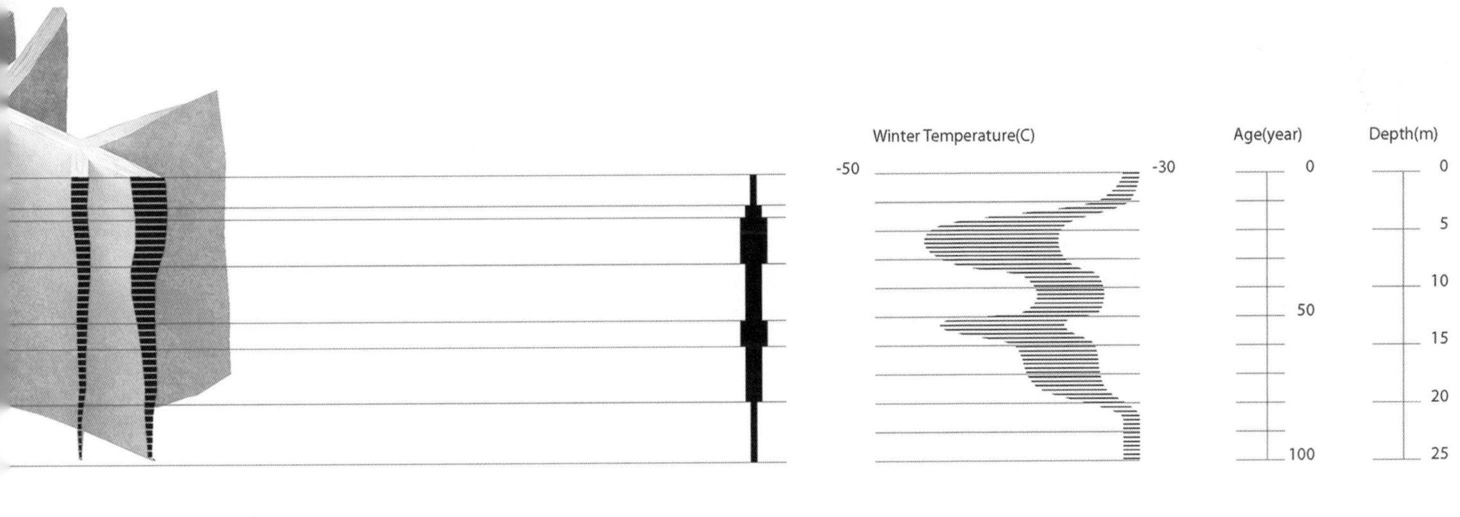

Winter Temperature(C)
-50
-30
Age(year)
0
50
100
Depth(m)
0
5
10
15
20
25

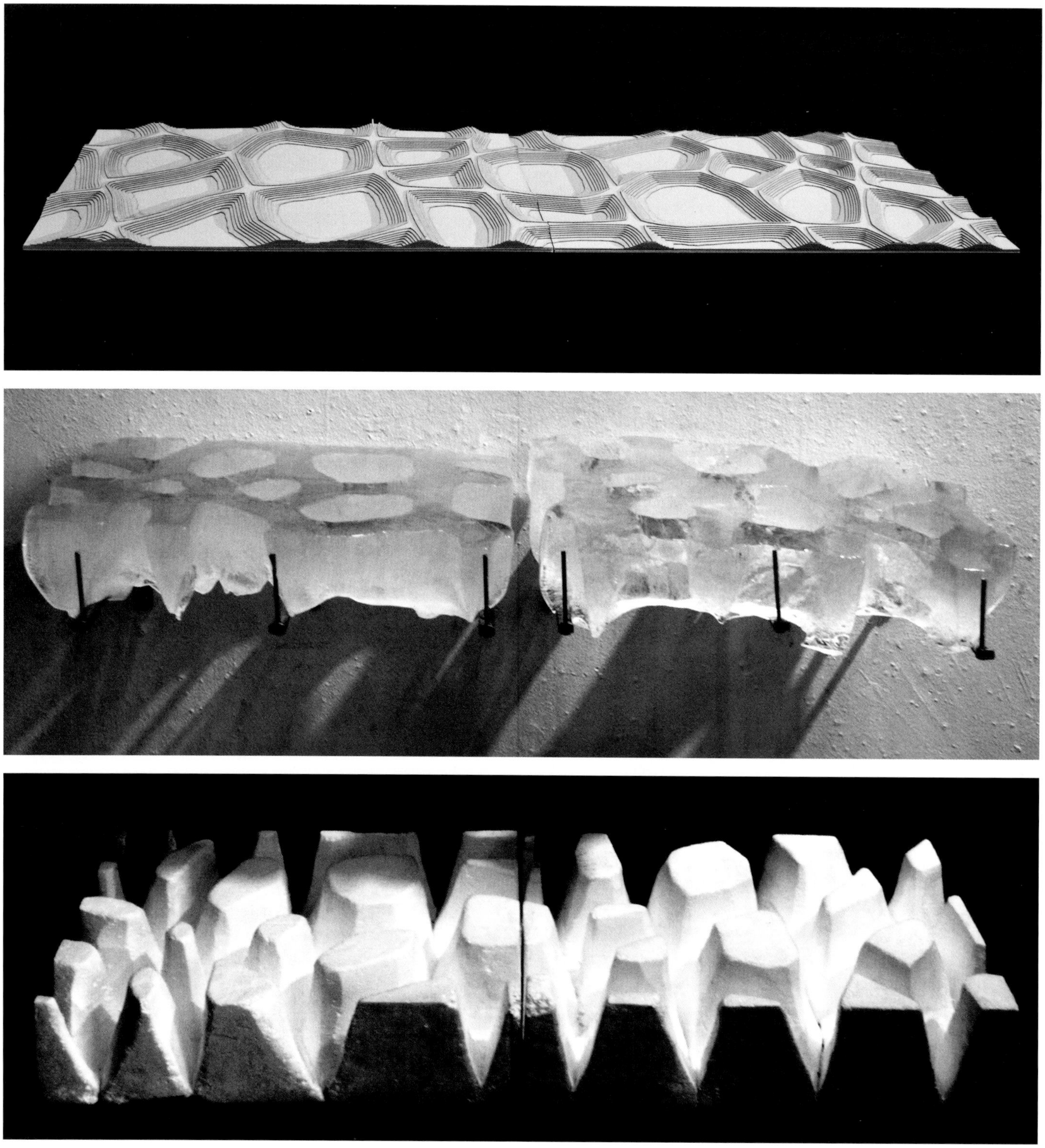

Above: Ice model experiment. As the ice forms, the refrigerator switch turns on and off to maintain the temperature and make layers of ice, visible in section.

Subterranean Channels

Snake River Plain, Idaho
Yael Agmon

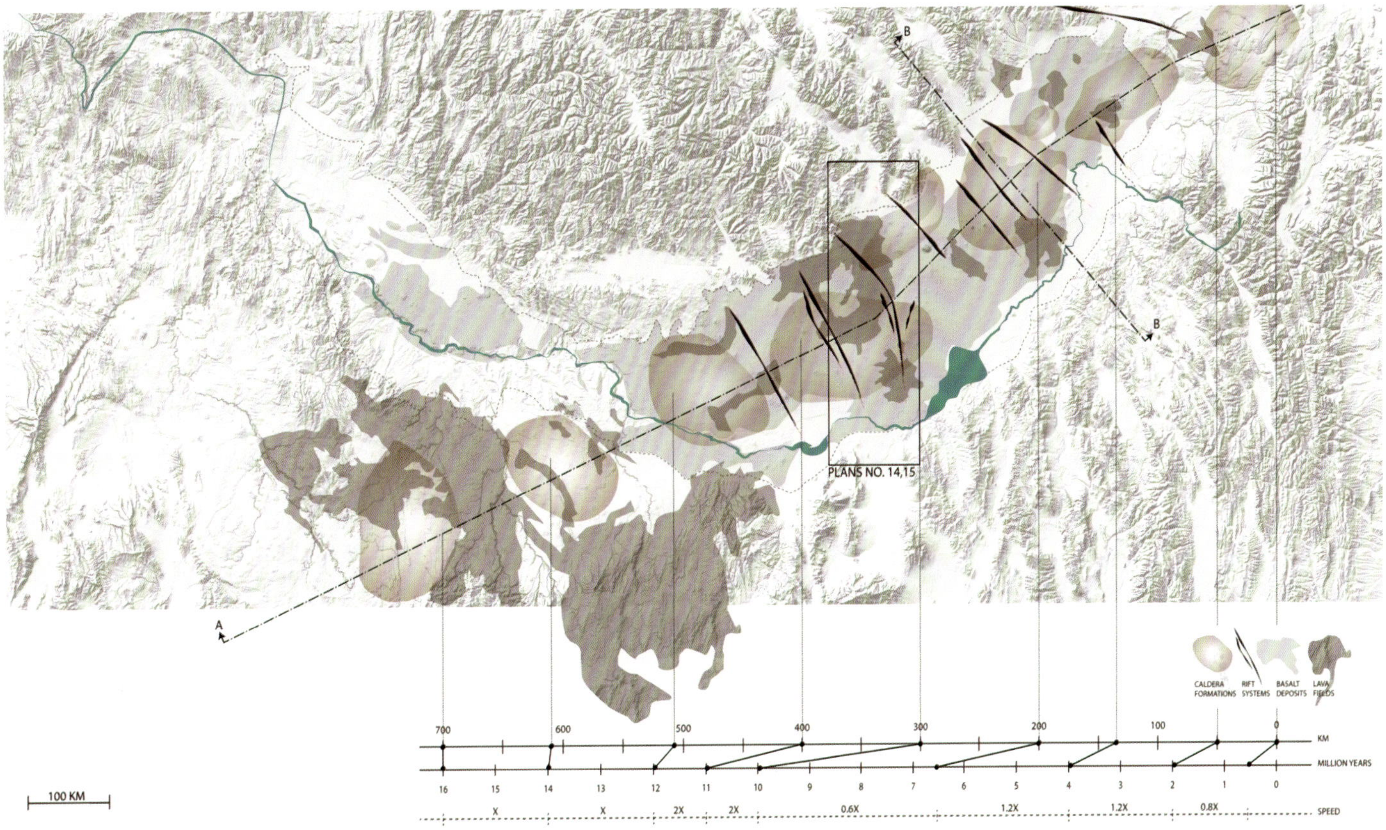

This project explores the complex interactions between different types of water bodies and geological formations through their respective state transformations. About 16 million years ago, a bulbous plume head known as the Yellowstone hotspot intercepted the base of the lithosphere and mushroomed out, causing widespread magmatic and tectonic activity centered in southwest Idaho. As the North American tectonic plate has moved eastward more than 1,000 kilometers, the friction between the plate and the Yellowstone hotspot has left a trail of calderas and volcanic features. As a result, a flat volcanic terrain surrounded by a crescent of mountain ranges was formed in Southern Idaho, which is known today as the Snake River Plain that stretches over 40,000 square miles and is surrounded by high mountains.

These mountains became a natural barrier to adiabatic clouds originating in the Pacific Ocean. Their accumulation over the plain generated vast amounts of precipitation, which penetrated the basalt rock forming an unusually large aquifer beneath—44,000 square miles and up to 5,000 feet deep. Throughout the past 100,000 years, the aquifer's water has been flowing through the labyrinth of basalt rock, weaving in and out, the broken pieces of rock mass connecting back to the Snake River. A dynamic relationship between solids and liquids is revealed in the Snake River Plain. The viscous lava, which melted its way up through the solid rock, later solidified and transformed into basalt and rhyolite. The porosity of these volcanic rocks allowed for the accumulation of water in the voids, continuously eroding the rock and creating more subterranean channels.

Top: Plan of the Snake River Plain, emphasizing the volcanic traces along a 16-million-year track of the northern tectonic plate over a mantle plume.

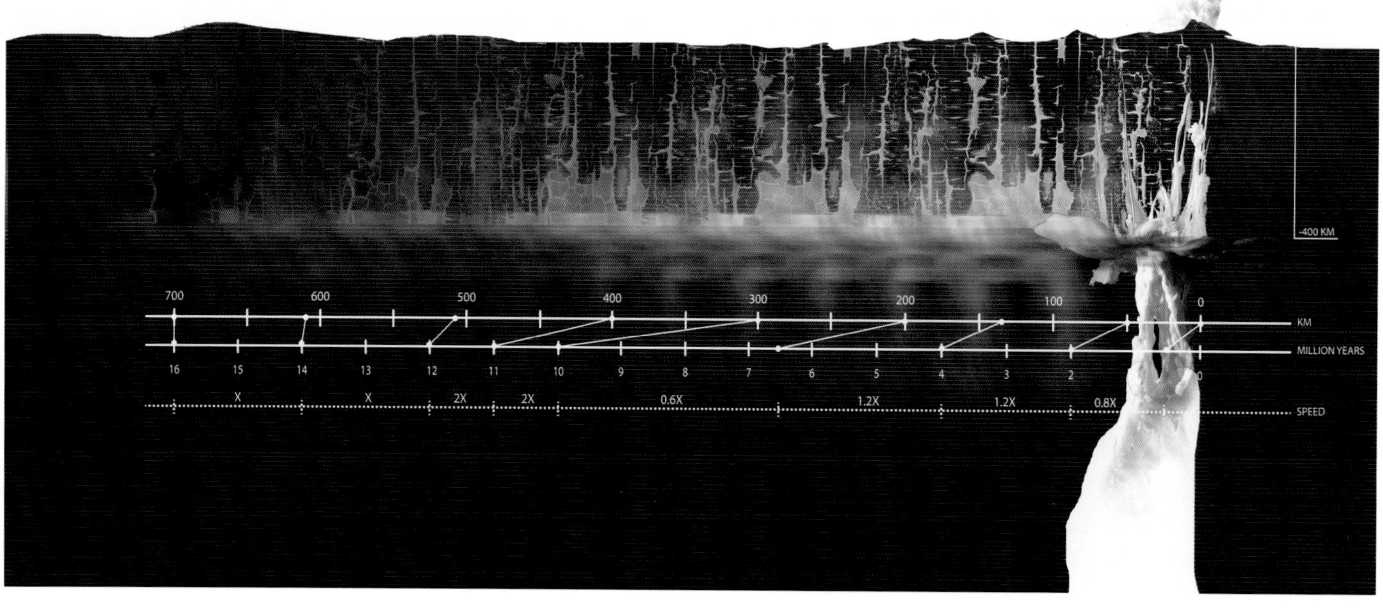
-400 KM
700
600
500
400
300
200
100
0
KM
MILLION YEARS
16
15
14
13
12
11
10
9
8
7
6
5
4
3
2
0
X
X
2X
2X
0.6X
1.2X
1.2X
0.8X
SPEED

Opposite top: Detailed view into the rock mass describing the gradual erosion of the vertical volcanic channels by the underground water, from about two million years ago (left) to present day (right).

Opposite bottom: Section along the Snake River Plain (SE-NW), depicting the interaction between the hotspot's mantle plume and the tectonic plate above it, which is constantly in motion.

Above: Section across the Snake River Plain (N-S), showing the three stages of the volcanic interactions with the lithosphere: a) The heat creates a bulge. b) Intensive heat melts the area and a caldera is formed. c) The surface sinks and a geological break is generated between the caldera and its surroundings.

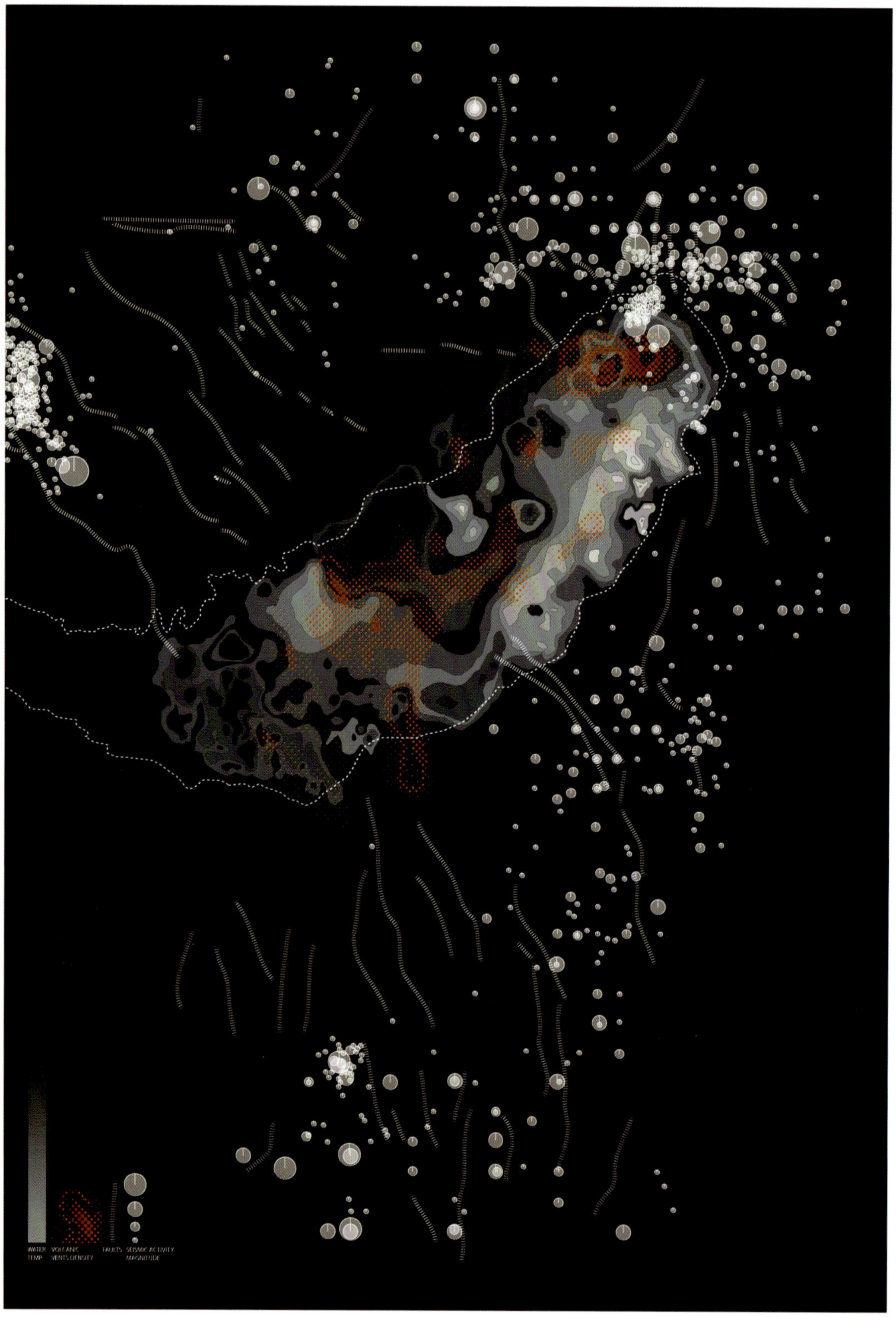

Above: Underground plan of the eastern Snake River Plain, which reveals the likelihood of potential explosive events. Water temperature, the density of the volcanic vents, and the seismic activity in the last century (along with the geological faults they generated) might help in predicting future potential lava-water interactions.

Top left: Section of the aquifer showing the interaction of the water with the vertical structure of the volcanic rift dikes. The water table rises in the dikes due to capillarity action.

Top right: Section of a potential event showing the explosive effect of an eruption across the aquifer in areas where volcanic activity is still present. In such an event, an enormous amount of energy will be released. As the magma meets the water a double reaction can occur as each of the forces will push inwards to the chamber that has been created. Be-sides the energetic potential of the event, a unique form of Tephra will be generated. Tephra is a material that can be used to create super-strong fibers that can bear extreme contusions of heat and water, and is a useful material for enriching agricultural soils.

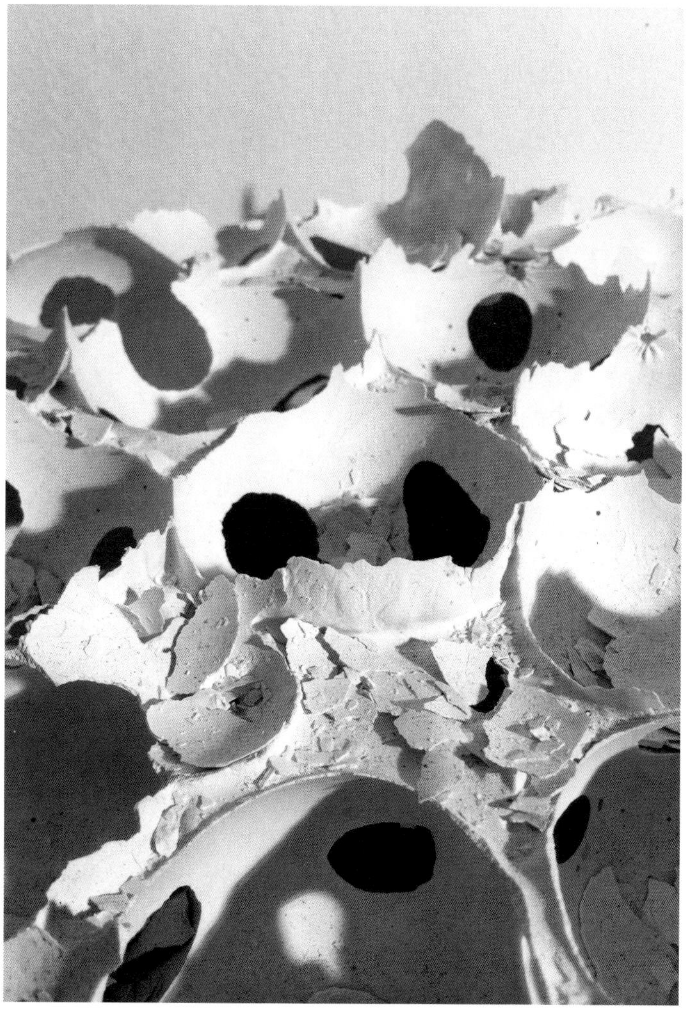

Above: Models of cavities created by water movement through the rock.

BASIN AND RANGE: GEOLOGIC TIME

John McPhee

One is tempted to condense time, somewhat glibly—to say, for example, that the faulting which lifted up the mountains of the Basin and Range began "only" eight million years ago. The late Miocene was "a mere" eight million years ago. That the Rocky Mountains were building seventy million years ago and the Appalachians were folding four hundred million years ago does not impose brevity on eight million years. What is to be avoided is an abridgment of deep time in a manner that tends to veil its already obscure dimensions. The periods are so long—the eighty million years of the Cretaceous, the forty-six million years of the Devonian—that each has acquired its own internal time scale, intricately constructed and elaborately named. I will not attempt to reproduce this amazing list but only to suggest its profusion. The stages and ages, as they are called—the subdivisions of all of the epochs and eras—read like a roll call in a district council somewhere in Armenia. Berriasian, Valanginian, Hauterivian, Barremian, Bedoulian, Gargasian, Aptian, Albian, Cenomanian, Turonian, Coniacian, Santonian, Campanian, and Maastrichtian, reading upward, are chambers of Cretaceous time. Actually, the Cretaceous has been cut even finer, with about fifty clear time lines now, subdivisions of the subdivisions of its eighty million years, The Triassic consists of the Scythian, the Anisian, the Ladinian, the Carnian, the Norian, and the Rhaetian, averaging seven million years. What survived the Rhaetian lived on into the Liassic. The Liassic, an epoch, comes just after the Triassic and is the early pan of the Jurassic. Kazanian, Couvinean, Kopaninian, Kimmeridgian. Tremadocian, Tournaisian, Tatarian, Tiffanian.... When geologists choose to ignore these names, as they frequently do, they resort to terms that are undecipherably simple, and will note, typically, that an event which occurred in some flooded summer 341.27 million years ago took place in the "early late-middle Mississippian." To say "middle Mississippian" might do, but with millions of years in the middle Mississippian there is an evident compunction to be more precise. "Late" and "early" always refer to time. "Upper" and "lower" refer to rock. "Upper Devonian" and "lower Jurassic" are slices of time expressed in rock.

In the middle Mississippian, there was an age called Meramecian, of about eight million years, and it was during the Meramecian that the Tonka—the older of the formations in the angular unconformity in Carlin Canyon, Nevada—was accumulating along an island coast. The wine-red sandstone and its pebbles may have been sand and pebbles of the beach. The island was of considerable size, apparently, and stood off North America in much the way that Taiwan now reposes near the coast of China. Where there were swamps, they were full of awkward amphibians, not entirely masking in their appearance the human race they would become. They struggled along on stumpy legs. The strait separating the Meramecian island from the North American mainland was about four hundred miles wide and contained crossopterygian fish, from which the amphibians had evolved. There were shell-crushing sharks, horn cora1s, meadows of sea lilies, and spiral bryozoans that looked like screws. The strait was warm and equatorial. The equator ran through the present site of San Diego, up through Colorado and Nebraska, and on through the site of Lake Superior. The lake would not be dug for nearly three hundred and forty million years. If in the Meramecian you were to have followed the present route of Interstate 80 moving east, you would have raised the coast of North America near the Wyoming border, and landed on a red beach. Gradually, you would have ascended through equatorial fern forests, in red soil, to a high point somewhere near Laramie, to begin there a long general downgrade among low hills to Grand Island, Nebraska, where you would have come to an arm of the sea. The far shore was four hundred miles to the east, where the Mississippi River is now, and beyond it was a low, wet, humid, flat terrain, dense with ferns and fern trees—Illinois, Indiana, Ohio. Halfway across Ohio, you would have come to a second epicratonic sea, its far shore in central Pennsylvania. In New Jersey, you would have begun to ascend mountains and ever higher mountains, their summits girt with ice and capped with snow, not unlike Mt. Kenya, not unlike the present peaks of New Guinea and Ecuador, with their snowfields and glaciers in the equatorial tropics. Reaching the site of the George Washington Bridge, you would have been at considerable altitude, looking at mountains and more mountains before you in future Africa.

If you had turned around and gone back to Nevada a million years later, still in Meramecian time, there would have been few variations to note along the way. The west coast would have moved east, but only a bit, and would still be approximately at the western end of Wyoming. There would have been a significant alteration, however, in the demeanor of the island over the strait. At a little over two inches a year, it would have moved forty miles or so eastward, compressing the floor of the strait and pushing up high mountains, like the present mountains of Timor, which have come up in much the same way to stand ten thousand feet above the Banda Sea. Up from the sea and within those Meramecian Nevada mountains can the wine-red pebbly sandstone of the Tonka formation.

Forty million years after that, when the Tonka mountains had been worn flat the Strathearn limestones were forming over their roots, the American scene was very different. It was now the Missourian age of late Pennsylvanian time (about three hundred million years ago), and the Appalachians were still high but they were no longer alpine. Traveling west, and coming down from the mountains around Du Bois, Pennsylvania, you would have descended into a densely vegetal swamp. This was Pennsylvania in the Pennsylvanian, when vegetation rioted on the earth and the big trees were kings. They were not huge by our standards but they were big trees, some with diamond patterns precisioned in their bark. They had thick boles and were about a hundred feet high. Other trees had bark like the bark of hemlocks and leaves like flat straps. Others had the fluted, swollen bases of cypress. In and out among the trunks flew dragonflies with the wingspans of great horned owls. Amphibians not only were walking around easily but some of them had become reptiles. Through the high meshing crowns of the trees not a whole lot of light filtered down. The understory was all but woven—of rushlike woody plats and seed ferns. There were luxuriant tree ferns as much as fifty feet high. The scene suggests a tropical rain forest but was more akin to the Everglades, the Dismal Swamp, the Atchafalaya basin—a hummocky spongy landscape ending in a ragged coast. All through Pennsylvanian time, ice sheets had been advancing over the southern continents, advancing and retreating, forming and melting, lowering and raising the level of the sea, and as the sea came up and over the land in places like the swamps of Du Bois it buried them, first under beach sand and later—as the seawater deepened—under lime muds. With enough burial, the muds became limestone, the sands became sandstone, the vegetation coal. When the sea fell, erosion wore away some of that, but then the sea would rise again to bury new generations of ferns and trees under successive layers of rock. The cyclothems, as they are called, contain the coals of Pennsylvania, and similar ones the coals of Iowa and Illinois. The shallow sea that reached Pennsylvania and eastern Ohio was a hundred miles wide in the Missourian age of Pennsylvanian time, and after crossing the water you would have reached a beach and another coal swamp and then, in light-gray soil, a low lush tropical forest that went on through Indiana to eastern Illinois, where it ended with more coal swamps, another sea. The far shore was where the Mississippi River is now, and beyond that was an equatorial rain forest, which ended in central Iowa with another swamp, another sea. The water here was clear and sparkling, with almost no land-derived sediments settling into it, just accumulating skeletons—clean deep beds of lime. Five hundred miles over the water, you would have raised the rose colored beaches of eastern Wyoming. Mountains stood out to the south. They were the Ancestral Rockies, and time would bevel them to stumps. Skirting them, in Pennsylvanian Wyoming, you would have traversed what seem to have been Saharan sands, wave after wave of dunal sands, five hundred miles of rose and amber pastel sands, ending at the west coast of North America, in Salt Lake City. As the Pennsylvanian sea level moved up and down here, it left alternating beds of lime and sand, which, two eras later, the nascent Oquirrh Mountains would lift to view. Two hundred miles out to sea was the site of Carlin Canyon, where muds of clean lime were settling. The Strathearn, the younger formation of the two in the Carlin unconformity, is an almost pure limestone.

The two formations, conjoined, were driven upward, according to present theory, in a collision of crustal plates that occurred in the early Triassic. The result was yet another set of new mountains—alpine mountains which erosion brought down before the end of the Jurassic, but not enough to obliterate the story that is told in Carlin Canyon. Still gazing at the Carlin unconformity, Ken Deffeyes said, "Profound as all the time is to build and destroy those mountain ranges, it is just a one-acter in the history of the Basin and Range—small potatoes, weak beer, just a little piece of time, a little piece of the action, lost in all the welter of all the other history." There had been two complete cycles of erosion and deposition and mountain building in this one place in one-fortieth of the time scale. That is what made John Playfair's mind grow giddy when James Hutton took him in 1788 to see the angular unconformity at Siccar Point. It was especially fortunate that Playfair was there, and that Playfair knew Hutton and Hutton's geology equally well, for when Hutton finally wrote his book most readers were trampled by the prose. Hutton was at best a difficult writer. Insights came to him but phrases did not. James Hall, who was twenty-seven when he went with Hutton and Playfair to Siccar Point, would say of Hutton years later, "I must own that on reading Dr. Hutton's first geological publication I was induced to reject his system entirely, and should probably have continued still to do so, with the great majority of the world, but for my habits of intimacy with the author, the vivacity and perspicuity of whose conversation formed a striking contrast to the obscurity of his writings." Hall, incidentally, melted rock in crucibles and saw how crystals formed as it cooled. He is regarded as the founder of experimental geology. John Playfair likewise assessed Hutton's literary style as containing "a degree of obscurity astonishing to those who knew him, and who heard him every day converse with no less clearness and precision then animation and force." One can imagine what Playfair thought when he read something like Hutton's two-volume *Theory of the Earth*:

"If in examining our land, we shall find a mass of matter which had been evidently formed originally in the ordinary manner of stratification, but which is now extremely distorted in its structure and displaced in its position,—which is also extremely consolidated in its mass and variously changed in its composition,—which therefore has the marks of its original or marine

Basin and Range, Image source Voyager UNAVCO

composition extremely obliterated, and many subsequent veins of melted mineral matter interjected; we should then have reason to suppose that here were masses of matter which, though not different in their origin from those that are gradually deposited at the bottom of the ocean, have been more acted upon by subterranean heat and the expanding power, that is to say, have been changed in a greater degree by the operations of the mineral region."

In that long sentence lies the discovery of metamorphic rock. But just as metamorphism will turn shale into slate, sandstone into quartzite, and granite into gneiss, Hutton had turned words into pumice. Unsurprisingly, his insights did not at once spread far and wide. They received a scattered following and much abuse. The attacks were theological, in the main, but, needless to say, geological as well—particularly with regard to his elastic sense of time. Even when people began to agree that the earth must be a great deal older then six thousand years, calculations were conservative and failed to yield the reach of time that Hutton's theory required. Lord Kelvin, as late at 1899, figured that twenty-five million years was the approximate age of the earth. Kelvin was the most august figure in contemporary science, and no one stepped up to argue. Hutton published his *Theory of the Earth* in 1795, when almost no one doubted the historical authenticity of Noah's Flood, and all species on earth were thought to have been created individually, each looking at the moment of its creation almost exactly as it did in modern times. Hutton disagreed with that, too. Writing a treatise on agriculture, he brought up the matter of variety in animals and noted, "In the infinite variation of the breed, that form best adapted to the exercise of the instinctive arts, by which the species is to live, will most certainly be continued in the propagation of this animal, and will be always tending more and more to perfect itself by the natural variation which is continually taking place. Thus, for example, where dogs are to live by the swiftness of their feet and the sharpness of their sight, the form best adapted to that end will be the most certain of remaining, while those forms that are less adapted to this manner of chase will be the first to perish; and, the same will hold with regard to all other forms and faculties of the species, by which the instinctive arts procuring its means of substance may be pursued." When he died in 1797, Hutton was working on that manuscript, no part of which was published for a hundred and fifty years.

People who admired Hutton's theory of the earth became known—because of the theory's igneous aspects, its molten basalts and intruding granites—as vulcanists or plutonists, and they quickly grew to be the intellectual enemies of the Wernerian neptunists, and others who believed that God had made the world through a series of catastrophes, notably the Noachian flood. The schism between these two groups would carry well into the nineteenth and even into the twentieth century, the ratio gradually reversing. In 1800, the Huttonians were outnumbered at least ten to one. In fact, a Werner-trained neptunist took over the chair of natural history at the University of Edinburgh and for many years neptunism was official in Hutton's own city.

All this can be presumed to have bestirred John Playfair, a handsome, life-loving, and generous man of "mild majesty and considerate enthusiasm," as a contemporary described him. Never mind that the contemporary was his nephew. With all those neptunists and men of the cloth on the one side and his friend's prose on the other, the battle to Playfair must have seemed unjust, and he betook himself to alter the situation. The least of his many verbal gifts was a slow-cooled lucidity, a sense of the revealing phrase, and his *Illustrations of the Huttonian Theory of the Earth*, published in 1802, was the first fully clear and persuasive statement of what the theory was about. It is testimony to Playfair's efficacity that the opposition stiffened.

"According to the conclusions of Dr. Hutton, and of many other geologists, our continents are of indefinite antiquity, they have been peoples we know not how, and mankind are wholly unacquainted with their origin," wrote the Calvinist geologist Jean André Deluc in 1809. "According to my conclusions, drawn from the same source, that of facts, our continents are of such small antiquity, that the memory of revolution which gave them birth must still be preserved among men; and thus we are led to seek in the book of Genesis the record of the history of the human race from its origin. Can any object of importance superior to this be found throughout the circle of natural science?"

As geologists built the time scale, their research and accumulating data imparted to Hutton's theory an obviously increasing glow. And in the early eighteen-thirties Charles Lyell, who said in so many words that his mission in geology was "freeing the science from Moses," gave Hutton's theory and his sense of deep time their largest advance toward universality. In three volumes, he published a work whose full title was *Principals of Geology*, Being and Attempt to Explain the Former Changes of the Earth's Surface, by Reference to Causes Now in Operation. Lyell was so anti-neptunist, so anti-catastrophist that he out-Huttoned Hutton both in manner and in form. He not only subscribed to the uniformitarian process—the topographical earth building and destroying and rebuilding itself through time—but was finicky in insisting that all processes had been going on at exactly the same rate through all ages. *Principles of Geology* was to be the most enduring and effective geological text ever published. The first volume was eighteen months off the press when H.M.S. Beagle set sail from Devonport with Charles Darwin aboard. "I had brought with me the first volume of Lyell's *Principles of Geology*, which I studied attentively; and the book was of the highest service to me in many ways. The very first place which I examined, namely St. Jago in the Cape de Verde islands, showed me clearly the wonderful superiority of Lyell's manner of treating geology, compared with that of any other author which works I had with me or ever afterwards read." When Darwin had first studied geology, he had heard lectures in Wernerian neptunism at Edinburgh, and they had very nearly put him to sleep. Nevertheless, the degree he later took at Cambridge University was in geology. He referred to himself as a geologist. His field identifications of the rocks he collected on his travels, and the minerals within the rocks, were essentially without error. The rocks are in Cambridge, where contemporary geologists have thin sectioned them, confirming Darwin's petrology. Voyaging on the Beagle, he was enhancing his sense of the slow and repetitive cycles of the earth and the giddying depths of time, with Lyell's book in his hand and Hutton's theory on his head. In six thousand years, you could never grow wings on a reptile. With sixty million, however, you could have feathers, too.

*Reproduced with permission from John McPhee and FSG. From John Mcphee, "Basin and Range," in *Annals of the Former World* (New York: Farrar, Strauss, and Giroux, 1981).

Permafrost: Interactions and Transformations of States of Matter

Alaskan Coast
Ming Yan

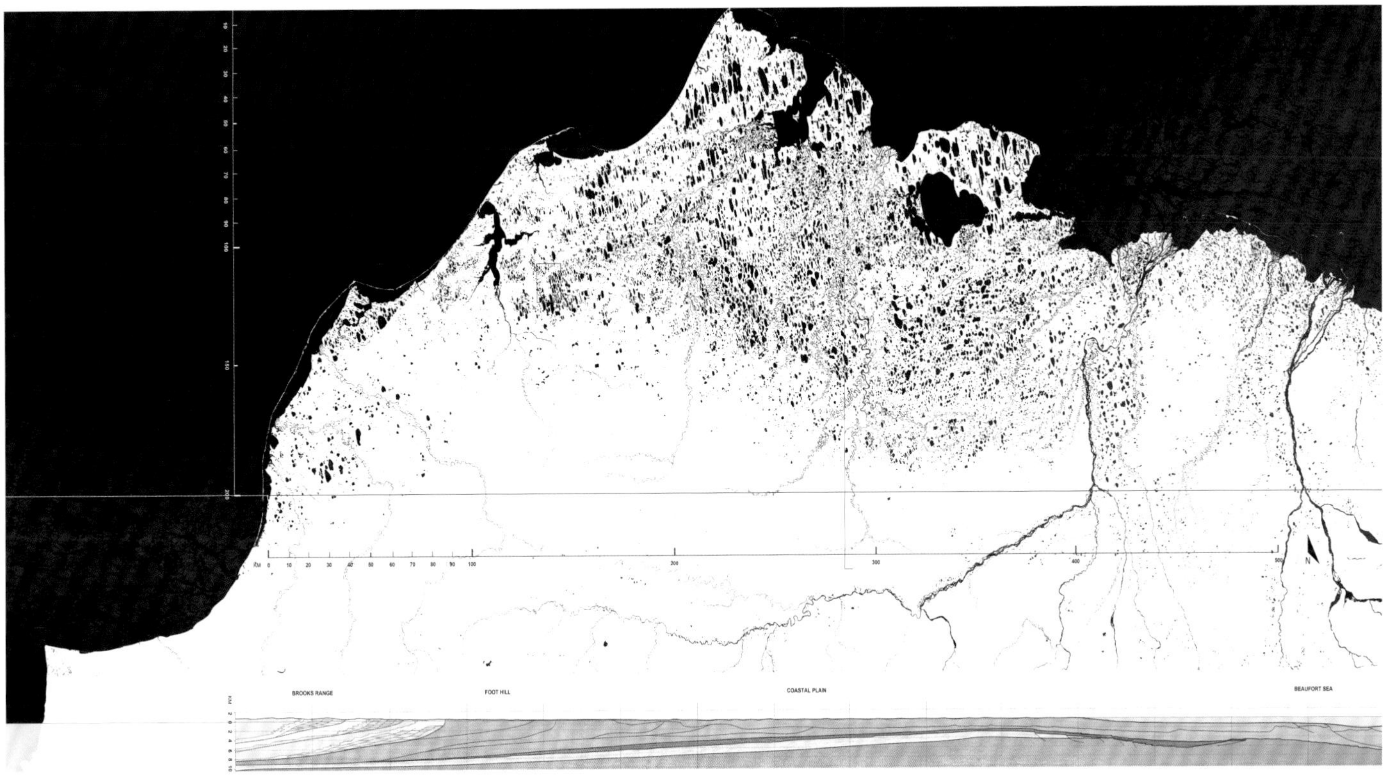

Permafrost, the frozen surface soil covering more than 27,000 square miles of Alaska's northern coastal region, is a crucial protection layer that prevents vast amounts of methane, a greenhouse gas, from being emitted into the atmosphere, and is the driving force behind Alaska's famous patterned ice landscape. The thawing and freezing of permafrost occurs seasonally, but as ocean temperatures rise thawing accelerates. Lake sizes increase and become closer together. Seven hundred and seventy-five thousand years old, the Alaskan coastal permafrost layer is about 400 meters thick, but it is diminishing every year due to global warming. With increasing annual mean temperatures, 100 meters of impermeable permafrost will likely thaw into permeable talik. Greenhouse gases trapped inside will be released into the atmosphere contributing to global warming and further accelerating this process.

Top: Plan of permafrost lakes in northern Alaska. (Bottom drawing): the geological formation of the northern Alaskan coastal slope as a result of a collision between two tectonic plates. The textured surface geology of the region is one contributing factor to the abundance of permafrost lakes.

Above: Plan and section through a lake. This large body of water protects soil below from freezing. In contrast, an area without the protection of surface water might have a 400-meter, impermeable layer of permafrost below.

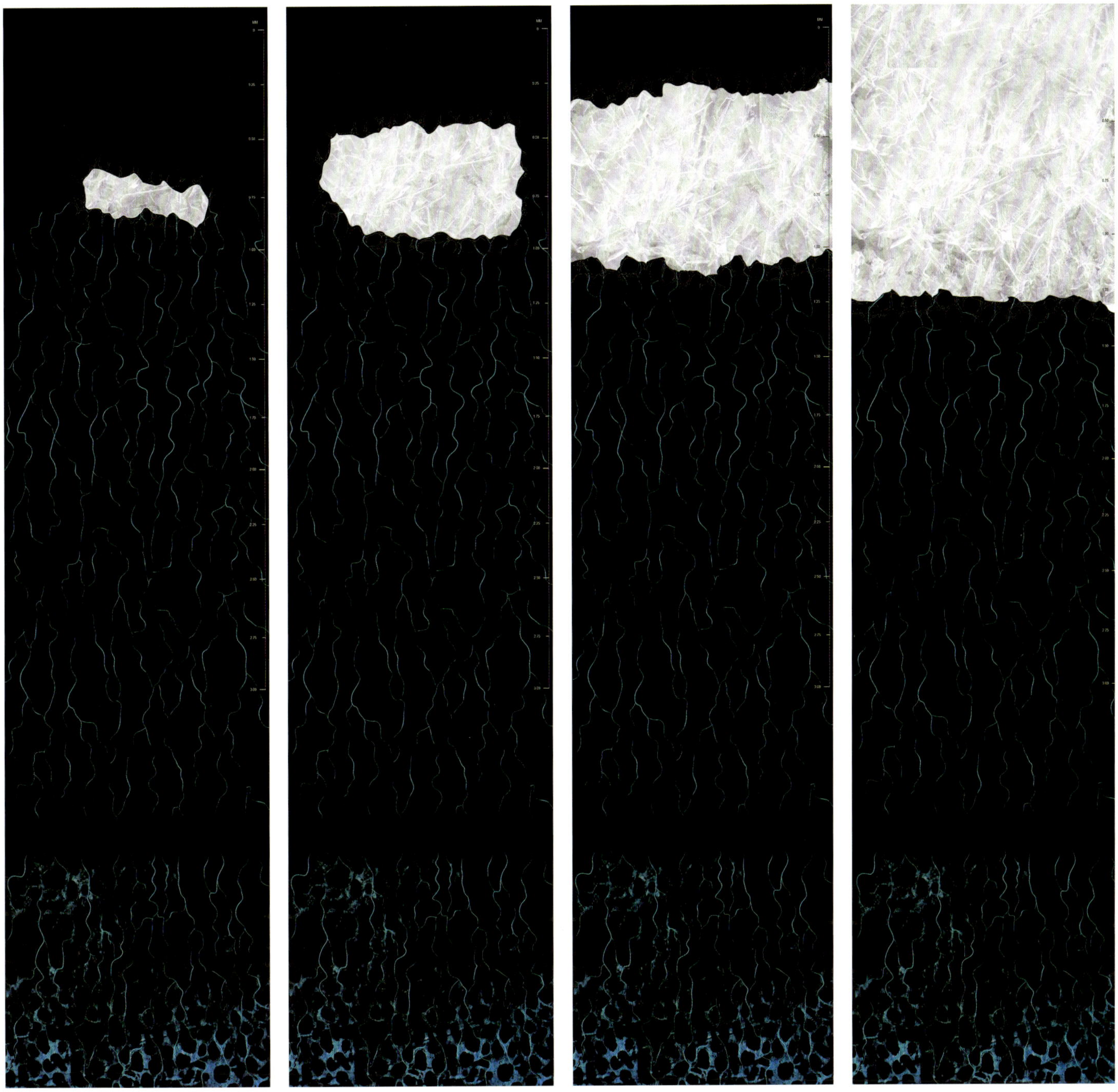

Above: Sections showing the diminishing layers of permafrost.

Next page: Sectional diagrams showing temperature variation through a lake with winter and summer landforms. Dashed red lines separate the areas not affected by temperature change (below) from those that change with seasonal temperature variations.

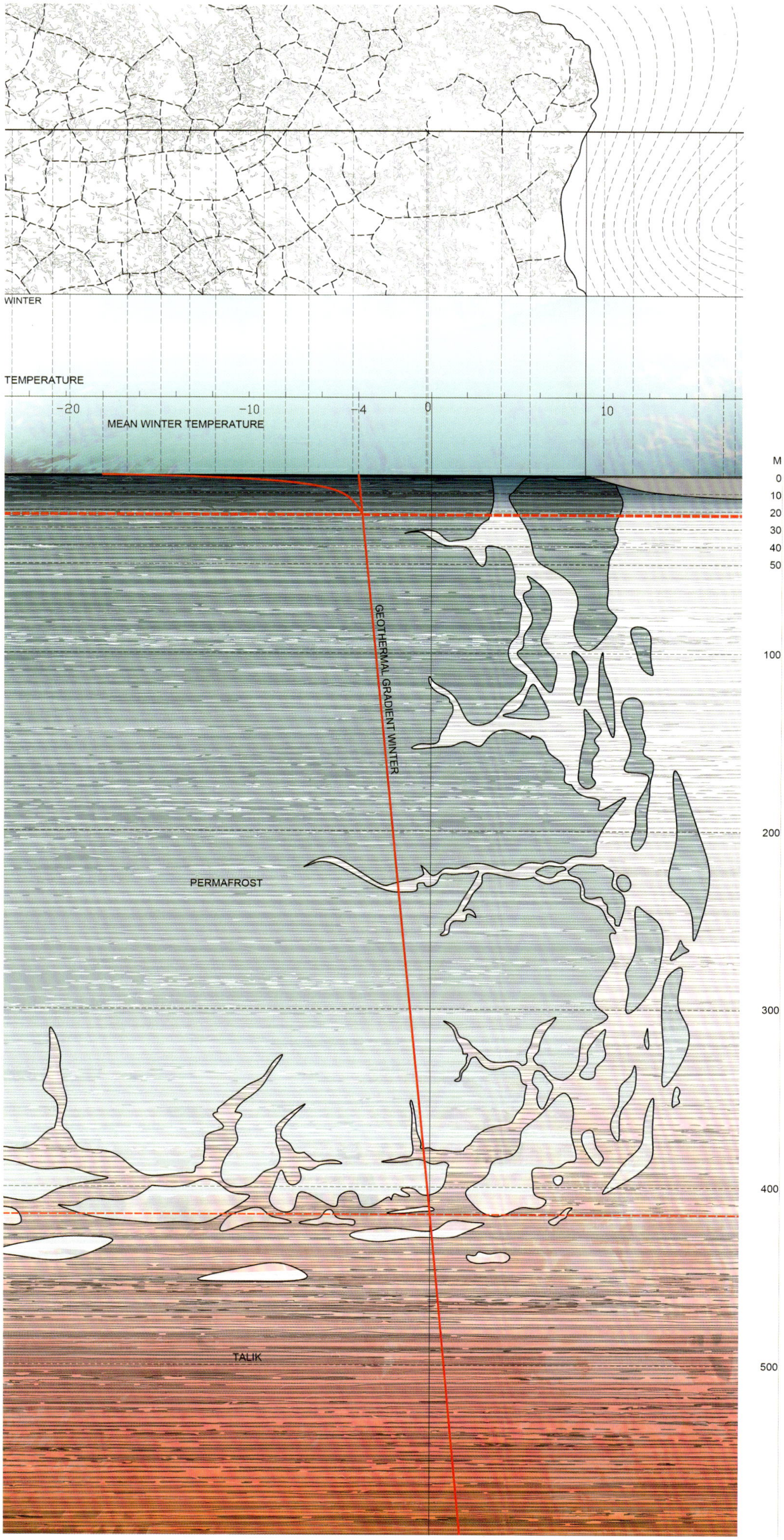
WINTER
TEMPERATURE
-20
-10
-4
0
10
MEAN WINTER TEMPERATURE
M
0
10
20
30
40
50
100
200
300
400
500
GEOTHERMAL GRADIENT WINTER
PERMAFROST
TALIK

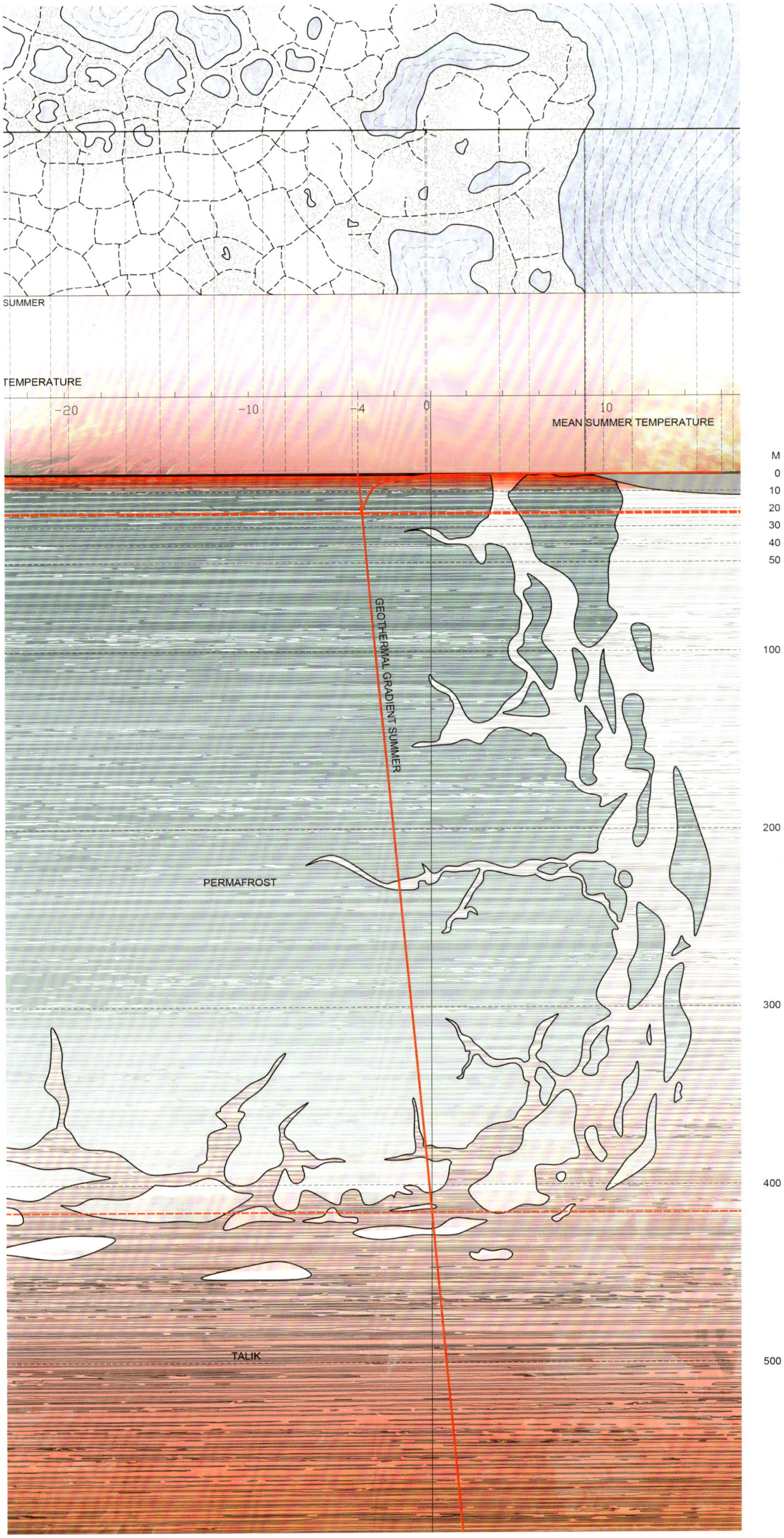
SUMMER
TEMPERATURE
-20
-10
-4
0
10
MEAN SUMMER TEMPERATURE
M
0
10
20
30
40
50
100
200
300
400
500
GEOTHERMAL GRADIENT SUMMER
PERMAFROST
TALIK

Salt of the Earth

Lake Bonneville, Utah
Adam Longenbach

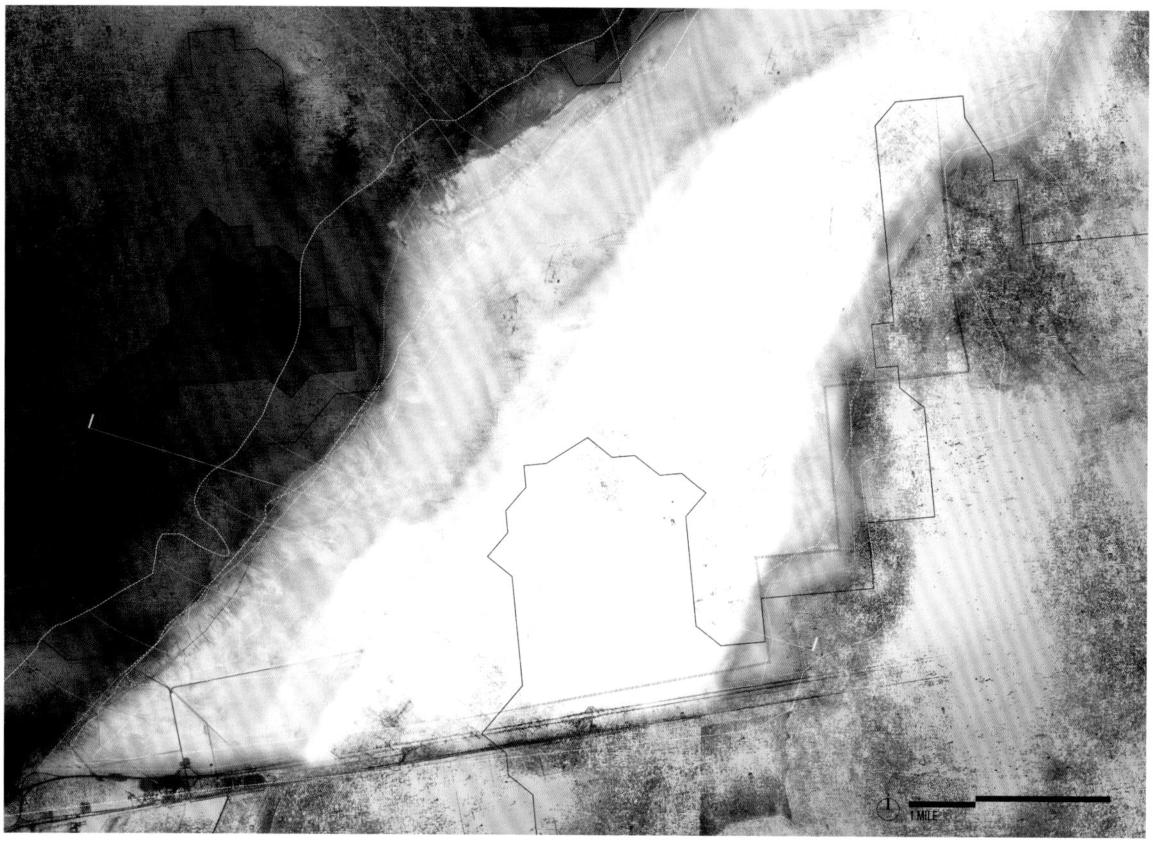

Sixteen thousand years ago, at its peak during the Upper Paleolithic Period, the ancient Lake Bonneville was the size of current Lake Michigan, with a surface area of 20,000 square miles and depth over 980 feet. In present-day Utah and Nevada, Lake Bonneville was formed out of the particular climatic conditions of that time, marked by low temperatures, low rates of evaporation, and increased precipitation in the Great Basin region. Due to climate change and receding glaciers since the Upper Paleolithic Period, Lake Bonneville has desiccated into two separate entities: water, which we call the Great Salt Lake, and residue, which we call the Bonneville Salt Flats.

The precipitous materialization and dematerialization of the ancient lake has had lasting effects on that region in northwestern Utah, which is still in the process of returning to an equilibrium state. The Earth's crust is sustaining isostatic rebound from the removal of the lake's mass, and the basin's subterranean fresh water and artesian aquifer is continually contaminated by residual lake salts that dissolve into its seasonal water cycle. As the crust continues to rebound, the salty alluvial deposits of Lake Bonneville are pushed upward and pass through the underground aquifer channels. When the aquifer surfaces on the basin floor through crustal fissures, the freshwater, turned brine-water, evaporates, leaving behind salt to recharge the Bonneville Salt Flats.

This project posits that, in 40,000 years when the basin crust is likely to reach its isostatic equilibrium, the aquifer will have completely purged the soil of Lake Bonneville's pernicious salts, re-amalgamating them into a single, isolated body: the Bonneville Salt Flats. Consequently, when the earth is relieved of its salt content and when the soil has been purged, the aquifer will once again transport potable water to the basin floor not covered by the salt flats. This water can provide for a diversity of vegetation and wildlife foreign to the landscape for nearly 55,000 thousand years.

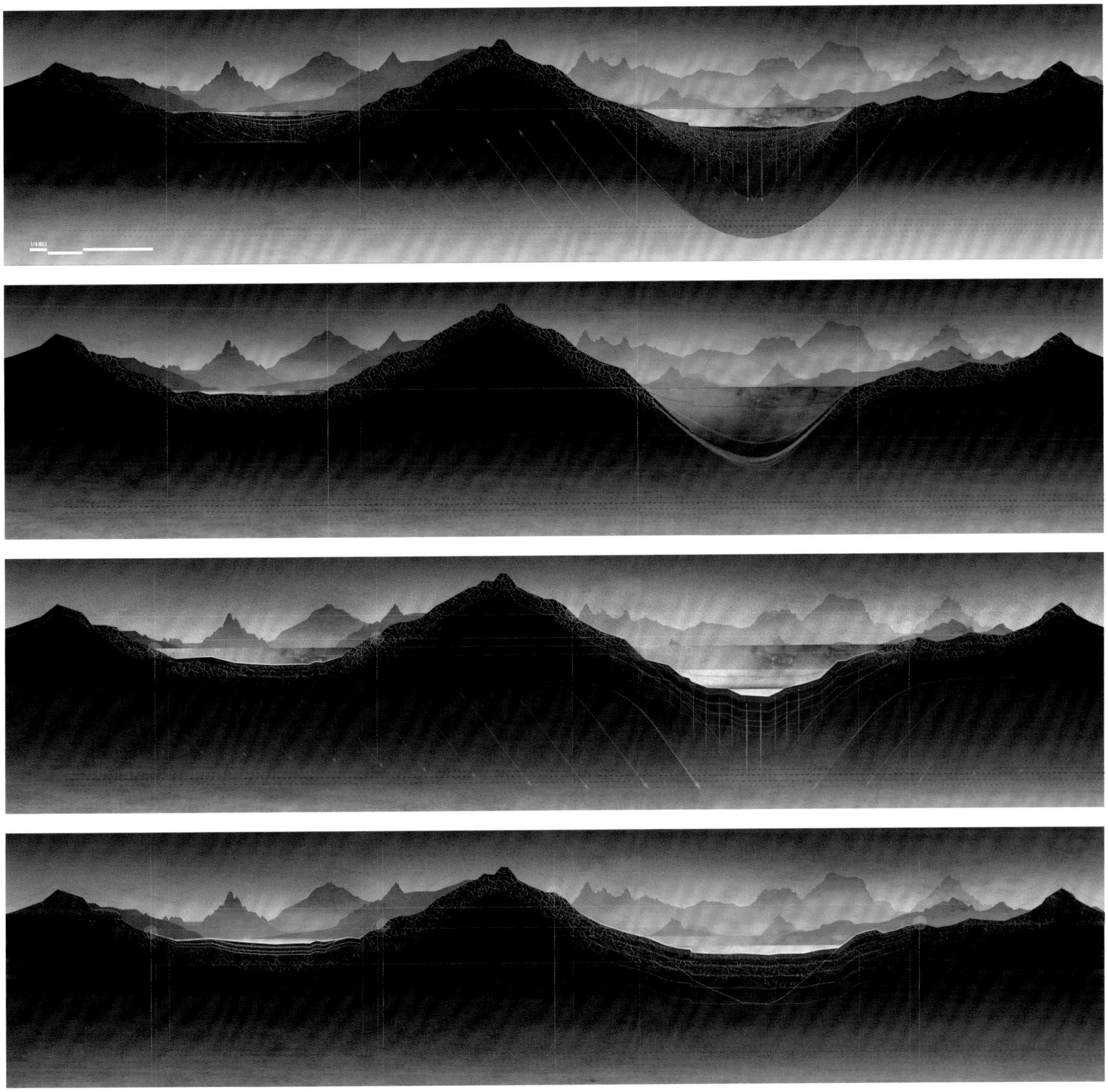

Opposite: Contemporary plan of the Bonneville Salt Flats, a 46-square-mile salt surface with salt deposits up to five feet thick.

Above: Series of sections representing the isostatic rebound of the Earth's crust due to the desiccation of Lake Bonneville over the last 16,000 years (from the Upper Paleolithic Period to today) to become both the Great Salt Lake and the Bonneville Salt Flats.

Above: Transverse sections of the Bonneville Salt Flats showing a new surface layer of salt formed by the annual dissolution and eventual resurfacing of salt content within the underground aquifers.

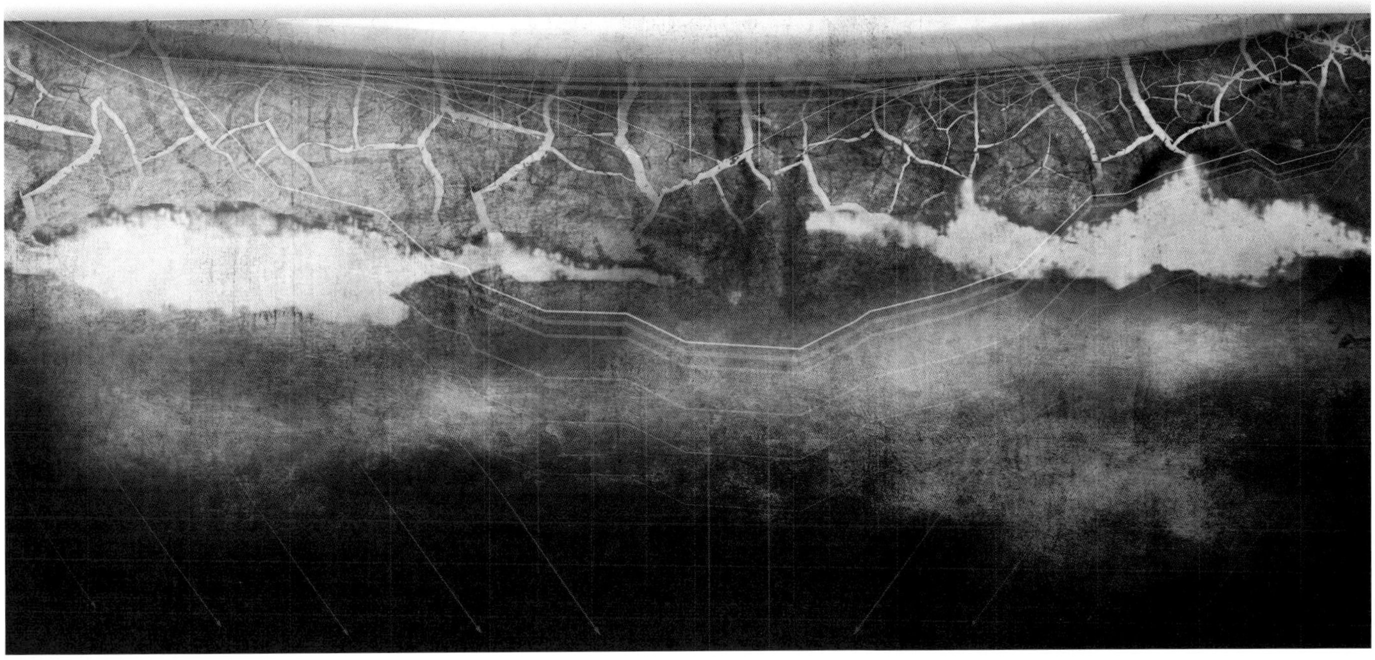

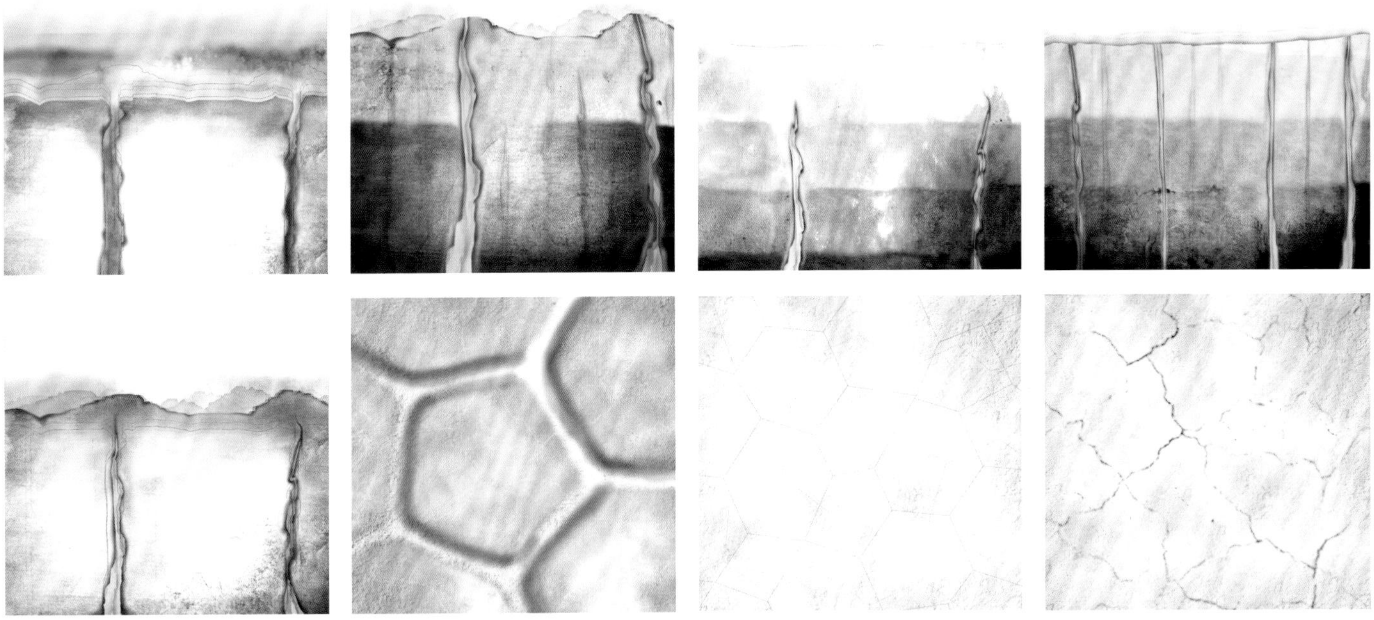

Top: Section of the current isostatic rebound of the Earth's crust pushing new salts upward and into the underground aquifer, which in turn carries those salts to the surface to form the salt flats annually.

Bottom: Plan and section of the three primary surface conditions and salt formations—carbonate, sulfate, and chloride—of the Bonneville Salt Flats.

Above: Material study model of the crystallization of salt on the surface of wood over a two-month period. Holes in the wood approximate the diameter of cracks and channels that form the underground aquifer below the Bonneville Salt Flats.

Rock, Fire, and Water: Interactions in Constant Motion

The Geysers, Sonoma County, California
Jaebong Jeon

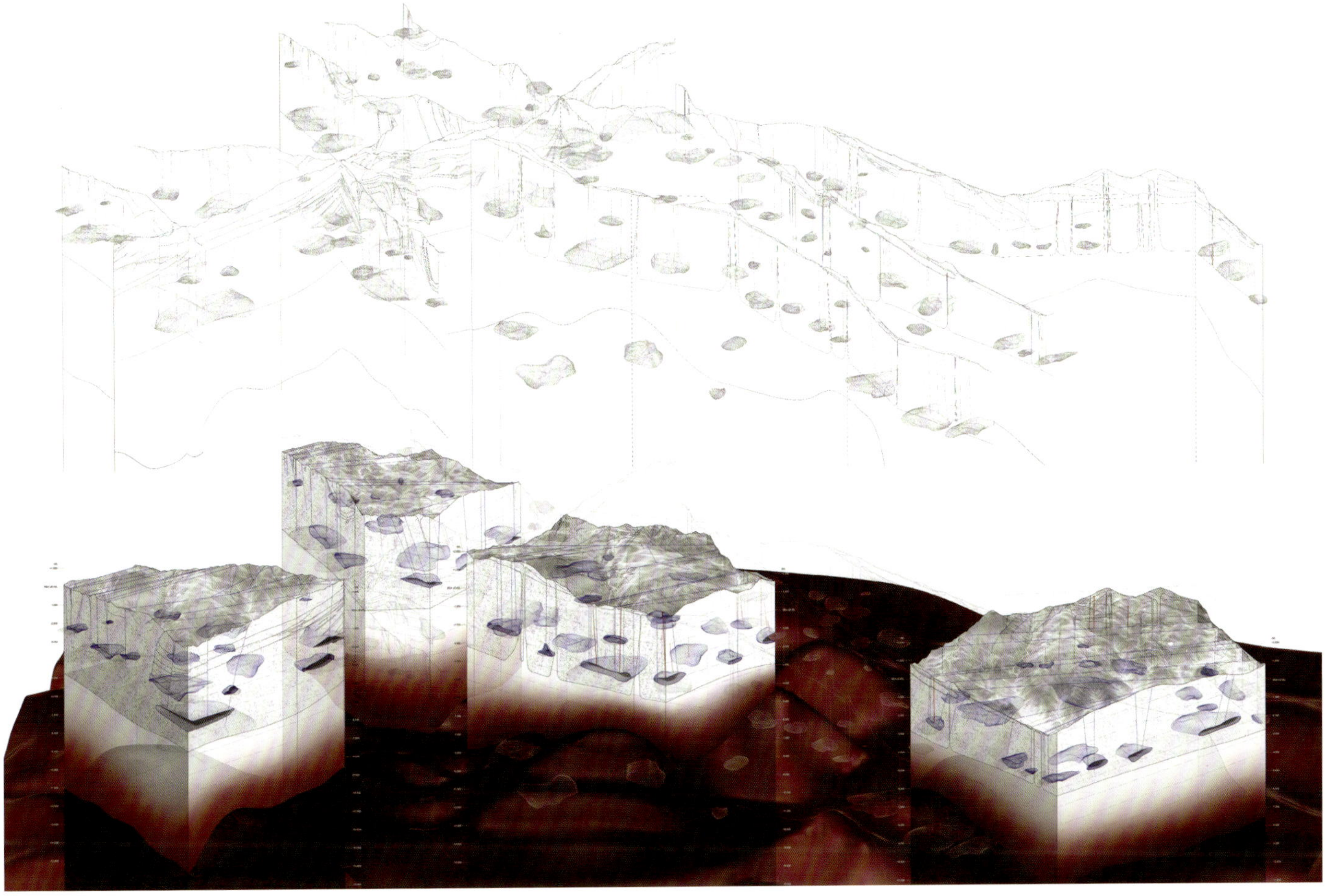

This project explores the relationships between various conditions and forces at play in the formation of the Sonoma County Geyser Field in northern California, the largest geothermal field in the world, revealing an "invisible" complex spatial and material interaction, with permeable and impermeable layers of rock, heat, and water in a constant process of transformation. Over the past 30 million years, due to the friction caused by the motion of tectonic plates, fractures and faults have emerged in Sonoma County. The upheaval of a magma chamber five million years ago also contributed to the formation of these fractures. As water penetrated the cracks in the earth, an underground reservoir developed in a permeable layer of rock. Currently, a magma chamber about four kilometers below the surface of the earth heats the impermeable layer surrounding the saturated rock. The entrapped water gradually turns into steam, and when it meets a heat peak a tremendous amount of pressure is released upwards, emerging above the surface as a visible geyser. The geysers jointly form a long, narrow strip and cover an area of about 30 square miles, erupting approximately every 30 minutes.

Top: Axonometric view of four selected sections showing the magma that soared up to four kilometers from the surface. This phenomenon resulted from a volcanic eruption that produced cracks and faults and allowed the rainwater to seep into the ground, creating a reservoir.

Above: Axonometric section of the San Andreas Fault in California, as two tectonic plates move in opposite directions in the mid-Cenozoic Era (about 30 million years ago). The fault caused the uplift of a magma chamber around Clear Lake about five million years ago, which erupted about two million years ago. The Clear Lake Volcanic Field led to the "Sister Faults," a series of faults that includes Big Valley fault.

Opposite: Axonometric drawing of the Clear Lake Volcanic Field. This geophysical data suggests there is currently a spherical to cylindrical magma chamber with a diameter of about 14 kilometers about seven kilometers from the surface. The magma chamber began to heat the underground water reservoir about 20,000 years ago.

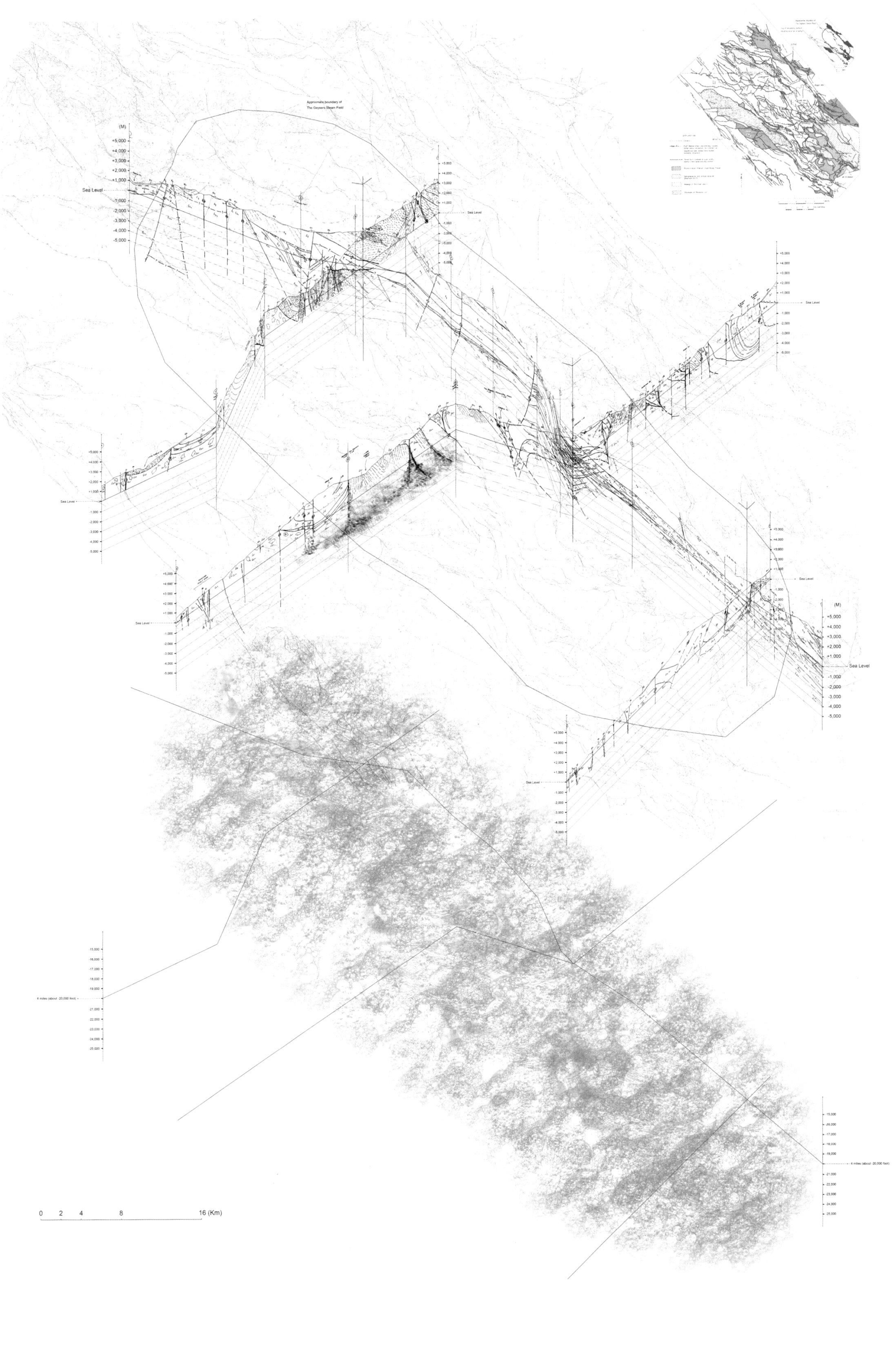
Approximate boundary of
The Geysers Steam Field
(M)
+5,000
+4,000
+3,000
+2,000
+1,000
Sea Level
-1,000
-2,000
-3,000
-4,000
-5,000
-15,000
-16,000
-17,000
-18,000
-19,000
4 miles (about -20,000 feet)
-21,000
-22,000
-23,000
-24,000
-25,000
0 2 4 8 16 (Km)

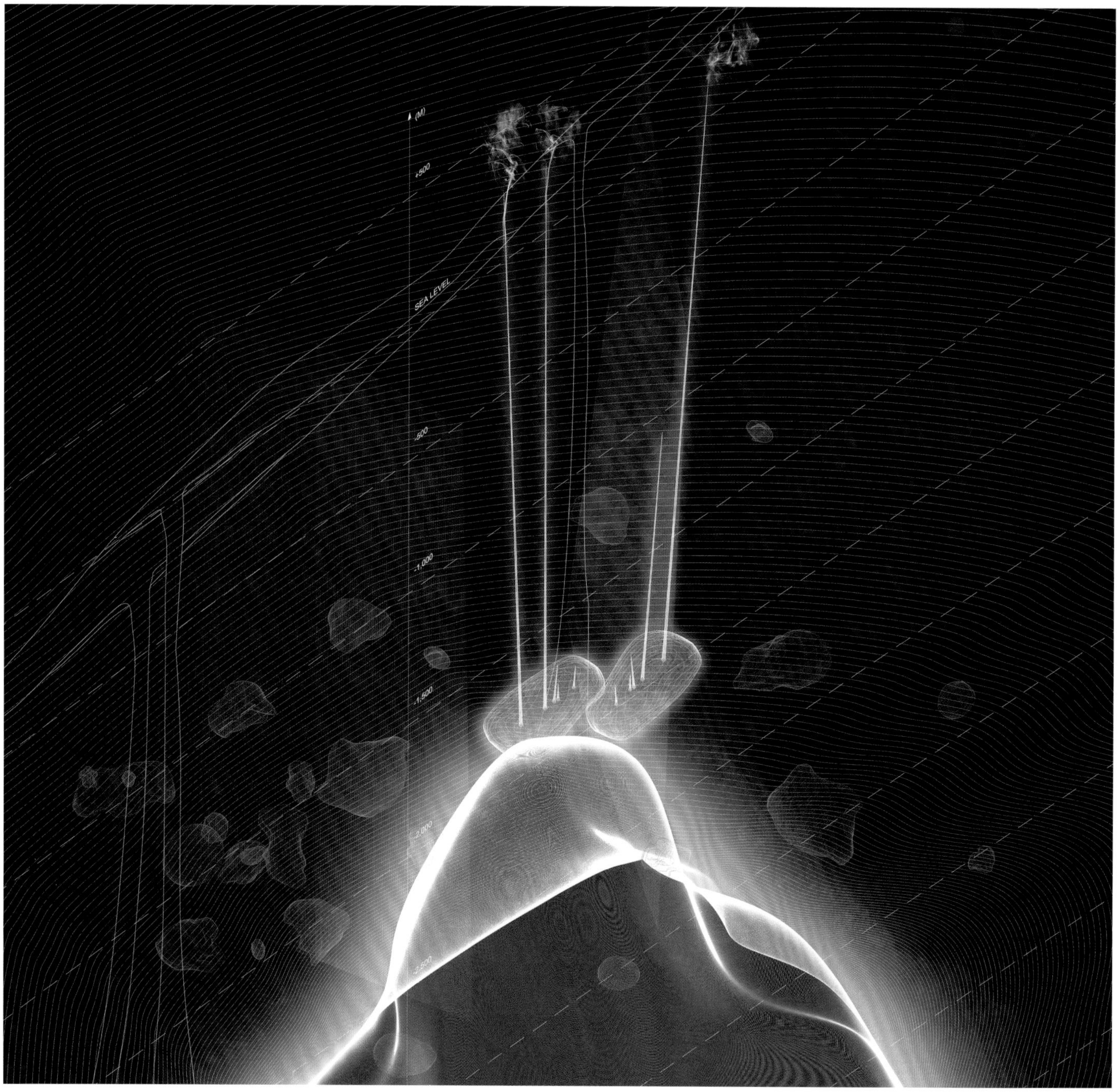
(M)
+500
SEA LEVEL
-500
-1,000
-1,500
-2,000

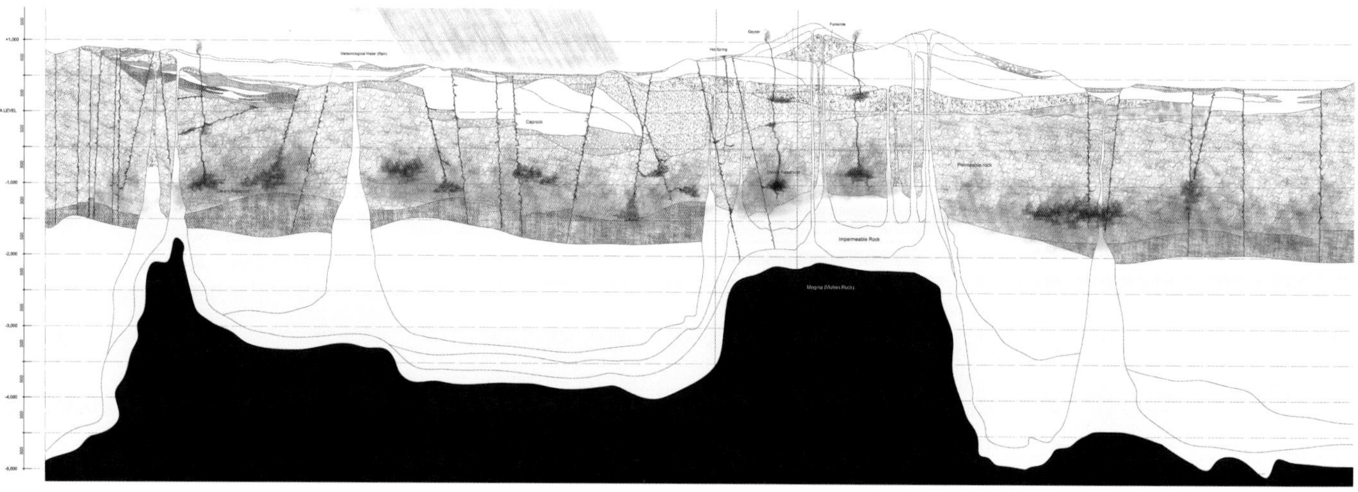
+1,000
SEA LEVEL
-1,000
Meteorological Water (Rain)
Hot Spring
Geyser
Fumarole
Caprock
Permeable rock
Impermeable Rock

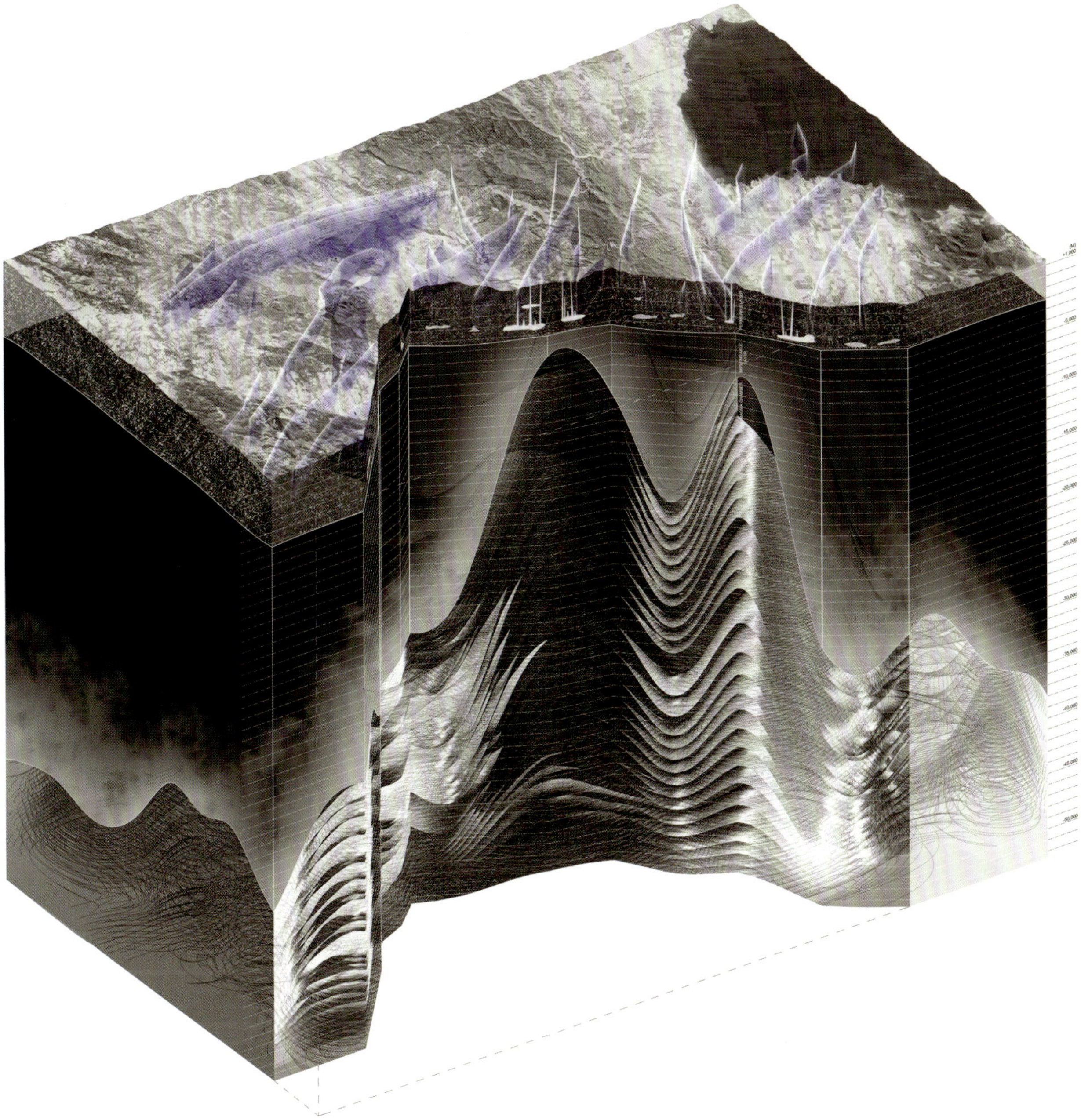

Opposite top: Section drawing of a geyser with a depth of at least two kilometers.

Opposite bottom: Section drawing showing geological layers. Permeable rock, impermeable rock, and magma chambers are striated underground. Water reservoirs are located in the permeable rock. The magma transfers heat through the impermeable rock.

Above: Section axonometric view of the relationship between the faults, magma chamber, and reservoir in the formation of the Great Geyser.

Above: Physical model showing the underground condition through the geysers.

Opposite: Physical model of a geyser, built from zip ties in order to represent the linear pathway and volumetric reservoir simultaneously.

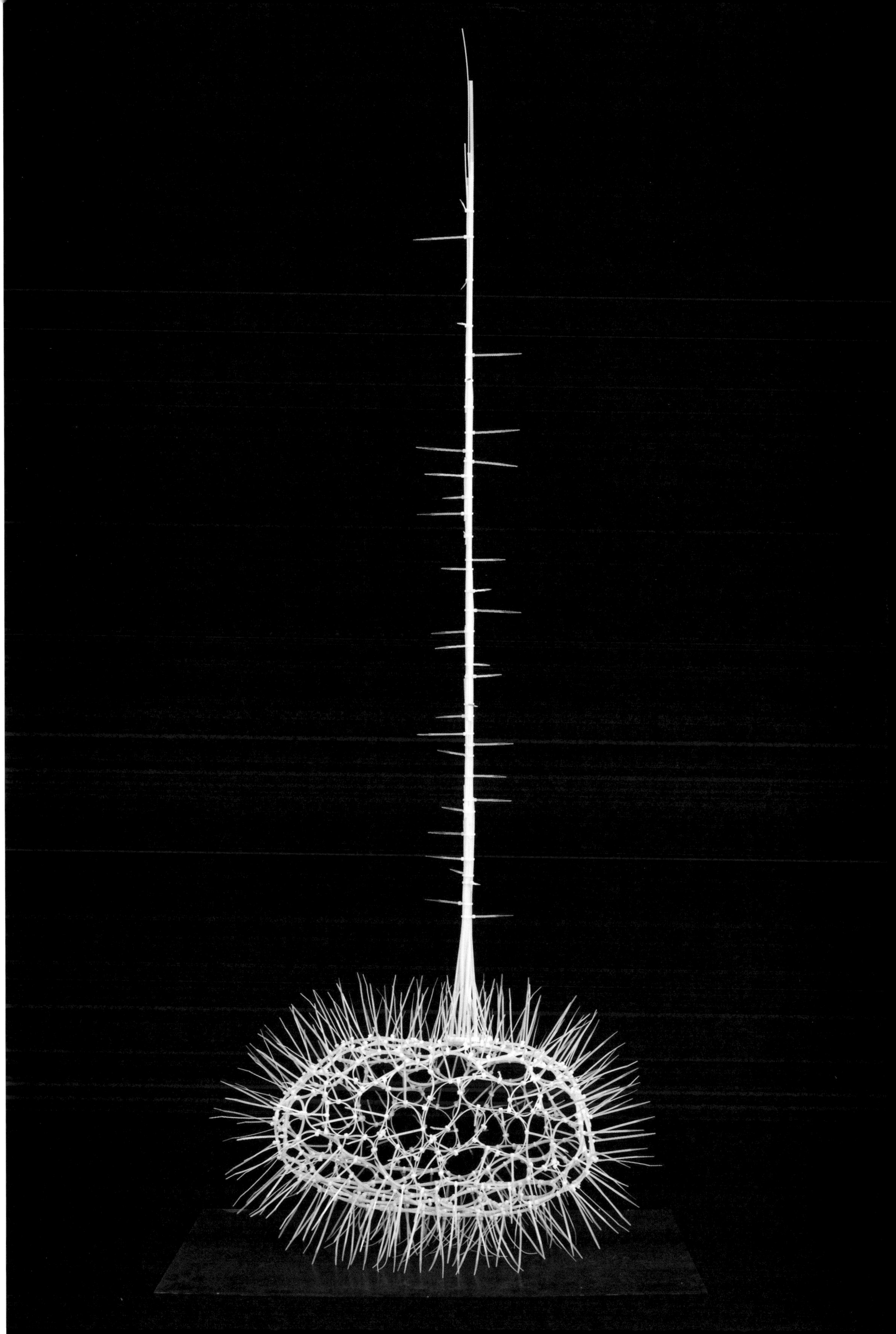

Algae as Habitat

Point Loma, California
Jihyun Lee

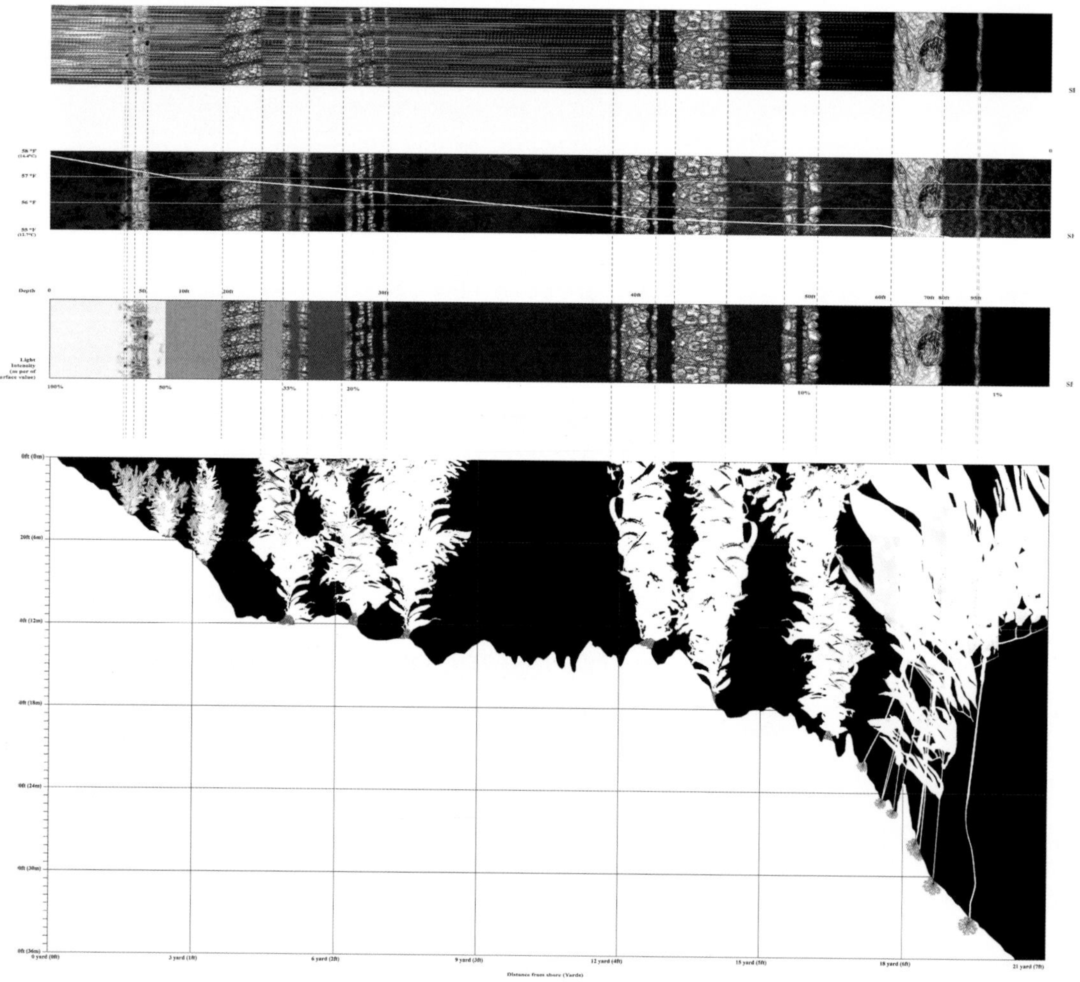

Ranging from microscopic marine fungi to large seaweed as tall as 260 feet, algae appear in abundant scales and formations. With a focus on the Macrocystis Pyrifera species, this project explores algae reproduction and growth patterns, structures, and morphological qualities by not only looking at external (macro-scale) qualities but also internal (micro-scale) properties. The project expands to a larger scale, considering algae communities as well as their relationship to the surrounding environment, which fosters the creation of new habitats for the growth of more diverse flora and fauna.

The locus of this exploration is Point Loma in southern California, the world's largest kelp bed, spreading over 18 square miles and containing 53 different types of algae. The kelp bed, or kelp forest, is structured vertically in the water column, stretching to a surface canopy. Macrocystis Pyrifera, or "Giant Kelp," is one of the fastest growing organisms in the world, dominating the underwater landscape in Point Loma.

In contrast, Procystis Fusiformis, a bioluminescent species, is closer to the scale of a micro-organism (300 nm = 0.0003 mm). Because of this light-emitting quality, this project uses this species as a tool for growing other algae species in order to create not only more complex flora but also more diverse fauna, providing habitats for macro- and micro-organisms alike. The combination of this algae species with an artificial element, also at the micro/nano-scale, brings light into dark ocean depths and enriches the complex ecological system that surrounds it. The intervention is minimal physically and visually, and invisible during the day, but its impact on its surroundings is immense.

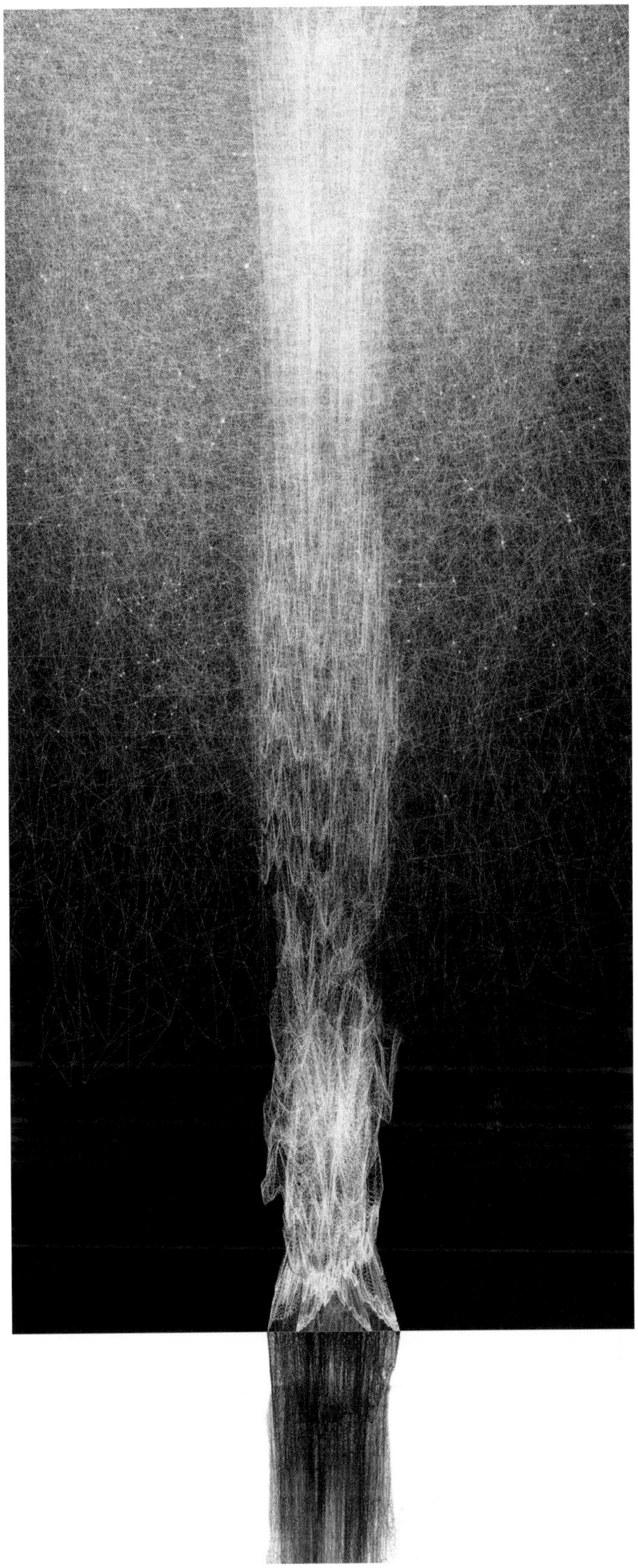

Above: While apparently similar to land plants, algae have an opposite life mechanism. It floats towards the surface of water by pnuematocysts, absorbs light and nutrition through the surface of blades (top), pneumatocysts transports nutrition throughout the kelp body by stipe, and the holdfast's only function is to anchor the body of kelp to a substrate; they have no root-like absorbent function.

Opposite: Sectional drawing (10 feet above the ground), representing ocean current pressure, temperature changes, and light penetration levels at a distance from shore of 0—12 yards, and sea level up to 120 feet deep.

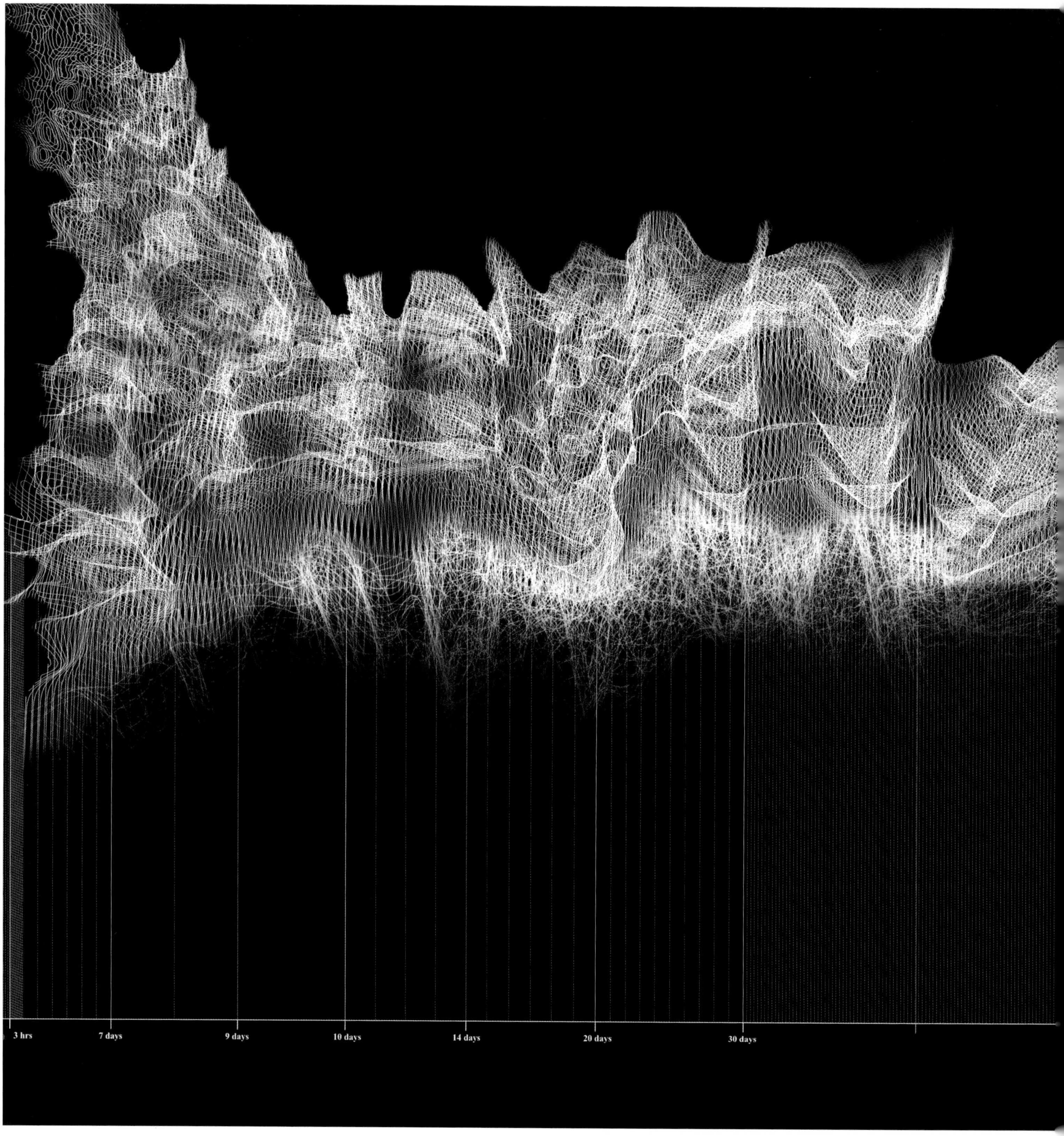

Above: Life cycle of Macrocystis Pyrifera interpreted through transitional points from one stage to the other in the reproduction process, from its outset to 2—3 years.

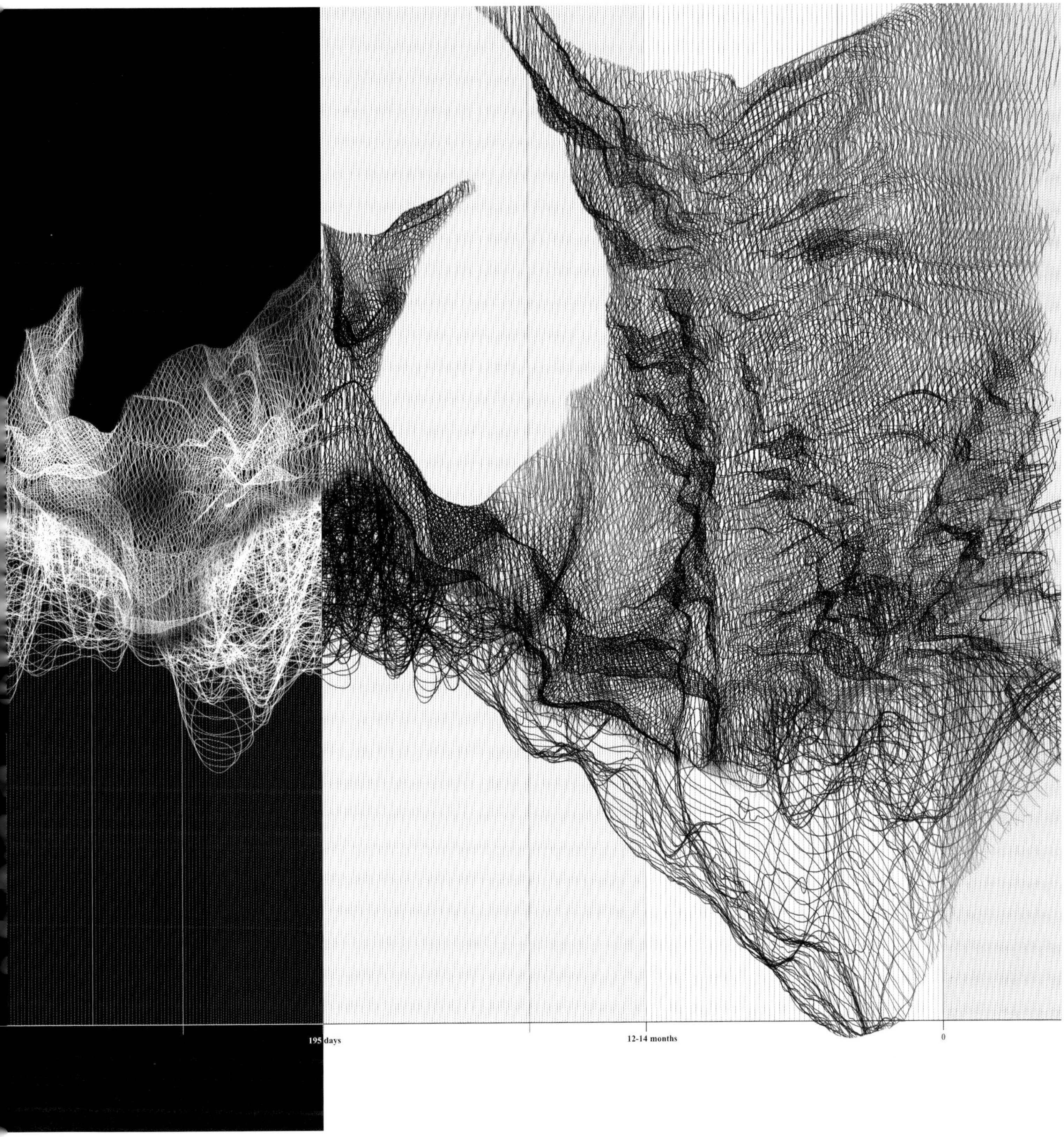
195 days
12-14 months
0

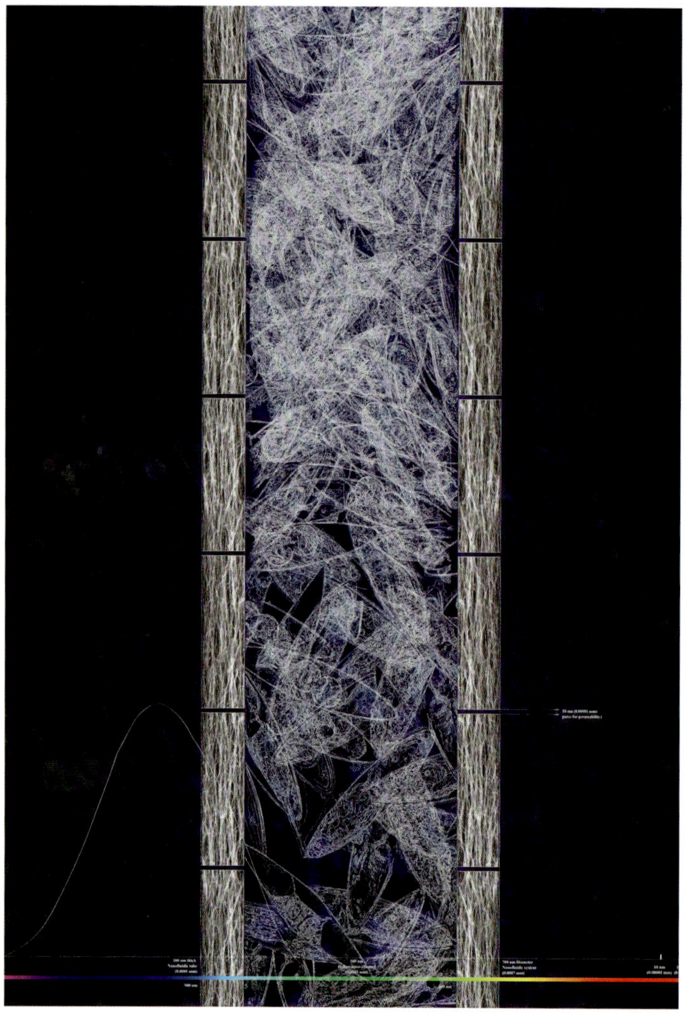

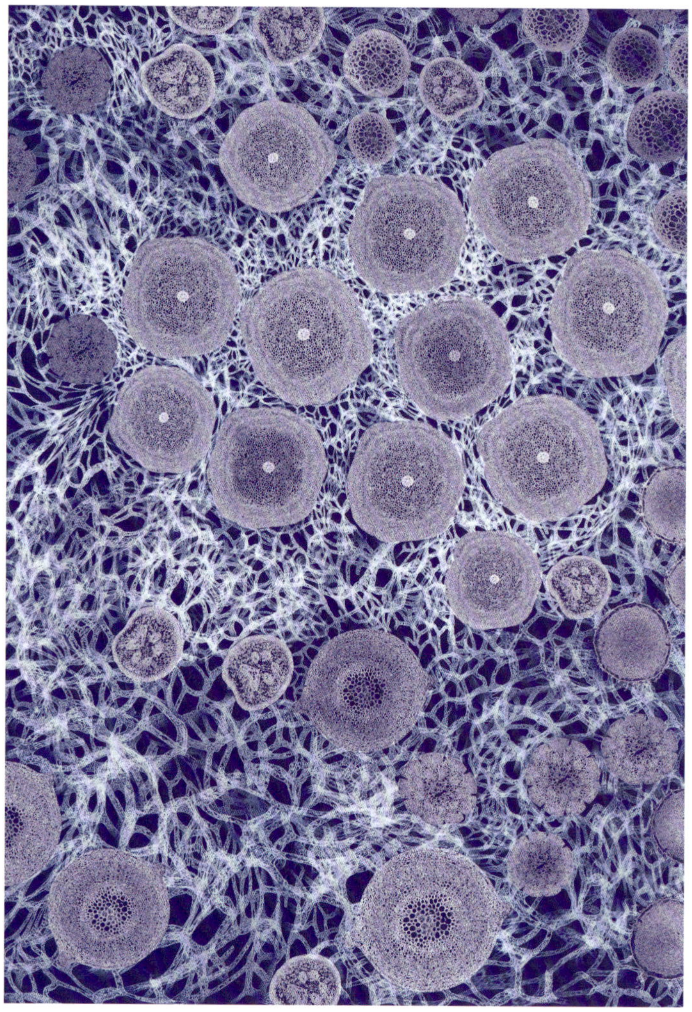

Top left: Longitudinal section of nano-fluidic tubes filled with Pyrocystis Fusiformis species illuminating during night (bioluminescence) in ocean water. The blue light of Pyrocystis Fusiformis can penetrate farther and deeper than any other light spectrum, down to the lower limits of the euphotic zone (scale 20,000:1).

Top right: Plan of the proposed prototypes, along with stipes, of Macrocystis and other small algae, when changes in the ocean occur, indicating increased growth rate and a tendency to inhabit nearby prototypes.

Left: Detail of tentacle-like holdfast's growth with gel-like adhesive ingredient, Algin, inside. Holdfast is a root-like structure anchoring system, adhering kelp to hard substrates with no absorbent function. Holdfasts do not correspond to the size of kelp. They are strong enough to anchor the giant kelp body to small rocks, withstanding the force of ocean currents (not to scale).

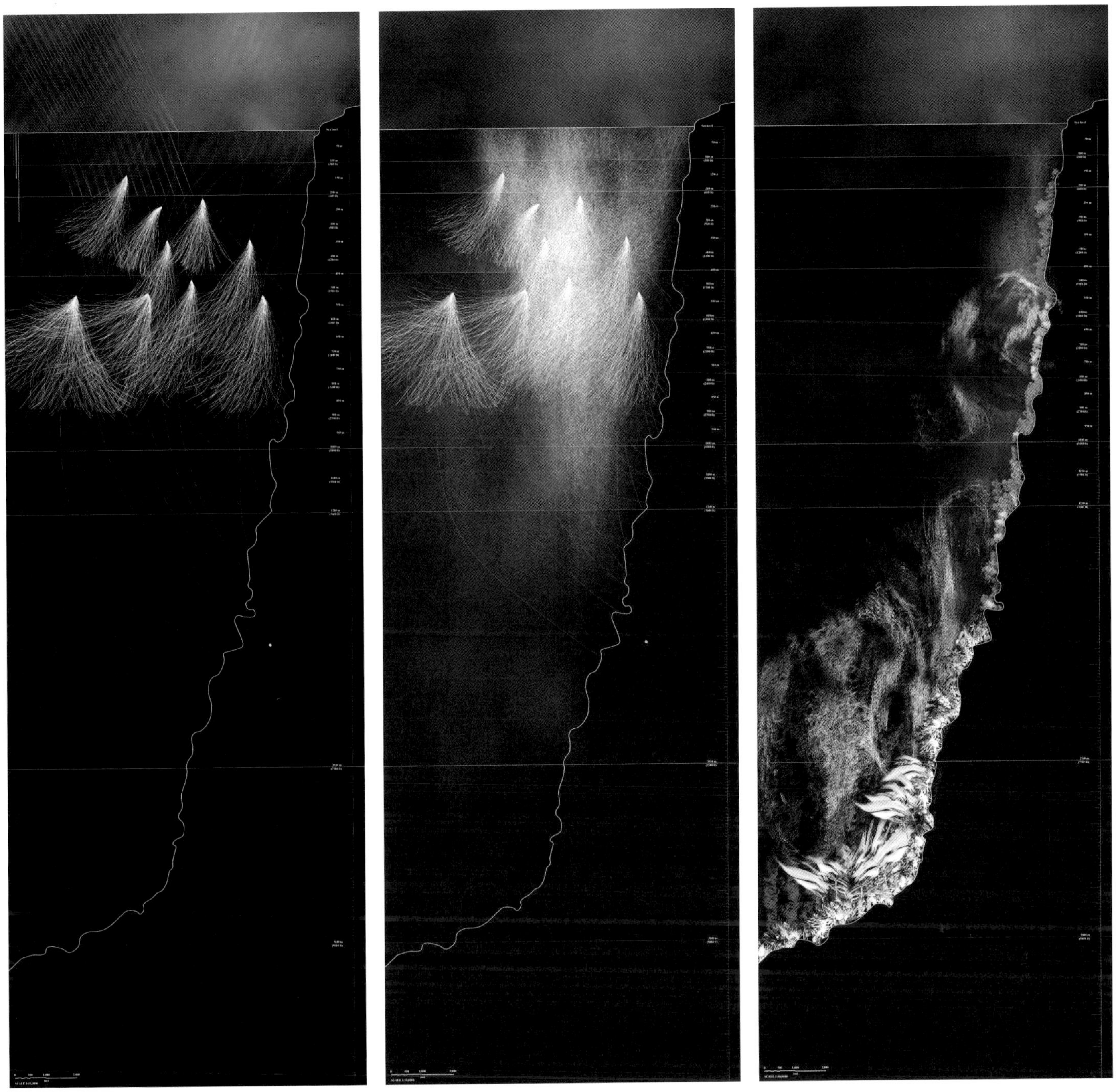

Above: Three sections showing changes over a few decades (from left to right) in kelp forest boundaries after installation of prototypes on site. 1. Prototypes are just installed. Collecting lights will be distributed throughout the deep ocean at night. 2. After a few years, changes in the kelp growth become visible. 3. After a few decades or more, kelp or algae will be fully grown and will have extend the boundaries of their habitat to the much deeper ocean. This new habitat may sponsor a greater variety of algae that are more likely to adapt to new environments and conditions (scale 1:50,000).

Above: Plan of the movement of algae spores between the proposed prototypes flowing through currents. Movement of spores is the beginning of reproduction process (scale 1:5).

Sequoia as Gestalt

Redwood National and State Parks, California
Rosannah Sandoval

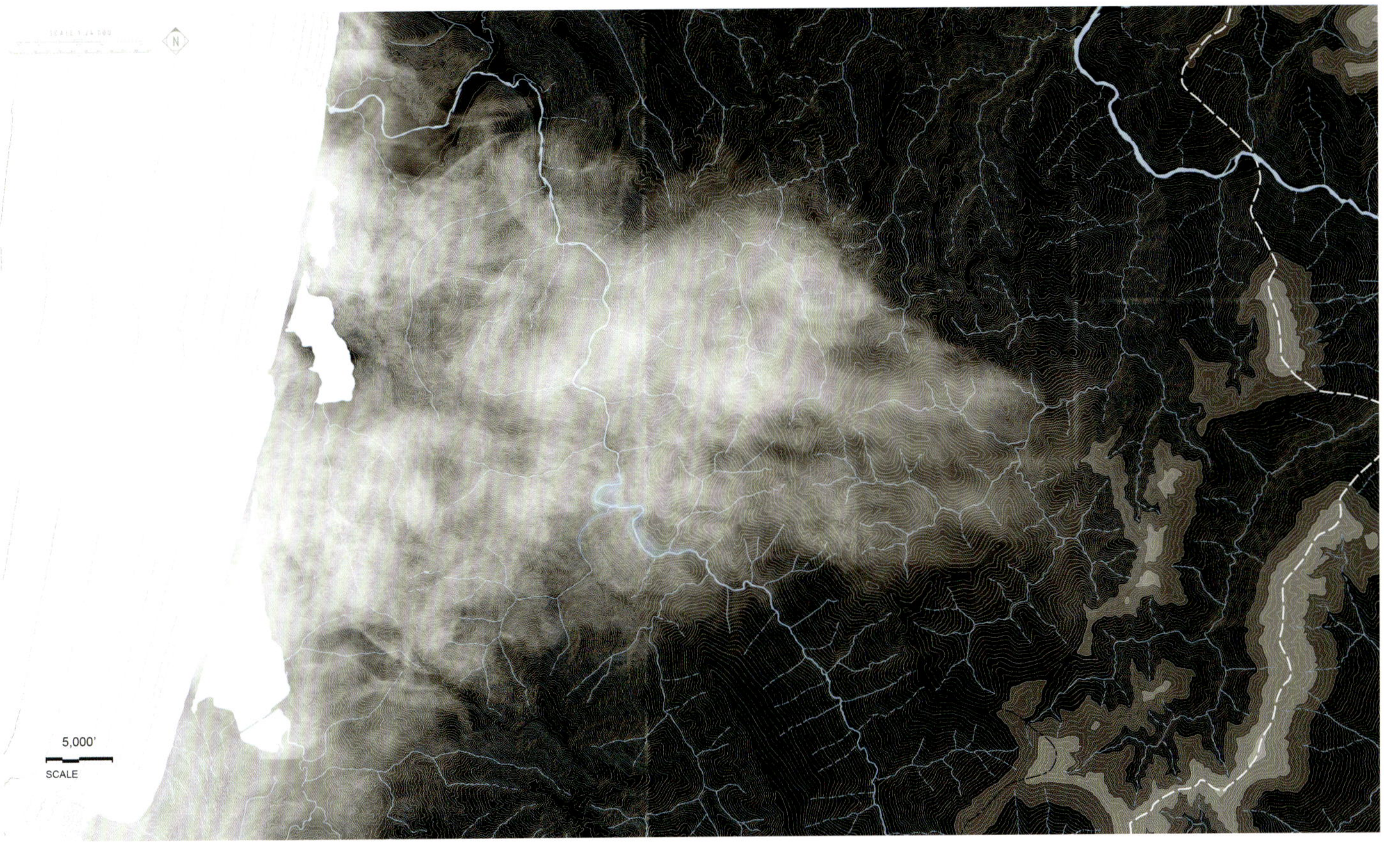

Condensation, coalescence, and capillarity are the delicate processes which are at the core of the survival of the largest living organism on Earth, the Sequoia Semperviren. These three processes occur in a cycle, made visible daily, as water changes state within the organism in relation to specific environmental conditions and millenary—a result of the accumulation of these processes over thousands of years. These two timeframes define the ecosystem of these unlikely creatures. One hundred and thirty-seven known Sequoia trees occupy a 26 square mile forest. On average, each Sequoia tree, as tall as 350 feet and with trunks over 13 feet in diameter, is 1,200—1,800 years old, but they can survive as long as 4,000 years.

As a whole, the Sequoia forest operates as a mega-organism, with each tree acting as a component within a larger structure. The forest network of trunks, branches, and needles capture fog, which provides the environmental conditions for the growth and subsistence of each tree. The regenerative process of the Sequoia depends on the dynamic relationships of cloning, burning, and flooding. The species' specific features (varying needle size, fiber density, and others) form an internal conduit for nutrients and water at a massive scale. Disturbance, decay, and digestion define reproduction in this complex system. Within the holistic system, all energy is maintained; the active convection of this energy substantiates the whole tree and forest.

Top: Plan view showing the daily fog resulting from the passage of warm, moist marine air over the cold surface water of the Pacific Ocean at dawn and dusk. This fog is key to the survival of the Coastal Redwood.

Top: Section of the Sequoia territory during the day when the temperature is higher than the dew point by more than 20 degrees, evaporating the fog between the Pacific Ocean and the Klamath Mountain range. During the day, the fog hovers over the ocean. The topography of peaks and valleys carries runoff from the mountains and creates pockets of shade and cool air.

Bottom: Section of the Sequoia forest at dawn and dusk when the temperature drops. At these times, the air cools to where it meets the dew point and becomes saturated, forming fog. Ocean currents carry the fog over the cool surface of the land to where it is captured by the dense forest canopy. The fog decreases the evaporation and transpiration of water from the Sequoias and adds moisture to the soil.

Opposite: Longitudinal section of a single Sequoia tree showing the water cycle within the tree. The sequoia generates its own rain through the harvesting of fog captured from the air. The moisture in the air condenses on the needle structure that densely populates the branches. When the weight of the water is greater than the needles can hold, the water drips down to the earth's surface. The droplets seep into the soil and the shallow roots absorb the moisture. When evaporation occurs on the tree's leaves, it creates a vacuum that pulls water up the trunk through capillarity.

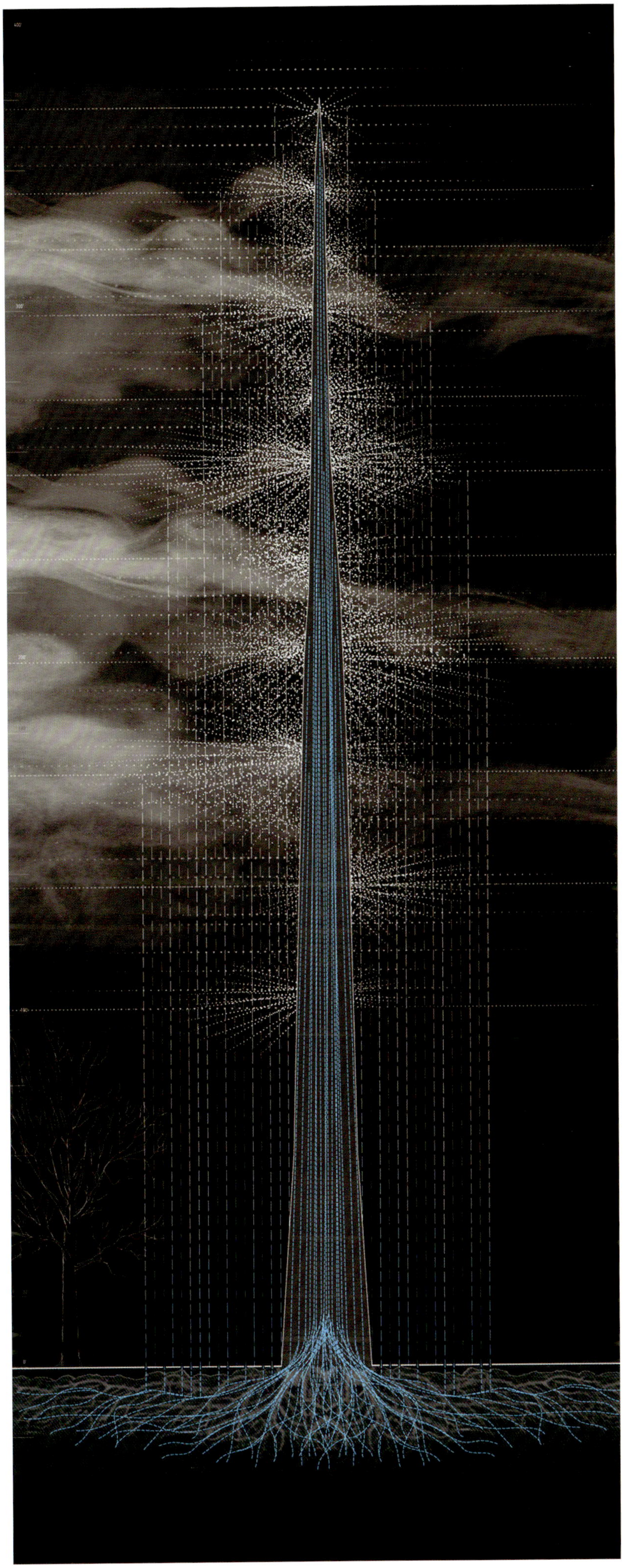

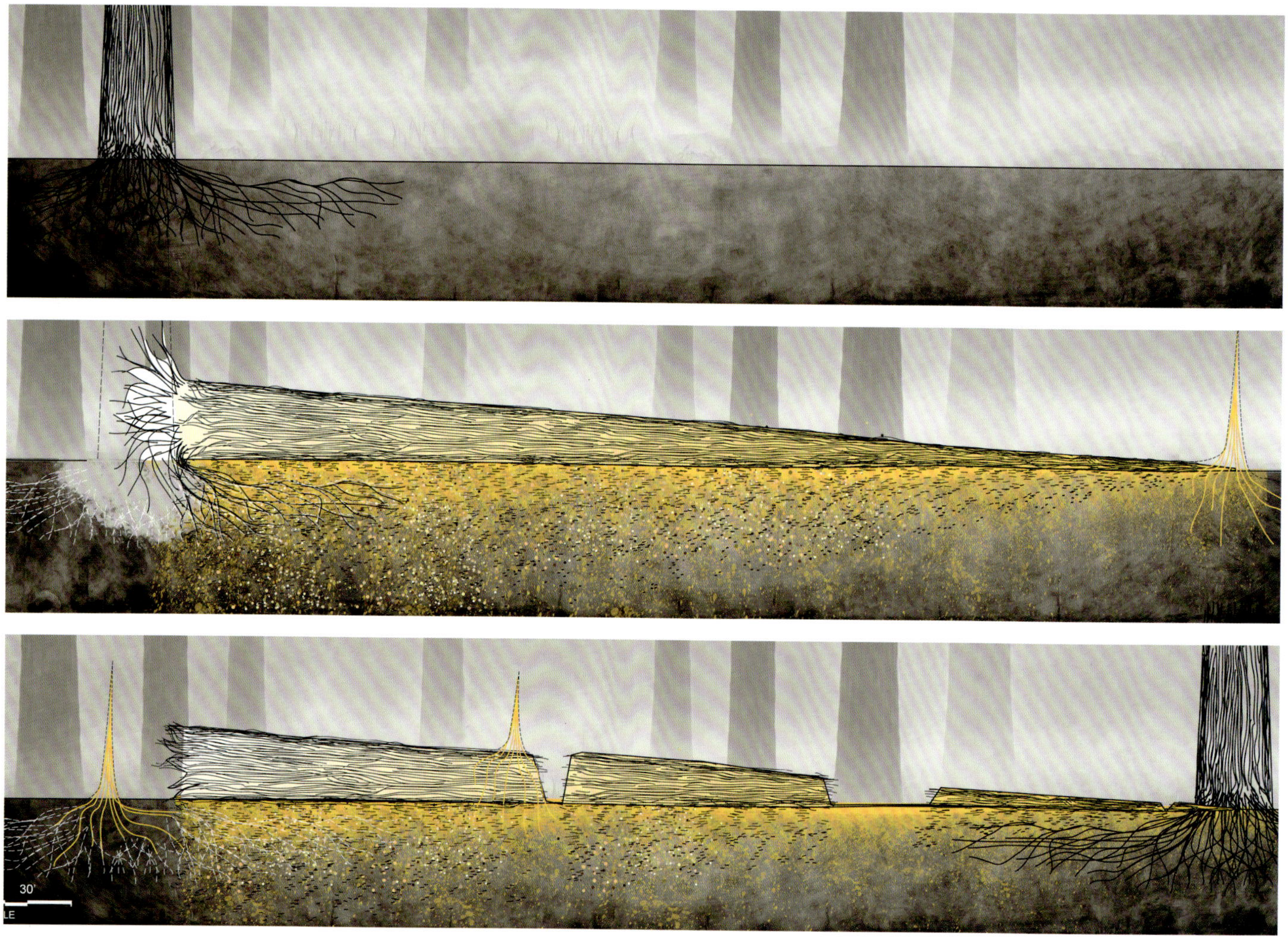

Top: Sections of the alternative reproductive capabilities of the Coastal Redwoods, cloning as stumps sprout from fallen, decaying trunks. The tree falls to the forest floor, activating a 100-year decaying process. Burls develop from dormant buds as a second generation Sequoia that uses the parent tree's existing root network.

Bottom: Plan of growth pattern of the Sequoia.

Opposite top: Sectional detail of the proposed enhanced grafting and cloning processes driven by the acceleration of current conditions. The Sequoia network grafts roots from tree to tree to strengthen its shallow base and create a mega-organism underground. This process could potentially occur three-dimensionally above the ground plane if a falling tree could be caught in midair by another tree's branch, which would allow more water and nutrients to move through the system.

Opposite bottom: Section of a proposal that would allow a new “super” Redwood system to emerge, potentially twice the height of the current 360-foot-high canopy.

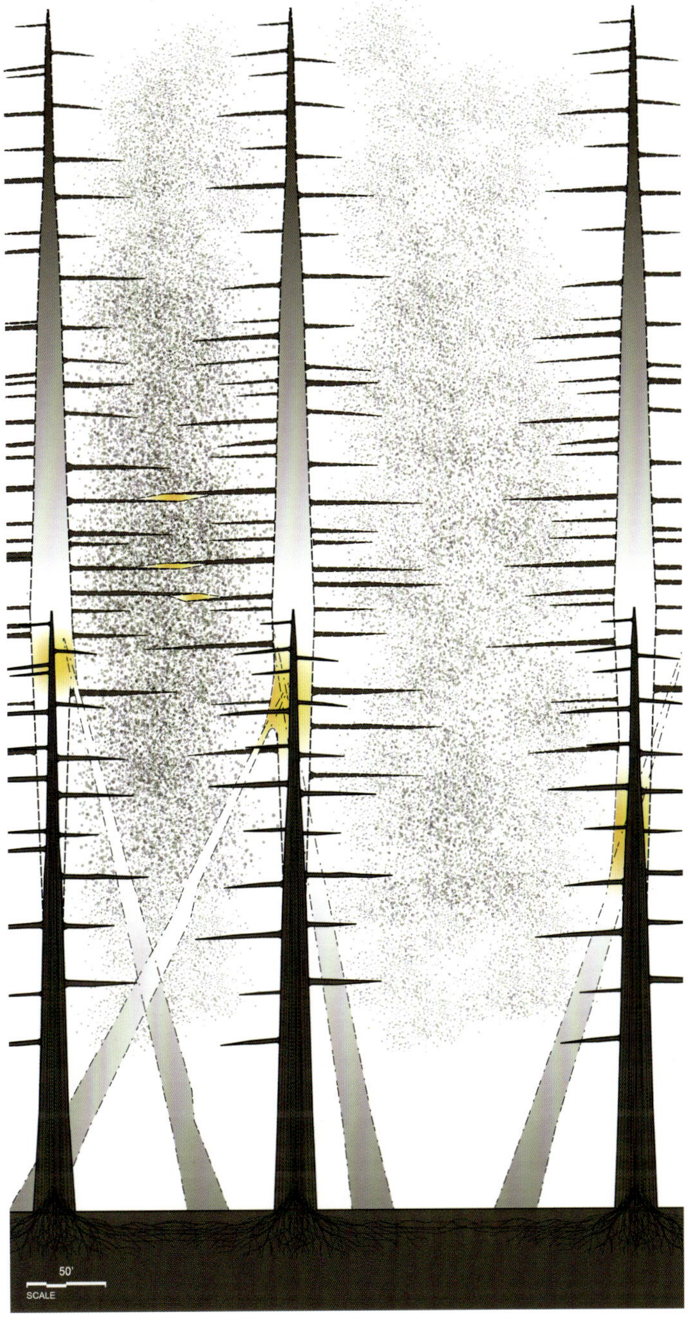
50'
SCALE

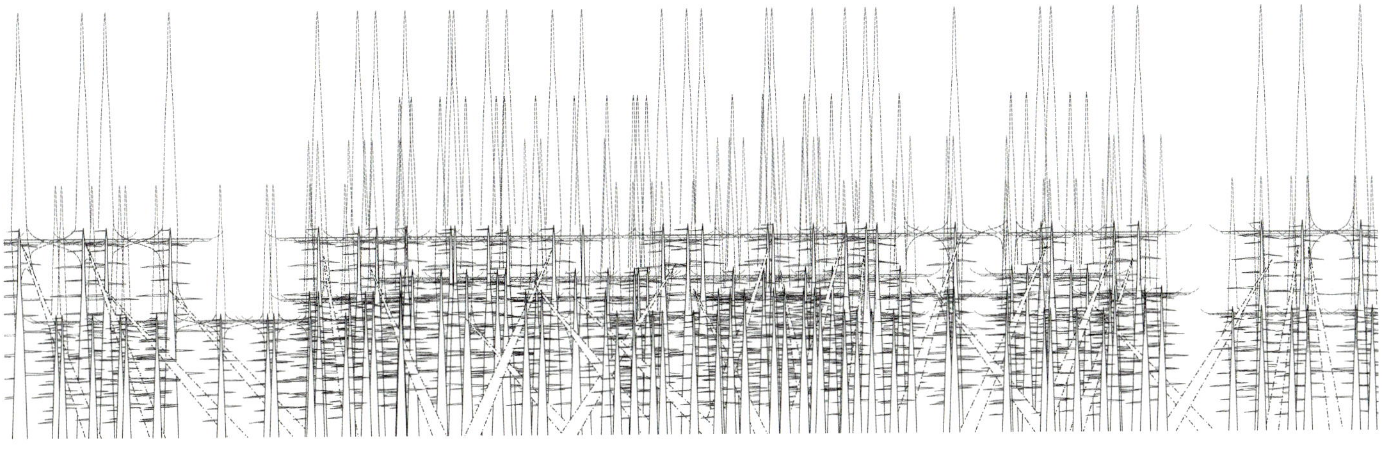

Clouds as Transformational Tools

Sahel Region, Africa
Chung-Wei Lee

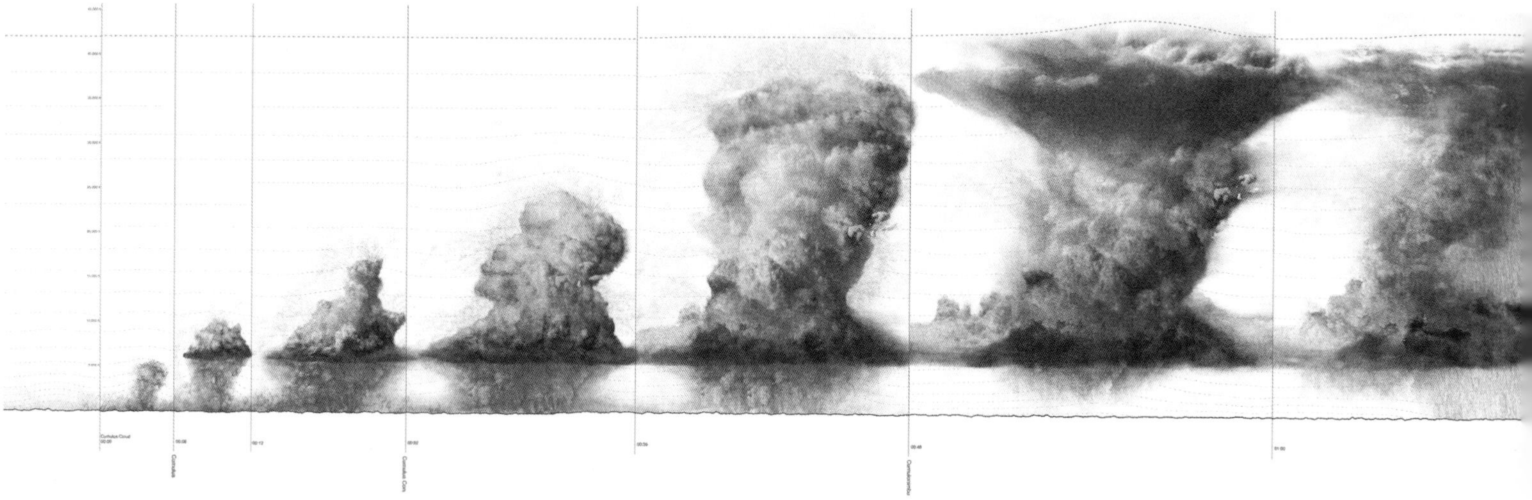

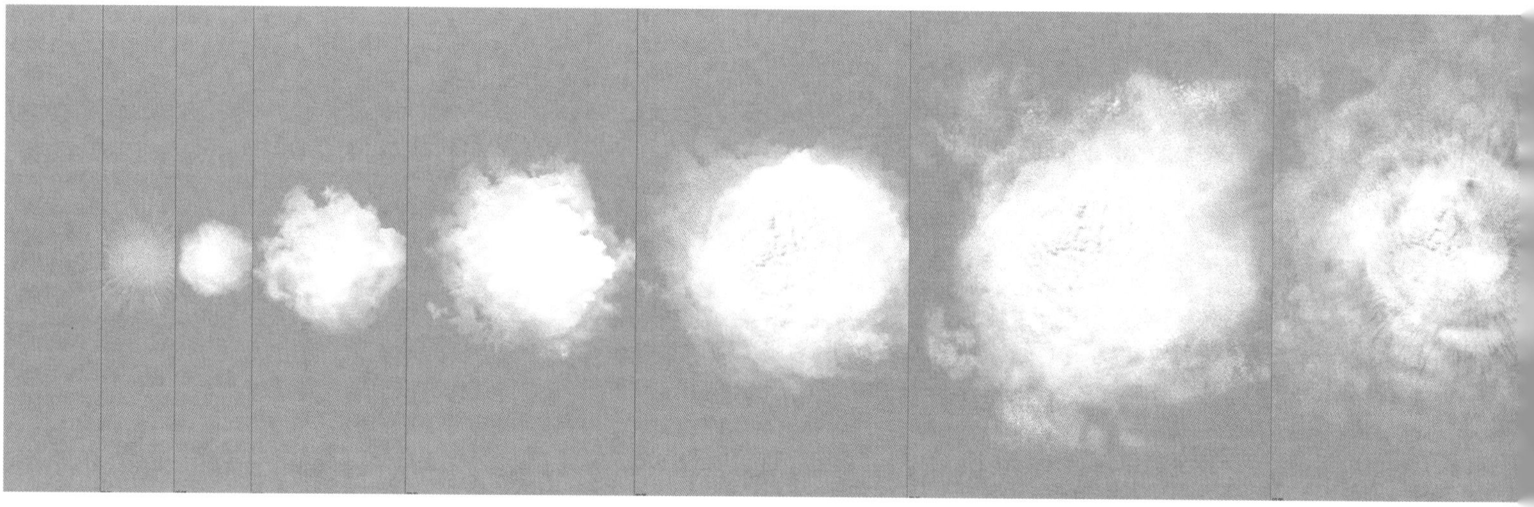

Based on principles of cloud formation, this project is an exploration into the possibilities of mitigating conditions in extremely dry, desert areas using the Earth's ground water resources to generate clouds. The locus of this exploration is the Sahel region in the Sahara. The Sahel region is a grassland belt that stretches across the African continent from the Atlantic Ocean to the Red Sea, which divides the vast, dry Sahara desert and the wet tropical rain forest. Its savannah ecosystem and agriculture activities depend on the precarious rainfall causing this region to be permanently threatened by food scarcity and desertification on the south Sahara fringe. At the same time, a trans-boundary fossil aquifer system—one of the world's largest groundwater systems—lies beneath the sandstone stratum covering the Sahara and Sahel. Most of these aquifers were recharged 5,000 years ago when the climate was tropical.

A new type of irrigation system reaching to the underground aquifer system is proposed to re-activate the water cycle over that region. This new system acts as a literal "cloud machine" that captures water vapor and triggers rainstorms. The heat and flatness of the landscape allow soil moisture patterns to trigger ground winds that favor the development of convective cumulus clouds—the cardinal engine that brings water vapor into the air, forming clouds, and resulting in rainfall. At a regional scale, these artificial patterns of soil moisture not only efficiently use the water vapor from the croplands' evapotranspiration but also capture the moisture brought by southwest winds from the southern tropical forests. Clouds become an environmental transformational tool fostering forest growth on the endangered fringe between the Sahel region and the Sahara Desert.

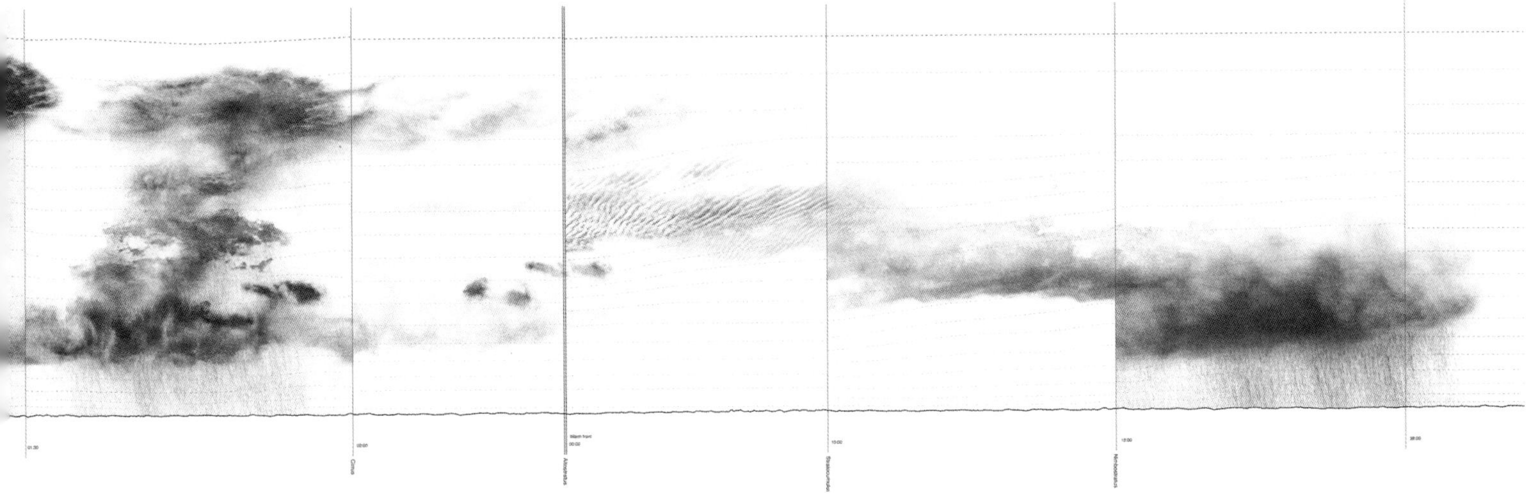

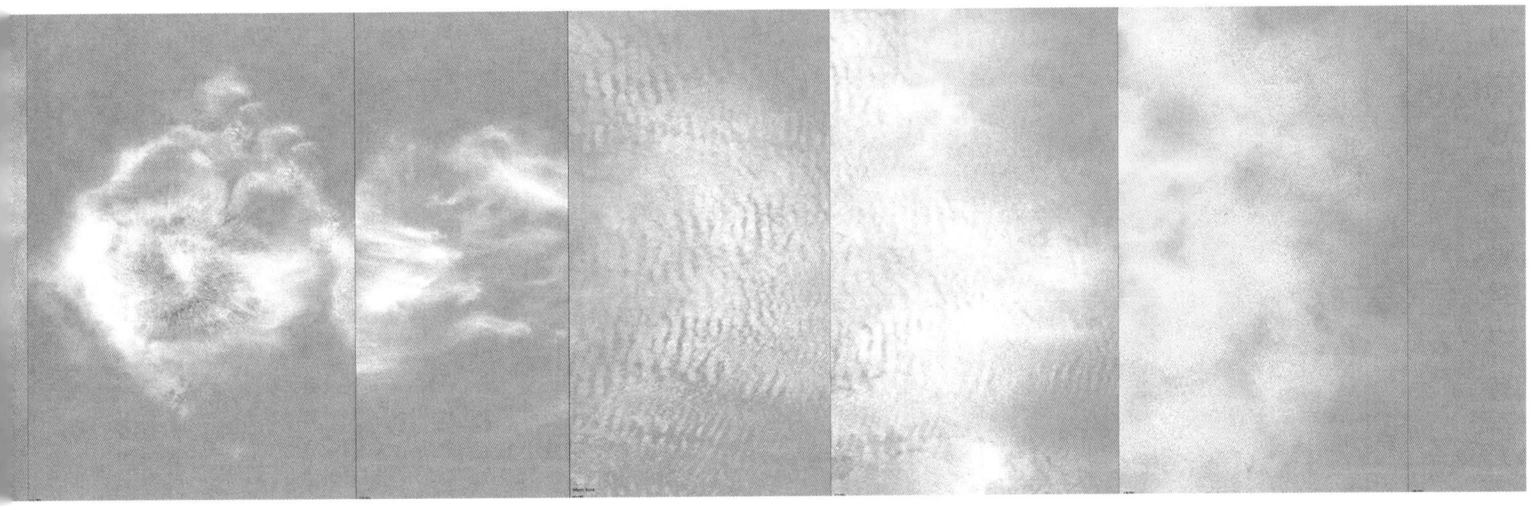

Top: Elevation of the convective cloud formation stages, a water circulation system that traverses the ground and the atmosphere. A water droplet can take several hours to several days to complete a full cycle.

Bottom: Plan of the convective cloud formation stages.

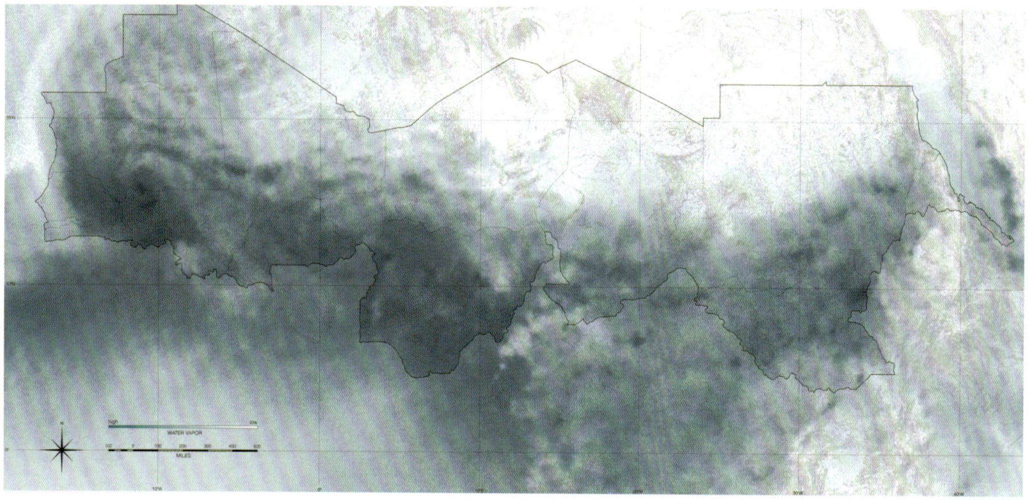
WATER VAPOR
MILES

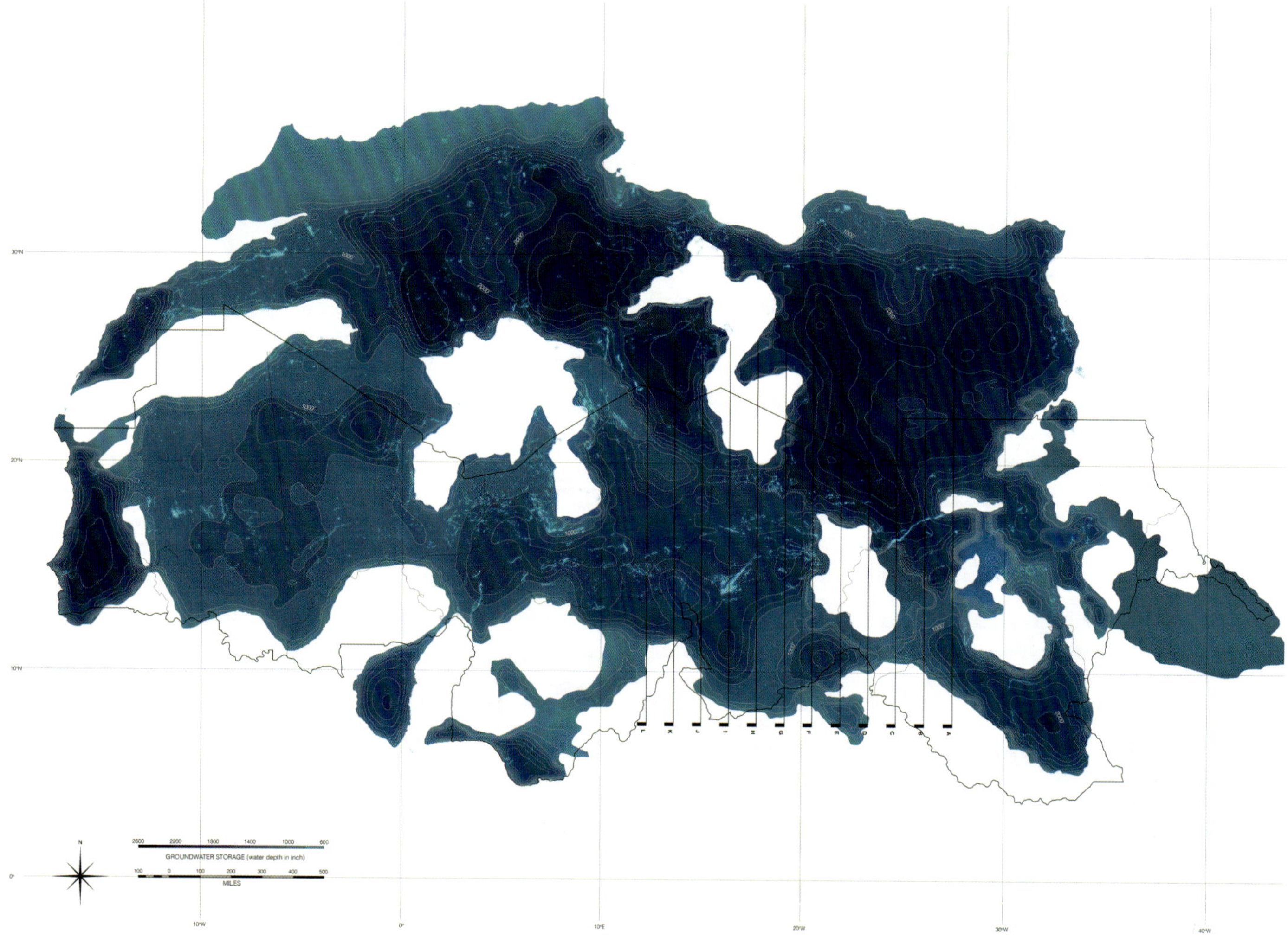
30°N
20°N
10°N
0°
N
2600 2200 1800 1400 1000 600
GROUNDWATER STORAGE (water depth in inch)
100 0 100 200 300 400 500
MILES
10°W
0°
10°E
20°W
30°W
40°W

Opposite top: Plan of the cloud cover over the Sahel region in one day.

Opposite middle: Plan of the water vapor distribution over the Sahel region.

Opposite bottom: Plan of the groundwater distribution over the Sahel region.

Above: Sections of the groundwater system and the climate types above. The Sahel region and the Sahara Desert have much more groundwater storage than the humid tropical areas adjacent to the Sahel region.

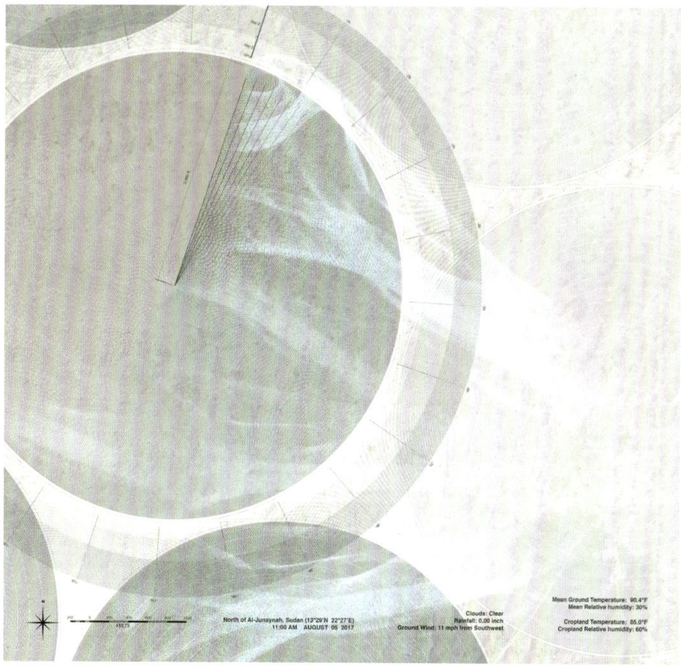

Top: Plan of the first phase of cloud-making, showing a single center-pivot irrigation system (each circle is one mile in diameter).

Bottom: By tracking the patterns of wind, humidity, and temperature, the proposed system creates drastic gradients of soil moisture resulting in a field of unbalanced temperature and humidity. The disequilibrium can catalyze the formation of up-currents of air over the hotter and dryer areas that suck water vapor from the surrounding lands and transforms it into cumulus cloud systems, generating rainfall.

Above: Experimental model that simulates the convection phenomena triggered by a surface with different temperatures as shown in the operating video. Size: 40" x 50" x 35" (LxDxH) Materials: wood, steel, burner, silicon pipes.

Cyclical Migration

Death Valley, California
David Ross

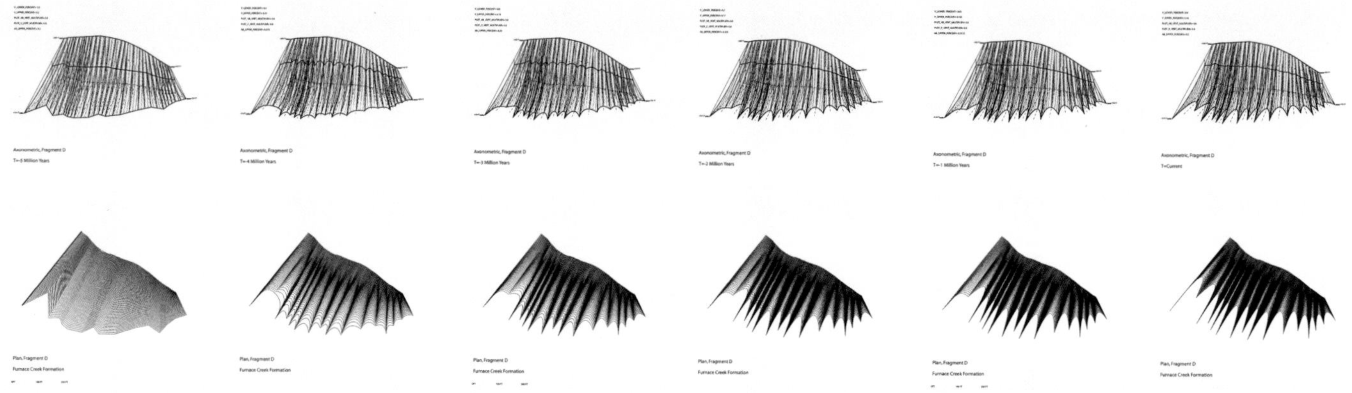

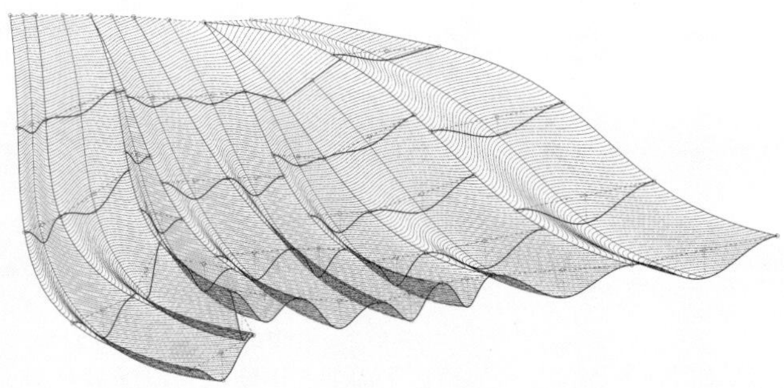

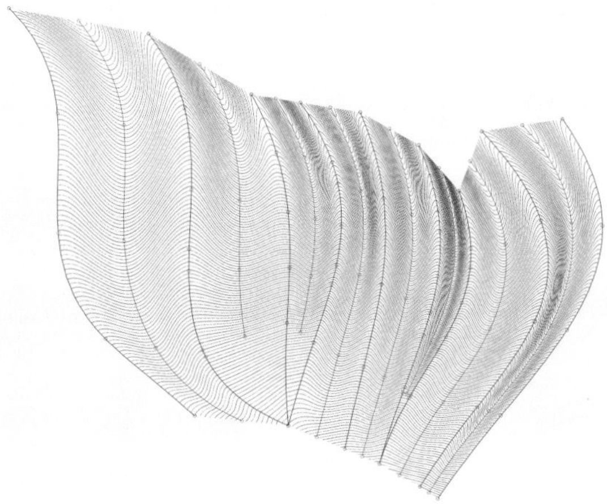

Death Valley is a triple threat. At 282 feet below sea level, Badwater Basin in Death Valley is simultaneously the hottest, driest, and lowest point in North America—an undisputed landscape of extremes. Over the course of 1,700 million years Death Valley has endured an aquatic inversion. It has not always been a valley, as the limestone and sandstone rocks indicate that it was a shallow sea for most of the Paleozoic Era (542—251 million years ago). Although now known for its lack of water, water flows have etched the site, leaving a morphological imprint on the land, from alluvial fans flanking both edges of the valley to the erosional badland formations at Zabriskie Point.

Focusing on Death Valley's orientation and its exposure, which offers no solar relief, this project explores through a set of speculative drawings, focusing on a 5,270-square-mile, designated U.S. wilderness and the relationship between water and light. The coexistent and competing flow of sunlight and water, marking the first light as the Sun rises above the Black Mountains to the first shadow as it sets in the west, are depicted in different phases. This migration of light and heat orbits around the lowest point of Death Valley, Badwater Basin, and describes a new solar contour.

Opposite: Furnace Creek Formations. A study of the hydrological geomorphology of Zabriskie Point at Death Valley, California. Hypothetical time-based computational model showing erosional landscape transformation over five million years.

Above: Furnace Creek Formation, Model. 150 x 300-foot erosional landscape fragment.

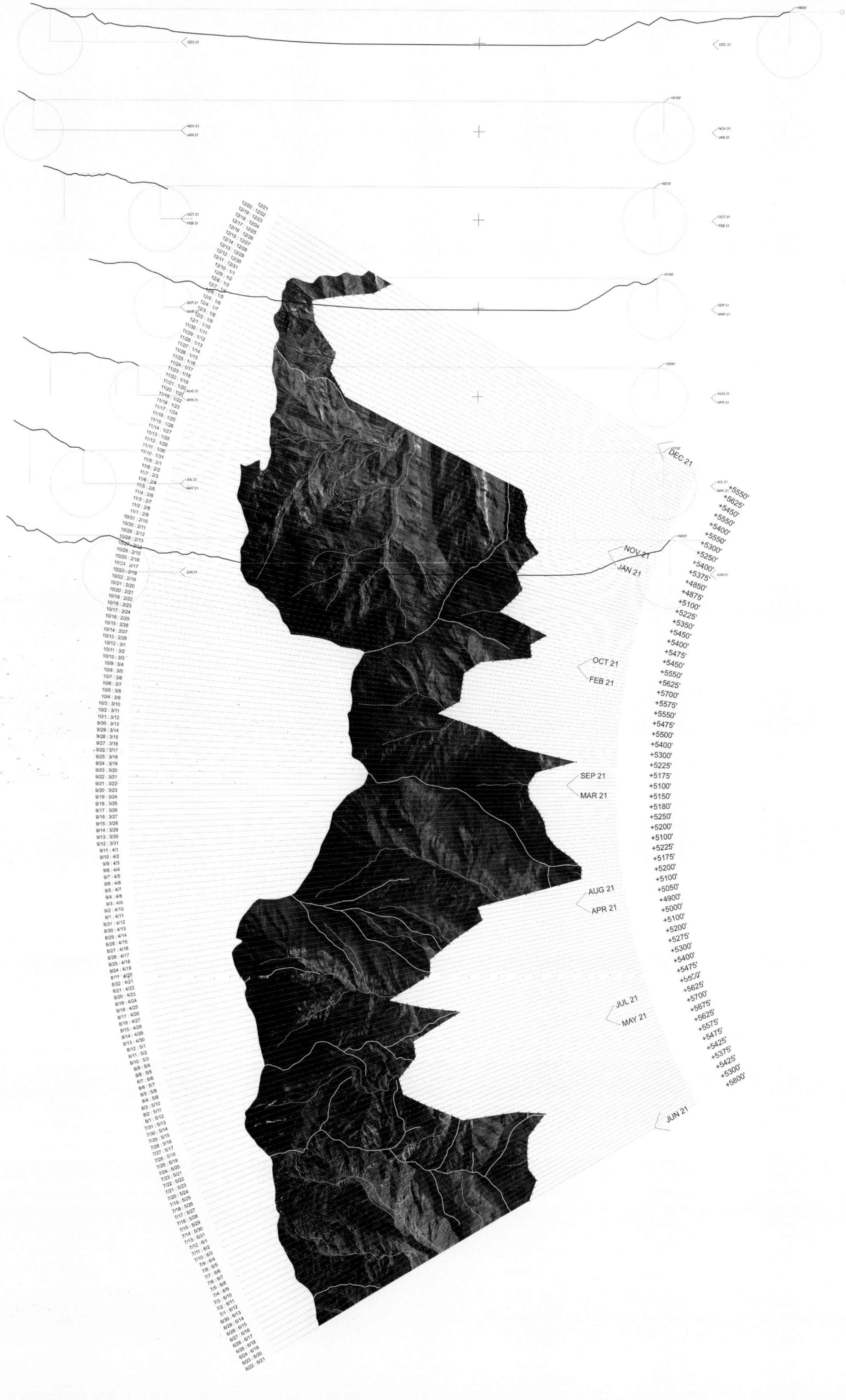
DEC 21
NOV 21
JAN 21
OCT 21
FEB 21
SEP 21
MAR 21
AUG 21
APR 21
JUL 21
MAY 21
JUN 21
+5550'
+5625'
+5450'
+5550'
+5400'
+5550'
+5300'
+5250'
+5400'
+5375'
+4850'
+4875'
+5100'
+5225'
+5350'
+5450'
+5400'
+5475'
+5450'
+5550'
+5625'
+5700'
+5575'
+5550'
+5475'
+5500'
+5400'
+5300'
+5225'
+5175'
+5100'
+5150'
+5180'
+5250'
+5200'
+5100'
+5225'
+5175'
+5200'
+5100'
+5050'
+4900'
+5000'
+5100'
+5200'
+5275'
+5300'
+5400'
+5475'
+5625'
+5700'
+5675'
+5625'
+5575'
+5475'
+5425'
+5375'
+5425'
+5300'
+5800'

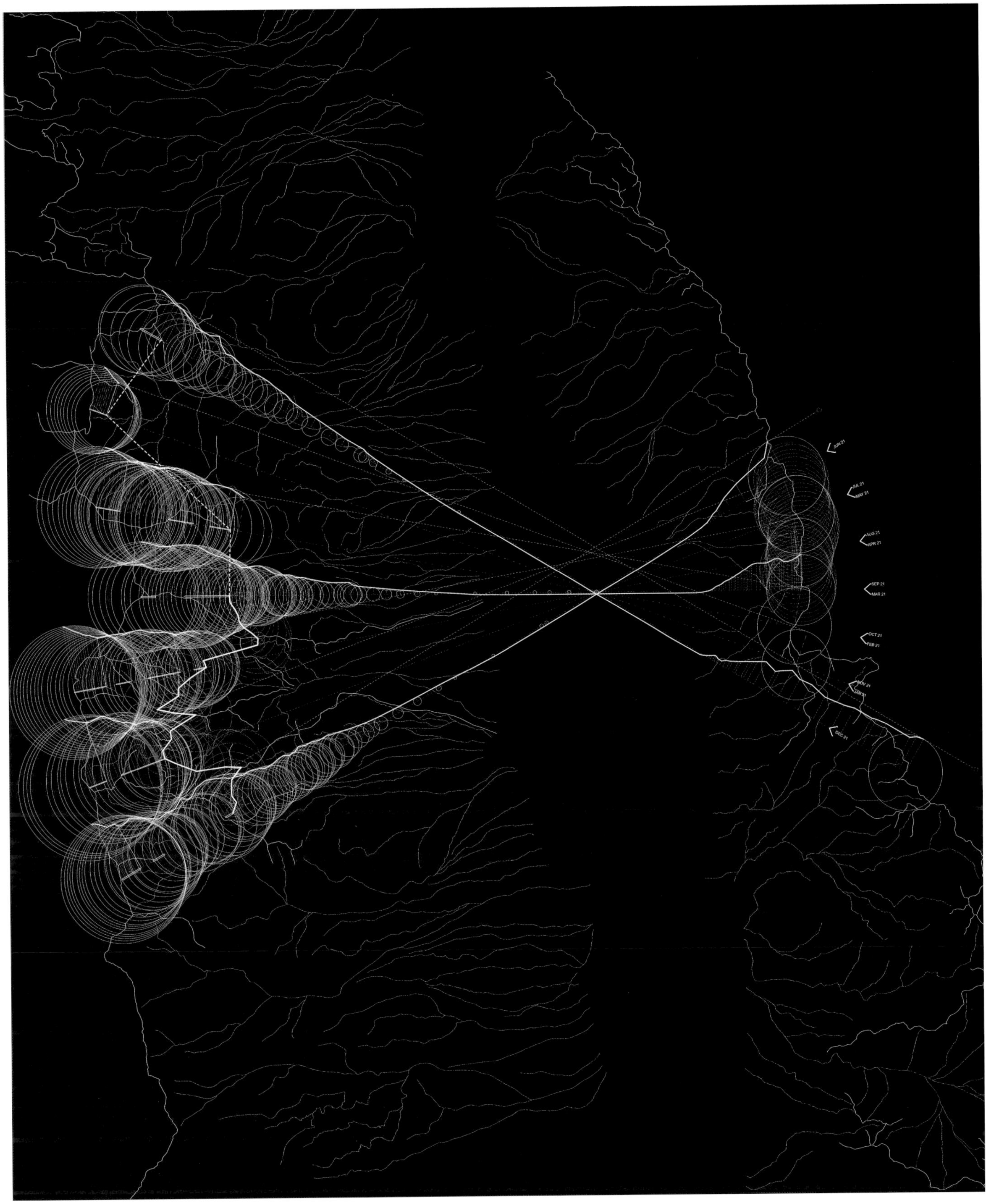

Opposite: Water Etchings. The terrain is in a state of continuous geological transformation, as water forms alluvial fans at the valley floor. These watermarks, amplified through tracing, denote the scarcity of precipitation at lower elevations with marginal annual increases at higher altitudes.

Above: Solar Contours, First Light. Three-hundred-and-sixty-five-day solar calendar locating Black Mountain eastern ridgeline (occluding contour) and constructed contour. This migratory line simultaneously locates Death Valley's first light and first shadow, defining the zero point of solar exposure. Key solstice days are superimposed in section, showing planetary axial alignment.

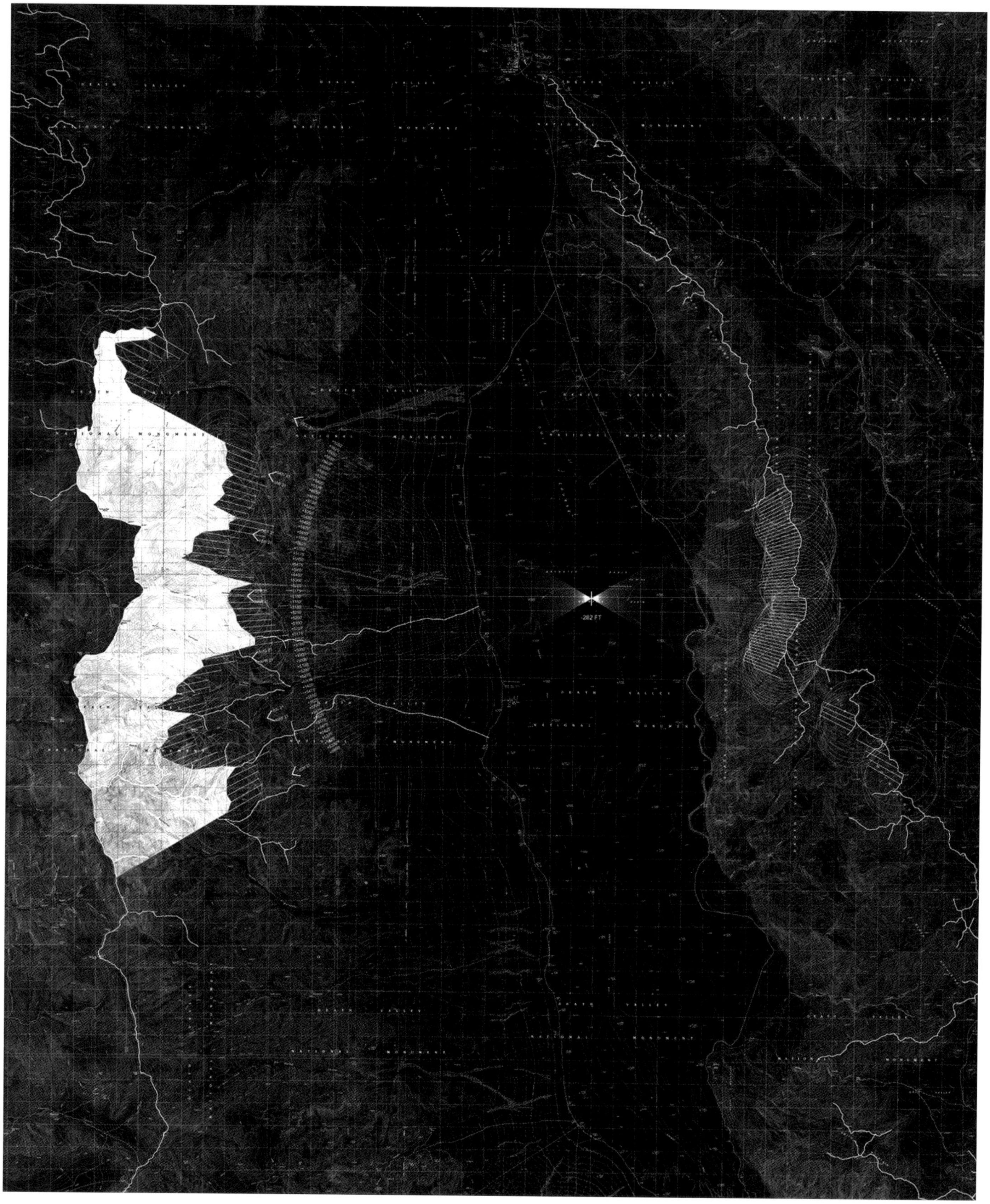

Above and opposite: Water and Light, Strategic Plan. Superimposition of solar contour and first light zones as defined by sunrise projection through Badwater Basin extremum point, including topographic watershed network.

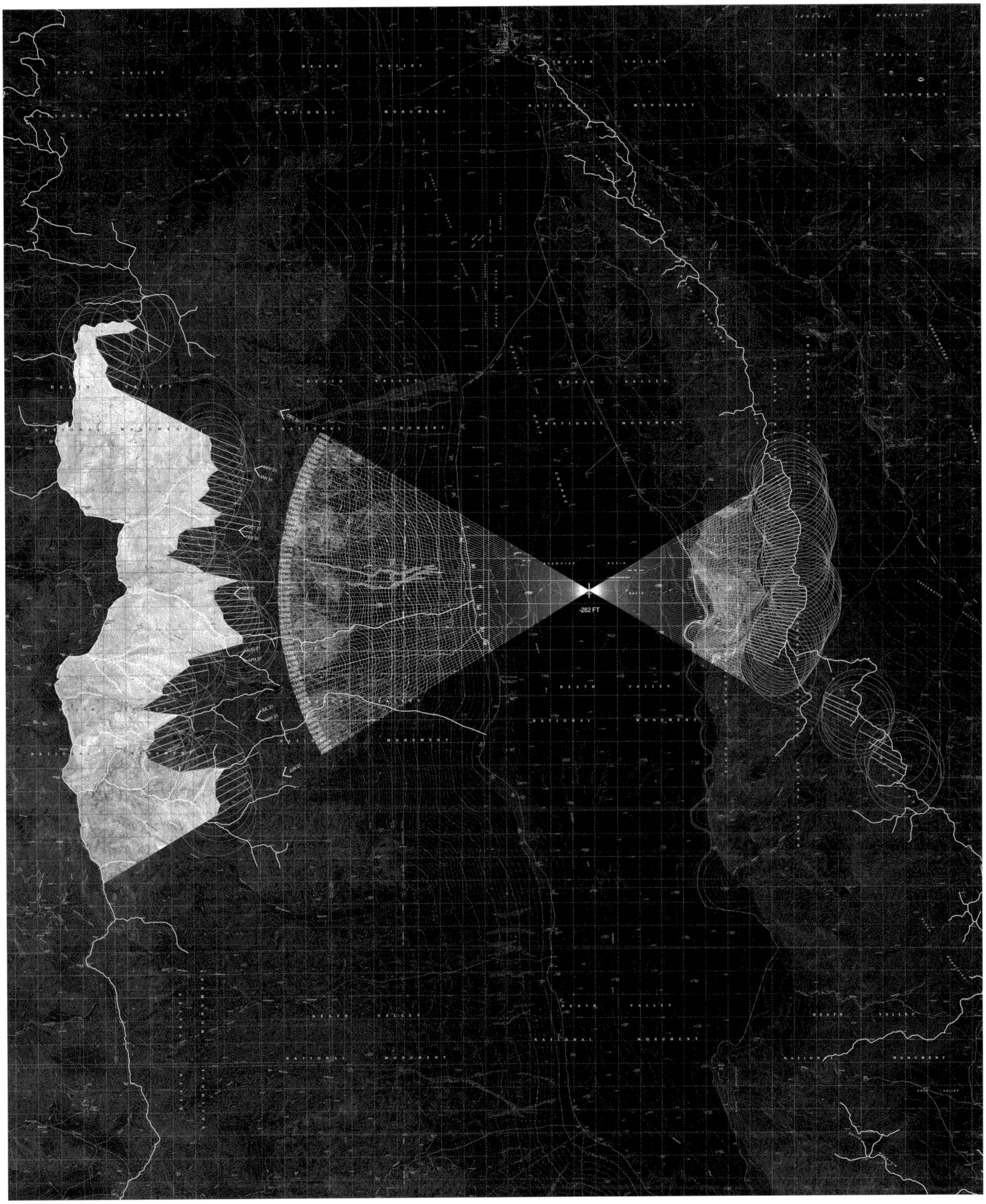
-282 FT

Colliding Matters

Meteor Crater, Arizona
Boreum Lee

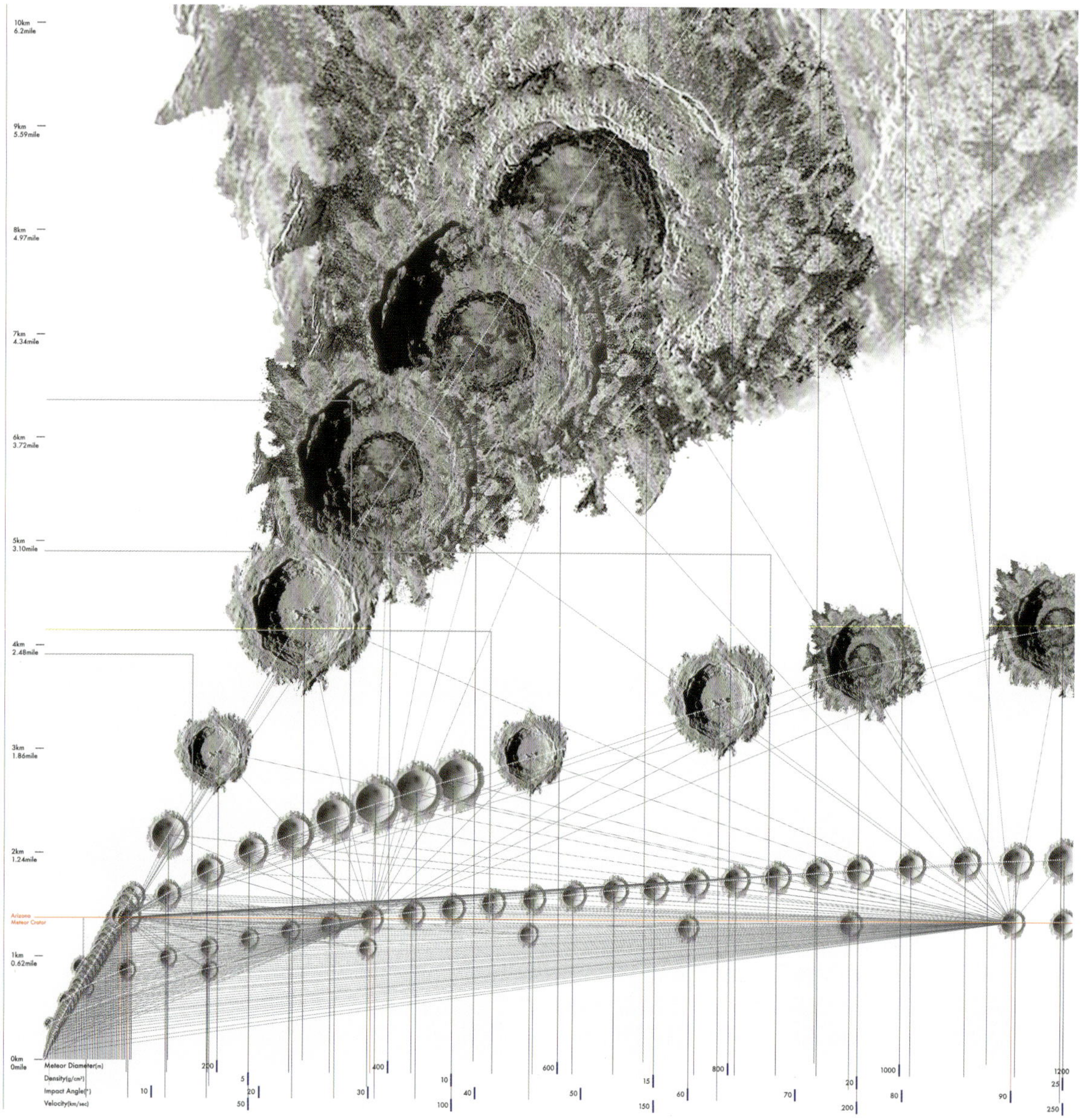

A meteor hit the Colorado Plateau in North Central Arizona 50,000 years ago, creating a .737-mile-wide, 560-feet-deep crater known as the Meteor Crater. This project attempts to reconstruct the entire journey of a meteorite to the Earth's surface. The hypervelocity impact of a large meteorite as such—approximately 60,000 metric tons impacting at a velocity of 15 km/s—created the propagation of powerful shock waves into the target rocks that were registered in the geophysical structure of the site. These traces found in the site reveal much about the materiality of the meteorite as well as the timeline of its journey, which apparently was not consistent. The level and type of friction of the rocky-metallic body with its surrounding environment constantly alternate, causing several transformations of its materiality. As a meteoroid enters the Earth's atmosphere it turns into a meteor turning into a meteorite when it collides with the surface of the Earth. Time plays a key role in this process, and it is through this lens that this phenomenon is explored here. Non-linear and inconsistent temporality is revealed as different temporal moments are juxtaposed.

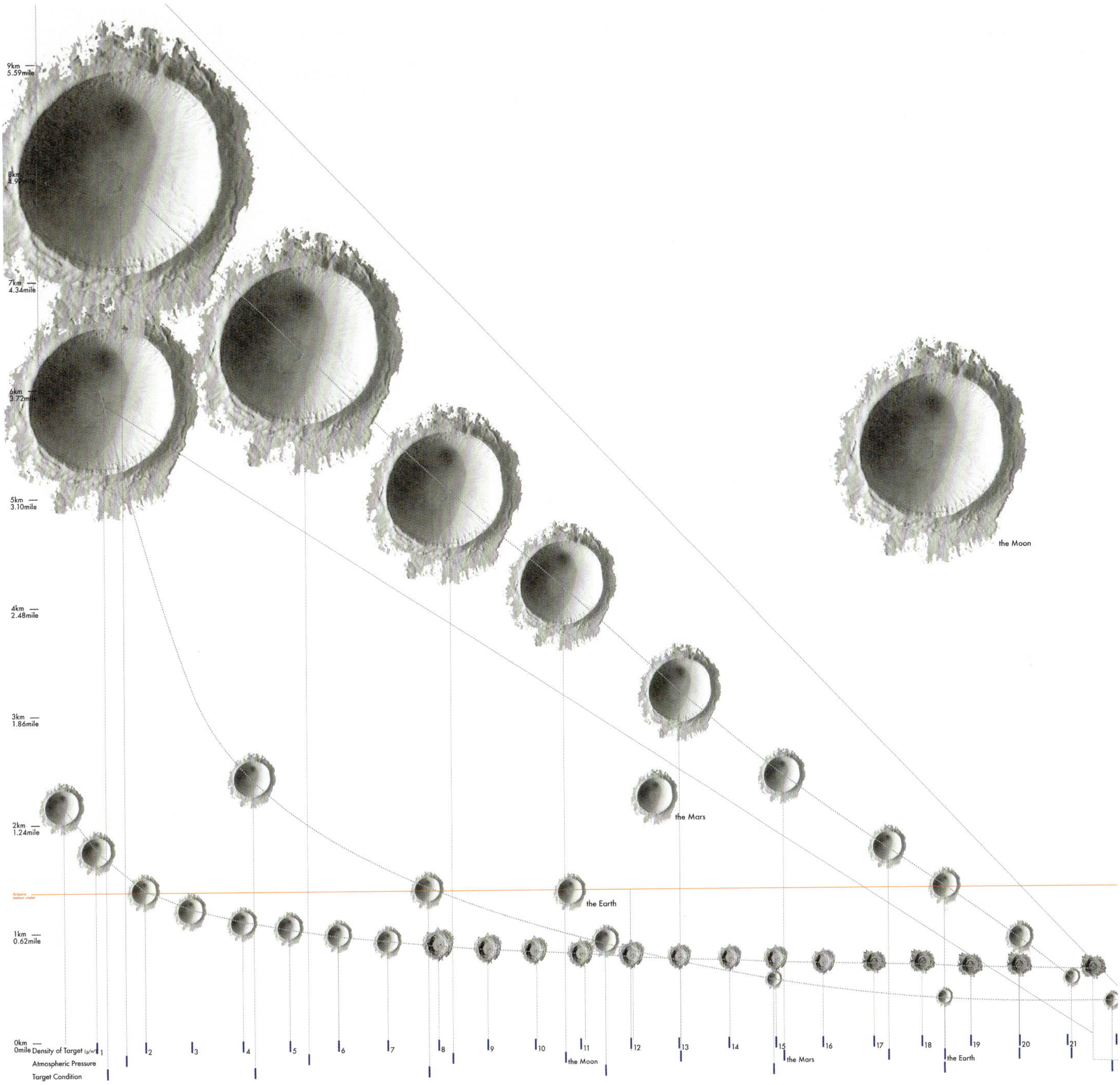

Opposite: Crater Variations. Drawing of hypothetical situation of different meteors hitting the same spot as the Arizona crater, depicting the relationship between the physical facts of the meteor, diameter, density, impact angle, initial velocity and chemical elements—and the resulting size and shape of the crater.

Above: Crater variations and environmental conditions. Environmental conditions affect the configuration of the resulting crater resulting from the meteor's impact. Speculative drawing of varying conditions and resulting craters in Mars, Jupiter, Earth's moon, and the Earth in relation to differences in gravity, density of soil, and atmospheric pressure.

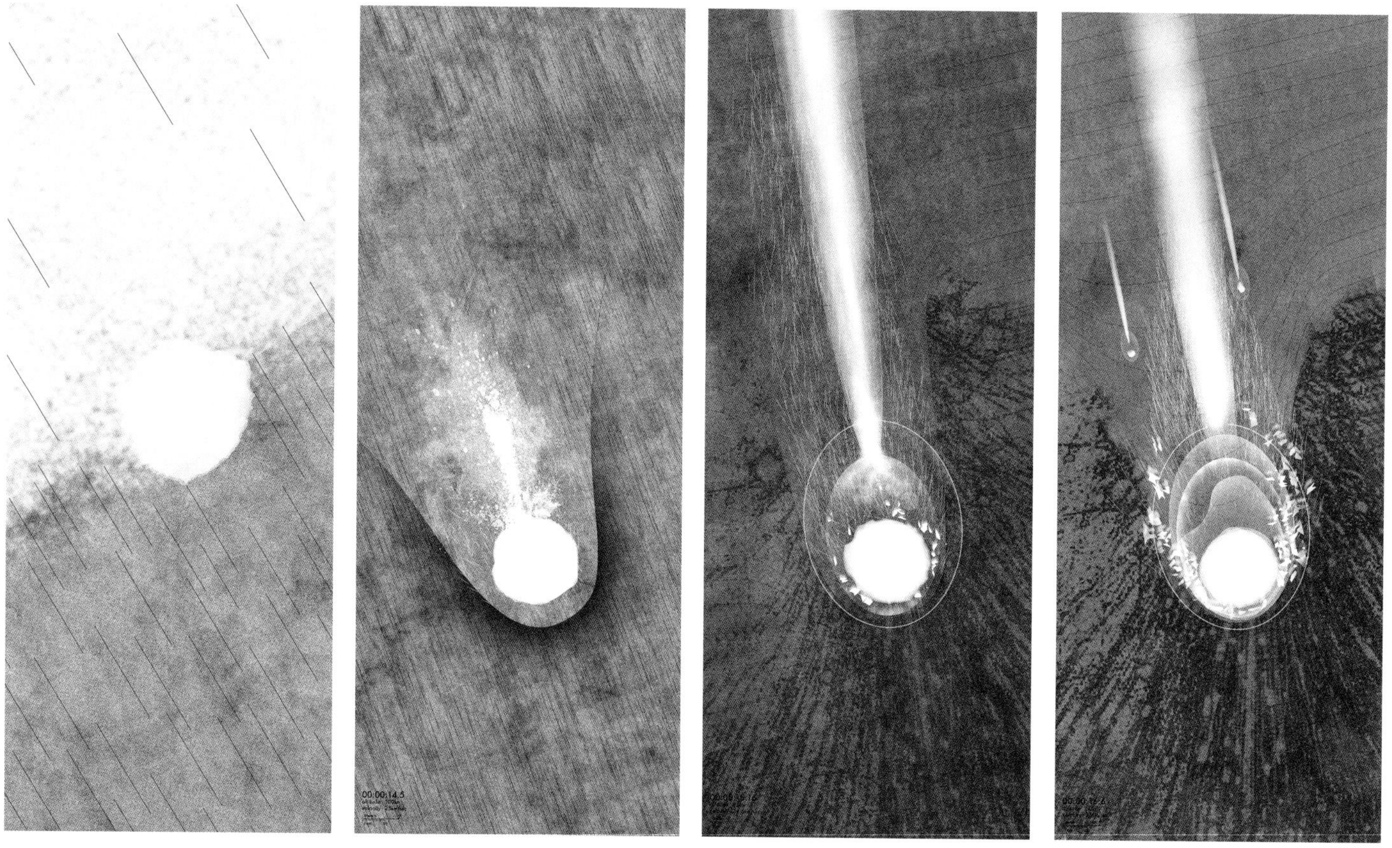

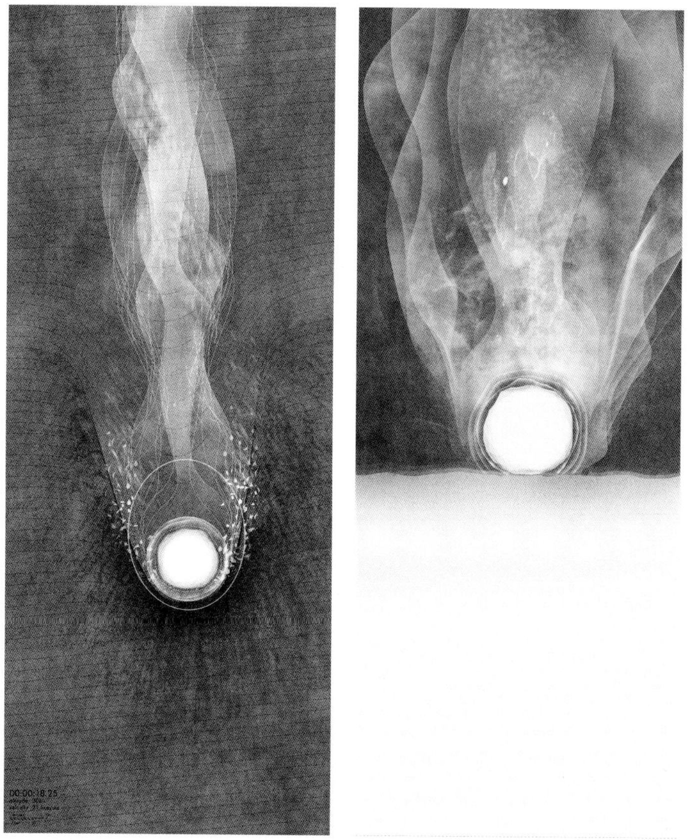

Above: Sectional drawings of meteor's changes as it enters the atmosphere according to time altitude and velocity in its travelling path before impact as a meteorite. 1. At atmosphere's threshold (t: 00:00:00; alt: 500 km). 2. Higher atmospheric density (t: 00:00:14.5; alt: 100 km; v: 25 km/s). 3. Meteor tail's appearance, increase in friction (t: 00:00:15.16; alt: 86 km; v: 24.6 km/s). 4. Increased tail length, decreasing brightness (t: 00:00:18.25; alt: 30 km; v: 21.5 km/s). 5. Decreasing meteor size, increasing tail brightness (t: 00:00:16.6; alt: 60 km; v: 23 km/s). 6. Impact, meteorite hits the ground (t: 00:00:20; alt: 0 km; v: 20 km/s).

Opposite top: Model exploring ground deformation through heat and gravity. As a highly heated metal ball is placed on a wax volume, it starts a melting process and accelerates downward as it penetrates through the wax.

Opposite bottom: Models exploring the forces of friction and pressure in ground deformation. High-pressure water erodes the series of boxes made from a plaster-salt mixture, depicting the formation of a crater as a result of multiple forces.

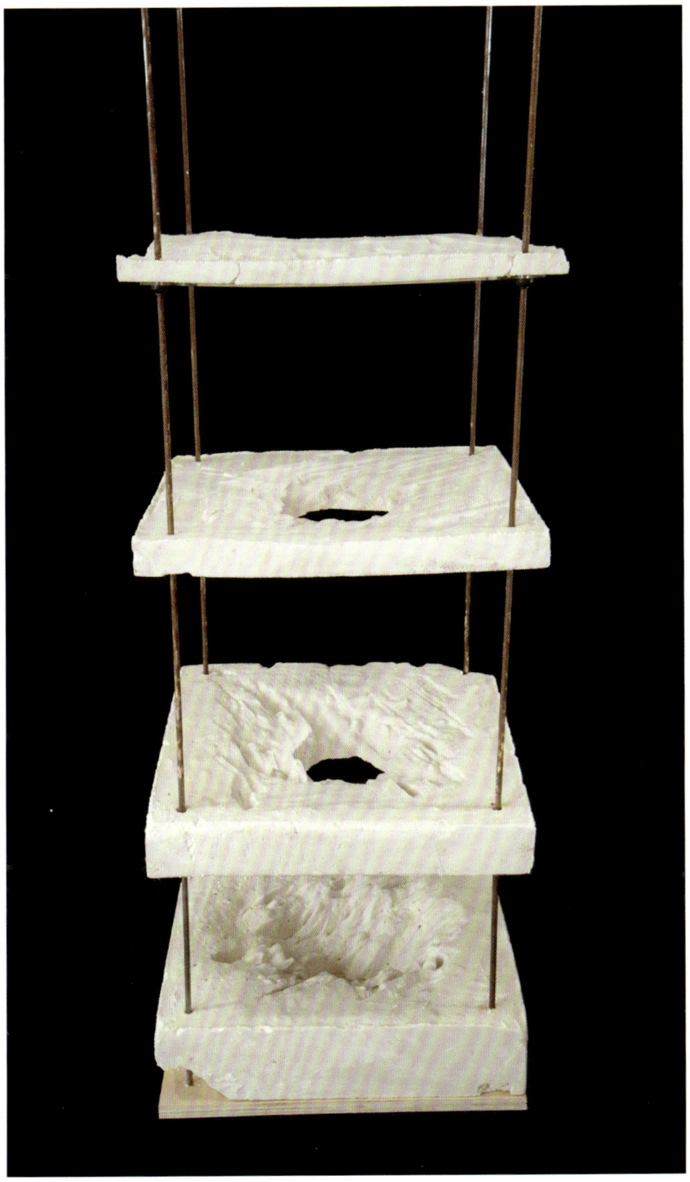

Tornadogenesis and Topography

Indiana, United States
Hsing-O Chiang

There are approximately 1,000 tornadoes annually, with more than 80 percent occuring in the United States and the vast majority in the Great Plains—a region of 20,000 cities and a population of 45,461,286 people. Although they last only seconds or minutes, tornadoes are natural disasters that cause massive destruction.

The first step of this project is to understand the forces at play in the formation of tornadoes and the paths, speeds, and conditions that induce them, and the second step is to propose a speculative scenario on mitigating strategies.

Between 1950 and 2014, 1,393 tornadoes struck Indianapolis. Due to this vulnerability, Indianapolis provides a prime site and prototype. Different topographic forms—depression, plains, hills, cliffs, etc.—with varying surface roughness created by vegetation, trees, sand, and boulders would ultimately allow the terrain to play an active role in the reduction of the devastating power of tornadoes.

Modifications to the one mile by one mile grid system of the suburbs surrounding Indianapolis can weaken and redirect the path of tornadoes away from the metropolitan area.

Top: Section of wind, traveling at different speeds, spinning along a horizontal axis from Canada. Very cold air is located in the middle levels of the atmosphere.

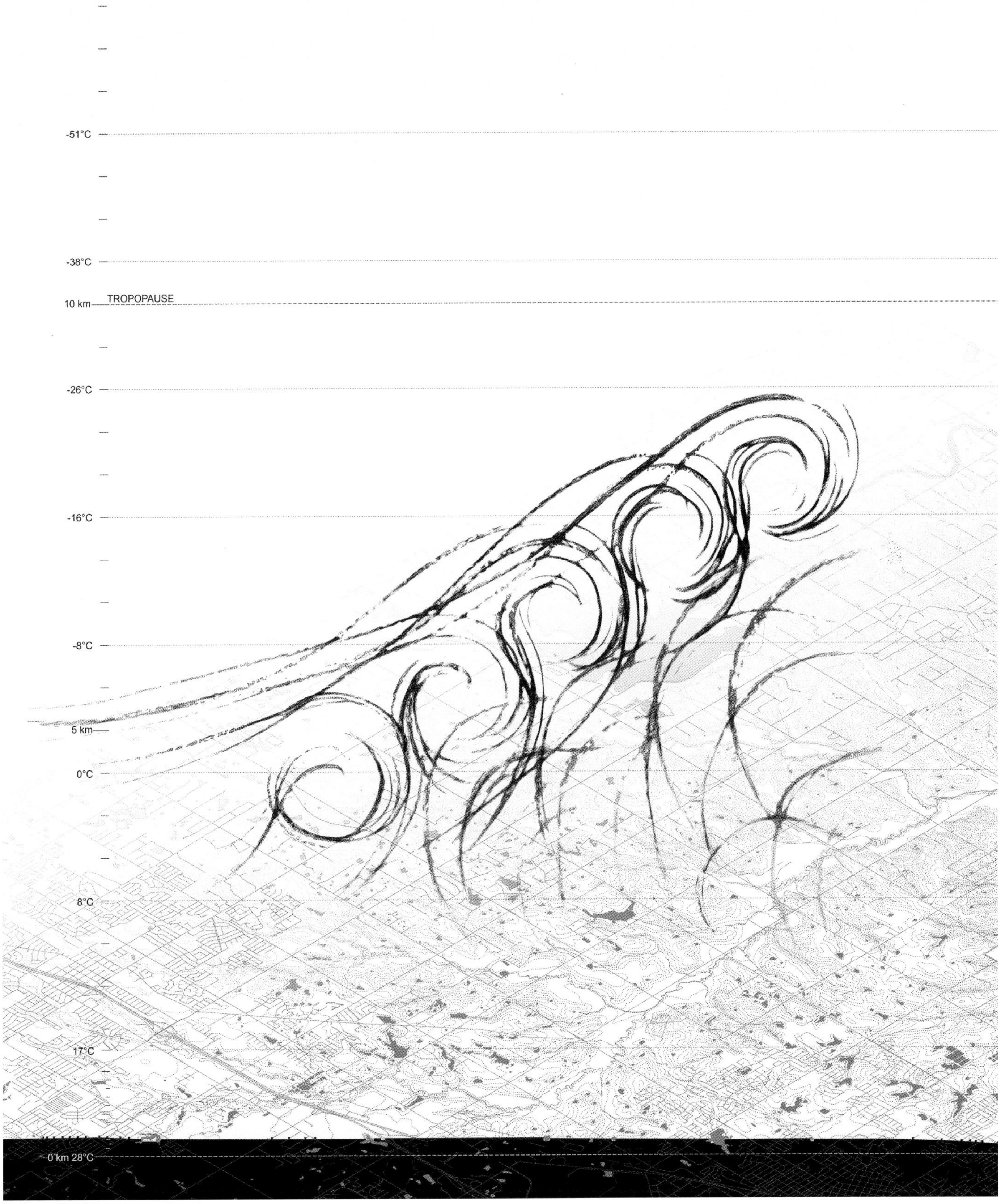

Above: Section of collision stage one between cool air from the northwest and warm moist air from the Gulf of Mexico as it is forced upwards.

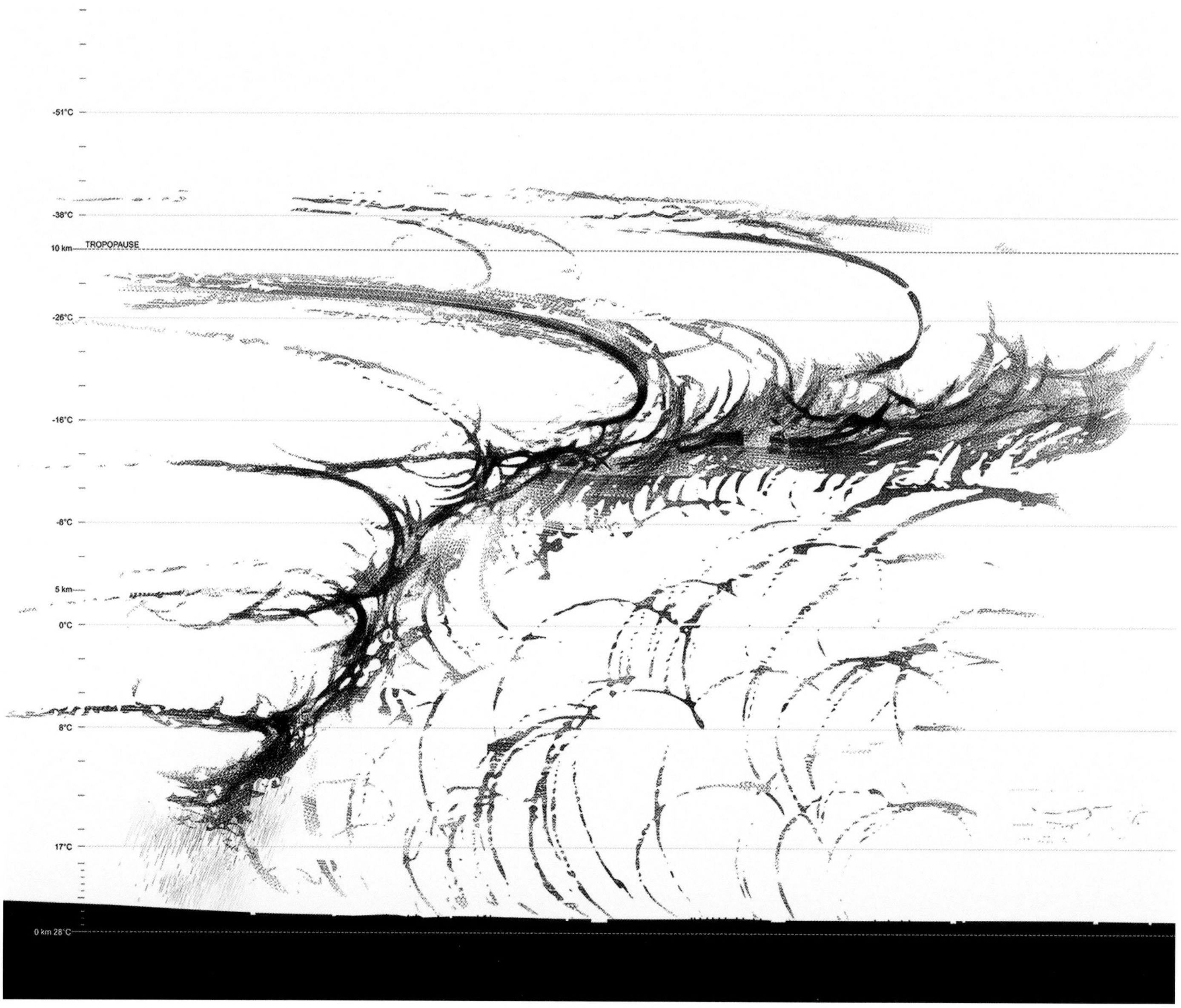

Above: Section of collision stage two between cool air from the northwest and warm, moist air from the Gulf of Mexico as the warm air is forced upwards.

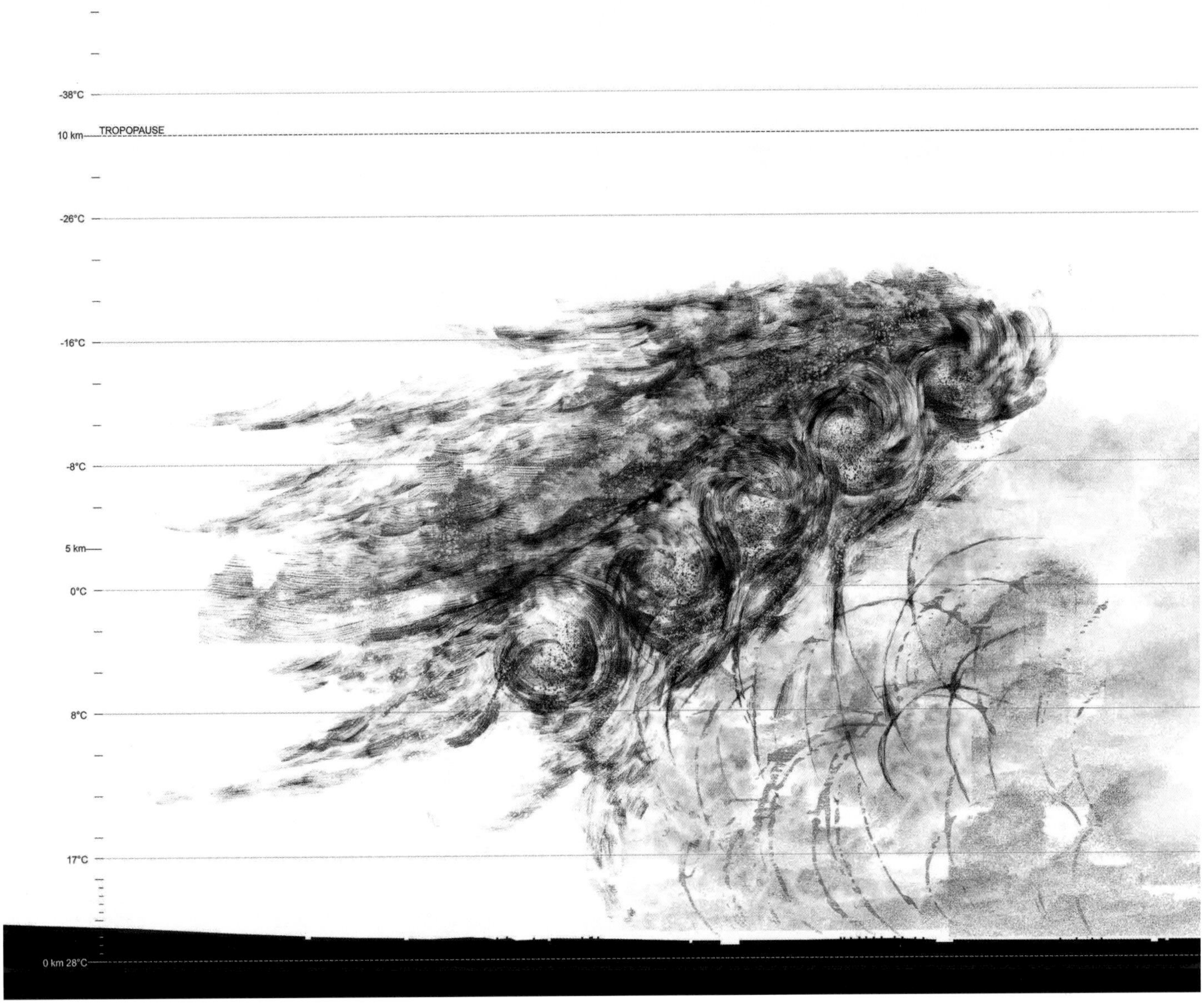

Above: Section of collision stage three between cool air from the northwest and warm, moist air from the Gulf of Mexico as the warm air is forced upwards.

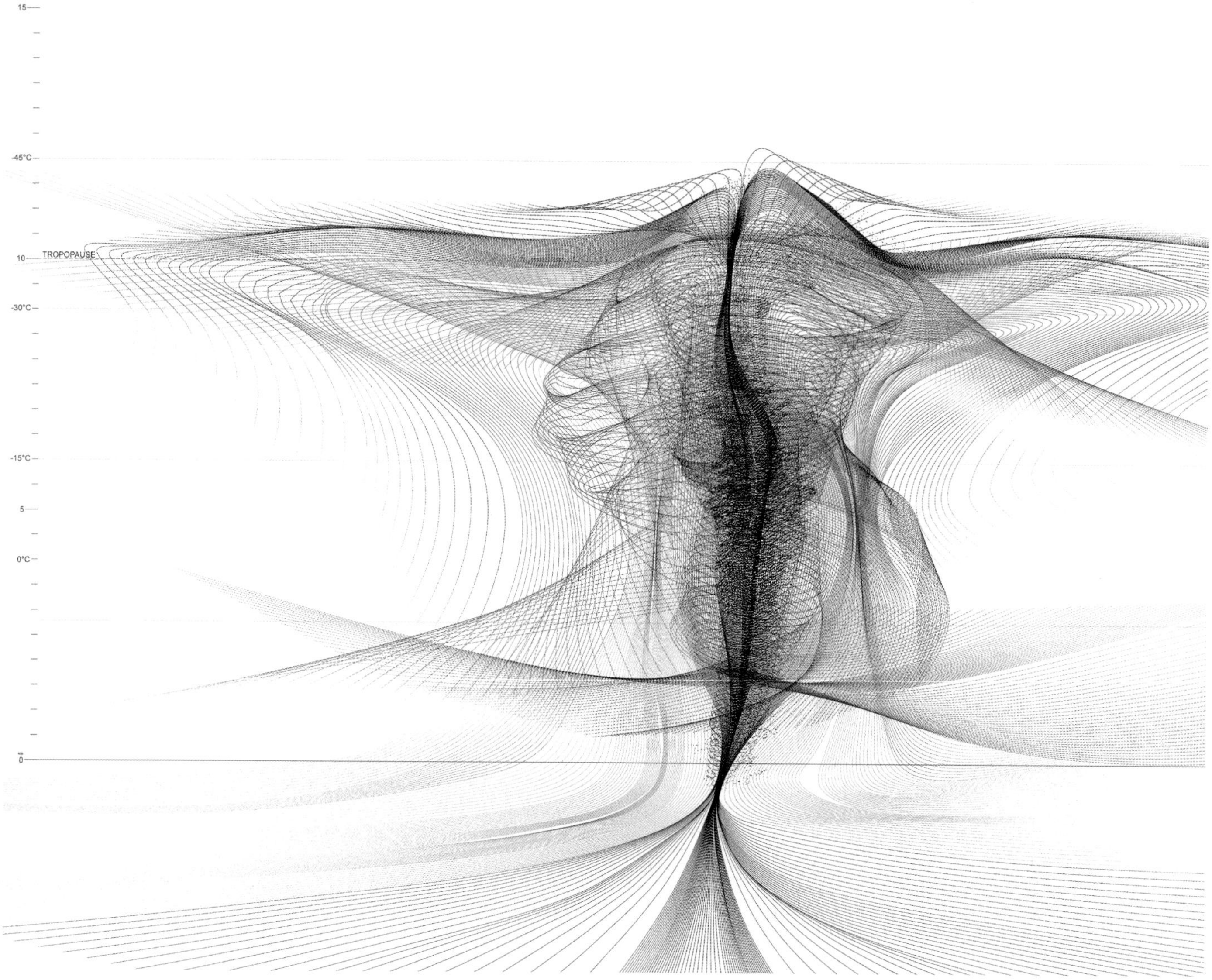
15
-45°C
10
TROPOPAUSE
-30°C
-15°C
5
0°C
0

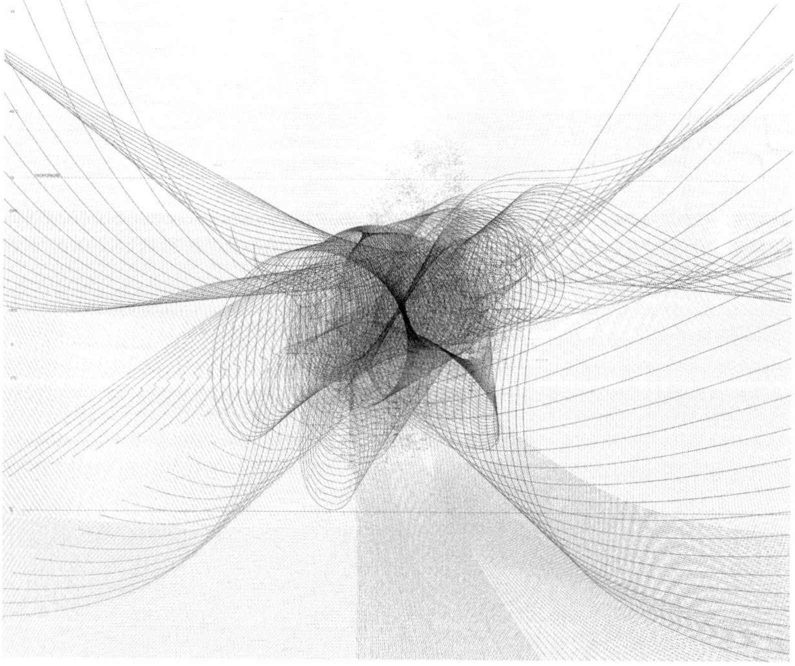

Opposite top: Section of a tornado formed by intertwining warm southeast and cold northwest wind forces.

Opposite bottom: Plan of rotation created by wind traveling at two speeds—fast and slow.

Above: Section of a tornado in the dissipating stage, when the cell starts to deteriorate and rainfall decreases in intensity.

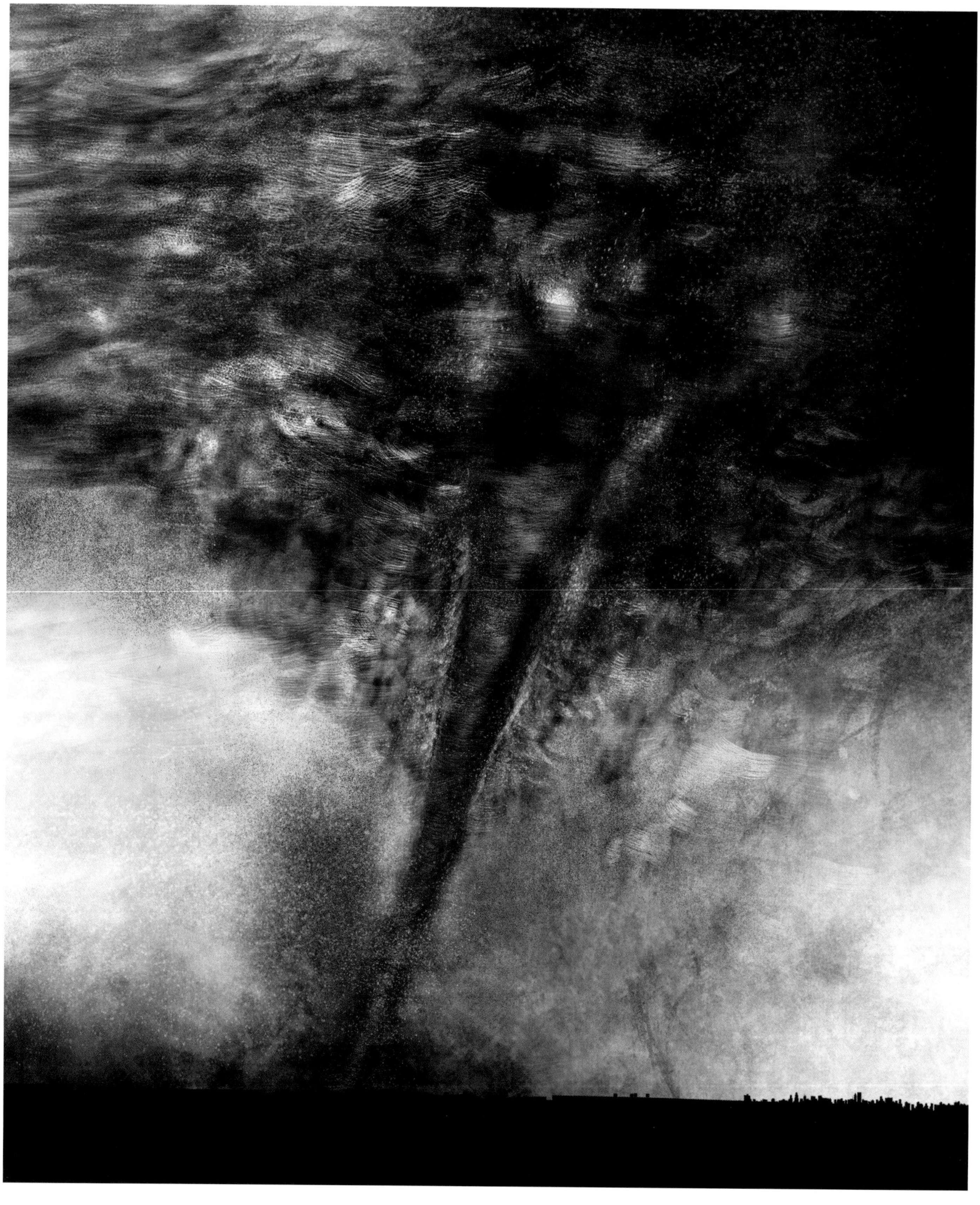

Above: View of a settlement being struck by a tornado.

Above: Models: Tornado forming wind patterns in different moments. Cut Plexiglass.

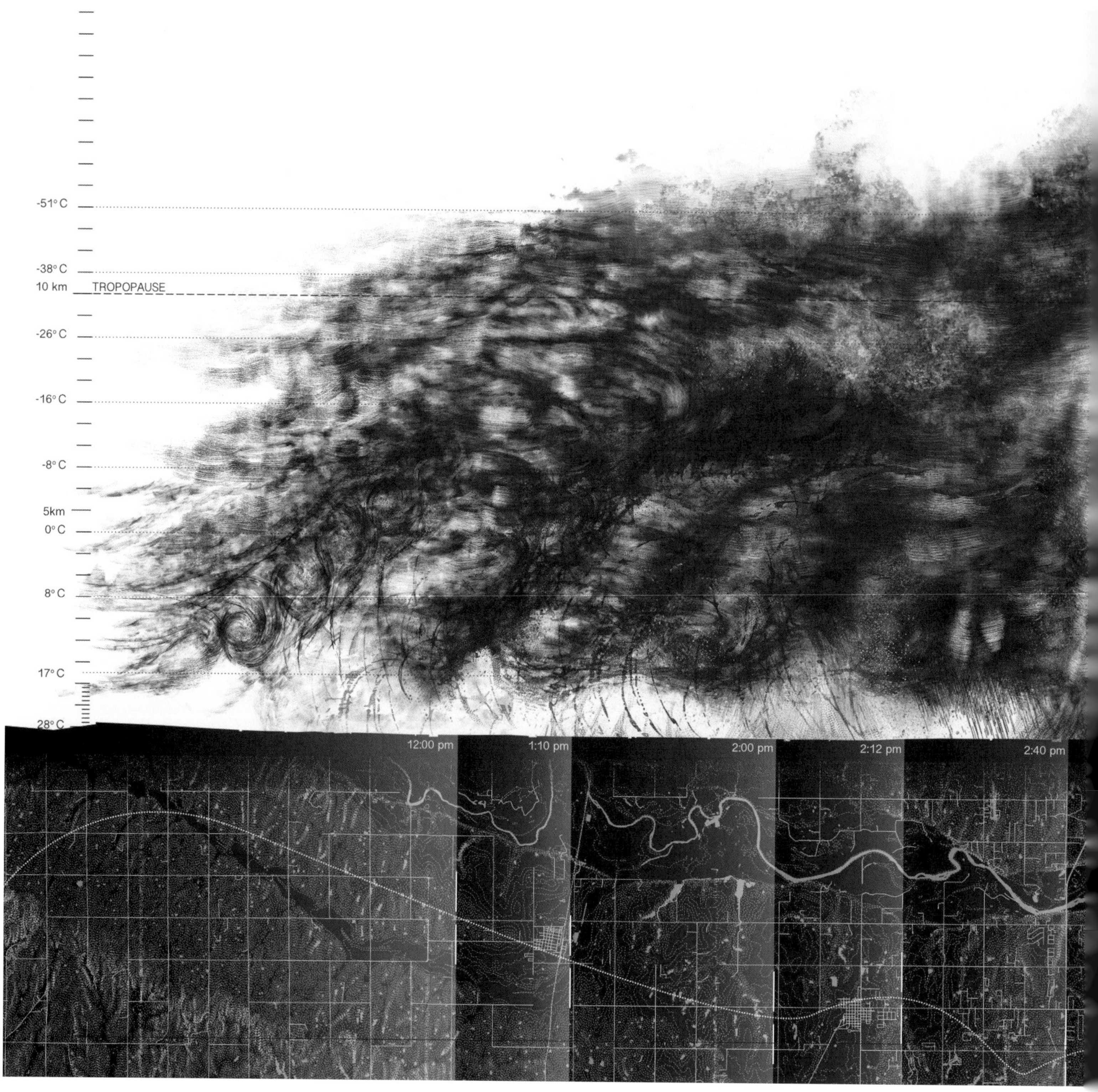

Above: Plan of Moore, Oklahoma during a tornado on May 20, 2013. The length of the damage path was 23.25 kilometers, with a maximum width of 1.74 kilometers.

Section showing how the tornado was formed.

2:46 pm

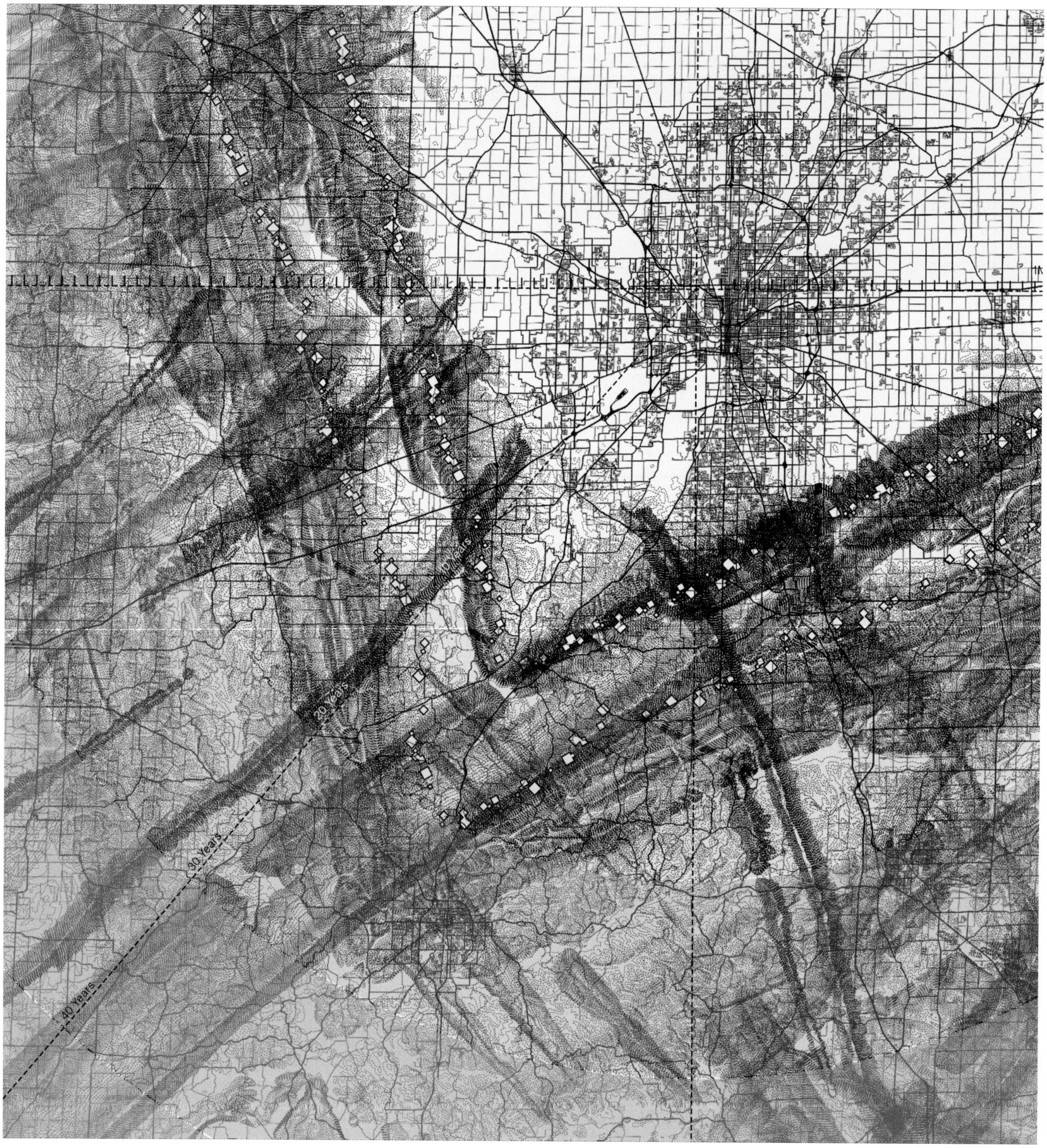

Above: Plan of landscape design proposal to protect cities by constructing topographic forms and surface roughness.

THE RETURN OF THE REPRESSED: NATURE

Diana Agrest

"As nature came to seem more like a machine, did not the machine come to seem more natural?"
—Sandra Harding [1]

This essay originated with the China Basin project, a theoretical urban proposal for San Francisco developed for the exhibition *Visionary San Francisco* held at the San Francisco Museum of Modern Art in 1990. A text from which to work developed around the China Basin area in San Francisco as the cause for intrigue and murder. This became the site for the project. While being an instinctive response to the question of the American city and urbanism today, its retrospective reading led me to focus on the question of nature. Although the project preceded the text, I have reversed the order of their presentation here, thus providing a framework for the understanding of the project rather than presenting the project as an application of it.

When this project was developed, the question of nature had been conspicuously absent from urbanistic discourse for almost 60 years. This symptomatic absence generated the critical examination of ideology that this text represents: it explores the conditions that articulate and structure the notions of nature, architecture, and gender in the ideology of modernist urbanism.

The American city, a city that regulates (suppresses or generates) enjoyment through the presence of object buildings, plays a key role in the unraveling of this complex articulation, indicating the repetition of a symptom that goes back to the original (American) urban scene/sin: the violation of nature by the machine; a confrontation where, in the struggle between the machine and the forces of nature, the woman is suppressed.

Nature has been a referent for Western architectural discourse from Vitruvius through the Renaissance, when beauty, the most important property of buildings, was supposed to result from the re-presentation of nature. Only in the nineteenth century, with Durand's critique of architecture as representation, was there a break with this tradition.[2] It is in the twentieth century, in Le Corbusier's Ville Contemporaine,[3] Plan Voisin, and Ville Radieuse,[4] that nature reappears in the urban discourse, not as part of an architectural metaphoric operation, but as an element in an urbanistic metonymic construct.

It is not only in the European urbanistic discourse that we find clues to the absence of nature, but also in the American ideological construction of the relationship between nature and city and its articulation with the process of urbanization. The current absence of nature in urban discourse is related precisely to the suppressed relationship between European urbanistic discourse and the

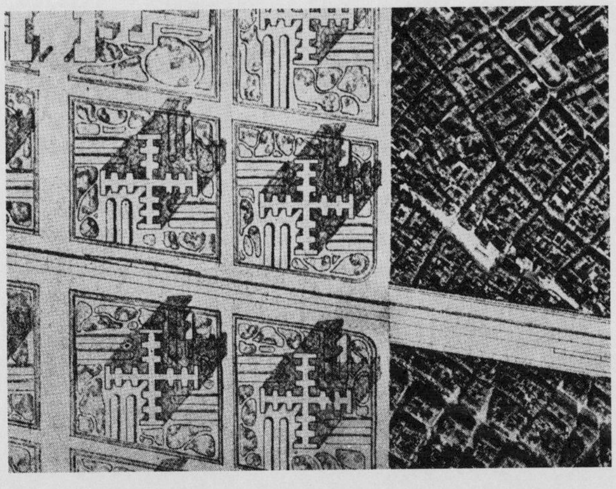

Le Corbusier, Collage Modern Contemporary City versus Historic City La Ville Radieuse, Editions L'Architecture d'Aujourd'hui, Boulogne, 1933, © FLC-ADAGP.

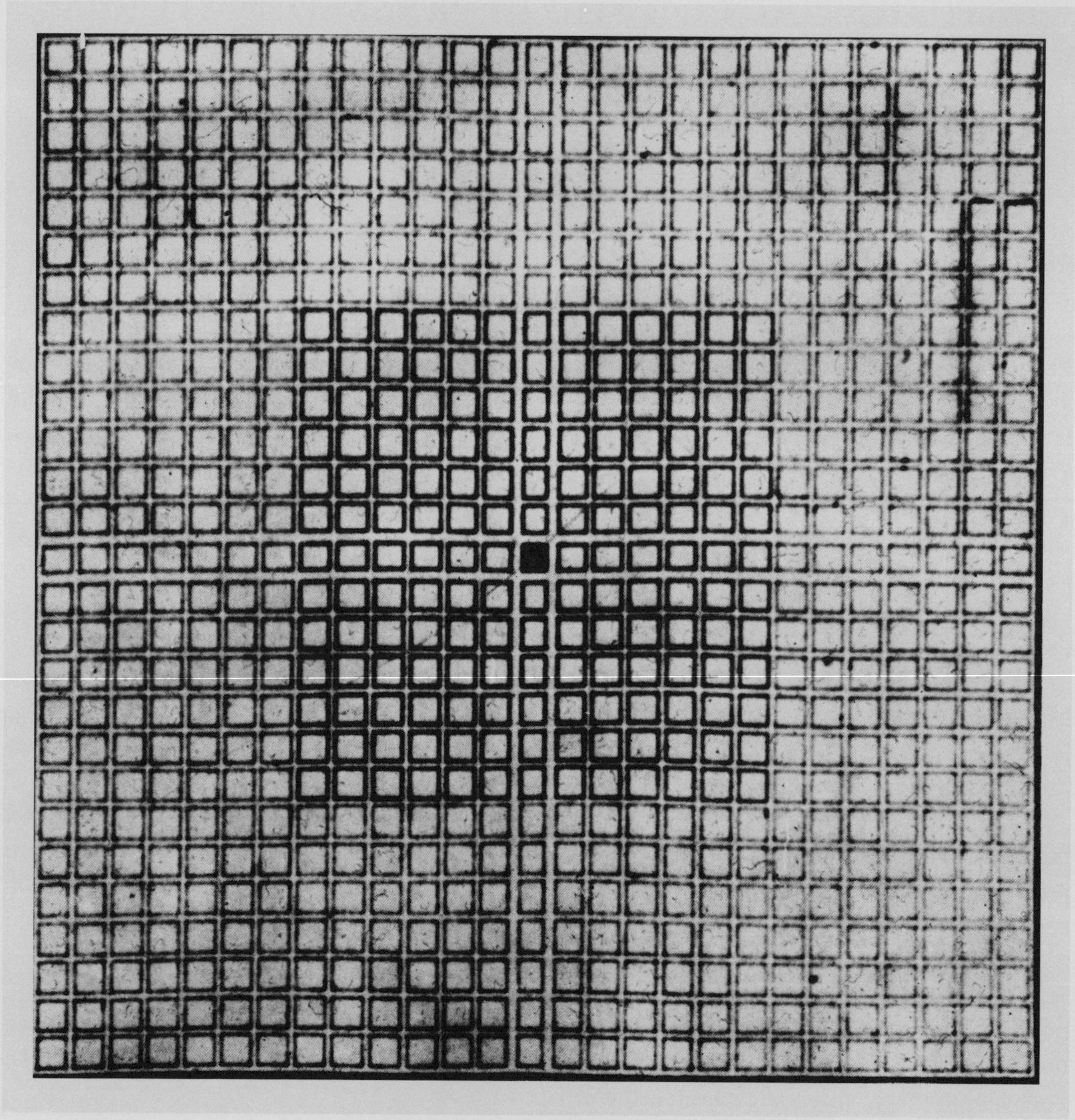

The "ideal" Cartesian grid as an American urban generator. Plan of Far West Missouri, 1836.

The grid on virgin land with the locomotive irrupting on the rural landscape. Bird's-eye view of Cheyenne, Wyoming, 1870, drawn by Augustus Koch, Wyoming State Archives, and Historical Department, Cheyenne, Wyoming.

American city. The American city—that place where urban development directly coincides with the westward displacement of the frontier, where a rational order was applied to virgin land—presents the most pertinent example of the relationship between nature and the city in twentieth-century urbanism as ideology and its articulation with the real.[5]

The development of the American city can be explained through the opposition between nature and culture, between wilderness and the city. In this equation the city was considered as evil, as the place of sin and was assigned a negative "sign," while nature, equated with God, embodied everything that was positive.

"By the time Emerson wrote *Nature* in 1836, the terms God and Nature could be used interchangeably." Ideas of God's nature and God in nature became hopelessly entangled.[6] The moral and aesthetic qualities with which nature was imbued were considered far superior to economic and urban forces and the potential for development those forces represented. The pastoral ideal was a distinctly American theory of society and an all-embracing ideology; America was seen by Europeans as a place that, as virgin land, offered the possibility of a new beginning for already developed Europe.[7]

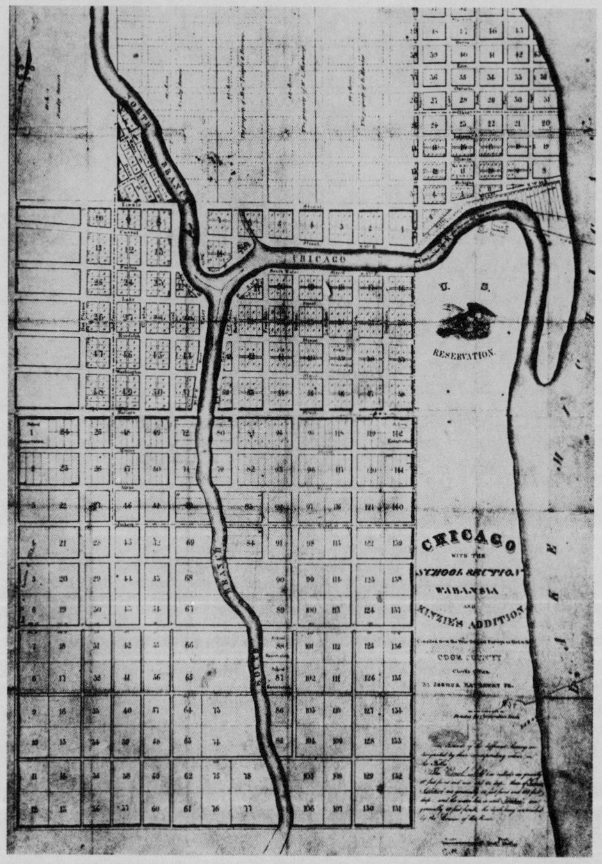

The open grid organizing the territory. Plan of Chicago, Illinois drawn by Joshua Hathaway Jr., 1834 Chicago Historical Society, Chicago, Ill.

However, when the frontier began to be pushed westward and wilderness was to be conquered, the city, by necessity, came to be seen as a positive term, since towns were necessary in order to facilitate the development of the land; and nature, which came to represent the danger of the unknown, became the negative sign.[8]

This conflict between city and country is already present in Jefferson's *Notes on Virginia*, in which he recognizes both the great political and economic potential of the machine and the fact that it will alter rural life.[9]

The machine, a product of and vehicle for the scientific revolution, made industrialization possible in a manner apparently consistent with the democratic project; at the same time, it both became and symbolized a threat to the pastoral ideal.

The greatest manifestation of this conflict appears in the form of the locomotive, the machine that disturbs the peaceful rural idyll, as Hawthorne so vividly describes in *Sleepy Hollow*, his reaction to the process of urbanization.[10]

The locomotive that slashes and scars the virgin land is the machine that makes possible the westward conquest of the wilderness, paradoxically destroying what it wants to discover. The more nature was conquered and exploited, the more a growing consciousness of its value as wilderness developed in anticipation of its ultimate destruction. Suddenly Americans came to the realization that as opposed to Europeans' historical past, their true past was nature itself. Extraordinary views of nature afforded by the new accessibility to the wilderness became equated with the beautiful and the sublime as defined by European Romantics;[11] and in the arts, it was in painting that the sublime in nature was most powerfully manifested.

Nature was equated with God, and painters who could portray nature as God's work were close to being emissaries of God on Earth. But paradoxically, "the new significance of nature and the development of landscape painting coincided with the relentless destruction of the wilderness into the early 19th century."[12] Thomas Cole represented this paradox in his series of paintings, *The Course of Empire*, "Savage State," "Pastoral State," "Consummation," "Destruction," and "Devastation."[13] However, the locomotive crossing the virgin land "was like nothing seen before," and in order to reconcile the power of the machine with the beauty and peacefulness of the rural countryside, a discourse in which the power of the machine could be praised, a technological sublime, had to be developed.[14]

The mid-nineteenth-century ideology of science in which the entire universe was seen as a mechanism and the machine was viewed as part of this natural universe provided the mediation that made the machine acceptable. However, this philosophy, neutralizing the contradiction of accepting the machine as a positive force, facilitated the destruction of the very landscape that represented the ideal of pastoralism.[15]

The ideological displacements that made possible the notion of the machine as mediator in the opposition between nature and city cannot be properly understood without introducing the problematic question of nature and science, in particular as it relates to scientific discourse, considered by philosophers as the "mirror" of nature. But for the ideology of that discourse to be understood in its many implications, another term needs to be added: that of gender, as it relates to both nature and to science.

In exploring the relationship between nature and science it is important to recognize the equivalence between nature and woman that, historically, scientific discourse has developed. Nature, gendered female, has been seen in philosophy and throughout the history of science as either an organism or a mechanism.[16]

According to the first view, nature was feminine and passive, while husbandry, the active exploitation of nature, was masculine. Thus the male was made essential to the cultivation of nature's latent fertility, just as in procreation, where the egg was seen as passive and the sperm as active, making the male "essential" to the process.[17]

This equivalence between nature and female is key to understanding the struggle for power and

Albrecht Durer: (1471—1528), *The Four Witches*, 1497. Engraving, 19.2 x 13.6 com. Albertina Museum, Vienna, Austria.

the engendering of the parties in that struggle where power is gendered male. It also makes possible the displacement of the double image of woman/nature. Nature is seen as a virgin nymph or fertile and nurturing mother "in loving service of mankind," or as "a wild willful creature generating chaotic states that needs to be controlled," and, even worse, the bearer of "plagues, famines, and tempests."[18]

Nature, identified with the female sex, was to be enslaved, inquisitioned, dissected, and exploited, an identification that justifies the search for power over nature and over women. Woman was seen as a virgin if subjected to male desires, or as a witch if rebellious; adored as a virgin, or burned as a witch. Witches, symbolizing the violence of nature, were believed to control natural forces like storms, illness, and death. (That "women also seemed closer to nature than men and imbued with a far greater sexual passion" became one of the major arguments in the witch trials of the sixteenth century.)[19]

After the scientific revolution of the sixteenth century the mechanistic view of the universe secured domination over the female attributes of nature. The virgin earth was subdued by the machine for the exploitation of the goods of the earth in a race where industrialization and technological progress, backed by an ever-more-rationalized view of the world, made the development of capitalism possible.[20] The process that privileged the mechanistic over the organic was also needed to control, dominate, and violate nature as female while excluding woman from socially and economically dominant ideology and practices. This approach to nature was based on a double system: one factual as it related to scientific laws; and one symbolic as machines transcended their own specific primary functions to give rise to a world of metaphoric and analogical relationships, ranging from the body to the entire universe.[21]

From a general opposition of *nature/culture*, other dichotomies more specific to architecture

Frederic Edwin Church, *Twilight in the Wilderness*, 1860. Cleveland Museum of Art, Cleveland, OH.

develop: *nature/city* and *nature/architecture*. Nature/city was already present, through the oppositional relationship between nature and machine, at the conquest of the American wilderness and concomitant development of the agrarian countryside.

Throughout this process the mechanistic view of nature prevailed in consonance with the scientific revolution, and it continued to prevail on both sides of the Atlantic, certainly until Le Corbusier's Ville Radieuse of 1922.

The locomotive, the machine that traversed the yet undeveloped land, generated another phenomenon: the appropriation and subdivision of land for towns and cities.

The formal instrument that shapes this appropriation is Jefferson's one-mile grid, which also became an urban footprint regardless of topographical conditions, transcending the opposition between country and city. Grids were drawn over the natural terrain as if on a blank piece of paper: cities without history. The grid as a spatially open-ended, nonhierarchical system of circulation networks anticipating what communications would produce later in a non-physical, spatial way.

The gridding of America should be seen as the creation of the real modern city, an abstract Cartesian grid with no past traced on virgin land. Le Corbusier appropriated this condition in his Plan Voisin of 1922 specifically, and it became a staple of early modernist urbanism in general.

While modern cities were being built in America, modern examples of urban theory such as Le Corbusier's Urbanisme, Plan Voisin, and Ville Radieuse were being developed in Europe.[22]

It is in these early-twentieth-century projects that nature appears as a major element in urban discourse. Ville Radieuse offers an excellent

Nature and the sublime in American painting. The painter as emissary of God on Earth, Frederick Edwin Church, 1825-1900, *Cotopaxi*, 1862, oil on painting, Detroit Institute of the Arts.

compendium of urbanistic ideology: *"I go where order is coming out of endless dialogue between man and nature, out of the struggle for life, out of the enjoyment of leisure under the open sky, in the passing of the seasons, the song of the sea ... The idea of the Radiant City was born over a period of years from observation of the laws of nature."*[23]

It is worth looking into the apparent paradox in Le Corbusier's urbanism, where nature has an essential role in his critique of the conditions of the historical city and in his development of an urbanism and architecture whose avowed referent is the machine. To understand this "return of nature" we must examine not only his writings but also his projects. Le Corbusier's critique of the historical city is based on establishing the opposition between historic city/nature, which could be translated formally into fabric/nature as stated in his critique of "the corridor street" in *Precisions*.[24] The green plane, as a metonymic presentation of nature, provides the formal background for the modernist notion of the city of object buildings as an alternative to the historical city of fabric.

In the Ville Contemporaine, a paradigmatic example of modern urbanism, the American city's "gridded nature" is metaphorically (and unconsciously) transformed into an abstract gridded green plane dedicated to the movement of cars, while buildings (on pilotis) and pedestrians are lifted from the ground.[25]

Nature becomes an element in the machinery of circulation, or part of the modernist visual field. This field is not an organic entity but an artificial construct formally organized as an abstract horizontal plane where geometry imposes order and formal control. "In order to save himself from ... chaos ... man has projected the laws of nature into a system that is a manifestation of the human spirit itself: geometry."[26]

While the incorporation of nature as an element of the modernist city was essential in generating the opposition between fabric and object, in its application this opposition becomes autonomous of nature, which, as if by a legerdemain, disappears. Nature is first suppressed, via a metaphorical maneuver representing it as a "green plane," as part of the urban machine; it is then relegated to a background, finally to be expelled by the economic-political forces of capitalism in a globalized market economy based on the exploitation and destruction of nature.

In modernist urbanism, where the city becomes the subject of architecture as a reaction to the historical city, the general opposition between nature and culture is transformed into the more specific opposition between nature and architecture. This new opposition is further articulated in the form of fabric/object, entering the architectural urban discourse as the historical city-of-fabric versus the modern city-of-objects on a green plane, thus generating a new morphology.

In its subsequent application, however, what remains of this morphology is just the object, while the green plane, nature, which was the essential condition for the emergence of this opposition and morphology, curiously disappears.

Nature then reappears in the discourse of modernist architecture and urbanism in a manner consistent with the mechanicism of the scientific ideology that is, at its base, represented in the imaginary of modernist urbanism as an artificial construct or as mechanized nature.

In Ville Radieuse sun, air, and light, absent from the historical city, reappear, managed and controlled by the machine (that is "exact air" and "artificial building site"). *"To build houses you must. Are they natural sites? Not at all: they are immediately artificialized. This means that the natural ground is limited to but one function: withstand the strains, the weight of the structure (law of gravity). Once this is done we say 'goodbye' to the natural site, for it is the enemy of man. A home on the ground (beaten earth) is frightfully unhealthful; you no longer find it anywhere but in artificial sites."*[27]

The countryside is now "gay, clean, and alive," always placed in the context of the machine age. It is the artificial architectural order of modernism that regulates the relations between nature, city, and technology. The ideology of modernist architecture and urbanism is still based on the mechanistic scientific ideology, taking the form of machinism, an ideology that implicitly sanctions the repression/suppression of woman. Le Corbusier writes once more in *Radiant City*, this time on "Laws":

The laws of nature and the laws of men.
We live in the presence of three spheres:
Our dictator, the sun
The globe on which we live out our destinies: the earth
And a companion forever whirling around us: the moon

...

Woman, that power in conjunction with which we work, is ruled by this lunar month.
We the men are ruled by the solar year.[28]

The urban realm thus discloses the historical role of the alignment of nature and gender, an identification that is once again key to the struggle for power and the engendering of power. The conception of the world as a machine in a fetishistic architecture that is the result of the application of the principles of modernist urbanism allows the double domination (or negation) of nature and women.

Inscription of Nature:
The China Basin Project

The city as object of desire is transformed into the city as the place where the forces of desire are set free. The China Basin project, much like Donna Haraway's cyborg, is "about transgressed boundaries, potent fusions and dangerous possibilities."[29] This project is a provocation. It is, to paraphrase Haraway, a fiction mapping our urban, social, and ideological reality, resolutely committed to partiality, irony, and perversity. It is antagonistic, utopian, and completely without innocence.[30] The project serves as a unique opportunity to examine some of the pressing questions concerning the place, role, and form of urban development and questions about nature in urbanistic discourse at this moment in time.

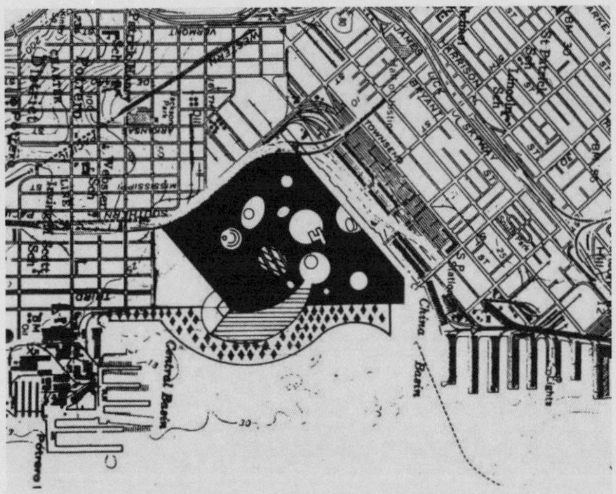

Diana Agrest, *Return of the Repressed: Nature.* The Machine in the Garden: Proposal, China Basin San Francisco, 1989. The site is located between US 280 the and the San Francisco Bay and adjacent to the Mission District.

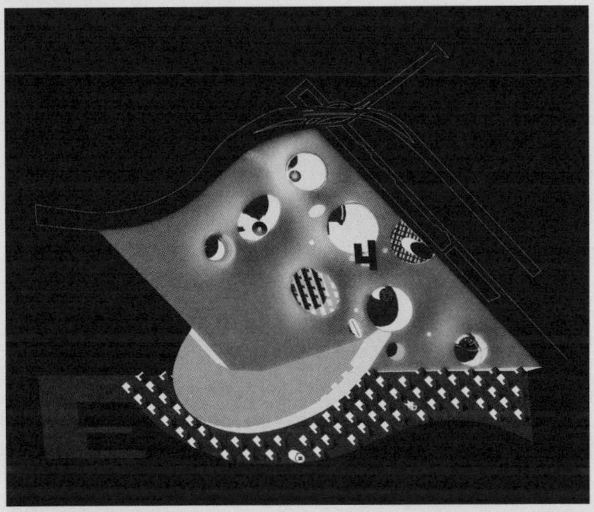

Diana Agrest, *Return of the Repressed: Nature.* The Machine in the Garden: Proposal, China Basin San Francisco, 1989. Plan, night view, green field level with public open courtyards accessible from various levels including the green area.

The China Basin is a 300-acre site sloping down from the Embarcadero Freeway toward San Francisco Bay. The scheme assumes the creation of a new natural urban datum plane related to that of the existing freeway, which in turn is rendered obsolete and transformed into a residential structure. The freeway both defines one edge of the site and indicates the highest point above sea level. The China Basin Canal bounds the northwestern edge of the site and the San Francisco Bay lies to the east. An undulating blanket of nature covers the site and is punctuated by curvilinear public spaces varying in function and depth.

In the China Basin project, the smooth surface of nature replaces the striated fabric of the city, in the form of various street grids, which is buried under the site: a seamless continuity of activity flows under the smooth surface of nature, continuous flux without delimitation. This project addresses and encourages active production rather than the frantic consumption that characterizes most urban developments, a condition manifested in the proposed program. Zones of programmatic superimposition and interrelation radiating out of each "courtyard" are created, thus defining a *public place*. The boundaries determining various programs are left in suspense, undetermined, creating areas of programmatic instability, dissolving the barriers of institutionalized practice and reflecting the chance process of urban change over time.

Intermediate levels provide most of the routes of movement. An intricate machine comprised of interlocking reels and platforms allows pedestrians to travel from one place to another in rotating, horizontal, vertical, and diagonal movement. At other levels, more traditional communication routes are present as well. This project proposes to explore the possibilities of using other geometries than Euclidean, which is at the core of the Cartesian grids of both the American city and early twentieth-century urbanism.

Diana Agrest, *Return of the Repressed: Nature.* The Machine in the Garden: Proposal, China Basin San Francisco, 1989. Section through various activity systems and open courtyards; Olympic Training Center, Museum of the XXth Century, Production workshops for multiple activities, Genome Research Center, etc. Boundaries between programs are left undetermined.

Endnotes

1. Jean Nicholas Louis Durand, *Précis des Leçons d'Architecture* (Paris: 1817).
2. Le Corbusier, *The City of Tomorrow* (London: John Rodker, 1929).
3. Le Corbusier, *Radiant City* (New York: The Orion Press, 1964).
4. John W. Reps, *The Making of Urban America* (Princeton, NJ: Princeton University Press, 1965).
5. Barbara Novak, *Nature and Culture: American Landscape and Painting 1825—1875* (New York and Toronto: Oxford University Press, 1980), 3.
6. Leo Marx, *The Machine in the Garden* (London, Oxford, and New York: Oxford University Press, 1964), 4, 99.
7. Reps.
8. Marx, 88.
9. Marx, 15.
10. Ibid., 96, and Novak, 5.
11. Novak, 4.
12. Ibid., 10.
13. Marx, 195, 206.
14. Ibid., 162, 165, and Carolyn Merchant, *The Death of Nature* (San Francisco: Harper and Row, 1989), 194, 227, 29.
16. Merchant, 2, 5, 20, 99, 214.
17. Ibid., 149, 163.
18. Ibid., 2, 20, 127.
19. Ibid., 130, 32.
20. Ibid., 2, 192.
21. Ibid., 192, 227.
22. Le Corbusier, *Radiant City* and *The City of Tomorrow.*
23. Le Corbusier, *Radiant City*, 85.
24. Le Corbusier, *Precisions* (Paris: Editions Vincent Freal, 1964).
25. Ibid.
26. Le Corbusier, *Radiant City*, 83.
27. Ibid., 55.
28. Ibid., 76.
29. Donna J. Haraway, "A Cyborg Manifesto," in *Simians, Cyborgs, and Women* (New York: Routledge, 1991), 154.
30. Ibid., 151

Work Appendix

17 Liquid Tectonics
Yellowstone Caldera
Chung-Wei Lee

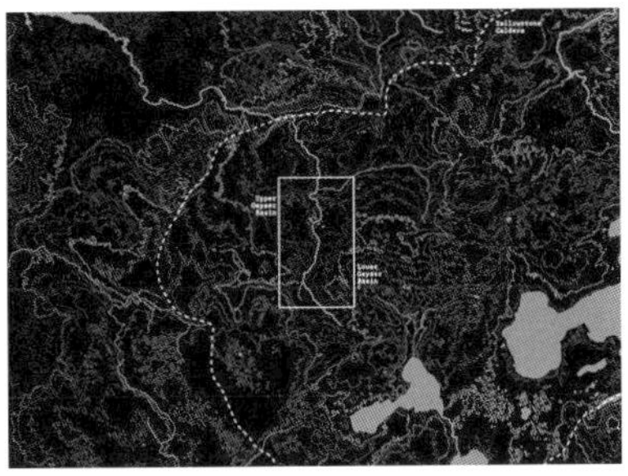

1. William J. Fritz and Robert C. Thomas, "Quaternary Volcanism," in *Roadside Geology of Yellowstone Country* (Sevierville, TN: Mountain Press, 2011), 62-76.
2. Kenneth L. Pierce and Lisa A. Morgan, "The Track of the Yellowstone Hot Spot: Volcanism, Faulting, and Uplift," in *Geological Society of America Memoirs* 179 (1992): 38.
3. Kenneth L. Pierce, Don G. Despain, Lisa A. Morgan and John M. Good, "The Yellowstone Hotspot, Greater Yellowstone Ecosystem, and Human Geography," Professional Paper 1717-A (U.S. Geological Survey: 2007): 9.
4. William R. Keefer, "Formation of the Yellowstone Caldera," Bulletin 1347 (U.S. Geological Survey, 1972).
5. Robert L. Christiansen and H. Richard Blank, Jr., "Volcanic Stratigraphy Of The Quaternary Rhyolite Plateau In Yellowstone National Park," Professional Paper 729-b (U.S. Geological Survey, 1972): B7.
6. Robert O. Rye and Alfred H. Truesdell, "The Question of Recharge to the Deep Thermal Reservoir Underlying the Geysers and Hot Springs of Yellowstone National Park," Professional Paper 1717 (U.S. Geological Survey, 2007): 266.
7. K. Eric Livo, Fred A. Kruse, Roger N. Clark, Raymond F. Kokaly and W.C. Shanks, III, "Hydrothermally Altered Rock and Hot-Spring Deposits at Yellowstone National Park—Characterized Using Airborne Visible- and Infrared-Spectroscopy Data," Professional Paper 1717 (U.S. Geological Survey, 2007): 495.
8. Jacob B. Lowenstern and Shaul Hurwitz, "Monitoring a Supervolcano in Repose: Heat and Volatile Flux at the Yellowstone Caldera," in *Elements* 4, no. 1 (2008): 38-39.

25 Phantom Surge
Seguam Island
Stefan van Biljon

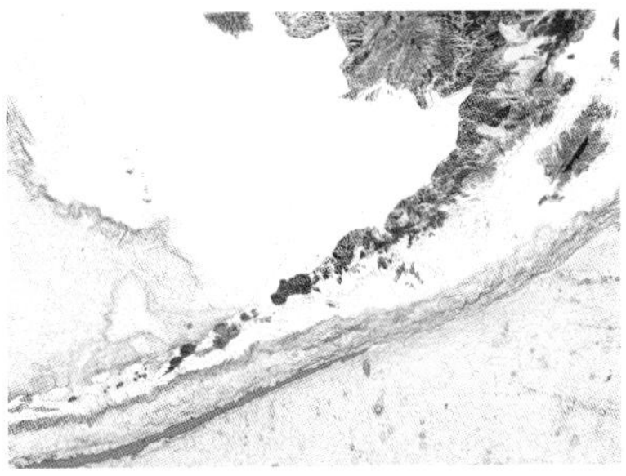

1. B. R. Jicha and B. S. Singer, "Volcanic History and Magmatic Evolution of Seguam Island, Aleutian Island Arc, Alaska," in *Geological Society of America Bulletin* 118, nos. 7-8 (Jul./Aug. 2006): 806.
2. E. L. Geist, J. R. Childs and D. W. Scholl, "The Origin of Summit Basins of the Aleutian Ridge: Implications for Block Rotation of an Arc Massif," in *Tectonics* 7, no. 2 (Apr. 1988): 329.
3. Jicha and Singer, "Volcanic History," 806.
4. J. P. Richards, "Magmatic to Hydrothermal Metal Fluxes in Convergent and Collided Margins," in *Ore Geology Reviews* 40 (2011): 1-26.
5. M. G. Best, *Igneous and Metamorphic Petrology*, 2nd ed. (Malden, MA: Blackwell Science Ltd., 2003): 210-12.
6. Jicha and Singer, "Volcanic History," 814-5.
7. C. DeMets, R. G. Gordon, D. F. Argus, and S. Stein, "Effect of Recent Revisions to the Geomagnetic Reversal Time Scale on Estimates of Current Plate Motions," in *Geophysical Research Letters* 21, no. 20 (Oct. 1994): 2191-94. Quoted in Jicha and Singer, "Volcanic History," 806.

29 Subduction and Transformations of the Mantle Rock
Mt. St. Helens
Hsing-O Chiang

1. Michael A. Clynne, David W. Ramsey and Edward W. Wolfe, "Pre-1980 Eruptive History of Mount St. Helens, Washington," Fact Sheet 2005-3045 (U.S. Geological Survey, 2005).
2. Steven R. Brantley, "Volcanoes of the United States," General Interest Publication (U.S. Geological Survey, 1994).
3. Linda Lawrance Noson, Anthony Qamar, and Gerald W. Thorsen, "Washington State Earthquake Hazards," Washington Division of Geology and Earth Resources Information Circular 85 (Washington State Department of Natural Resources, 1988).
4. G. C. Rogers, "An Assessment of the Megathrust Earthquake Potential of the Cascadia Subduction Zone," in *Canadian Journal of Earth Sciences* 25, no. 6 (1988): 844-852.
5. Donald Hyndman and David Hyndman, *Natural Hazards and Disasters*, 3rd ed. (Pacific Grove, CA: Brooks Cole, 2010).
6. U.S. Geological Survey, "Juan de Fuca Volcanics," *volcanoes.usgs.gov* (U.S. Geological Survey, 2002).
7. David D. Alt and Donald W. Hyndman, *Roadside Geology of Oregon*, 19th ed. (Missoula, MT: Mountain Press, 1978): 3.

34 Fire and Ice
Mount St. Helens
Minibum Koo

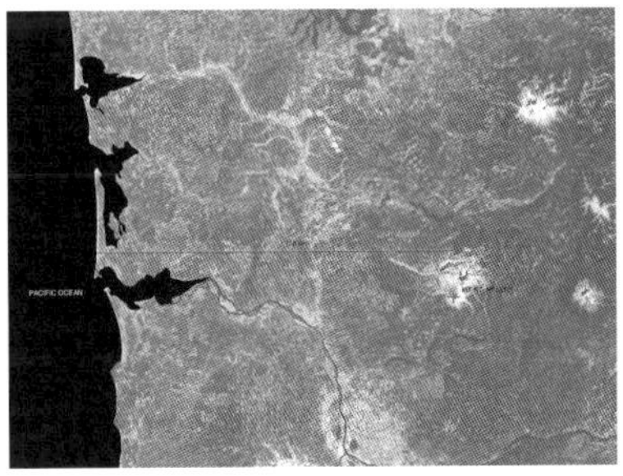

1. Jonathan S. Fruchter et al., "Mount St. Helens Ash from the 18 May 1980 Eruption: Chemical, Physical, Mineralogical, and Biological Properties," in *Science* 209, no. 4461 (1980): 1116—25.
2. Marc J. Defant and Mark S. Drummond, "Mount St. Helens: Potential Example of the Partial Melting of the Subducted Lithosphere in a Volcanic Arc," in *Geology* 21, no. 6 (1993): 547—50.
3. Peter W. Lipman and Donal Ray Mullineaux, "The 1980 Eruptions of Mount St. Helens, Washington," Professional Paper 1250 (U.S. Geological Survey, 1981).

40 Fire and Water
Crater Lake
Aikaterini Olga Kefalogianni

1. Stephen L. Harris, *Fire Mountains of the West: The Cascade and Mono Lake Volcanoes*, 3rd ed. (Missoula, MT: Mountain Press Publishing Company, 1988): 1-60, 133-56.
2. Richard L. Hill, *Volcanoes of the Cascades: Their Rise and their Risks* (Guilford, CT: Globe Pequot, 2004): 1-16, 65-74.
3. David Ritchie, *The Ring of Fire* (New York: Atheneum, 1981).
4. William L. Sullivan, *Trails of Crater Lake National Park & Oregon Caves National Monument* (Oregon: Navillus Press, 2010).
5. Charles R. Bacon and Manuel Nathenson, "Geothermal Resources in the Crater Lake Area, Oregon," Open-File Report 96-663 (U.S. Geological Survey, 1996).
6. R. J. Kurzeja and M. M. Pendergast, "Comparison of MTI Water Temperatures with Ground Truth Measurements at Crater Lake, OR" (U.S. Department of Energy, 2002).
7. Manuel Nathenson, "Water Balance for Crater Lake, Oregon," Open-File Report 92-505 (U.S. Geological Survey, 1992).
8. Victor T. Neal, Steven J. Neshyba and Warren W. Denner, "Vertical Temperature Structure in Crater Lake, Oregon" (Corvalis: Oregon State University, 1972).

44 Oblique Tectonics
Kilauea Volcano
Lawrence Lek

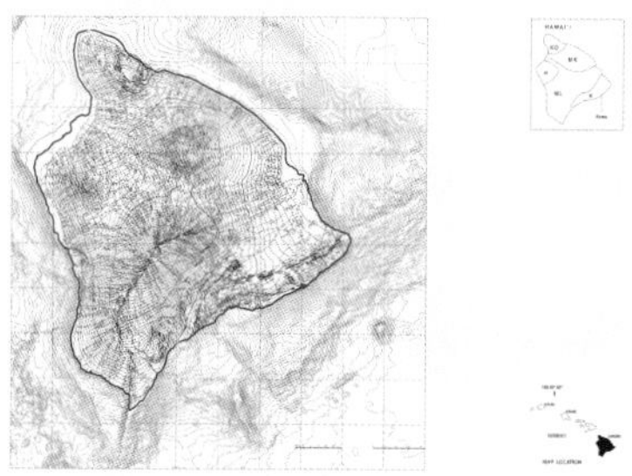

1. Donald A. Swanson, Wendell A. Duffield and Richard S. Fiske, "Displacement of the South Flank of Kilauea Volcano: The Result of Forceful Intrusion of Magma into the Rift Zones," Professional Paper 963 (U.S. Geological Survey, 1976).
2. Thomas L. Wright and Richard S. Fiske, "Origin of the Differentiated and Hybrid Lavas of Kilauea Volcano, Hawaii," in *Journal of Petrology* 12, no. 1 (Feb. 1971): 1—65.
3. V. J. Realmuto, A. J. Sutton and T. Elias, "Multispectral Thermal Infrared Mapping of Sulfur Dioxide Plumes: A Case Study from the East Rift Zone of Kilauea Volcano, Hawaii," in *Journal of Geophysical Research* 102, no. B7 (Jul. 1997): 15057—72
4. Michael P. Ryan, "The Mechanics and Three-Dimensional Internal Structure of Active Magmatic Systems: Kilauea Volcano, Hawaii," in *Journal of Geophysical Research* 93, no. B5 (May 1988): 4213—48.
5. Robert I. Tilling, Christina Heliker and Donald A. Swanson,"Eruptions of Hawaiian Volcanoes," 2nd ed., General Information Product 117 (U.S. Geological Survey, 2010).
6. R. S. Fiske and E. D. Jackson, "Orientation and Growth of Hawaiian Volcanic Rifts," in *Proceedings of the Royal Society Of London A* 329, no. 0115 (Royal Society Publishing, 1972): 299-326.

48 Moving Plates and Stationary Hotspots
Hawaiian Islands
Wei Che Yu

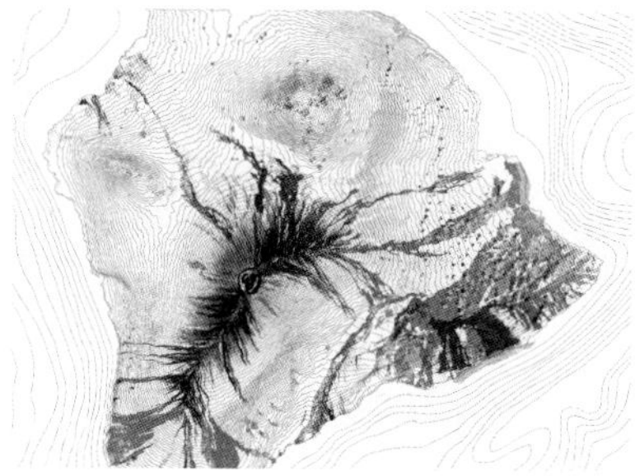

1. Donald W. Peterson, Robin T. Holcomb, Robert I. Tilling, and Robert L. Christiansen, "Development of Lava Tubes in the Light of Observations at Mauna Ulu, Kilauea Volcano, Hawaii," in *Bulletin of Volcanology* 56, no. 5 (Nov. 1994): 343—60.
2. Francis G. Howarth, "Cavernicoles in Lava Tubes on the Island of Hawaii," in *Science* 175, no. 4019 (Jan. 1972): 325-26
3. Ronald Greeley, "The Role of Lava Tubes in Hawaiian Volcanoes, Volcanism in Hawaii," vol. II, Professional Paper 1350 (U.S. Geological Survey, 1987).

54 Life, Death, and Regeneration of Coral Reefs
Hawaii and The Marshall Islands
Hancheng Chen

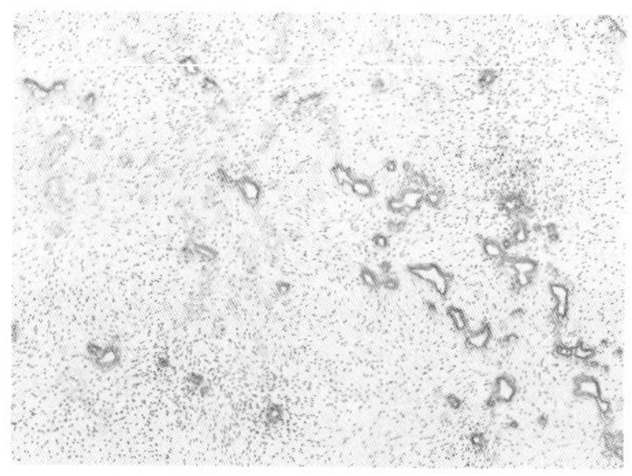

1. Urmila Phadnis and Ela Dutt Luithui, *Maldives, Winds of Change in an Atoll State* (New Delhi: South Asian Publishers, 1985).
2. Heiko HüNeke and Thierry Muldur, eds., *Deep-Sea Sediments*, Developments in Sedimentology, vol. 63 (Amsterdam: Elsevier, 2011).
3. Chris Perry and Kevin Taylor, eds., *Environmental Sedimentology* (Hoboken, NJ: Wiley-Blackwell, 2006).
4. Craig Taylor and Erik van Marcke, eds., *Infrastructure Risk Management Processes: Natural, Accidental, and Deliberate Hazards* (Reston, VA: American Society of Civil Engineers, 2005).
5. Lauretta Burke, Dirk Bryant, John McManus and Mark Spalding, *Reefs at Risk: A Map-Based Indicator of Threats to the World's Coral Reefs* (Washington, D.C.: World Resources Institute, 1998).
6. Colin D. Woodroffe, "Reef-Island Topography and the Vulnerability of Atolls to Sea-Level Rise," in *Global and Planetary Change* 62 (2008): 77-96.
7. Ryan T. Bailey and John W. Jenson, "Groundwater Resources Analysis of Atoll Islands in the Federated States of Micronesia Using an Algebraic Model," Technical Report 134 (Guam: Water and Environmental Research Institute of the Western Pacific University of Guam, October 2011).
8. Alexandre S. Ganachaud, Alex Sen Gupta, James C. Orr, Susan E. Wijffels, Ken R. Ridgway, Mark A. Hemer, Christophe Maes, Craig R. Steinberg, Aline D. Tribollet, Bo Qiu, and Jens C Kruge, "Observed and Expected Changes to the Tropical Pacific Ocean," in *Climate Change 2007: The Physical Science Basis Contribution of Working Group I to the Fourth Assessment Report of the IPCC* (Cambridge, UK: Cambridge University Press, 2007).
9. Thomas J. Goreau, "Marine Electrolysis for Building Materials and Environmental Restoration," in Janis Kleperis, ed., *Electrolysis* (London: IntechOpen, 2012).

81 Invisible Clouds: Nuclear Testing and Radioactive Spaces
The Marshall Islands
Daniel Meridor

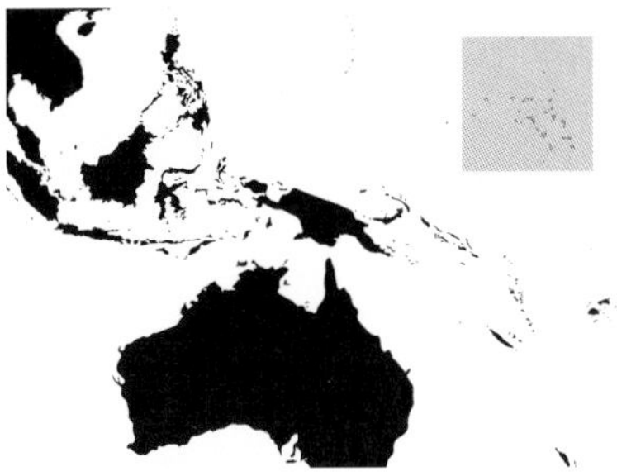

1. Giff Johnson, "Pardise Lost," in *Bulletin of the Atomic Scientists* 36, no. 10 (Dec. 1980): 24-29.
2. Defense Nuclear Agency "The Radiological Cleanup of Enewetak Atoll" (Washington, D.C.: Defense Nuclear Agency, 1981)
3. Peter Goin, *Nuclear Landscape* (Baltimore and London: Johns Hopkins University Press, 1991).
4. Neal O. Hines, *Proving Ground: An Account of Radio-Biological Studies in the Pacific, 1946-1961* (Seattle: University of Washington Press, 1962).
5. Terry Hamilton, "Renewing Hopes for Full Resettlement of Bikini, Enewetak and Rongelap," in *Marshall Islands Monitor* 1, no. 2 (May 2009): 5-6.
6. V. E. Noshkin, I. W. L. Robison, K. M. Wong and R. J. Eagle, "Behavior of Plutonium Isotopes in the Marine Environment of Enewetak Atoll," in *Journal of Radioanalytical and Nuclear Chemistry* 234, nos. 1-2 (1998): 243—49.
7. V. E. Noshkin, R. J. Eagle, and W. L. Robison, "Fine and Coarse Components in Surface Sediments from Bikini Lagoon" (Livermore, CA: Lawrence Livermore National Laboratory, 1997).
8. U.S. Department of Energy, National Nuclear Security Administration Nevada Field Office, "United States Nuclear Tests July 1945 through September 1992," DOE/NV--209-REV 15 (Nevada: U.S. Department of Energy, Dec 2000).
9. Phillip H. Muller, "Republic of the Marshall Islands: Views Regarding the Possible Security Implications of Climate Change" (New York: Permanent Mission of the Republic of the Marshall Islands to the United Nations, July 2009).
10. K. V. Marsh, K. M. Wang, G. Holladay, V. E. Noshkin, and R. Buddemeier, "Radiological and Chemical Studies of the Groundwater at Enewetak Atoll, Sampling, Field Measurements, and Analytical Methods" (Livermore, CA: Lawrence Livermore National Laboratory, 1975).

86 A Dissolving Landscape
Mammoth Cave Region
Chih-Wei Hsu

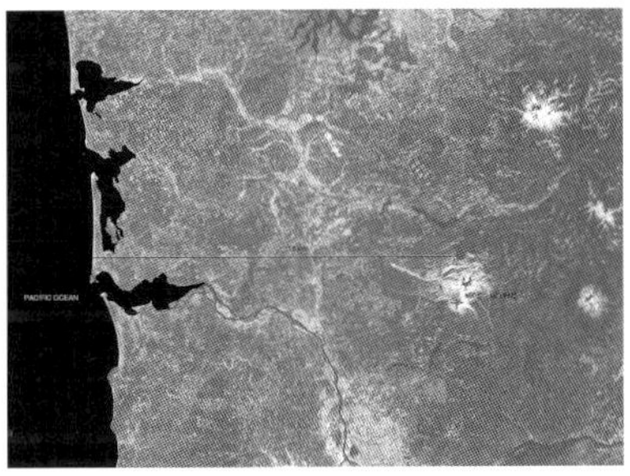

1. National Park Service, Geologic Resources Division, "Mammoth Cave National Park: Geologic Resources Inventory Report," Natural Resource Report NPS/NRSS/GRD/NRR—2011/448 (Fort Collins, CO: U.S. Department of the Interior, Sept. 2011).
2. Derek Ford and Paul Williams, *Karst Hydrogeology and Geomorphology* (Hoboken, NJ: John Wiley & Sons, 2007).

90 Traces of Choreography of Fractures
Lechuguilla Cave
Bahar Avanoglu

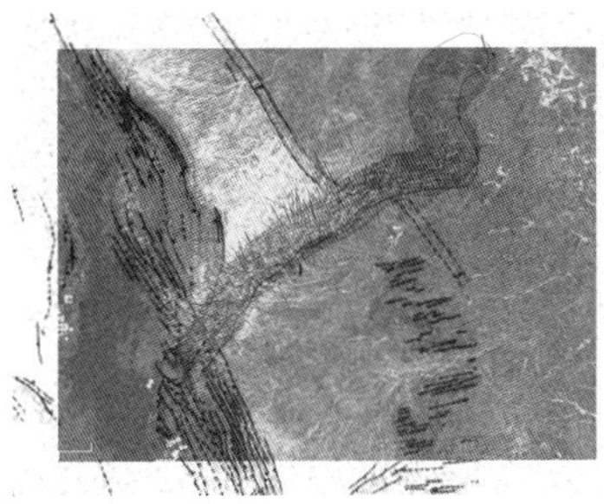

1. J. Michael Queen and Leslie A. Melim, "Biothems: Biologically Influenced Speleothems in Caves of the Guadalupe Mountains, New Mexico, USA," in *Caves and Karst Southeastern New Mexico*, New Mexico Geological Society 57th annual Fall Field Conference Guidebook (Socorro, NM: New Mexico Geological Society, 2006): 167-74.
2. Patricia Kambesis, "Lechuguilla Cave, New Mexico, U.S.A.," in *Encyclopedia of Caves*, 2nd ed., ed. William B. White and David C. Culver (Amsterdam: Elsevier, 2012): 103-07, 280-84, 374-77, 456-64, 528-31, 598-603, 603-08, 777-86, 810-19.
3. National Park Service, *Canyons & Caves* nos. 14, 15, 19, 22, 25, 27, 29, 30, 32, 35, 38, 39, 42 (Carlsbad, NM: Resource Management Offices, Carlsbad Caverns National Park, Fall 1999—Winter 2010).
4. National Park Service, "Half a Century Later, a National Geological Society Cavern Map (1953) and a Picture (1952) Bring Cavern into More Focus," in *CAVE History Update: A Newsletter from CAVE Cultural Resources in the Resource Stewardship and Science Division* 10 (Carlsbad, NM: National Park Service, August 2004): 1-3.
5. Louise D. Hose, ed., *Journal of Cave and Karst Studies* 62, no. 2 (August 2000).
6. Malcolm S. Field, ed., *Journal of Cave and Karst Studies* 69, no. 1 (April 2007).
7. Malcolm S. Field, ed., *Journal of Cave and Karst Studies* 69, no. 3 (December 2007).

97 Residual Surface
Mammoth Hot Springs
Betty F. Bluvshtein

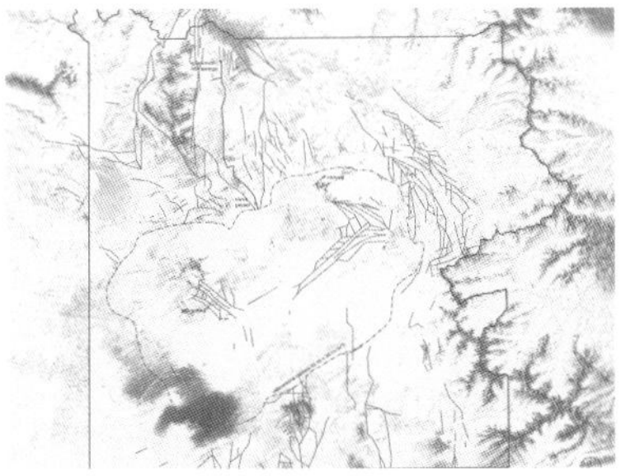

1. K. E. Bargar, "Geology and Thermal History of Mammoth Hot Springs, Yellowstone National Park, Wyoming," Technical Report USGS-BULL-1444 (Laramie: Wyoming Geological Survey, 1978).
2. K. Eric Livo, Fred A. Kruse, Roger N. Clark, Raymond F. Kokaly, and W. C. Shanks, III, "Hydrothermally Altered Rock and Hot Spring Deposits at Yellowstone National Park—Characterized Using Airborne Visible- and Infrared-Spectroscopy Data," Professional Paper 1717 (U.S. Geological Survey, 2007).
3. Ibid.
4. Donald E. White, R. A. Hutchinson, and T. E. C. Keith, "The Geology and Remarkable Thermal Activity of Norris Geyser Basin, Yellowstone National Park, Wyoming," Professional Paper 1456 (Washington, D.C.: U.S. Geological Survey, 1988).
5. R. Blaine McCleskey, James W. Ball, D. Kirk Nordstrom, JoAnn M. Holloway and Howard E. Taylor, "Water-Chemistry Data for Selected Hot Springs, Geysers, and Streams in Yellowstone National Park, Wyoming, 2001-2002," Open-File Report 2004-1316 (U.S. Geological Survey, 2004).
6. Tami Blackford, ed., *Recording Change at Mammoth Hot Springs: Microbial Diversity from Harsh Environments,* Yellowstone Science 18, no. 3 (2010).

102 Between Erosion and Sedimentation: Water Flow and Land Mass
The Mississippi River Delta, The Gulf of Mexico
Ja-Sheng Chen

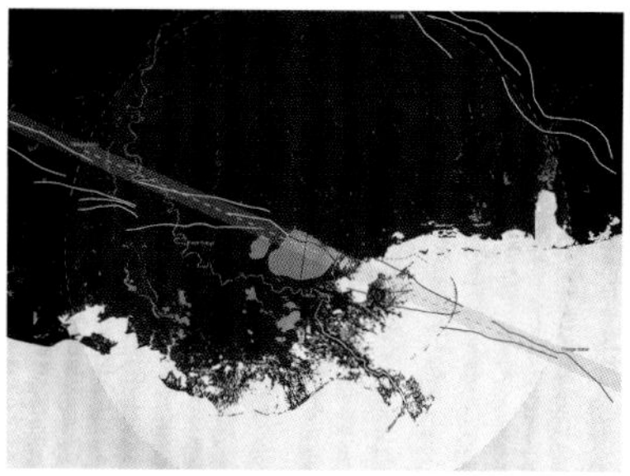

1. Coalition to Restore Coastal Louisiana, eds., "Coastal Louisiana, Here Today and Gone Tomorrow? A Citizens' Program for Saving the Mississippi River Delta Region, to Protest Its Heritage, Economy and Environment" (Baton Rouge, LA: Coalition to Restore Coastal Louisiana, 1988).
2. U.S. Army Corps of Engineers, New Orleans District, "Beneficial Use of Dredged Material," *mvn.usace.army.mil*.
3. Brian Davis, "The Mississippi River: Land-Making Machine," *faslanyc* (28 May 2011).
4. Bob Bobson, "Southeastern Louisiana Fault Scarp," *geocaching.com* (22 Oct. 2009).
5. Meg Sutton, "Coastal Restoration as a Climate Change Adaptation Strategy," *mississippiriverdelta.org* (12 June 2012).
6. "Why Do Wetlands Matter?" *GuttertoGulf.com.*
7. "Sediment from the Mississippi Floods," *NASA Earth Observatory*.
8. Coastal Wetlands Planning, Protection & Restoration Act, Public Law 101-646.
9. US Army Corps of Engineers, New Orleans Region, "Mississippi Delta Hydrographic Survey Book," mvn.usace.army.mil (2014).
10. Robert Stewart, *Our Ocean Planet: Oceanography in the 21st Century—An Online Textbook*, Our Ocean World (College Station, TX: Texas A&M University, 2017).

116 Growth in Anoxic Conditions
Mangroves in the Florida Wetlands
Lenia Pachy

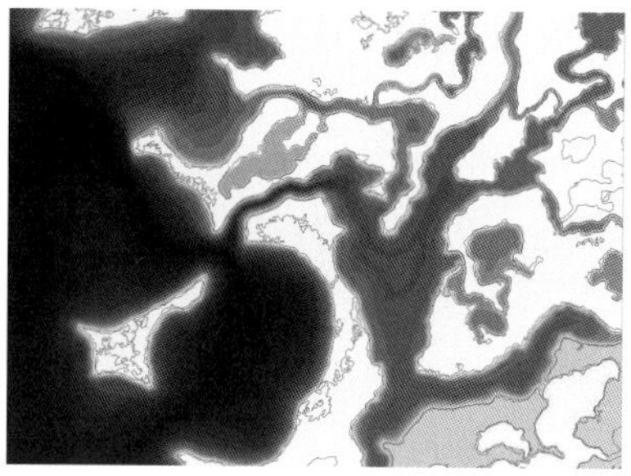

1. A. M. Gill and P. B. Tomlinson, "Studies on the Growth of Red Mangrove (Rhizophora mangle L.) 2. Growth and Differentiation of Aerial Roots," in *Biotropica* 3, no. 1 (Jun. 1971): 63-77.
2. R. Allen Brooks and Susan S. Bell, "A Multivariate Study of Mangrove Morphology (Rhizophora mangle) Using Both Above- and Below-Water Plant Architecture," in *Estuarine, Coastal and Shelf Science* 65 (2005): 440-8.
3. Arunika H. L. A. N. Gunawardena, "Programmed Cell Death and Tissue Remodelling in Plants," in *Journal of Experimental Botany* 59, no. 3 (2008): 445—51.
4. David J. Longstreth and Olga N. Borkhsenious, "Root Cell Ultrastructure in Developing Aerenchyma Tissue of Three Wetland Species," in *Annals of Botany* 86 (2000): 641-6.
5. Elisabeth E. Schussler and David J. Longstreth, "Changes in Cell Structure During the Formation of Root Aerenchyma in Sagittaria Lancifolia (Alismataceae)," in *American Journal of Botany* 87 (2000): 12—19.
6. D. J. Gibbs, W. C. Dennison, R. J. Lawn, and A. J. McComb, "Waterlogging and Submergence: Surviving Poor Aeration," in Brian J. Atwell, Paul E. Kriedemann, Colin G.N. Turnbull, and D. Macmillan, eds., *Plants in Action: Adaptation in Nature, Performance in Cultivation* (Melbourne: Macmillan, 1999).

109 Between Two Waters: Disaster as Opportunity
Lake County
Ling Li Tseng

1. A. B. Tihansky, "Sinkholes, West-Central Florida," in Devin Galloway, D. R. Jones, and S. E. Ingebritsen, eds., *Land, Subsidence in the United States*, Circular 1182 (U.S. Geological Survey, 1999): 121—40.
2. W. C. Sinclair, J. W. Stewart, R. L. Knutilla, A. E. Gilboy, and R. L. Miller, "Types, Features, and Occurrence of Sinkholes in the Karst of West-Central Florida," Water-Resources Investigations Report 85-4126 (U.S. Geological Survey, 1985).
3. Leslie A. Northa, Philip E. van Beynena, and Mario Pariseb, "Interregional Comparison of Karst Disturbance: West-Central Florida and Southeast Italy," in *Journal of Environmental Management* 90, no. 5 (April 2009): 1770-81.
4. Dean Whitman, Timothy Gubbels, and Unda Powell, "Spatial Interrelationships between Lake Elevations, Water Tables, and Sinkhole Occurrence in Central Florida: A GIs Approach," in *Photogrammetric Engineering & Remote Sensing* 65, no. 10 (October 1999): 1169-78.

133 Salt Domes
The Gulf of Mexico
Yu-Chun Lin

1. Susan Bratek, "Salt Tectonics: An Advanced Examination of Rock Salt," *smbratek.wordpress.com*.
2. Scot W. Krueger, "Dynamics of Tear Faults in the Salt-Detached Systems of the Northern Gulf of Mexico," in *Search and Discovery* 50346 (2010).
3. S. W. Krueger and Neil T. Grant, "The Growth History of Toe Thrusts of the Niger Delta and the Role of Pore Pressure," in K. McClay, J. Shaw and J. Suppe, eds., *Thrust Fault-Related Folding: AAPG Memoir* 94 (2011): 1-34.
4. S. W. Krueger and N. T. Grant, "Evolution of Fault-Related Folds in the Contractional Toe of the Deepwater Niger Delta," in *Search and Discovery* 40201 (2006).
5. M. G. Rowan, M.P.A. Jackson and B.D. Trudgill, "Salt-Related Fault Families and Fault Welds in the Northern Gulf of Mexico," in *AAPG Bulletin* 83, no. 9 (1999): 1454-84.
6. Krystal Pearson, "Geologic Models and Evaluation of Undiscovered Conventional and Continuous Oil and Gas Resources—Upper Cretaceous Austin Chalk, U.S. Gulf Coast," in Scientific Investigations Report 2012—5159 (U.S. Geological Survey, 2012).

140 Chronicle of Eroding Forces
Apostle Islands
Boreum Lee

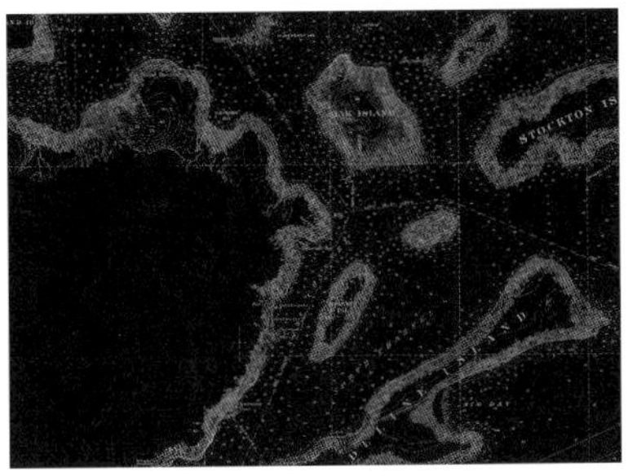

1. Wayne N. Engstrom, "Beach Foreshore Sedimentology and Morphology in the Apostle Islands of Northern Wisconsin," in *Journal of Sedimentary Petrology* 44, no. 1 (Mar. 1974): 190-206.
2. E. A. Pendleton, E. R. Thieler, and S. J. Williams, "Coastal Change-Potential Assessment of Sleeping Bear Dunes, Indiana Dunes, and Apostle Islands National Lakeshores to Lake-Level Changes," Open-File Report 2005-1249 (U.S. Geological Survey, 2005).
3. J. D. Anderson, C. H. Wu, and D. J. Schwab, "Wave Climatology in the Apostle Islands, Lake Superior," in *Journal of Geophysical Research: Oceans* 120 (2015): 4869—90.

144 An Aeolian Sense: Configuring Power of an Invisible Force Field
Great Sand Dunes of Colorado, CO
Katerina Kourkoula

1. S. L. Forman et al., "Episodic Late Holocene Dune Movements on the Sand-Sheet Area, Great Sand Dunes National Park and Preserve, San Luis Valley, Colorado, USA," in *Quaternary Research* 66 (2006): 97—108.
2. National Park Service, "Great Sand Dunes National Park and Preserve: Geologic Resource Evaluation Report," Natural Resource Report NPS/NRPC/GRD/NRR—2006/011 (March 2006).
3. Richard F. Madole, "On the Origin and Age of the Great Sand Dunes, Colorado," in *Geomorphology* 99 (2008): 99—119.
4. V. P. Tchakerian, *Desert Aeolian Processes* (New York: Springer, 1995).
5. K. Pye and H. Tsoar, *Aeolian Sand and Sand* (New York: Springer, 1990).

150 Water Motion in a Topographical Vessel
Bay of Fundy
Mando Fytou

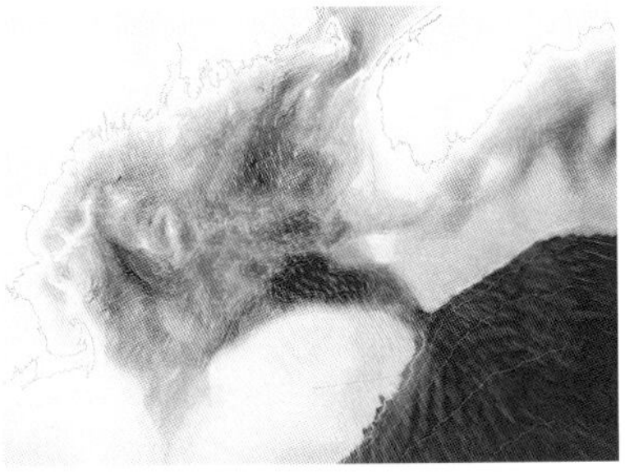

1. Con Desplanque and David J. Mossman, Bay of Fundy Tides, in *Geoscience Canada* 28, no. 1 (Mar. 2001).
2. R. H. Karsten, J. M. McMillan, M. J. Lickley and R. D. Haynes, "Assessment of Tidal Current Energy in the Minas Passage, Bay of Fundy," in *Institute of Mechanical Engineers* 222, no. 5 (Jul. 2008): 493-507.
3. Carl L. Amos, G. R. Daborn, H. A. Christiana, A. Atkinson and A. Robertson, "In Situ Erosion Measurements on Fine-Grained Sediments from the Bay of Fundy," in *Marine Geology* 108, no. 2 (Oct. 1992): 175-96.

154 Impact and Flow
Lituya Bay Mega Tsunami
Yeqing Cao

1. Charles L. Mader and Michael L. Gittings, "Modeling the 1958 Lituya Bay Mega-Tsunami, II," in *Science of Tsunami Hazards* 20, no. 5 (2002): 241.
2. Hermann M. Fritz, Fahad Mohammed and Jeseon Yoo, "Lituya Bay Landslide Impact Generated Mega-Tsunami 50th Anniversary," in *Pure and Applied Geophysics* 166, nos. 1-2 (Feb. 2009): 153-75.
3. Steven N. Ward and Simon Day, "The 1958 Lituya Bay Landslide and Tsunami: A Tsunami Ball Approach," in *Journal of Earthquake and Tsunami* 04, no. 285 (2010).
4. Don J. Miller, "The Alaska Earthquake of July 10, 1958: Giant Wave in Lituya Bay," in *Bulletin of the Seismological Society of America* 50, no. 2 (April 1960): 253-66.

162 Manipulated Life Cycles
Bering Strait
Melanie Fessel

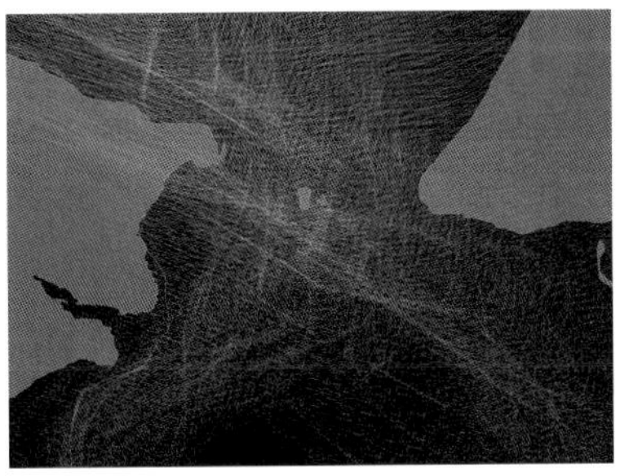

1. Bruce H. Ramsay, "The Interactive Multisensor Snow and Ice Mapping System," in *Hydrological Processes* 12 (1998): 1537-46.
2. Lawrence K. Coachman, Knut Aagaard and R. B. Tripp, *Bering Strait: The Regional Physical Oceanography* (Seattle: University of Washington Press, 1975).
3. M. Brady Olson and Suzanne L. Strom, "Phytoplankton Growth, Microzooplankton Herbivory and Community Structure in the Southeast Bering Sea: Insight into the Formation and Temporal Persistence of an Emiliania Huxleyi Bloom," in *Deep Sea Research Part II: Topical Studies in Oceanography* 49, no. 26 (Dec. 2002): 5969—90.
4. M. J. Dagg, J. Vidal, T. E. Whitledge, R. L. Iverson and J. J. Goering, "The Feeding, Respiration, and Excretion of Zooplankton in the Bering Sea during a Spring Bloom," in *Deep Sea Research Part A: Oceanographic Research Papers* 29, no. 1 (Jan. 1982): 45—63.
5. Rick Riewe, "Inuit Use of the Sea Ice," in *Arctic and Alpine Research* 23, no. 1 (Feb. 1991): 3-10.
6. John E. Walsh, "The Role of Sea Ice in Climatic Variability: Theories and Evidence," *Atmosphere-Ocean* 21, no. 3 (1983).
7. Robert H. Mattlin, John E. Reynolds, III, Henry P. Huntington, and Caleb Pungowiyi, "Impacts of Changes in Sea Ice And Other Environmental Parameters in the Arctic" (Girdwood, AK: Marine Mammal Commission, Aug. 2000).

167 Frozen Flow
Hubbard and Columbia Glaciers
Josefina Poroli

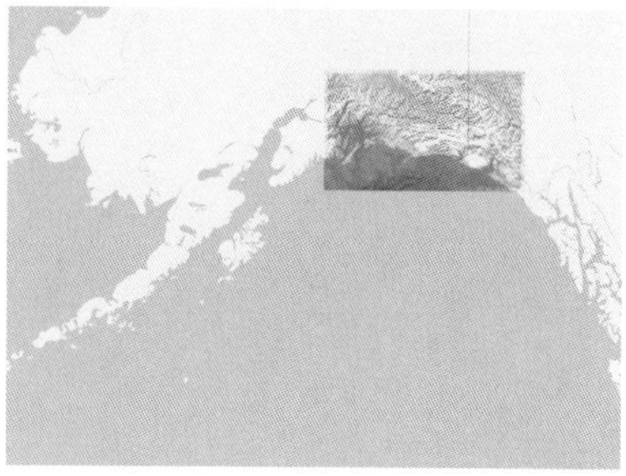

1. Bruce Molnia, "Glaciers of Alaska," Professional Paper 1386-K, (U.S. Geological Survey, 2008): 52-74.
2. Dennis Trabant, Robert Krimmel and Austin Post, "A Preliminary Forecast of the Advance of Hubbard Glacier and Its Influence on Russell Fiord, Alaska," Water Resources Investigations Report 90-4172 (U.S. Geological Survey, 1991).
3. Peter G. Knight, "Glacier Composition, Mechanics and Dynamics," in *Glacier Science and Environmental Change* (Malden, MA: Blackwell, 2006).
4. Michael Hambrey and Jürg Alean, *Glaciers* (Cambridge, UK: Cambridge University Press, 2004).
5. Austin Post and Edward R. Lachapelle, *Glacier Ice* (Seattle: The Mountaineers, 1971).
6. Robert P. Sharp, *Living Ice: Understanding Glaciers and Glaciation* (Cambridge, UK: Cambridge University Press, 1988).
7. Joan Eamer, Hugo Ahlenius and Pål Prestrud, *Global Outlook for Ice & Snow* (Nairobi, Kenya: United Nations Environment Programme Division of Early Warning and Assessment, 2007).
8. Matthew Bennett and Neil F Glasser, *Glacial Geology: Ice Sheets and Landforms* (New York: Wiley, 1996).
9. Roger LeB. Hook, *Principles of Glacier Mechanics* (Cambridge, UK: Cambridge University Press, 2005).
10. K. M. Cuffey and W. S. B. Burlington, *The Physics of Glaciers* (Burlington, MA: Butterworth-Heinemann/Elsevier, 2010).

172 Transformative Materiality
Bering Glacier
Jonathan Heckert

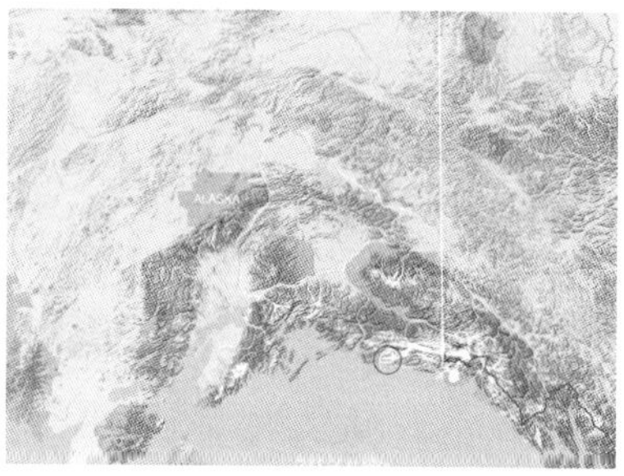

1. Anthony A. Arendt et al., "Rapid Wastage of Alaska Glaciers and Their Contribution to Rising Sea Level," in *Science* 297 (19 July 2002): 382-385.
2. Jane Bennett, *Vibrant Matter: A Political Ecology of Things* (Durham, NC: Duke University Press, 2010).
3. Bruce F. Molnia, "Satellite Image Atlas of Glaciers of the World: Glaciers of North America: Glaciers of Alaska," Professional Paper 1386-K (U.S. Geological Survey, 2008): K1-K36.
4. Bruce F. Molnia and Austin Post, "Surges of the Bering Glacier," in *The Geological Society of America* 462 (2010): 291-316.
5. Bruce F. Molnia and Austin Post, "Introduction to the Bering Glacier System, Alaska/Canada: Early Observations and Scientific Investigations, and Key Geographic Features," in *The Geological Society of America* 462 (2010): 13-42.
6. Austin Post and Edward LaChapelle, *Glacier Ice*, (Seattle: University of Washington Press 2000).
7. Michel Serres, *The Natural Contract* (Ann Arbor: University of Michigan Press, 1995).
8. Robert A. Shuchman et al., "Bering Glacier Ablation Measurements," in *The Geological Society of America* 462 (2010): 83-104.
9. "Young's Modulus Graph," *ffden-2.phys.uaf.edu.*

180 [Perma]Frost Landscape
Northern Alaska Currents
Seongmo Ahn

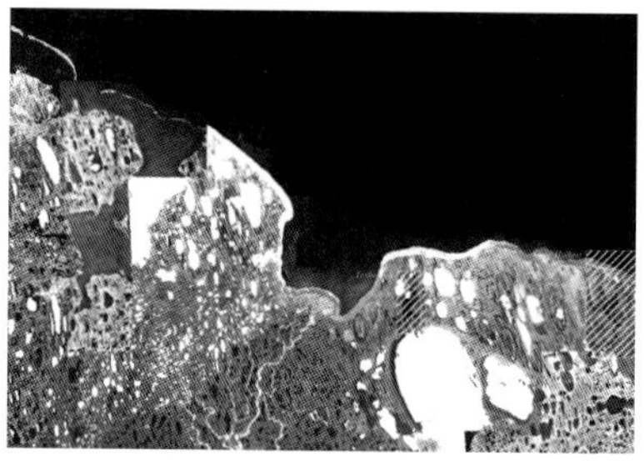

1. M. Torre Jorgenson and Yuri Shur, "Evolution of Lakes and Basins in Northern Alaska and Discussion of the Thaw Lake Cycle," in *Journal of Geophysical Research* 112, no. F02S17 (2007).
2. Robert F. Black and William L. Barksdale, "Oriented Lakes of Northern Alaska," in *The Journal of Geology* 57, no. 2 (Mar. 1949): 105-11.
3. "Permafrost - International Conference," (Lafayette, IN: National Academy of Science, 11-15 November 1963, Lafayette, Indiana).
4. "Permafrost—Second International Conference," (Yakutsk, U.S.S.R: National Academy of Science, 13-28 July 1973).

187 Subterranean Channels
Snake River Plain
Yael Agmon

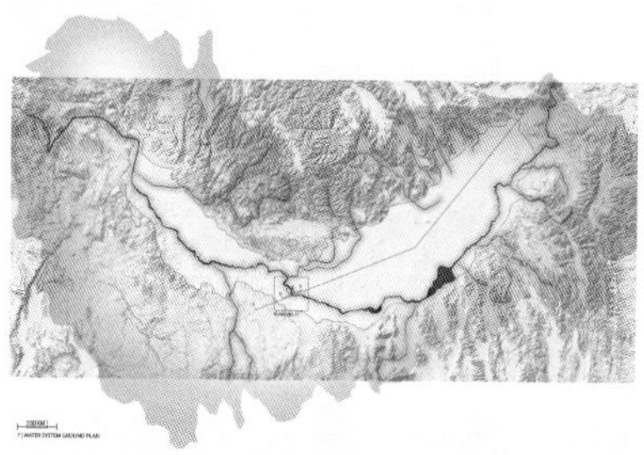

1. Robert B. Smith and Lawrence W. Braile, "The Yellowstone Hotspot," in *Journal of Volcanology and Geothermal Research* 61 (1994): 121—87.
2. Kenneth L. Pierce and Lisa A. Morgan, "The Track of The Yellowstone Hot Spot: Volcanism, Faulting, and Uplift," in *Geological Society of America, Memoir* 179 (1992).
3. William P. Leeman, Derek L. Schutt and Scott S. Hughes, "Thermal Structure Beneath the Snake River Plain: Implications for the Yellowstone Hotspot," in *Journal of Volcanology and Geothermal Research* 188 (2009): 57—67.
4. I. W. D. Dalziel, L. A. Lawver and J. B. Murphy "Plumes, Orogenesis, And Supercontinental Fragmentation," in *Earth and Planetary Science Letters* 178, nos. 1-2 (2000): 1-11.
5. Joachim R. R. Ritter and Ulrich R. Christensen, eds., *Mantle Plumes: A Multidisciplinary Approach*, (Berlin: Springer, 2007).
6. Robert B. Smith et al., "Geodynamics of The Yellowstone Hotspot and Mantle Plume: Seismic and GPS Imaging, Kinematics, and Mantle Flow," in *Journal of Volcanology and Geothermal Research* 188 (2009): 26—56.
7. D. J. Ackerman, "Transmissivity of the Snake River Plain Aquifer at the Idaho National Engineering Laboratory, Idaho," in *Water-Resources Investigations Report* 91-4058 (Idaho Falls, Idaho: U.S. Department of Energy, 1991).
8. Warren W. Wood and Walton H. Low, "Aqueous Geochemistry and Diagenesis in the Eastern Snake River Plain Aquifer System, Idaho," in *Geological Society of America Bulletin* 97, no. 12 (1986): 1456-1466.
9. Xiaohua Peng and Eugene D. Humphrey, "Crustal Velocity Structure Across the Eastern Snake River Plain and the Yellowstone Swell," in *Journal of Geophysical Research* 103, no. B4 (Apr. 1998): 7171-7186.
10. Scott S. Hughes et al., "Mafic Volcanism and Environmental

Geology of the Eastern Snake River Plain, Idaho," in Scott S. Hughes and Glenn D. Thackray, eds., *Guidebook to the Geology of Eastern Idaho: Idaho Museum of Natural History* (Idaho Museum of Natural History, 1999): 143-68.

201 Permafrost: Interactions and Transformations of States of Matter
Alaskan Coast
Ming Yan

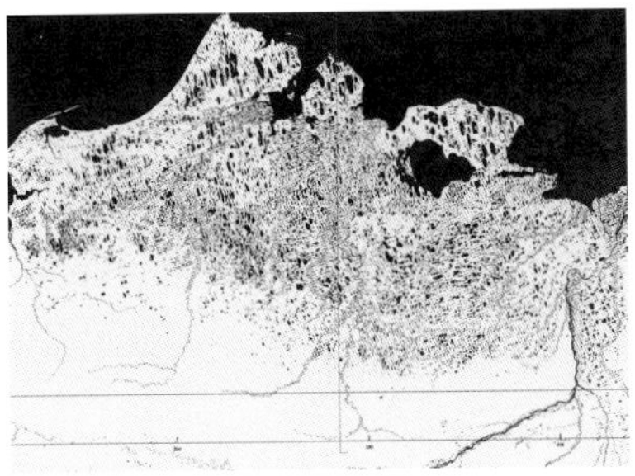

1. M. Torre Jorgenson, Yuri L. Shur, and Erik R. Pullman, "Abrupt Increase in Permafrost Degradation in Arctic Alaska," in *Geophysical Research Letters* 33, no. 2 (January 2006).
2. David Moody Hopkins, "Permafrost and Ground Water in Alaska," Professional Paper 264-F (U.S. Geological Survey, 1955).
3. T. E. Osterkamp, "A Thermal History of Permafrost in Alaska," in Marcia Phillips, Sarah M. Springman and Lukas U. Arenson, eds., *Permafrost* (London, UK: Taylor & Francis, 2003).

206 Salt of the Earth
Lake Bonneville
Adam Longenbach

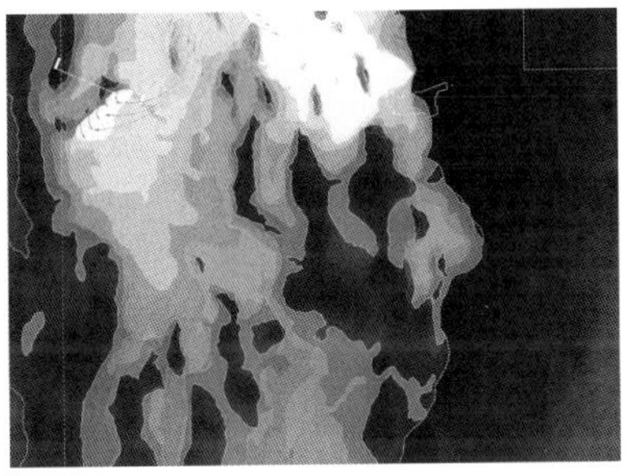

1. Bureau of Land Management, "Bonneville Salt Flats FAQs," *blm.gov*.
2. Max D. Crittenden, "New Data on the Isostatic Deformation of Lake Bonneville," Professional Paper 454-E (U.S. Geological Survey, 1963).
3. Donald R. Currey, "Lake Bonneville: Selected Features of Relevance to Neotectonic Analysis," Open-File Report 82-1070 (U.S. Geological Survey, 1982).
4. U.S. Geological Survey, Utah, "Geological Investigations of the Wasatch Fault Zone in Salt Lake City" (U.S. Geological Survey, 2010).
5. Wallace J. Gwynn, "Brine Properties, Mineral Extraction Industries and Salt Load of Great Salt Lake" (Utah Department of Natural Resources, 1997).
6. Paul Link and Shuhab Khan, "History of Lake Bonneville," in *Digital Geology of Idaho, geology.isu.edu*.
7. Keenan Lee, "The Bonneville Flood," *geology.mines.edu* (2004).
8. Gregory C. Lines, "Hydrology and Surface Morphology of the Bonneville Salt Flats, Pilot Valley Playa, Utah," Water Supply Paper 2057 (U.S. Bureau of Land Management, 1979).
9. James L. Mason and Kenneth L. Kipp, "Investigation of Salt Loss from the Bonneville Salt Flats, Northwestern Utah," Fact Sheet 135-97 (U.S. Geological Survey, 1997).
10. W. W. White, III, "Replenishment of Salt to the Bonneville Salt Flats: Results of the 5-Year Experimental Salt Laydown Project" (U.S. Bureau of Land Management, 2003).

211 Rock, Fire, and Water: Interactions in Constant Motion
The Geysers, Sonoma County
Jaebong Jeon

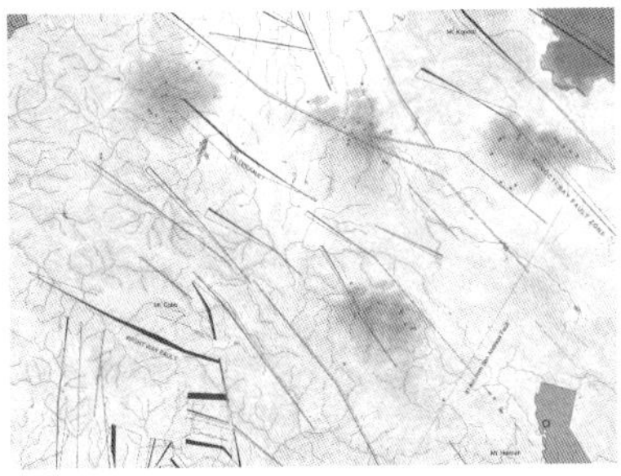

1. E. T. Allen and Arthur L. Day, *Steam Wells and other Thermal Activity at "The Geysers", California* (Washington, D.C.: Carnegie Institution of Washington, 1927).
2. R. J. Mclaughlin, V. E. Langenheim, A. M. Sarna-Wojcicki, R. J. Fleck, D. K. Mcphee, C. W. Robert, C. A. Mccabe and Elmira Wan, "Geological and Geophysical Framework of The Santa Rosa 7.5' Quadrangle, Sonoma County, California," Open-File Report 2008-1009 (U.S. Geological Survey, 2008).
3. Minh Pham and Anthony J. Menzies, "Results From a Field-Wide Numerical Model of the Geysers Geothermal Field, California" in *Geothermal Resources Councill Transactions* 17 (Oct. 1993).
4. Bu Paul Brophy, Marcelo J. Lippmann, Patrick F. Dobson and Bastien Poux, "The Geysers Geothermal Field Update 1990-2010," Special Report 20 (Geothermal Resources Council, 2010).
5. Jacob B. Lowenstern, Cathy J. Janik, Lynne S. Fahlquist, and Linda S. Johnson, "A New Compilation of Gas and Steam Analyses from The Geysers Geothermal Field, California, USA," in *Proceedings 21st New Zealand Geothermal Workshop* (1999): 55-60.
6. Wendell A. Duffield and John H. Sass, "Geothermal Energy—Clean Power from the Earth's Heat," Circular 1249 (U.S. Geological Survey, 2003).
7. Jacob B. Lowenstern, Cathy J. Janik, Lynne S. Fahlquist and Linda S. Johnson, "Gas and Isotope Geochemistry of 81 Steam Samples from Wells in The Geysers Geothermal Field, Sonoma and Lake Counties, California, U.S.A.," Open-File Report 99-304 (U.S. Geological Survey, 1999).
8. B. C. Hearn, Jr., J. M. Donnelly-Nolan, and F. E. Goff, "Geologic Map and Structure Sections of the Clear Lake Volcanics, Northern California," Miscellaneous Investigations Map I-2362 (U.S. Geological Survey, 1995).

218 Algae as Habitat
Point Loma
Jihyun Lee

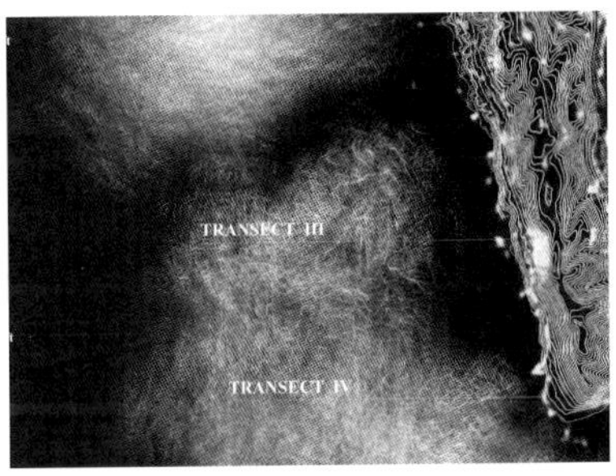

1. Catriona L. Hurd, Paul J. Harrisona, Kai Bischof, and Christopher S. Lobban, *Seaweed Ecology and Physiology* (Cambridge, UK: Cambridge University Press, 2014): 100-35.
2. David R. Schiel and Michael S. Foster, "The Biology and Ecology of Giant Kelp Forests," (Berkeley, CA: University of California Press, 2015): 101-39.
3. Charles Harper Turner, "The Marine Environment Offshore from Point Loma, San Diego County" (California: Scripps Institution of Oceanography Library, 1968).
4. Edith A. Widder and James F. Case, "Distribution of Subcellular Bioluminescent Sources in a Dinoflagellate, Pyrocystis Fusiformis," in *Biological Bulletin* 162, no. 3 (Jun. 1982): 423-48.
5. M. S. Doty, J. F. Caddy, B. Santelices, "Case Study of Seven Commercial Seaweeds Resources," FAO Fisheries Technical Paper

281 (Rome: Food and Agriculture Organization of the United Nations, 1987).
6. David R. Schiel and Michael S. Foster, *The Biology and Ecology of Giant Kelp Forests* (Berkeley, CA: University of California Press, 2016).

225 Seaquoia as Gestalt
Redwood National and State Parks
Rosannah Sandoval

1. Stephen C. Sillett and Robert Van Pelt, "Trunk Reiteration Promotes Epiphytes and Water Storage in an Old-Growth Redwood Forest Canopy," in *Ecological Monographs* 77, no. 3 (Aug. 2007): 335-359.
2. W. A. Cannon, "On the Relation of Redwoods and Fog to the General Precipitation in the Redwood Belt of California," in *Torreya* 1, no. 12 (December, 1901): 137-139.
3. Vladimir Douhovnikoff, Adelaide M. Cheng and Richard S. Dodd, "Incidence, Size and Spatial Structure of Clones in Second-Growth Stands of Coast Redwood Sequoia Sempervirens (Cupressaceae)," in *American Journal of Botany* 91, no. 7 (Jul., 2004): 1140-1146.
4. John D. Stuart, "Fire History Of An Old-Growth Forest Of Sequoia Sempervirens (Taxodiaceae) Forest In Humboldt Redwoods State Park, California," in *Madroño* 34, no. 2 (April-June 1987): 128-141.
5. Alana R. Oldham, Stephen C. Sillett, Alexandru M. F. Tomescu and George W. Koch, "The Hydrostatic Gradient, Not Light Availability, Drives Height-Related Variation in Sequoia Sempervirens (Cupressaceae) Leaf Anatomy," in *American Journal of Botany* 97, no. 7 (2010): 1087-1097.

230 Clouds as Transformational Tools
Sahel Region, Africa
Chung-Wei Lee

1. Hans R. Pruppacher and James D. Klett, *Microphysics of Clouds and Precipitation* (Netherlands: Springer, 2010).
2. James C. McWilliams, *Fundamentals of Geophysical Fluid Dynamics* (Cambridge, UK: Cambridge University Press, 2006.
3. James R. Fleming, "The Climate Engineers," in *Wilson Quarterly* 31, no. 2 (Washington, D.C.: Woodrow Wilson International Center for Scholars, 2007).
4. Jost Heintzenberg and Robert J. Charlson, *Clouds in the Perturbed Climate System* (Cambridge, MA: The MIT Press, 2009).
5. C. M. Taylor, A. Gounou, F. Guichard, P. P. Harris, R. J. Ellis, F. Couvreux and M. De Kauwe, "Frequency of Sahelian Storm Initiation Enhanced over Mesoscale Soil-Moisture Patterns," in *Nature Geoscience* 4 (2011): 430-433.
6. A. M. MacDonald, H. C. Bonsor, B. E. O. Dochartaigh and R. G. Taylor, "Quantitative Maps of Groundwater Resources in Africa," in *Environmental Research Letters* 7, no. 2 (2012).
7. Hubert H. G. Savenije, "New Definitions for Moisture Recycling and the Relationship with Land-Use Changes in the Sahel," in *Journal of Hydrology* 167 (1995): 57-78.

236 Cyclical Migration
Death Valley
David Ross

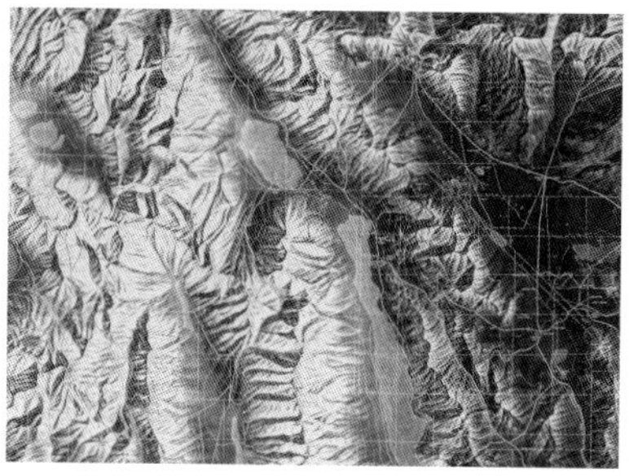

1. Charles Storrow Denny, "Alluvial Fans in the Death Valley Region, California and Nevada," Professional Paper 466 (U.S. Geological Survey, 1965).
2. Roger LeB. Hooke, "Geomorphic Evidence for Late-Wisconsin and Holocene Tectonic Deformation, Death Valley, California," in *GSA Bulletin* 83, no. 7 (1972): 2073-98.
3. Richard J. Blakely, Victoria E. Langenheim and David A. Ponce, "Summary of Geophysical Investigations of the Death Valley Regional Water-Flow Modeling Project, Nevada and California," Open-File Report 2000-189 (U.S. Geological Survey, 2000).
4. Michael N. Machette, "Terrestrial Cosmogenic-Nuclide Dating of Alluvial Fans in Death Valley, California," Professional Paper 1755 (U.S. Geological Survey, 2008).
5. A. M. Harvey, A. E. Mather and M. Stokes, "Alluvial Fans: Geomorphology, Sedimentology, Dynamics,"Special Publication 251 (Geological Society of London, 2005).
6. Athol D. Abrahams and Anthony J. Parsons, *Geomorphology of Desert Environments* (Netherlands: Springer, 2009).

242 Colliding Matters
Meteor Crater
Boreum Lee

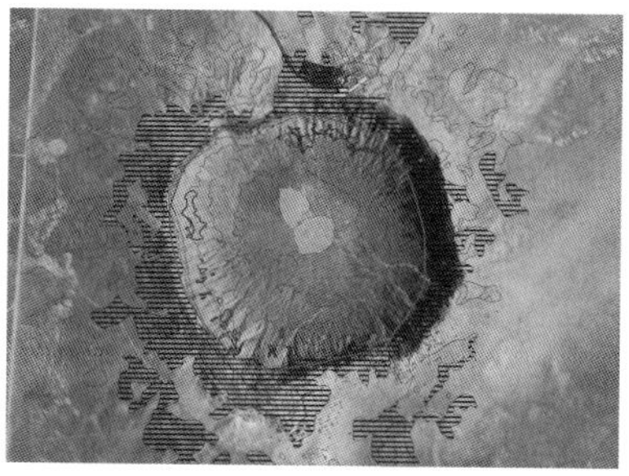

1. David A. Kring, *Guidebook to the Geology of Barringer Meteorite Crater, Arizona* (*a.k.a. Meteor Crater*), LPI Contribution 1355 (Lunar and Planetary Institute, 2007).
2. John A. Grant and Peter H. Schultz, "Erosion of Ejecta at Meteor Crater, Arizona," in *Journal of Geophysical Research* 98, no. E8 (Aug. 1993): 15, 133-15, 147.
3. David C. Fritts, Daniel Goldstein, and Tom Lund, "High-Resolution Numerical Studies of Stable Boundary Layer Flows in a Closed Basin: Evolution of Steady and Oscillatory Flows in an Axisymmetric Arizona Meteor Crater," in *Journal of Geophysical Research* 115 (2010).
4. Robert D. Regan and William J. Hinze, "Gravity and Magnetic Investigations of Meteor Crater, Arizona," in *Journal of Geophysical Research* 80, no. 5 (Feb. 1975).
5. Jason B. Burt et al., "Petrographic, X-Ray Diffraction, and Electron Spin Resonance Analysis of Deformed Calcite: Meteor Crater, Arizona," in *Meteoritics & Planetary Science* 40, no. 2 (2005): 297—306.
6. Pavel Koten et al., "The Beginning Heights and Light Curves of High-Altitude Meteors," in *Meteoritics & Planetary Science* 41, no. 9 (2006): 1305—20.
7. Bevan M. French, Traces of Catastrophe: *A Handbook of Shock-Metamorphic Effects in Terrestrial Meteorite Impact*

Structures, LPI Contribution No. 954 (Lunar and Planetary Institute, 2003).

246 Tornadogenesis and Topography
Indiana
Hsing-O Chiang

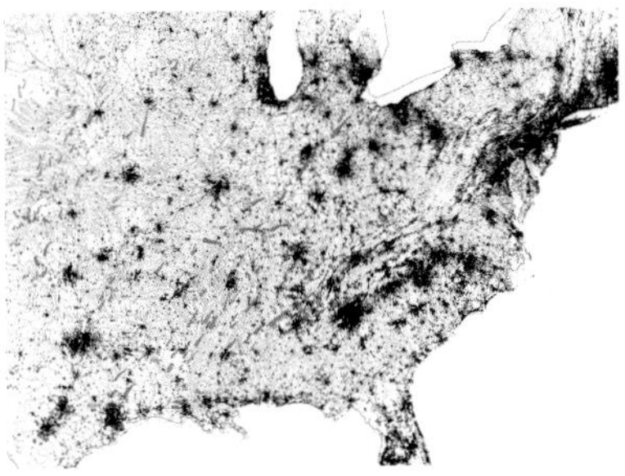

1. D. C. Lewellen, "Effects of Topography on Tornado Dynamics: A Simulation Study," (paper presented at 26th Conference of Severe Local Storms, West Virginia University, Morgantown, WV, November 2012).
2. Chris J. Diamond and Eugne M. Wilkins, "Translation Effects on Simulation Tornados," in *Journal of the Atmospheric Sciences* 41 (1984).
3. Lewellen, "Effects."
4. Diamond and Wilkins, "Translation."
5. Johannes M. L. Dahl "Supercells: Their Dynamics and Prediction" (Berlin: Free University of Berlin, 2006).
6. R. Jeffrey Trapp And Robert Davies-Jones, "Tornadogenesis with and without A Dynamic Pipe Effect," in *Journal of Atmospheric Sciences* 54 (1997).
7. Anthony W. Lyza and Kevin R. Knupp, "An Observational Analysis of Potential Terrain Influences on Tornado Behavior" (paper presented at the 27th Conference on Severe Local Storms, University of Alabama in Huntsville, November 2014).
8. D. C. Lewellen, Baiyun Gong and W. S. Lewellen, "Effects of Finescale Debris on Near-Surface Tornado Dynamics," in *Journal of Atmospheric Sciences* 65 (2008).
9. Ronald L. Holle and Michael W. Maier, "Tornado Formation from Downdraft Interaction in the FACE Mesonetwork," in *Journal of Atmospheric Sciences* 108 (1980).
10. Amanda K. Kis and Jerry M. Straka, "Nocturnal Tornado Climatology," in *Journal of Atmospheric Sciences* 25 (2010).

Author and Contributor Bios

Diana Agrest

Diana Agrest, FAIA is a New York architect internationally renowned for her critical pioneering approach to architecture and urbanism in both practice and theory. The founder and principal of Agrest and Gandelsonas Architects (1980), she has been involved since 1975, in the design and building of projects from master plans and urban design projects to civic and residential buildings globally recognized with numerous awards. She is a professor at the Irwin S. Chanin School of Architecture of The Cooper Union and has taught at Princeton, Columbia, and Yale. Agrest's belief in architecture as an interdiscursive field is reflected in her books including: *Architecture from Without: Theoretical Framings for a Critical Practice* (MIT Press, 1991); *Agrest and Gandelsonas: Works* (Princeton Architectural Press,1995); *The Sex of Architecture*, ed. with P. Conway and L. K. Weisman (Abrams,1996), which won the International Book Award from the AIA in 1997; and *A Romance with the City*, ed. (The Cooper Union,1982). She was also an editor of the journal *Oppositions*. Her work has been exhibited in the Museum of Modern Art (and is in its permanent collection), the Museum of Contemporary Art, Los Angeles, the San Francisco Museum of Modern Art, the Walker Art Center, Center Pompidou, Paris, and the Milano Triennale, among others. She has written, produced and directed the documentary film "The Making of an Avant-Garde: The Institute for Architecture and Urban Studies 1967-1984," which premiered at MoMA in New York in 2013 having received grants from the Graham Foundation, New York State Council of the Arts, AIA Brunner, and others. Agrest graduated in Architecture and Urbanism from the University of Buenos Aires and did postgraduate studies at the Centre de Recherche d'Urbanisme and the École Pratique des Hautes Études, VI Section, Paris, France from 1967—1969.

D. Graham Burnett

D. Graham Burnett is a historian of science, writer, editor, and 2013-2014 Guggenheim Fellow in residence as at the Bard Graduate Center in New York City. The recipient of a 2009 Mellon New Directions Fellowship, he is currently working on connections between the sciences and the visual arts. Burnett graduated from Princeton in 1993 and completed a Ph.D. in the History and Philosophy of Science at Cambridge University (1997 [2001]). Prior to joining Princeton in 2001, he taught at Yale, was a Mellon Fellow in the Humanities at Columbia University (1997—1999) and was an inaugural Fellow in the Center for Scholars and Writers at the New York Public Library (1999—2000). He has published *Masters of All They Surveyed: Exploration, Geography, and a British El Dorado* (University of Chicago Press, 2000), which examines the relationship between cartography and colonialism in the nineteenth century, *Descartes and the Hyperbolic Quest* (American Philosophical Society, 2005), *Trying Leviathan: The Nineteenth-Century New York Court Case that Put the Whale on Trial and Challenged the Order of Nature* (Princeton University Press, 2007), which won the 2007 Hermalyn Prize in Urban History and the New York City Book Award in 2008, and *The Sounding of the Whale: Science and Cetaceans in the Twentieth Century* (University of Chicago Press, 2012). In 2008 he became an editor at *Cabinet*. He is a member of the New York Institute for the Humanities and is affiliated with Princeton's Program in History of Science, Law and Public Affairs Program, Center for Architecture, Urbanism and Infrastructure, and The Princeton Environmental Institute.

Peter Louis Galison

Peter Louis Galison is the Joseph Pellegrino University professor in history of science and physics at Harvard University and Director of the Collection of Historical Scientific Instruments. He received his Ph.D. at Harvard University in both physics and in the history of science in 1983. In 1997, Galison was named a John D. and Catherine T. MacArthur Foundation Fellow; in 1999, he won the Max Planck Prize. Galison's main work explores the complex interaction between the three principal subcultures of twentieth-century physics—experimentation, instrumentation, and theory. He has published *How Experiments End* (University of Chicago Press, 1987) and Image and Logic (University of Chicago Press, 1997), which won the Pfizer Award in October 1998. *Einstein's Clocks, Poincaré's Maps* (W.W. Norton, 2003) considers how the theory of relativity stood at the crossroads of technology, philosophy, and physics. He has published (with Lorraine Daston) *Objectivity* (Zone Books, 2007), which considers how visual representation has shaped the concept of scientific objectivity. Further work includes *Picturing Science, Producing Art* (Routledge, 1998; ed. with Caroline A. Jones), and *Einstein for the 21st Century: His Legacy in Science, Art, and Modern Culture* (Princeton University Press, 2008; ed. with Gerald Holton and Silvan S. Schweber). He has directed, with Robb Moss, the feature documentary films "Secrecy" (2008) about the invisible world of government secrecy, which competed at the Sundance Film Festival and at the Berlin Film Festival (2008); and "Containment" (2015), which premiered at Full Frame, about the need to guard radioactive materials for the 10,000-year future.

Caroline A. Jones

Caroline A. Jones studies modern and contemporary art, focusing on its technological modes of production, distribution, and reception. Trained in visual studies and art history at Harvard, she did graduate work at the Institute of Fine Arts in New York before completing her Ph.D. at Stanford University in 1992. She has held positions at the Museum of Modern Art in New York (1977-83) and the Harvard University Art Museums (1983-85), and her exhibitions and/or films have been shown at the San Francisco Museum of Modern Art, the Hirshhorn Museum and Sculpture Garden in Washington, D.C., and the Hara Museum Tokyo. She has received fellowships from the National Endowment for the Humanities, the John Simon Guggenheim Foundation, the Radcliffe Institute for Advanced Studies (2013-14), the Newhouse Center for the Humanities at Wellesley College (2009-10), Institute National d'Histoire de l'Art in Paris (2006-07), the Wissenschaftskolleg zu Berlin and the Max Planck Institüt (2001-02), the Institute for Advanced Studies in Princeton (1994-95), and the Stanford Humanities Center (1986-87). Her books include *The Global Work of Art, World's Fairs, Biennials, and the Aesthetics of Experience* (University of Chicago Press, 2017), *Eyesight Alone: Clement Greenberg's Modernism and the Bureaucratization of the Senses* (University of Chicago Press, 2005), *Machine in the Studio: Constructing the Postwar American Artist* (University of Chicago Press, 1996; winner of the Charles Eldredge Prize in 1998), and *Bay Area Figurative Art*, 1950-1965 (University of California Press, 1990; awarded the silver medal from San Francisco's Commonwealth Club). She has edited *Sensorium: Embodied Experience, Technology, and Contemporary Art* (MIT Press, 2006) and co-edited *Experience: Culture, Cognition, and the Common Sense* with D. Mather and R. Uchill (MIT Press, 2016) and *Picturing Science, Producing Art* with P. Galison (Routledge, 1998).

John McPhee

John McPhee is an American writer and a pioneer of creative nonfiction. He is professor of writing at Princeton University, where he has taught since 1974. He has been a staff writer at *The New Yorker* since 1965 and has written nearly 30 books, among them *The Pine Barrens* (Farrar, Straus and Giroux, 1968), *The Control of Nature* (FSG, 1989), and most recently, *Draft No. 4: On the Writing Process* (FSG, 2017). McPhee won the Pulitzer Prize in General Nonfiction in 1999 for *Annals of the Former World*, a compilation of five books on the geological history of North America. He has also received the Award in Literature from the American Academy of Arts and Letters (1977), the George Polk Career Award (2008), and the Wallace Stegner Award (2011). McPhee received a Litt.D. from Bates College in 1978, an honorary Doctorate of Letters from Yale University in 2009, and an honorary Doctorate of Humane Letters from Amherst College in 2012.

Acknowledgments

While I started my work on the subject of nature many years ago outside the frame of my teaching, it was the Irwin S. Chanin School of Architecture of The Cooper Union, where I taught for most of my life as an educator, that provided the context of it's inquiring and creative spirit and the support to explore and develop critical pedagogical approaches under the deanships of John Hejduk, Anthony Vidler, and now Nader Tehrani. John Hejduk's pedagogical principles set the tone for the school and the critical role of drawing still resonates today. That was a different historical moment and so were the issues. While the ethos and principles remain, many of the questions critical to architectural discourse have since changed.

I first introduced the "Architecture of Nature/Nature of Architecture" studio in the fourth-year design studio of the undergraduate program in 2008 as a way of dealing with the environmental issues in a way that could bring together philosophical inquiry, scientific research, and architecture by emphasizing the critical importance of representation and of drawing in the process. In bringing this approach to the Advanced Research Design Studio of our newly created MArch II Program, I decided to continue developing it even further. The pleasure of exploring new areas of study was matched by that of devising different modes of representation as tools for thought and production of knowledge. I want to specially thank Anthony Vidler, former Dean, for providing the intellectual space, academic freedom, and trust necessary for testing and exploring the new intellectual and pedagogical territories that this studio and work represent.

This work is the result of eight years of an extraordinary partnership with my graduate students at the Irwin S. Chanin School of Architecture in the and of my initial "Architecture of Nature/ Nature of Architecture" studio in the undergraduate fourth-year studio. They had none of the familiar territory of architecture to hold on to but our tools of representation and our architectural gaze, but they met the challenge with passion and creativity. I want to thank each and every one of them, whether their work is represented in this book or not, as the inquisitive energy and discussion were shared experiences that everyone greatly benefitted from. I also want to thank the very dedicated (then junior) faculty that have taught this studio with me over the years: Yael Agmon, Lis Cena, Elena Fanna, Evangelos Kotsioris, Tomas Leeser, Masha Panteleyeva, Laila Seewang, Lydia Xynogala, and Michael Young for his participation in the 2016 thesis summer studio.

Elizabeth O'Donnell, as acting dean between 2013 and 2015 and then as associate dean, has been the most committed supporter of this book project. As I proposed the do such a book, she embraced the project with wholehearted enthusiasm, belief, rigor, and collegial generosity, together with her unfailing calm, sound advice, pointed observations, and incredible professionalism. It has been both a privilege and a pleasure to share in this process with Elizabeth. I owe her a great debt of gratitude.

Special thanks to Nader Tehrani, dean since 2015 and colleague, for his support, interest in and commitment to this book since embarking on his leading role at the school.

I am grateful to Yael Agmon, who acted as an editorial and production assistant, for her most generous dedication and commitment as well as intelligence, organizational skills, good judgment, and a great spirit overall. I could not have done it without her.

It is a privilege to have the contributions of Peter Galison, Caroline Jones, and D. Graham Burnett, all outstanding intellectuals and scholars whose minds and work I admire. I want to thank them for taking the time and interest to enter the world of the work that this book represents and to address the questions it poses with genuine attentiveness and insight. I also want to thank them for their dedication in the back-and-forth of editing the interview transcripts. John McPhee, whose writings and approach to the American geological past never cease to fascinate me, was most generous in his exchanges with me and in supporting the publication of the excerpt reproduced here.

Mario Gandelsonas has always been a supporter of the making of this book and my approach to the subject of nature, but I specially want to thank him for being a reader of my introduction and offering comments with sharpness, objectivity, and insight.

Our publisher, Gordon Goff, from ORO Publisher and its AD+R imprint, has believed in this project from the start and has had the most enthusiastic and generous attitude in making it a reality. Jake Anderson, managing editor, has always been ready to help and provide the necessary advice and assistance on all fronts with professional grace.

My special thanks to our graphic designer Alex Lin for the book's beautiful design and for his patient and consistent dedication to excellence.

The Architecture Archive is an essential part of our school and its work of photographically recording models and archiving the digital records is invaluable. For that I want to thank Steven Hillyer, its director and a trusted colleague, and the team working at the Archive throughout these years: Lea Bertucci and Chris Dierks, collaborating when asked with the best disposition. I also want to thank Steven for his input as well as Mindy Lang, director of the Center for Design and Typography, who offered insight in the nascent stages of this project. Monica Shapiro, our academic administrator, and Robyn Fitzsimmons, administrative assistant, have helped over all these years in ways that are many and hard to classify, including some in relation to the book. Frank Kurtzke and Kevin Leonard, co-heads of the shop, have guided students in the production of many of the models that are featured here. I want to thank Julia Chapman for her initial editing of the projects texts and Phillip Polefrone for his invaluable editing assistance.

Last, but not least, I want to acknowledge with gratitude that the project was made possible by the generosity of the many contributors to the School of Architecture Dean's Circle and by the Faculty Development Fund, established by an anonymous gift to The Cooper Union.